Marxism and the failure of organised Socialism in Spain, 1879–1936

Marxism and the failure of organised Socialism in Spain, 1879–1936

PAUL HEYWOOD
Lecturer in Politics, University of Glasgow

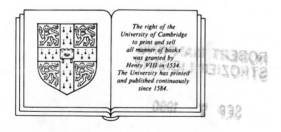

The right of the
University of Cambridge
to print and sell
all manner of books
was granted by
Henry VIII in 1534.
The University has printed
and published continuously
since 1584.

CAMBRIDGE UNIVERSITY PRESS
Cambridge
New York   Port   Chester
Melbourne   Sydney

Published by the Press Syndicate of the University of Cambridge
The Pitt Building, Trumpington Street, Cambridge CB2 1P
40 West 20th Street, New York, NY 10011, USA
10 Stamford Road, Oakleigh, Melbourne 3166, Australia

First published 1990

Printed in Great Britain at the University Press, Cambridge

British Library cataloguing in publication data
Heywood, Paul
  Marxism and the failure of organised Socialism in
  Spain, 1879–1936.
  1. Spain. Political events, 1868–
  I. Title
  946.08

Library of Congress cataloguing in publication data
Heywood, Paul.
  Marxism and the failure of organised socialism in Spain, 1879–1936
  Paul Heywood.
    p.   cm.
  Bibliography.
  Includes index.
  ISBN 0-521-37492-8
  1. P.S.O.E. (Political party) – History.   2. Socialism – Spain –
  History.   3. Spain – Politics and government – 1875–1885.   4. Spain –
  Politics and government – 1886–1931.   5. Spain – Politics and
  government – 1931–1939.   1. Title.
  JN8395.P15H43   1990
  324.246'07409034 – dc20   89–36111   CIP

ISBN 0 521 37492 8

wv

Contents

Preface

This study sets out to examine the relationship between the theory and practice of a major European Socialist party, the Partido Socialista Obrero Español (PSOE), from its foundation in 1879 to the outbreak of the Spanish Civil War in 1936. During this period, the PSOE was, despite its slow growth, the largest working-class party in Spain, and for a crucial spell in the 1930s, the largest parliamentary party. Indeed, its political significance in both the creation and the collapse of the ill-fated Second Republic (1931–6) can hardly be overstated. As a result, published studies of the Spanish Socialist movement have understandably shown a marked tendency to concentrate on the PSOE's role during this five-year period. In particular, attention has been focussed on the divisions within the party which culminated in its notorious post-1933 'radicalisation', often seen as central to the breakdown of political stability in the Second Republic. Moreover, the divisions which so damaged the PSOE during the Republic have been seen as all the more noteworthy in that they represent a marked contrast to its apparently traditional unity and discipline: although relatively small in terms of membership, the PSOE prior to 1931 had supposedly manifested an organisational cohesion unique amongst the political groups opposed to the Restoration Monarchy (1875–1931). Remarkably, for all the PSOE's significance, there still exists no comprehensive study of the Spanish Socialist Party from its formation to the Civil War. This book aims to serve as a contribution to filling that gap.

Nonetheless, the main focus of the book – the relationship between theory and practice in the Spanish Socialist movement – may at first sight appear somewhat curious. Although the PSOE held explicitly to a Marxist self-image, it has become almost axiomatic to refer to the poverty of Marxism in the Spanish labour movement. Spanish Socialism has produced no Marxist theorists of international stature, and few who could be regarded as particularly important even in a local context. So much is this the case that most published studies of the PSOE have virtually excluded issues of theory as a factor in the party's divisions. The present study does not demur from the observation that Spain has never been noted for the fecundity or quality of its Marxism. Indeed, rather than 'illumine what was dark', Spanish Marxism prior to the Civil War merely manifested rigidity, schematism and a striking lack of originality. The PSOE remained inflexibly attached to a distinctively narrow vision of Marxist theory, imported originally from France and unsatisfactorily superimposed on a very different socio-political environment.

However, this study is informed by the belief that there is an important ontological distinction to be drawn between Marxist and non-Marxist political parties. The former, to be meaningfully termed as such, have to *believe* that their political praxis is derived from theoretical formulations in a conscious manner. Thus, even though the quality of their Marxism was poor, most leaders of the PSOE genuinely saw themselves as Marxists and attempted to act accordingly, or at least thought they were acting accordingly. This is not to suggest that the elaboration of Marxist theory figured prominently within the concerns of the PSOE leadership, still less, that Marxism provided a constant reference point for the party's day-to-day political functioning. Rather, it is to argue that Marxist theory, no matter how poorly conceived or understood, set the *parameters* within which the PSOE formulated its political policies, or its strategy for socialism. It is therefore my contention that the importance of Marxism in Spain lay precisely in its poverty: the influence of the PSOE leaders' devotion to a distorted vision of Marxism was paramount in determining the broad outlines of their political conduct.

I investigate three main inter-related issues. First, I attempt to analyse *why* Marxist theory in Spain has been so poverty-stricken. I have sought answers by returning to the period when Marxism was introduced into Spain and examining how the particular manner of its introduction influenced the origins and early development of the PSOE. Second, in doing so, I confront the question of whether the Spanish Socialist movement really was characterised by unity, discipline and cohesion prior to the Second Republic. Third, following on from this, I look at the question of what effect the poverty of its Marxism had upon the development of the Spanish Socialist movement, both before and during the Second Republic. It would be as well to mention here, however, two further things I specifically do *not* do: I do not argue that the poverty of the PSOE's Marxism was the only aspect of that party's complex make-up which contributed to its strategic and tactical deficiencies. In addition, I do not attempt to provide a detailed organisational or social history of the PSOE. Instead, in examining the relationship between theory and practice in the PSOE, I aim to provide a broad ideological and organisational overview through which to construct an explanatory framework for the party's failure in the period under consideration.

By its very nature, this study has had to marry different intellectual approaches and thus is to some degree deliberately syncretic. Indeed, the historical narrative and the political theory are informed by an awareness of their constant mutual interplay. Neither narrowly archival, nor based wholly on secondary literature, the book offers an original analysis of the development of Spanish Socialism before 1936. Inevitably, given that the study covers a period of nearly sixty years, it contains some variations in emphasis. Chapter 1, which deals with the period 1879–1914, serves as an extended introduction and sets out the main issues of the study. Since it provides a basic background, its approach is more thematic than narrative. Emphasis is laid upon the manner in which Marxism was introduced to Spain, how it was adopted as the ideology of the newly created PSOE, and the factors which led to its peculiar distortion. In addition, the chapter provides a brief analysis of the development of the Spanish state in the nineteenth century and of the nature of the Restoration Monarchy, established in 1875. This serves as a historical template against which are measured the pronouncements and activities of the PSOE in its early years.

Chapters 2, 3 and 4 tend more obviously towards political narrative. There are two main reasons for this. On the one hand, they cover the PSOE between 1914 and 1931, the period about which least is known or has been written. They thus serve to some degree as expositional chapters, providing the first systematic account in English of the Socialist movement during these years. On the other hand, the theoretical debates of the period, although clearly of importance for the development of the PSOE, were hardly of transcendental significance. Moreover, since virtually nothing has been written by historians about the Socialist movement in these years, there is as yet no standard orthodoxy with which to engage in debate. Hence the approach in these three chapters is more conventionally histori-cal, although the main emphasis remains that of the relationship between the PSOE's Marxist theory and its political practice.

Chapter 2, on the years 1914–19, examines the Socialist movement's response to the First World War and the Bolshevik Revolution, as well as its involvement in the so-called 'crisis of 1917'. The chapter also analyses the emergence of a clear polarisation between an increasingly reformist leadership and a growing number of radical militants within the PSOE. The results of this polarisation form the subject of chapter 3, which covers the period 1919–23. In these years, the PSOE's activity was both domin-ated and disrupted by the issue of whether or not to join the Leninist Third International, formed in early 1919. The chapter examines in detail the three Extraordinary Congresses, held between 1919 and 1921, which culminated in the first major splits in the PSOE and the eventual formation of the Partido Comunista de España (PCE). In particular, new light is thrown on the selection of delegates and the manipulation of proceedings during the definitive 1921 Congress. Chapter 4 covers the PSOE during the Primo de Rivera Dictatorship and the collapse of the Restoration

Monarchy, 1923–31. It centres on the question of why the Socialists collaborated with the Dictator, and suggests that the most common explanation, opportunism, merits some degree of qualification. The chapter also analyses the emergence of the PSOE as the central force within the opposition to the Monarchy and its role in the declaration of the Second Republic.

Chapters 5 and 6 deal with the Republic. In these chapters, the approach adopted moves away from straightforward political narrative towards a greater emphasis on theoretical debates. In part, this is dictated by the existence of a large literature on the Republic, both in English and ever more so in Spanish. Rather than repeat basic information that is widely available elsewhere, I have assumed a degree of familiarity with the main events of the Republic and concentrated instead on interpretation. This has allowed detailed consideration of much of the existing literature on the Socialist movement during the Republic. It is demonstrated that the divisions which so damaged the PSOE between 1931 and 1936 were in large measure the logical culmination of theoretical ambiguities which had marked the party since its inception. Chapter 5, on 1931–4, concentrates in particular on the PSOE's ideological response to the Republic and the theoretical debates which led to its leaving the government in 1933 as well as its subsequent involvement in the insurrectionary movement of October 1934. Chapter 6 covers the period from October 1934 to July 1936. It examines the debate over the causes and impact of the PSOE's 'radicalisation', and concludes that the establishment of the Popular Front coalition at the start of 1936 not only represented the final triumph of the reformists over the revolutionists, but also the effective abandonment of Marxism as the party's guiding ideological principle.

In addition, in order to contrast the Marxism of the PSOE with that of other leftist organisations in Spain during a period when Marxist theory was at its most fecund, chapters 5 and 6 briefly analyse the ideological development of the Bloc Obrer i Camperol (BOC) and the Izquierda Comunista Española (ICE) – which merged in 1935 to become the Partido Obrero de Unificación Marxista (POUM) – as well as that of the PCE. This allows a comparison to be drawn between the relationship of revolutionary Marxism to the PSOE and that which obtained in two very different groups: on the one hand, dissident Communists untrammelled by either a large organisation or the responsibility of power; on the other, official Communists with no independent control over theoretical production, but nonetheless with the credibility and power of the Soviet state behind them. It is shown that greater sophistication in terms of Marxist theory was of little consequence while the PSOE retained political hegemony on the parliamentary Spanish Left: theories of revolution found no automatic translation into practice. Ultimately, the growing threat of fascism in 1930s Spain obliged even the radicals of the POUM to abandon their Marxist principles in face of the harsh realities of *Realpolitik* and join the expressly reformist Popular Front coalition.

This book is based upon a doctoral thesis presented at the London School of Economics. In the process of completing the original study and subsequently preparing it for publication, I have incurred a number of debts which it is a pleasure to acknowledge. In their different styles, both my supervisors have had a significant impact upon the elaboration of this study. Professor Tom Nossiter of the LSE has been a source of continued intellectual stimulation. He also cajoled and encouraged in the right measure to ensure that, although a long time in the making, the thesis appeared sooner than might otherwise have been the case. Professor Paul Preston of Queen Mary College has similarly been unstinting in his support. His vast knowledge of modern Spain is matched only by the infectious readiness and kindness with which he shares it. Indeed, his is the leading, and often guiding, influence on this work.

While researching in Spain, I received much warm support, advice and hospitality from Professors Santos Juliá, José Manuel Macarro Vera, Francisco Laporta, and, especially, Elías Díaz. Professor Juan Trías and Luis Arranz were also kind with their time and assistance. Among others who helped make my stay in Spain productive, if not always in an academic sense, Isabel Espuelas, Antonio Oporto, Maite Villar and Sheelagh Ellwood merit special mention.

Several friends have read all or part of various drafts of this study. I would like to thank Tom Buchanan, Julián Casanova, Nick Ellison, Helen Graham and Brendan O'Leary. I am indebted above all to Mary Vincent, whose advice and support were and continue to be of inestimable value. In a less direct but no less important way, Dave Edgerton and James Dunkerley have helped maintain morale in a period when academe has found itself increasingly beleaguered by financial constraints. I was, nonetheless, fortunate enough in the course of preparing this study to receive financial support from the then Social Science Research Council, the Vicente Cañada Blanch Fellowship Committee of the University of London, and the Centre for Contemporary Spanish Studies, Queen Mary College.

Finally, it is a pleasure to acknowledge the patience and assistance of staff at the following libraries and archives: in London, the British Library of Political and Economic Science, the British Library Reading Room, and the Marx Memorial Library; in Madrid, the Fundación Pablo Iglesias, the Fundación de Investigaciones Marxistas, the Biblioteca Nacional, the Archivo Histórico Nacional, the Hemeroteca Nacional and the Hemeroteca Municipal. In fact, amongst the very few things for which I can claim complete responsibility are the inevitable errors and misjudgements contained in what follows.

Abbreviations used in text

1 Spanish parties and organisations

ASM	Agrupación Socialista Madrileña (Madrid Socialist Group)
BOC	Bloc Obrer i Camperol (Workers' and Peasants' Bloc)
CEDA	Confederación Española de Derechas Autónomas (Spanish Confederation of Autonomous Right-Wing Groups)
CGTU	Confederación General del Trabajo Unitario (General Unitarian Confederation of Labour, PCE union movement)
CNT	Confederacíon Nacional del Trabajo (National Labour Confederation)
CSR	Comités Sindicalistas Revolucionarios (Revolutionary Syndicalist Committees)
FJSE	Federación de Juventudes Socialistas de España (Federation of Socialist Youth of Spain, PSOE youth movement)
FNTT	Federación Nacional de Trabajadores de la Tierra (National Federation of Landworkers)
FRE	Federación Regional Española (Spanish Regional Federation)
ICE	Izquierda Comunista Española (Spanish Communist Left)
ILE	Institución Libre de Enseñanza (Free Institute of Education)
IRS	Instituto de Reformas Sociales (Institute of Social Reforms)
JAP	Juventud de Acción Popular (Popular Action Youth Movement, CEDA youth movement)
JCI	Juventud Comunista Ibérica (Iberian Communist Youth, ICE youth movement)
JSU	Juventudes Socialistas Unificadas (Unified Socialist Youth)
NFM	Nueva Federación Madrileña (New Madrid Federation)
OCN	Organización Corporativo Nacional (General Miguel Primo de Rivera's National Corporatist Organisation)
PCE	Partido Comunista de España (Spanish Communist Party, post-March 1922)
PCE	Partido Comunista Español (Spanish Communist Party, pre-March 1922)
PCOE	Partido Comunista Obrero Español (Spanish Communist Workers' Party)

POUM   Partido Obrero de Unificación Marxista (Workers' Party of Marxist Unification)

PSOE   Partido Socialista Obrero Español (Spanish Socialist Workers' Party)

SOMA   Sindicato de los Obreros Mineros de Asturias (Syndicate of Asturian Mineworkers)

UGT   Unión General de Trabajadores (General Workers' Union)

UJC   Unión de Juventudes Comunistas (Union of Communist Youth, PCE youth movement)

2 Non-Spanish parties and organisations

ECCI   Executive Committee of the Communist International

KPD   Kommunistische Partei Deutschlands (German Communist Party)

PCF   Parti Communiste Français (French Communist Party)

PCI   Partito Comunista Italiano (Italian Communist Party)

PSI   Partito Socialista Italiano (Italian Socialist Party)

SFIC   Section Française de l'Internationale Communiste (French Section of the Communist International)

SFIO   Section Française de l'Internationale Ouvrière (French Section of the Workers' International)

SPD   Sozialdemokratische Partei Deutschlands (German Social Democratic Party)

USPD   Unabhängige Sozialdemokratische Partei Deutschlands (Independent German Social Democratic Party)

I Decaffeinated Marxists: weak version
the PSOE, 1879–1914

Introduction

Studies of the Spanish labour movement prior to the Second Republic, established in 1931, have tended to concentrate on the Anarchists. This is unremarkable, given the enormous strength and influence of Spanish Anarchism until its repression during the three-year civil war which destroyed the Republic. The war was marked by an unstated, unholy – and wholly unlikely – community of purpose between Francoists and Communists. Their mutual hatred barely masked a common desire: the stamping out of Anarchist revolutionary initiatives unleashed by the collapse of the Republic. The Second Republic itself, though, was intimately associated with the Spanish Socialists: its creation was above all their triumph, its collapse their tragedy (some argue, their fault).[1] As the largest political party of the Left, the Partido Socialista Obrero Español (PSOE) played a pivotal role, both in government and in opposition, during the Republic's all too brief five-year existence. For this reason, historians of Spanish Socialism have properly focussed their attention mainly on the PSOE's turbulent experiences between 1931 and 1936. Indeed, in recent years a lively historiographical debate has developed over the role of the PSOE's internal divisions in the polarisation of politics during the Second Republic.[2] However, the strength of Spanish Anarchism before 1931 and the centrality of the PSOE in the Republic have combined to obscure the fact that organised Socialism goes back a long way in Spain. In fact, the PSOE was originally founded in 1879, making it one of the oldest Socialist parties in Europe. The PSOE's early development is of the greatest significance: many of the divisions which so damaged the party during the Republic find their origins in the struggle to establish a political presence in late nineteenth-century Spain.

The central feature of the early Socialist movement was what might be termed 'decaffeinated Marxism'.[3] This refers to the insistence of early PSOE leaders that the party's political praxis was derived from Marxist theory, even though the theory they espoused was rigid, schematic and derivative, bearing little obvious relation to the socio-economic or political situation in Spain. In turn, the praxis at times bore little obvious relation to the theory, thereby giving rise to an ideological confusion which continued to encumber Spanish Socialism throughout much of the twentieth century. Essentially, the first PSOE leaders believed themselves to be Marxists, but understood neither Marxist theory nor how it might be applied specifically to Spain. Whilst proclaiming the necessity and inevitability of Socialist revolution to end the corruptions of bourgeois democracy under the Monarchy, they engaged in precisely the legalist reformism which their own arguments dismissed as useless. Whilst calling for the establishment of a Republic, they shunned all collaboration with other Republican forces on the grounds that they represented the bourgeoisie. Isolationist and arrogant, the PSOE leaders made the crucial mistake of failing to see that Spanish democracy was more Bourbon than bourgeois, a dynastic deception designed to protect the Monarchy and ensure that the population had no effective voice. One result of this misconception was that the Socialist movement remained trapped by an interpretative schema which condemned it to the margins of political life. Only in 1909, when the PSOE finally abandoned its haughty isolationism and entered into an electoral alliance with the Republicans, did the Socialists begin to have an impact in Spain.

That indigenous Marxism in Spain has never been noted for its innovative theory hardly needs emphasising. Indeed, it has become almost axiomatic to comment on the marked poverty of theoretical production by Spanish Marxists, a point expressed most succinctly by Luis Araquistáin in the remark, 'I think we Spaniards have contributed nothing original to the theme of modern socialism.'[4] Less agreement exists, however, as to why this should be so. There have been three main approaches to providing an answer. First, emphasis has been placed on issues of personality and contingency: the Internationalist message arrived via Bakunin's emissary Giuseppe Fanelli, whose strength of character laid the basis for the implantation of Anarchism rather than Marxism in Spain.[5] Second, a slightly more sophisticated view argues that the industrial backwardness of the Spanish economy favoured the implantation of Anarchism rather than Socialism, although this explains neither why Anarchism should have taken root in the most advanced industrial region, Catalonia, nor Socialism in later years amongst the landless peasants of Andalusia and Estremadura in the south.[6] Third, there is the perennial chestnut of Spanish idiosyncrasy: quasi-metaphysical speculations about the innate Anarchism of the Spanish national character.[7]

All three explanations boil down to the basic assertion that Marxist Socialism was weak in Spain because Anarchism was strong. The present study seeks to move beyond this truism by analysing why this should be so; more specifically, it seeks to analyse why the Socialists remained committed to espousing Marxist revolutionism whilst engaging in often timid reformism, and the effect it had on the development of organised Socialism in Spain.[8] Emphasis will be laid upon the nature of the Spanish state and how it inhibited the implantation of Socialism; the dependence of the first Spanish Socialists on their French colleagues for an introduction to much of Marx's work, thereby allowing a simplistic and mechanistic reading through the distorted lenses of Jules Guesde, Paul Lafargue and Gabriel Deville to penetrate Spain; the overriding preoccupation of Spanish Socialists with questions of organisation rather than theoretical analysis, leading to virtual silence on such vital matters as the agrarian problem and regional diversity in Spain; the ideological inheritance of both Catholicism and 'Krausism', an obscure philosophical system of Germanic origin which had a remarkable impact upon many of the early Socialist leaders; and, finally, the intransigent dominance within the PSOE of its founder, Pablo Iglesias, whose determination to make Madrid the centre of Socialist operations allowed the Anarchists to establish a presence virtually without challenge within the more industrial Barcelona. The Catalan capital was always more likely to provide a focus for challenges to the power of the state, as evidenced in both 1909 and 1917, and the Socialists' failure to organise effectively there was of considerable significance.

Socialism and the Spanish state

Fundamental in the development of the Spanish state was the lack of a bourgeois-democratic revolution from below in which the structures of the *ancien régime* were broken. Unlike in Britain and France, there was no establishment during the nineteenth century of a relatively democratic polity able to adjust to and absorb new social forces. Instead, the Spanish state developed along what might be termed 'Prussian' lines, with the one notable difference that industrial capitalism in Spain remained under-developed. Although Spanish history throughout the nineteenth, and indeed much of the twentieth century, has been marked by a counterpoint between the forces of progress and reaction, it was the latter which generally remained dominant. By the last quarter of the nineteenth century a 'reactionary coalition' had become established between a powerful political oligarchy, made up of the monarchy, landowners and the Church, and a politically weak commercial and manufacturing bourgeoisie.[9] This laid the basis for the development in Spain of *agrarian* capitalism, no less exploitative than the industrial variant. Despite the immense diversity of Spanish agriculture, the politically dominant sectors were, broadly speaking, the large landowners. Their *latifundios* were generally concentrated in the central and southern parts of the country, Andalusia and Estremadura, although there were also powerful *latifundistas* in Old Castile and particularly in Salamanca. Industrial development, by contrast, was sporadic, being concentrated mainly on textile production in Catalonia and mining in the Basque Country.

The roots of the reactionary coalition had been established during the 1830s and the 1850s when Church lands were disentailed as part of an ultimately unsuccessful attempt at social reform. These lands were bought up mainly by existing landlords, but also by members of the embryonic commercial and industrial bourgeoisie. However, rather than using their capital to modernise agricultural production and invest in industry, the bourgeoisie allowed itself to be 'co-opted' by the political oligarchy. Attracted by the prestige conferred by land ownership, a substantial proportion of the new *haute bourgeoisie* was easily persuaded to collaborate in the coalition's basic aim: the maintenance of the prevailing social system against any reformist threats to agrarian dominance. Threats certainly existed. Although numerically weak, and still further emasculated by the existence of the reactionary coalition, the northern-based commercial and mercantile bourgeoisie did make sporadic efforts to alter the manifest injustices which abounded in nineteenth-century Spain. Their lack of genuine revolutionary drive, however, was demonstrated in the period 1868 to 1874; these six years of political chaos culminated in the establishment of an ultimately abortive republic, created more by accident than design. Population growth since the middle of the century had intensified pressure on the land, provoking widespread internal migration to urban centres by peasants desperate to leave the countryside. This exacerbated the already high rates of urban unemployment, whilst at the same time economic depression, worsened by the collapse of cotton supplies to the Catalan textile industry during the American Civil War, engendered morale-sapping inflation.

Poorly organised and inarticulate, Spanish workers increasingly expressed their growing resentment through violence. In turn, the monarchy's ever-growing corruption and disdain for the politically powerless angered liberal army officers, disgusted by the hypocrisy of Queen Isabella's clerico-conservative leanings. A series of *pronunciamientos* combined with urban riots to oust her in 1868. In the ensuing power vacuum, the liberal bourgeoisie let slip its golden opportunity. Lacking coherent leadership and direction, the working class and peasantry were able to do little more than stage a number of poorly coordinated cantonalist risings.[10] These were easily put down, but the spectre of proletarian disorder dampened liberal enthusiasm for progress. Unable to establish its authority, the First Republic, formally established in February 1873, was crushed by the army in December 1874. Once more, the bourgeoisie ceded its right to rule in return for the provision of political stability in which to make money. The monarchy was restored in the person of Alfonso XII; reform was abandoned.

The 'Restoration Monarchy' ruled over Spanish political life until 1923. Up until 1897 it was dominated by the politician Antonio Cánovas de Castillo, architect of the so-called *turno pacífico*.[11] The idea behind the *turno* was to maintain the configuration of political power in Spain basically unaltered, while presenting a façade of parliamentary democracy. Two political parties, the Conservative and the Liberal, were created to represent the two principal sections of the landed oligarchy, the wine and olive growers of the south and the wheat growers of the centre. These landed classes, whose economic power rested on their *latifundios*, were linked to the political centre in Madrid, alongside the Church and the higher-ranking military, through the system of *caciquismo*.[12] *Caciques* were local political bosses who, through a variety of more or less corrupt means, ensured that electoral results approximated to the predetermined outcomes decided upon in Madrid. Since the only options were Conservative government under Cánovas, or Liberal government under Práxedes Sagasta, it was effectively impossible for alternative interests to find political expression. The Canovite system, modelled on its founder's admiration for British parliamentary procedures, had little to do with democracy, even less did it cater for the representation of workers' and peasants' interests.

The crucial point to note, however, is the weakness of the commercial and manufacturing bourgeoisie in Spain. In terms of socio-political development, the majority of these middle classes were

Catholic and conservative, imitators in their modest sphere of aristocratic attitudes and without a proud, independent bourgeois culture.[13]

There was no sizeable middle class in nineteenth-century Spain linked to the development of an industrial economy at the forefront of political transformation. In other words, in Marxist terms, the political revolution which brought about the modern constitutional state in Europe and thereby 'destroyed all the estates, corporations, guilds and privileges which expressed the separation of the people from its community',[14] had not occurred in Spain. Rather than the Spanish state being a reflection of bourgeois civil society, the ruling class remained an oligarchy comprising the latifundist nobility, the Church, the *haute bourgeoisie* and the higher-ranking military. Its concerns were conservative, its determination to guard against revolutionary initiatives fierce.

Revolution, of course, was precisely the supposed *raison d'être* of the Partido Socialista Obrero Español (PSOE), founded in Madrid on 2 May 1879 by a small group of men, many of whom had been members of the minority 'authoritarian' branch of the International in Spain.[15] The division in Spain between 'authoritarians' and 'anti-authoritarians' reflected the struggle for control within the First International between Marx and

Bakunin, with the difference that in the Iberian peninsula it was followers of the latter who managed to establish initial hegemony. The mouthpiece of the first Marxists in Spain had been *La Emancipación* (1871–3), which moved away during 1872 from the Bakuninist current of the Federación Regional Española (FRE) towards a more explicit identification with Marx.[16] Under the prompting of Marx's son-in-law, Paul Lafargue, who had fled to Spain from the Paris Commune in 1871, the editor of *La Emancipación*, José Mesa y Leompart, tried to keep the FRE faithful to the orientations of the General Council of the First International. However, Mesa's main concern was to attack the 'anti-authoritarian' positions derived from Proudhon and Bakunin, which were being propagated by the Catalan-based *La Federación*, rather than to use Marxist theoretical postulates as a basis for analysing the situation in Spain.

Mesa was the guiding impulse behind the creation of the Nueva Federación Madrileña (NFM), supposedly faithful to the Hague Congress of the International.[17] In fact, the NFM failed to supersede the anti-electoral line of the early Spanish workers' movement. Abstentionist mistrust of electoral participation was out of line with Marx's emphasis on the need to struggle to win reforms from the existing state. However, even though abstentionist attitudes could be justified on the grounds that the Spanish state had not reached the stage at which it was meaningful to seek reform through it, these grounds were not used. Instead, the line of *La Emancipación* on the August 1872 elections, for example, was unequivocal in its erroneous assertion:

Internationalists! Do not go to the elections. . .we workers have nothing to do in bourgeois parliaments.[18]

If the prescription made sense, the diagnosis remained faulty. This rigid anti-electoral stance, derived from a simplistic understanding of both Marxism and the Spanish state, led to a costly inflexibility: thus it was that the proclamation of the First Republic in February 1873 was treated as if nothing had happened, producing no change in the NFM's political line.

José Mesa left Spain for France in 1872. There he established close contact with Jules Guesde, a leader of the French Socialist movement who was subsequently to have an important influence on the nascent Spanish movement. In Madrid, meanwhile, the Asociación General del Arte de Imprimir, a typesetters' union originally constituted in 1871, was reformed in 1874. Under the presidency of Pablo Iglesias, who was to become the central figure in the Spanish workers' movement, the Asociación was to be the driving force behind the eventual formation of the Socialist Party: the majority of the founding members of the PSOE were affiliated to it. However, although the Socialist Party was very much a creation of workers, the predominance of members of the Asociación General del Arte de Imprimir, an artisanal union of the labour aristocracy, gave it an elitist hue which at times was to verge on sectarianism. The typographers associated with the Asociación formed a closely knit nucleus, headed by Iglesias, which was to create difficulties in terms of collaboration both with other workers felt to be of inferior status, and with intellectuals.[19] This was an important factor contributing to the slow progress made by the group between the fall of the First Republic at the end of 1874, and the official constitution of the Socialist Party, in conditions of illegality, in 1879.

The first formal constitution of the Socialist Party was Madrid-based, initially known as the Grupo Socialista Madrileño.[20] Its primary concern was to set up a commission to write a programme and formulate the organisation of a country-wide party. The commission comprised Pablo Iglesias, Victoriano Calderón, Alejandro Ocina, Gonzalo Zubiaurre, and Jaime Vera, although Vera did not take part in the actual writing of the programme nor in formulating the organisation. The election of Iglesias to the position of Secretary of the Executive Committee confirmed him in the leading position which he was to retain until his death in 1925. He was challenged, though, by Francisco Mora, who played an important part in the formulation of the 1880 revised version of the first party programme. It has been suggested that this first programme of 20 July 1879 was probably sent for revision to Marx and Engels.[21] If so, they would surely have been left aghast at its 1880 reformulation which was based in large measure on the 1872 Manifesto of the Federal Committee of the Federación Regional Española, in turn constructed from tenets taken mainly from Bakunin and Proudhon. The main elements of the 1872 Manifesto had been twofold. First, there were two principal affirmations couched in a Bakuninist framework: 'in the economy, collectivism; in politics, anarchism', alongside a conception of political power based on a theory of a revolutionary state made up of workers' collectives and autonomous local federations. Second, a Proudhonian conception of Justice was seen as the leading principle of social equilibrium once capitalist exploitation had been eliminated.[22]

The Mora text of 1880 made a few significant changes to this. References to Anarchist faith were dropped and, in line with the London and Hague conferences of the International, political action was accepted as a necessity for the workers.[23] Nonetheless, much of what remained was clearly in the line of Bakuninist rather than Marxist conceptions. The three aspirations defined by the 1880 programme were: the possession of political power by the working class; the transformation of individual or corporative ownership of the means of production into common ownership by the whole society; and the organisation of society on the basis of economic federalism, guaranteeing to all members of the workers' collectives the full proceeds of their work. Marx's likely reaction to the third aspiration can be deduced from his 'Critique of the Gotha Programme', in which he ridiculed the Lassallean notion of each worker receiving the undiminished proceeds of his labour. As Marx pointed out, there would always be a number of inescapable deductions to be made, and in any case the notion of distribution involved remained trapped within categories derived from capitalist society. Moreover, though, coupled to the Spanish Socialists' concern with distribution was a notion of a rational and egalitarian social order, presided over by the figure of Justice, with clear reference to Proudhon. This went hand in hand with a Bakuninist theory of the state being reduced to merely administrative functions.

What all this reflected was the lack of any systematic study of the works of Marx by the early Spanish Socialists, with a resultant poor understanding of Marxist economic analysis. The upshot of these theoretical inconsistencies was that the political action called for in the Socialist programme had a strongly 'reformist' hue, with a passive conception of inevitable revolution. Thus, the 'minimum' demands of the 1880 programme amounted to gradualism in both the political and economic planes, an orientation that continued to underlie the various reworkings of the programme throughout the 1880s, and formed the basis of the definitive programme of 1888. It was here that the disjuncture between revolutionary rhetoric and reformist tactics was established, for throughout the 1880s Pablo Iglesias in particular spoke of the proximity and inevitability of revolution which would come about as a necessary effect of the evolution of capitalism, in a manner completely external to political class action.[24]

This is the central striking feature of the early PSOE. As has been shown, the Spanish state at the end of the nineteenth century remained imbued with pre-capitalist features and had made scant and uneven progress along the transitional road towards industrial capitalism. Nonetheless, this did not inhibit the early PSOE leaders from proclaiming loud and often that Spain did indeed exhibit what was perhaps the most basic characteristic in Marxist terms of the capitalist mode of production. Thus, Pablo Iglesias, in just one example of what was to become virtually an incantation, proclaimed

Class antagonism has now lost its complexity of former times, and today is reduced to its simplest expression – the struggle between...the bourgeoisie and the proletariat.[25]

Iglesias was not alone in such pronouncements, even if he was the most insistent. Jaime Vera, the major intellectual of early Spanish Socialism and a man elevated to hagiologic status in the history of the Spanish workers' movement, was equally guilty. This was perhaps most clearly illustrated in the responses of the Agrupación Socialista Madrileña to the Comisión de Reformas Sociales, set up in a rare progressive act by Royal Decree in

December 1883. Organised by the Liberal administration of Sagasta, its brief was to investigate the living conditions of the working class in Spain.[26]

The two most important Socialist responses to the Comisión were presented by Vera and Iglesias. The former eschewed the official question-naire and instead produced a written report, which has come to be known simply as the *Informe*, while the latter presented two oral reports. Vera's *Informe* has provoked extraordinary responses. Rarely studied closely, it has nonetheless been widely acclaimed, in the words of Juan José Castillo, as 'the greatest theoretical expression of Marxism in Spain at the end of the nineteenth century.' Juan José Morato, founder member and first biographer of the Socialist movement, went so far as to suggest that 'Spanish Socialist thought is Jaime Vera in the *Informe*.'[27] It is thus somewhat surprising to discover that the *Informe* is something of a naked monarch: an eclectic admixture of various ideas, some mutually exclusive, put together with little seeming consideration of their applicability to the situation in Spain. Iglesias, meanwhile, was far less concerned than Vera with questions of theory, and effectively argued that the crucial issue was the organisation of the workers' struggle.

The PSOE leaders were plainly labouring under severe misapprehensions about the socio-political and economic situation in Spain. Less obvious is why this should have been so. There are perhaps three major reasons which converged and which contribute towards an explanation. The first of these concerns the influence of French interpretations of Marxism. Clearly, the early Spanish Marxists had a decidedly limited firsthand knowledge of the works of Marx and Engels. This, in fact, is hardly surprising: not only was it exceedingly hard to gain access to what was proscribed by the state as subversive literature, but even if central Marxist texts had been available in good translations it is unlikely that the PSOE leaders would have found time to internalise them.[28] The majority of early members of the PSOE came from a working class which enjoyed neither leisure nor the facilities to acquire more than basic levels of education. Moreover, Marx's *Das Kapital*, for instance, is hardly light reading, nor indeed would it have provided many obvious clues as to the political nature of the Spanish state.

In the light of these constraints, the early PSOE leaders not unnaturally turned to the French Socialists for guidance and advice. It was far more likely that the Spanish Socialists would have a working knowledge of French than of German or English, and this fact, together with geographical proximity, contributed to a heavy French influence on early Hispanic Socialism. Moreover, this link was fortified by José Mesa who, it will be remembered, had left Madrid for Paris in the early 1870s. Once in France, Mesa established contact with Carl Hirsch and Guerman Alexandrovitch Lopatin, friends of Marx and Engels, who in turn introduced him to the

Café Soufflet group, which included Jules Guesde and Gabriel Deville. Heavily involved with the Parisian circle associated with the journals *Les Droits de l'Homme, La Révolution* and later *L'Egalité*, Mesa became an intermediary between Paris and Madrid, transmitting to the Spaniards ideas formulated by the French.[29]

In many ways, this was a disaster for the Spanish Socialists. The influential Guesdist version of Marxism

rested upon the monotonous expression of a single theme: the coming 'expropria-
tion of the expropriators'.... In the Guesdist scheme...the antagonism of capital
and labour is seen as leading inevitably to a dramatic confrontation which transfers
the means of production to the collectivity.[30]

Guesde's ideas derived ultimately from Malthus, via Ricardo and in particular Ferdinand Lassalle with his 'iron law of wages', an idea scorned by Marx. Essentially, Guesdist Marxism was reductionist and determin-istic, characterised by the rigidity and simplicity of most of its postulates. In turn these derived from a lack of knowledge of some of the fundamental works of Marx and Engels, the survival of ideological influences of pre-Marxist Socialism and an incapacity to relate theoretical perspectives to concrete conditions. The simplistic appeals of Guesdist formulations, in which revolution was seen as both easy and on the political agenda, had much to commend them to the theoretically unsophisticated early Spanish Socialists.[31]

The second reason relates to the manner in which Pablo Iglesias stamped his authority upon the PSOE. While it is certainly the case that the potential for fruitful theoretical developments in Spain was in any case limited, it remains equally true that the character and actions of Iglesias compounded an already unpromising situation. At the same time, however, it must be conceded that he played a fundamental and vital role in the organisational formation and development, such as it was, of the Spanish Socialist movement – a paradox symptomatic both of the man and of the interpretations to which he has been subject. Perhaps the fundamen-tal characteristic of Iglesias was pragmatism wedded to a basic mistrust of whatever lay outside his own personal ambit. Thus, he mistrusted not just Republican politicians, but also the few intellectuals who, at an early stage, joined the PSOE. Both of these antipathies, it could be argued, incurred heavy costs for the Spanish Socialist movement. In many ways, though, Iglesias personified Spanish Socialism. The victim of many personal attacks from Anarchists and Republicans alike, his puritanical laic sanctity and total commitment to Socialist ideals is undeniable. In this he was represen-tative of a tradition which came to mark the Spanish Socialists – a tradition of ascetic morality which derived from the Socialist ideal of an all-embracing code of conduct.[32]

The attempted glorification of Iglesias, particularly after his death, by leading Socialists such as Julián Besteiro, Julián Zugazagoitia, and Indalecio Prieto, was later challenged by some of those who moved to the left following the 1921 split in the PSOE. Joaquín Maurín, for example, perhaps the most accomplished Marxist theorist Spain has ever known, saw Iglesias as a *cacique*, and accused him of eliminating from the leadership of the Socialist movement the very individuals who should have been there: Jaime Vera, Antonio García Quejido and Facundo Perezagua. He also saw Iglesias' political strategy as inadequate, since it was centred in Madrid where there was no significant industrial development. His overall judgement was harsh indeed:

Iglesias was neither a revolutionary, nor intelligent. . . Intellectually, Iglesias was a man of complete mediocrity. If anyone were today to reread his speeches and articles – totally empty, without a single original idea of his own, without a hint of passion – they would be astonished that he could have been the moving spirit of a large part of the Spanish proletariat. . . Iglesias fostered a rigid, mean working-class movement which contributed in large measure to the intellectual poverty of our socialism.[33]

Juan Andrade, a founder member of the Communist Party who later joined forces with Maurín in the ill-fated POUM, added to this his definition of *pablismo* as the 'peculiar psychology of Spanish reformism', characterised by a rudimentary workerism which led to the abandonment of revolutionary principles, and to scarce attention being paid to problems of theory. It cannot be doubted that theory played but a small part in the concerns of Iglesias. As Morato was to concede in his largely hagiographic biography of the Socialist leader, organisational questions took up so much of his time that there was little left to devote to studying the works of Marx and Engels.[34]

The dominant characteristic of the PSOE's political activities under the leadership of Iglesias was to be a pragmatism which seemingly had little to do with Marxist theory, even though the party continued to insist on its Marxist nature. The crucial point is that the Marxism of the PSOE remained static, a fixed and distant lodestar which threw little light. Iglesias was almost obsessed with the idea of building up an efficient and powerful organisation, a legacy which was to cost the party dear in terms of flexibility. Fear of seeing the PSOE organisation damaged was a main reason behind the party's hesitancy to take the political initiative between 1917 and 1923, when the state, torn apart by a combination of social disorder and economic decline, tottered on the verge of collapse. A similar reason lay behind the PSOE's collaboration with the Dictatorship of Primo de Rivera, established in 1923 – two years before Iglesias' death – to shore up the nearly moribund Restoration Monarchy. Again, as will be seen, a central dimension of the splits within the PSOE during the Second Republic was the issue of organisational integrity versus revolutionary goals.

The Socialist leader's overriding concern with organisational matters existed alongside a dismissive attitude towards the role of intellectuals in the PSOE. Indeed, a division between workers and intellectuals was a marked feature of the PSOE in the nineteenth century. As Carr states, 'to Socialists they appeared as individualists whose intellectual aestheticism removed them from practical politics.'[35] An indicative example of this concerns Miguel de Unamuno, the Spanish philosopher and essayist, who was perhaps the major figure who could have acted as a catalyst for the development of Marxist thought in Spain. He became thoroughly disillusioned with the PSOE on account of Valentín Hernández, editor of *La Lucha de Clases* (Bilbao), to which Unamuno was a regular contributor while a member of the party between 1894 and 1897.[36] Hernández's attitude towards intellectuals at times verged on contempt, particularly in relation to the lack of importance he felt they attached to questions of political organisation. Unamuno, for his part, began to see the PSOE as marked by narrow-mindedness and dogmatism, as evidenced by his letter of May 1895 to his friend Pedro Múgica:

I'm a convinced socialist, but my friend, those who go by that name here are impossible; fanatics ignorant of Marx, poorly educated, obsessed by order, intolerant, full of prejudices of bourgeois origin, blind to the virtues and uses of the middle class, unaware of the evolutionary process. In fact they've got everything except any social sense.[37]

Unamuno left the PSOE in disgust in 1897, and it was not until after the 1909 alliance with the Republicans that any significant number of intellectuals joined the party.

The third main reason for the poor development of Marxism in Spain was that the First International showed little interest in the Iberian peninsula. While it is true that Marx and Engels themselves demonstrated some degree of interest in Spanish affairs,[38] and also that the International was actually outlawed in Spain in 1871, in the final analysis very little attention was paid to the Iberian mainland by the Internationalists. Giuseppe Fanelli, as is well known, went to Spain on behalf of the First International, but he in fact took with him a highly vulgarised version of the statutes of the International Working Men's Association, in which it was suggested that the prime aim of the workers should be to attack the state. The point of this was to lend credence to the positions of Bakunin's Alliance of Socialist Democracy, which Fanelli really represented, and to create confusion over the different tactical lines being pursued by the two associations. Thus, the early numbers of *La Emancipación*, up until early

1872, exalted the importance of organisation, yet also took a clear 'anti-authoritarian' line. After Fanelli, the representative of the First International in Spain was Paul Lafargue who had arrived in the Iberian peninsula after the collapse of the Paris Commune in 1871. Lafargue, though, was given his role more on account of his happening to be in Spain, and his ability to speak Spanish (he was of Cuban descent), than because of any intimate knowledge of Spanish affairs. Moreover, his abilities as a populariser of Marxism were probably overestimated on account of his familial connection with the grand master himself. Certainly, his period in Spain cannot be judged a great success.

The combination of these three factors helps to explain the poverty of early Marxist theory in Spain. Together with periodic state repression of the workers' movement, and the strength of rival groupings such as the Anarchists and the Republicans, ideological stagnation contributed to the painfully slow growth of the PSOE in the last quarter of the nineteenth century. Also important, though, was the PSOE's failure, for all its emphasis on organisation, to organise an effective propaganda machine. Certainly the necessity for some national party organ was well recognised, and to this end there was convened the Asamblea de Accionistas on 27 January 1886 in order to found a party newspaper. This meeting of the party activists was in fact the scene of the first major internal crisis of the PSOE, and it was to have important and long-lasting repercussions, for it represented the moment at which Iglesias took sole control of the party. After acerbic arguments at the meeting it was agreed to set up a party newspaper, *El Socialista*, constituted on the basis of four aims: to defend the programme of the PSOE as developed in the replies to the Comisión de Reformas Sociales; to support openly strike action by the working class; to propagate constantly the principle of a workers' association, with a view to creating a national association of resistance; and to oppose all bourgeois parties, particularly the advanced ones, while at the same time asserting that a republic was always preferable to the monarchy.

It was the last point which was to be the major source of acrimony. Jaime Vera and Francisco Mora hotly disputed the tactic of intransigence towards all Republican parties, arguing both that this would leave the Socialists dangerously isolated, and that it was necessary to distinguish between different forms of Republicanism. Iglesias, on the other hand, saw all Republicans as linked to the bourgeois classes and therefore necessarily against the interests of the workers. Antonio García Quejido, one of the members of the Asociación General del Arte de Imprimir who had founded the Socialist Party, and who was to become increasingly important in the party's development, attempted to formulate a compromise arrangement. In this he was unsuccessful. As a result, Jaime Vera withdrew from active political life for four years, while Francisco Mora left the party altogether, only rejoining in 1901. This left Iglesias effectively free to dictate the direction of the party in the years that followed. While García Quejido was later to engage in important theoretical work, generally underplayed in the history of the Spanish workers' movement, this neither attained significant influence nor led him to challenge Iglesias until the start of the twentieth century.[39]

The Asamblea de Accionistas set up a Board, comprising Iglesias, García Quejido, Hipólito Pauly, Diego Abascal and Matías Gómez Latorre, to produce the newspaper. Iglesias, of course, was appointed editor. García Quejido was forced to leave Madrid to seek work because of his known Socialist connections and his participation in strikes during the two previous years, and Abascal and Pauly 'couldn't write'. Pauly, in fact, was later expelled for embezzlement. The vacancies were filled by Atonio Atienza and Juan José Morato, both primarily translators rather than original contributors. Thus, when *El Socialista* eventually appeared, in mid-March 1886, it became the mouthpiece for the Socialist doctrine according to Iglesias. The first eight numbers carried his orthodoxy in the form of a series of articles under the title 'El programa de nuestro partido'. The programme was somewhat lacking in sophistication. Reductionism was to the fore:

Of the distinct social classes which existed in previous times, today there only remain the bourgeois and working (classes).[40]

Since parliament was seen as devoted exclusively to the interests of the bourgeoisie, it was held that the working class must therefore take political power. The justification for this, however, clearly demonstrated the 'moralistic', ethical aspect, with its Proudhonian overtones, of the conception of Socialism espoused by Iglesias. Society, it was held, was

Condemned by Justice. . . In its turn, Reason too condemns and rejects a society like the present one.[41]

Such an appeal to Reason in History was clearly at odds with Marx's trenchantly materialistic analysis. It also highlighted the tension within Iglesias between a revolutionary and a reformist perspective. The reconciliation of the two positions was never clearly worked out, thereby compounding the growing impression of schizophrenia within the PSOE.

El Socialista, which should have been the major vehicle for the propagation of Socialist ideas in Spain, had to wage a constant battle against bankruptcy. Furthermore, it reflected, and suffered through, the paucity of original theoretical analysis. Indeed, in many ways it was little more than a direct copy of the French Socialist newspaper, *Le Socialiste*, from which it took both its title and its design for a masthead. Most of its content in the early years of publication was either a copy or translation of news and texts taken from French publications, mainly *Le Socialiste* and *L'Egalité*.[42] This simply reinforced the schematism now so marked amongst the Spanish Socialists, leaving them increasingly marginal to developments in the wider European Socialist movement. Of course it could be argued that none of the European Socialist parties manifested any outstanding theoretical sophistication in the last quarter of the nineteenth century. Indeed, theoretical stagnation was actually reinforced by the political line of the Second International. However, the important point is that the Spanish Socialists seemed unaware of very major differences between French and Spanish socio-political and economic development. It might have been more fruitful to look to Germany, although more difficult for reasons mentioned earlier, but even though the *pattern* of development in Germany and Spain was similar in some important respects, the *rate* of change was much slower and more uneven in the Iberian mainland. Unfortunately, though, in many ways the imported extreme determinism manifested by the PSOE meant that once the general orientation of the party became established, the theoretical debate remained suspended: neither practice nor theory were adapted to changing political circumstances. Indeed, the political activities of the PSOE seemed to bear increasingly little relation to the theoretical ideas from which they were supposedly derived.

Despite the repeated assertions that all reformist actions were useless, and that the inevitable revolution was on its way, Iglesias was consistently concerned to set up a national union structure to regulate political strike actions by the working class. This reached fruition with the founding of the Unión General de Trabajadores (UGT), 12–14 August 1888, with García Quejido as its first president. The UGT represented a logical development of previous initiatives in Spain, associated principally with the FRE, the Asociación General del Arte de Imprimir and the Barcelona-based Federación Tipográfica y de las Industrias Similares.[43] This was reflected in the three main elements of its founding statutes: the absence of any strict ideological definition, in order to attract workers who were not necessarily Socialist; a moderate attitude with regard to union struggles; and organisational centralism. It is arguable that the UGT was to be more successful in the first of these elements than the leaders of the PSOE might have liked. As Juan Pablo Fusi has suggested, the mismatch between UGT membership and support for the PSOE raises the question of whether the UGT before 1931 was effectively a Socialist union at all.[44] With regard to the question of organisational centralism, this meant that the UGT was effectively run from Madrid, even though initially its headquarters were in Barcelona, since in reality UGT and PSOE leaders were the same people. Indeed, under Pablo Iglesias the Socialist movement never expended sufficient effort on organising in Barcelona, which was potentially a far more important centre for radical politics than Madrid. This was to be demonstrated clearly in 1909 and again in 1917. Despite the existence of regionalist problems in both Catalonia and the Basque Country, these were never analysed theoretically as issues with importance for the Socialist movement. Instead, regionalism and patriotism were dismissed as purely bourgeois notions.[45]

Like the PSOE, which also held its first Congress in August 1888, the UGT was marked during the rest of the century by painfully slow growth. At the time of the PSOE Congress there existed only 28 Socialist groups throughout Spain, of which just 20 were represented. The Congress approved the party programme with slight modifications to the 'maximum' positions, and thus confirmed the diremption between reductionist revolutionary rhetoric and essentially pragmatic political practice. In many ways this confirmed the PSOE as marginal to Spanish politics, a position in which it was to remain until the 1909 Republican–Socialist alliance. Despite Prime Minister Sagasta's introduction of the Law of Universal Suffrage in May 1890, which in reality was circumscribed by a partial continuance of *caciquismo*, the PSOE made little impact in the elections of 1891, 1893, 1896 and 1898, reaching just 20,000 votes in the last of these.[46]

The PSOE 1898–1909: political wilderness

The first cracks in the *caciquismo*-based system known as the *turno pacífico* appeared at the end of the nineteenth century; arguably, the seeds of the system's collapse were sown outside Spain. The 'Cuban Question', which had been a long-standing sore for Madrid, re-emerged during the 1880s and 1890s despite the belief that it had been resolved by the 1878 Peace of Zanjón imposed by General Martínez Campos. A resurgence of Cuban nationalism led to full-scale war breaking out in 1895; the Spaniards were unable this time to quell the nationalists, and the struggle was brought to an end only by the interested intervention of the United States in 1898. A seven month's war resulted in Spain losing her last remaining colonies outside Africa – a deeply traumatic experience.

The disaster of 1898 was the catalyst for the appearance in Spain of

regionalism, anti-clericalism, militant anarchism, army frustration and a general *fin de siècle* pessimism which reacted violently against the clichés of parliamentary liberalism.[47]

While the PSOE was outspoken and virulent in its denunciation of Spanish involvement in the war, its voice was weak and became lost amongst the welter of forces calling the system into question. The beneficiaries of this surge of discontent, therefore, were not the Radicals and the Socialists, but the 'regenerationists' – the proponents of 'revolution from above', best exemplified by Antonio Maura.[48] The *caciquista* system effectively functioned to exclude the PSOE from any parliamentary role, and the party's posturings remained largely irrelevant to a Spanish political process in which the working class and peasant masses were definitely *personae non gratae*.

A further hindrance to the PSOE was one which may appear a little paradoxical. The Second International had been founded in Paris in 1889, and the PSOE was to be assiduous in its attendance of its Congresses, as well as in following their majority line. This, in fact, was unpropitious, for

the tactical behaviour and the theoretical beliefs of one Socialist party often had a profound influence on other parties; and, indeed, one of the main themes of the history of the Second International is the imposition by the strongest Socialist party of Europe, the German Social Democratic Party, of doctrines and tactics on other parties. . .[49]

The Second International showed little concern over events in Spain, providing no specific guidance to the Iberian Socialists. Again, the PSOE was to suffer through its attempt to apply to the Spanish situation tactical measures formulated in response to different socio-political and economic situations, tactics, moreover, formulated by people who had little interest in, and even less knowledge of, Spain.

A more positive move for Spanish Socialism, however, was the realisation in 1901 of Antonio García Quejido's long-cherished dream: the publication of a Marxist theoretical journal, *La Nueva Era*. Unfortunately, the journal was short-lived, collapsing in 1902, but during its brief life, particularly in 1901, it was the source of a number of important articles which helped to expand the horizons of Spanish Socialism. During its first year the pages of *La Nueva Era* were filled predominantly by foreign authors, amongst them Adler, Bebel, Engels, Jaurès, Kautsky, Plekhanov, Sorel and Turati.[50] However, there were also a number of pieces by Spaniards which manifested the first signs of a movement away from reductionist and schematic articulations of Marxism. It is noteworthy that Pablo Iglesias did not contribute to the journal.

Taking up themes expressed by Unamuno in *La Lucha de Clases*, where, following the Italians Loria and Nitti, he had argued that there were all-round advantages to be gained by winning wage rises through strike actions, García Quejido and Morato began to question the revolutionist reductionism which had been derived from the Lassallean/Guesdist 'iron law of wages'. Morato, who had published in 1897 *Notas para la historia de los modos de producción en España*, analysed living conditions in Madrid, and called on the Socialists to stimulate capitalist development in Spain through wage claims, since the bourgeoisie had shown itself incapable of doing so.[51] García Quejido, meanwhile, embarked on a series of explanatory articles on economic concepts in Marxist theory, a labour he was to continue until his death in 1927. The most important of these was

'La ley de los salarios, ¿está bien formulada?', in which he attacked the 'iron law of wages' and proposed a formula much closer to Marx. García Quejido saw early Spanish Socialism as 'mere phraseology', and called for the abandonment of the short-term revolutionary perspective it had encompassed up to that time. Revolution, he argued, must be seen as an ultimate goal which would come onto the political agenda only after a series of reforms had been carried out.[52]

Other articles of note were contributed by Vicente Barrio, future Secretary of the UGT, and Manuel Vigil, president of the Federación Socialista Asturiana. They both attacked the revolutionary postures of the Anarchists, and emphasised the need for constant propaganda work by the PSOE in order to prepare the workers 'to play the role History has prepared for them'.[53] This evolutionist perspective was characteristic of most of the Spanish contributors to *La Nueva Era*. The main strength of the journal, however, lay in the contributions by foreign authors, a point recognised by García Quejido himself:

> It is like that because in our wretched country we don't have, unfortunately, in the militant Socialist movement any real thinkers, and virtually no one who is even literate.[54]

By 1902, interest in *La Nueva Era* had fallen off considerably, matched by a similar decline in the quality of its articles. Theoretical pretensions were abandoned, and the journal was forced to close in October as being no longer financially viable.

The importance of *La Nueva Era* was that it opened the way towards more flexible postures within the PSOE, and was the stimulus behind the *renovador* movement which would eventually force Iglesias to abandon his simplistic militant anti-Republicanism. Essentially the arguments of the *renovador* faction revolved around the need to form some sort of electoral pact with the Republicans. Although García Quejido's proposal to this effect was defeated in 1903, the movement gathered momentum in the following years, especially after the formation in 1904 of the Federación de Juventudes Socialistas de España (FJSE) by Tomás Meabe and José Medinabeitia in Bilbao.[55] Meabe, passionately anti-clerical (he was described by Perezagua as 'un loco'), was concerned to inject greater intellectual content into the PSOE, and attempted to enlist the assistance of Unamuno and the philosopher, José Ortega y Gasset. While Meabe himself contributed nothing of lasting importance in terms of theory – he was the archetypal angst-ridden, soul-searching intellectual in a constant state of mental tension – his efforts can be seen as helping to ensure that the party reconsidered its tactical positions.[56]

The result of the reconsideration was to be the Republican–Socialist electoral alliance, established at the end of 1909. Fusi has argued that in fact such an alliance had already become a reality in various regional sectors of the PSOE, most notably in the Basque Country during provincial elections in 1907.[57] The immediate catalyst of the alliance was the so-called Tragic Week in Barcelona, but the question had been posed earlier by Vicente Barrio at the 8th Congress of the party in 1908. Barrio, who had succeeded García Quejido as head of the UGT, was particularly concerned at the continued failure of strike actions, and at the success of the Radical Republican Alejandro Lerroux, who had been able to capitalise on anti-Maura feeling. Maura, along with Francisco Silvela, was a proponent of 'regenerationism'. His essentially conservative solutions, carried out in collaboration with army generals such as Polavieja and Weyler, were based as much on a concern to introduce 'sincerity' and 'morality' into politics as to restructure the financial system which desperately needed attention. Maura did initiate some tax reforms aimed at bringing down inflation, and while this was partially successful, at least more so than his bid to rid Spain of *caciquismo*, it relied on an alliance with 'reactionary Catalanism', and alienated both the Liberal Party and the Republicans.[58] The gravest doubts about Maura's attempted local government reforms, widely seen by opponents to the Monarchy as an attempt to ensure that the political oligarchy maintained its hegemonic position, were expressed in Catalonia, which stood to suffer most from atavistic Madrid-based 'dynastic' politics. Complaints against Madrid *laissez-faire* policies were hardly new, but under the dynamism of Lerroux, Republicanism in a radical and demagogic guise was to experience a resurgence, tapping the growing social and political unrest in Barcelona. The success of Lerroux stood in stark contrast to the ineffective efforts of the PSOE, and highlighted the costs of previous failures to organise effectively in the Catalan capital.[59]

The spark which ignited the events of the Tragic Week was Maura's ill-considered call-up of Catalan reservists for a minor campaign in Morocco. Resentment against Madrid had been building up for years in Catalonia. A strike call towards the end of July 1909 by the quasi-Anarchist movement Solidaridad Obrera, supported by both Anarchists and the Federación Socialista de Cataluña, all long opposed to Spanish colonial involvement in North Africa, degenerated in Barcelona into an urban riot of extreme intensity. Throughout Catalonia, particularly in the capital, the Catholic Church became the target of pent-up resentment over its long-established position as pillar of the established order. Many churches and convents were sacked and burned, and several religious lost their lives in the disturbances.[60] The repression unleashed in response by government forces under the hardline Governor-General, Juan de la Cierva, was ferocious: 175 workers were shot in the streets, and many executions followed. The most important of these was that of the Anarchist Francisco Ferrer, who almost certainly had little to do with the events of the Tragic Week.

The European outcry at Ferrer's execution forced Maura's resignation, but more importantly from a Socialist point of view, the Tragic Week confirmed the Anarchists as the leaders of any revolutionary movement in Catalonia. In danger of being marginalised by the pincer movement of the Anarchists on their left and the Republicans on their right, the PSOE had to reconsider its tactical stance.

Caught within the confines of an interpretative scheme which could not have been simpler – the proletariat was right, the bourgeoisie was wrong[61] – Iglesias increasingly found himself not just unable to explain the failure of Socialism in Spain to develop in line with his messianic pronouncements, but also faced with ever greater challenges to his political line from within the PSOE. His response was predictably pragmatic, with the Republican–Socialist Conjunction agreed upon on 7 November 1909. The shift in the PSOE's tactical line, however, marked an important development in official theory. It was now recognised that even if the transition to Socialism remained inevitable, Spain had yet to pass through the vital preliminary stage of bourgeois revolution. Iglesias now accepted that Spain was in need of political modernisation, and that to achieve this a republic must be reinstated. This, however, would be impossible for the Socialists to bring about on their own owing to the 'exceptional' situation of repression existing at the time.[62] The PSOE must therefore ally with the Republicans, for now there was a degree of shared interest between the workers and the bourgeoisie. At last Iglesias was to concentrate his attack on the monarchy and its representative politicians, Maura, Dato and Canalejas, although he remained fundamentally preoccupied with maintaining a coherent organisation. This concentration on the electoralist, organisational aspect of the Conjunction effectively converted the PSOE into one more Republican party.[63] It also, however, transformed the party into a national force for the first time in its history.

The Conjunction also had another important effect: it induced a number of liberal intellectuals to join the PSOE. Amongst these were figures who were to play an important role in the PSOE's, and in some cases Spain's, history – Luis Araquistáin, Julián Besteiro, Oscar Pérez Solís, Manuel Núñez de Arenas, and Antonio Fabra Ribas. The other major intellectual figure of the PSOE, Fernando de los Ríos, did not join the party until ten years later in 1919. The influx of intellectuals did not, however, lead to a flourishing development of Marxist thought within the PSOE. Rather, it led to the elaboration of an increasingly reformist 'humanist' Socialism, similar in some respects to that of the British Fabians, couched in the appeals to 'justice' and 'morality' already so familiar within the party. That anti-revolutionary gradualism should become so marked amongst these PSOE intellectuals was due in large measure to the ideological inheritance of Catholicism, 'Krausism' and the Institución Libre de Enseñanza (ILE).

In order to understand the importance of all three to the Spanish Socialist movement, a slight digression is necessary.

Catholicism, Krausism and Socialism

Throughout the Restoration Monarchy, the organised Catholic Church held state-sanctioned virtual hegemony in all cultural and ideological spheres.[64] The Church in Spain appeared all-pervasive, above all in the area of education. While the influence of Catholic ideology should not be exaggerated, it would be remarkable if even its most bitter opponents did not bear the mark of Abel as well as that of Cain. Of course, the importance of anti-Catholicism as a spur to political radicalism has often been commented upon. In Spain, Catholicism's counterpart has traditionally been seen as Anarchism, classically described by Gerald Brenan as a 'religious heresy', a reaction against the claimed hypocrisies of the Catholic Church.[65] Although overstated, Brenan's view contains at least an element of truth. However, while the supposed millenarian overtones of Anarchism have been widely commented upon, religious influences within the Socialist movement are rarely referred to. Nonetheless, it is worthwhile devoting some attention to this, for it is possible to identify a number of parallels between patterns of behaviour amongst 'practising' Socialists and practising Catholics.[66]

Most obviously, there exists faith in a doctrine and devotion to its progenitor, either Karl Marx or, more often, Pablo Iglesias, the almost mythological 'laic saint' of Spanish Socialism. From 1925 onwards, the year of Iglesias' death, the UGT in Galicia organised an annual 'visit to the apostle's tomb'; this, it should be said, never quite managed to rival Galicia's more traditional annual pilgrimage to the tomb of St James at Santiago de Compostela. Further parallels exist in, for instance, devotion to a specific doctrine, and its redemptive aspects. There is a strong streak of salvific moralism to *pablista* socialism. Indalecio Prieto, the reformist PSOE leader from the Basque Country, stated in a letter of 2 January 1935 to his long-time confidant, Ricardo de Bastida, that 'between Socialism and Christianity there are fundamental, absolutely fundamental, similarities.'[67] Like the Catholic Church, Spanish Socialism placed major emphasis on organisation as the means to propagate its message and win converts to it. Indeed, organisation became exalted as an end in itself: hence the overarching concern, demonstrated most obviously during the Primo de Rivera Dictatorship, to maintain intact the organisational structures of the Socialist movement. This organisation was the means by which society would be saved: on the day of redemption, inevitable because of the laws of historical progress, the moral values of Socialist organisation would become universal.

The moral asceticism associated with *pablista* Socialism remained a powerful influence even into the 1930s. The defence of the Second Republic was often pitched in terms of moral duty: it was a necessary stage *en route* to Socialist salvation. In a remarkable address in the Cortes on 3 October 1931, during the debate on the religious clauses of the Republican constitution, Fernando de los Ríos declared:

Has it not been said that we, at times, are not Catholic, not because we are not religious, but because we want to be even more so. Our spiritual life is saturated to its very last cell by religious emotion; some of us have spent our entire lives prostrated before the idea of the absolute and we breathe into every one of our acts a yearning to uplift.[68]

Elsewhere, it has even been reported that during the Second Republic, the following canticle was intoned by members of the UGT: 'Hosannah, hosannah, glory be to Marx in the heights of his enormous glory, and peace and good will to workers wherever they may be (*en el llano de su existencia*)'.[69]

Many elements of Catholic ideology find a close parallel in Krausism. Indeed, that this obscure doctrine should have taken root at all in the normally barren soil of Spanish philosophical thought was probably due in no small measure to the fertilisation provided by Catholicism. Karl Christian Friedrich Krause (1781–1832) was a relatively minor German philosopher who claimed to have achieved the much-desired reconciliation between the subjective idealism of Kant and Fichte, and the absolute idealism of Hegel and Schelling. All of their particular contributions to the German philosophic tradition were embraced, he believed, in his notion of 'harmonic rationalism'.[70] In fact, though, Krause's doctrines represented simply a direct inheritance from Kant, attempting to overcome the dualism between the *questio quid facti* and the *questio quid juris*. In so doing he stressed Harmony and Unity in opposition to the Dialectic of Hegel, and believed that with his fivefold concept of the Spirit no type of knowledge would remain unattainable by Man. This left him operating within the framework of a logical account of validity, rather than attempting a transcendental epistemological account of how knowledge could be acquired.[71]

Although Catholic theology was obviously transcendental in the sense that it held that true knowledge could be revealed only after death, there are quite striking similarities with Krausism in the emphasis upon Harmony and Unity. Official Catholicism bitterly rejected Krausist notions as an affront to papal infallibility, but in fact Pope Leo XIII's encyclical *Aeterni Patris* (1879), with its clear Thomist influence, shared certain fundamental notions with the German idealist. The medieval scholastic thought of St Thomas Aquinas, based upon Aristotelian organicism, held an obvious appeal for Leo XIII, who rejected dialectical materialism in favour of an emphasis on class harmony. Likewise, Krause's notion of 'harmonic rationalism' rejected dialectical thought. In contradistinction to Hegel, Krause's philosophy wished to avoid the dissolution of the individual into the Absolute, and thus placed Man at the centre of an essentially humanist philosophy in which unity was the foundation of, rather than the result of, contradiction.[72]

Krausist 'harmonic rationalism' arrived in Spain under the auspices of Julián Sanz del Río, professor of the History of Philosophy in Madrid during the 1840s and 1850s. Sanz del Río had interpreted his mission as one of discovering a political philosophy adequate to the needs of Spain at the time. It should be borne in mind that

In philosophical matters...Spanish thought had yielded its most mature fruits in the sixteenth century. But of essentially new philosophy, the philosophy that began with Descartes, almost nothing was known...[73]

Such a context helps to explain why Sanz del Río felt that Spain 'needed' a political philosophy. He believed that in Krausism he had found the answer to that need. That Krausism took hold in Spain has less to do with the German philosopher's ideas in and of themselves than with the

immense attraction it held for Spanish intellectuals who had no desire to repudiate religious or even Christian experience and sensibility, but disliked the doctrinal formulations and narrow ecclesiastical discipline of Roman Catholicism.[74]

Indeed, in its Spanish variant, Krausism is best understood as an intellectual and ethical mode of being, a system of life, rather than as a strict philosophy. The main elements of this *Weltanschauung* comprised what might be termed rationality, morality and religiosity.[75] The rationality found expression in a commitment to scientific reasoning in investigation as against scholasticism and traditionalism; the morality in a commitment to the liberty of thought, of the press, of teaching and association, the inviolability of the person and of property, the rejection of privilege and arbitrary power, and the condemnation of violence from any quarter; and the religiosity was all-pervasive, though committed to reason and freedom against the prevailing Catholic integrationism of the time. The implications of all this for political action were much more in line with Fourier and Saint-Simon than with Marx. They included the belief that the only way to transform society was through gradual peaceful evolution. Social injustices, according to Krausism, derived from predominantly moral factors: egoism, avarice, lack of neighbourly love. Thus, in order to bring about change in a liberal direction, it was necessary first to achieve through education the ethical transformation of Man, which represented precisely the primary objective of Krausist philosophy.

It is somewhat ironic that one of the impulses that lay behind Sanz del Río seeking a philosophical system on German terrain was his strongly held Francophobia. He was convinced that the culture of France was harmful to the natural Spanish genius.[76] Whether genius was harmed by the influence of Guesde and Deville on the early Spanish Socialists is an open question, but the implantation and development of Marxist thought was certainly not helped either by their influence or by that of Krausism. Nonetheless, one of the most positive and concrete achievements of the Krausists was the creation in 1876 by Francisco Giner de los Ríos, a disciple of Sanz del Río, of the Institución Libre de Enseñanza (ILE). It was intended to be a free university designed, through an expressly liberal education, to nurture a progressive, democratic, modernising sector in Spain. However, economic constraints restricted the enterprise to primary level education. The *Institucionistas* were never revolutionaries. On the other hand, they *were* committed to a Krausist-inspired Liberalism which was against the rigid ideological hegemony of the reactionary Catholic political oligarchy, and they did perform an important role in opening channels for the development of progressive ideas in Spain.

Of course, of the wealth of creative talent which at one time or another came under the influence of Krausism and the ILE, only a relatively small number established direct links with the PSOE.[77] Those who did, though, included leading figures, such as Jaime Vera, Julián Besteiro or Fernando de los Ríos. In all of them it is possible to detect the imprint of austere morality and ethicism so characteristic of the Krausist 'spirit'. In no case was this truer than that of Pablo Iglesias, '*el abuelo*', whose incorruptible and spartan lifestyle bore testimony to his inflexible moral code. Within the Spanish Socialist movement, intense anti-clericalism like that of Tomás Meabe was not the norm; indeed, a motion to have practising Catholics expelled from the PSOE was heavily defeated at its 1899 Congress after Iglesias made clear his opposition.[78] It is unsurprising that in an era in which Marx's ideas were seen through either Guesdist or Second Internationalist lenses, and therefore considered essentially amoral, Marxism was never wholly internalised by the Spanish Socialists. The Marxist dogma as it was understood in Spain could be mouthed, and indeed it was, but the political implications deriving from it would always be avoided when these involved recourse to violence. Herein lay the roots of a later affinity on the part of Spanish Socialists with Jean Jaurès and Karl Kautsky.

The PSOE 1910–14: rifts and rupture

Following the 1909 Republican–Socialist Conjunction both the PSOE and the UGT experienced an impressive increase in membership.[79] However, the most immediate impact of the Conjunction, the election of Iglesias as the first PSOE deputy to the Cortes in 1910, also marked the beginning of the decline in his ability to dominate the Socialist movement. This decline intensified as his health deteriorated and as many of the 'second generation' of leaders – Besteiro, Prieto, Araquistáin, De los Ríos – joined the party in the following years. In fact, the years 1910 to 1914 witnessed the growth of internal divisions within the PSOE which would leave it severely weakened on the eve of the First World War. The pre-war period was marked by extraordinary ideological tergiversations, a reflection of the PSOE's confused ideological heritage. Iglesias, who for so many years had been associated with rigid dogmatism, now adopted the 'flexible' postures of the revisionist Julián Besteiro, a philosophy don who joined the PSOE in 1912. Besteiro, who would take over from *el abuelo* as leader of the Socialist movement following the latter's death in 1925, came to Socialism after an ILE-funded period of study in Germany. There he fell under the influence of neo-Kantianism which, together with the obligatory Krausism, was to remain a guiding philosophical point of reference throughout his political career and served as bridge to the Marxism of Karl Kautsky.[80] Meanwhile, many of those involved in the successive attempts to move away from *pablista* orthodoxy towards more open positions – García Quejido through *La Nueva Era*, Tomás Meabe through the FJSE, and Manuel Núñez de Arenas through the Escuela Nueva – were precisely those who now called for a 'hardening' of the PSOE's tactics. They would later argue for the PSOE's accession to the Third International, and break away to form the Partido Comunista Obrero Español (PCOE) in 1921 when it failed to do so.

The founding of the Escuela Nueva in 1910 by Núñez de Arenas followed very much in the tradition of *La Nueva Era* and the FJSE in attempting to widen the intellectual horizons of the PSOE. Núñez de Arenas proposed to introduce both science and culture to the working class, as well as to ensure its moral elevation, reflecting once more the strongly ethical strand of Spanish Socialist thought. Indeed, the Escuela Nueva group later defined itself as similar to the British Fabians.[81] However, somewhat against the dominant trend within the group, one of its leading members, the erstwhile *pablista* Jaime Vera, stressed his belief in the scientific character of socialism, and eschewed the moralistic appeals of the majority of PSOE leaders. His insistence on the need to analyse political action in terms of the relationship between theory and practice which characterised Marxism marked a distinct progress in the context of prevailing conceptions, but his was a voice lost in the wilderness. Moreover, Vera did not persist with this line. Like many of his colleagues, he became increasingly influenced by Jean Jaurès and, after the outbreak of war in 1914, increasingly disillusioned with politics.[82]

The appeal of Jaurès is easy to understand. In the words of Lichteim,

For Jaurès…the question was how Marxism could be incorporated…without doing fatal damage to the basic assumptions of eighteenth-century rationalism and moralism. Philosophically, the issue presented itself in terms of moral idealism versus scientific determinism…[83]

Jaurès' belief in the peaceful transformation of society through the democratic process was couched in evolutionary terms. He represented the fusion in France of the democratic and Socialist traditions, and effectively presided over the practical, if not verbal, distancing of the SFIO (Section Française de l'Internationale Ouvrière) from Marxism. Indeed, Jaurès was 'so fervent a moralist as to define his position almost exclusively in ethical terms.'[84] This refusal to separate Socialism from humanism, the appeal to Justice, found an echo amongst the Spanish Socialists, some of whom had effectively been Jaurèsian malgré eux since the 1880s, while others who joined after 1910 were explicitly so.

However, by 1914, considerations of developing Marxist theory in accordance with the political situation in Spain, never confronted directly by the leadership, were being forced ever further into the background in the PSOE. Instead, the issue of trade union tactics was provoking ever more open splits within the party. The ailing Iglesias consistently propounded the twin line of propaganda efforts supported by organised local strikes, but was opposed to all revolutionary initiatives. In fact, though, strike actions by the UGT were becoming increasingly independent of the central apparatus of the PSOE, particularly under powerful local leaders such as Eladio Fernández Egocheaga and Facundo Perezagua, who represented an embryonic izquierda socialista, or hard left. Perezagua had clashed with the leadership of the PSOE over the miners' strike in the Basque Country in 1910, and later the railway workers' strike of 1912 which started in Catalonia and extended to cover large areas of Spain. The bitterest clash, though, came over the 1913 Rio-Tinto miners' strike, which Perezagua and Egocheaga wanted to convert into a general strike with the ultimate aim of radicalising the PSOE. Iglesias, in collaboration with Manuel Llaneza, leader of the Asturian miners, opposed this move for fear of the PSOE's tactical line being undermined.[85] The upshot was the expulsion of Egocheaga from the UGT when he denounced the 'treason' of the Unión Ferroviaria at the Congress of 1914; Perezagua walked out of the Congress in solidarity, and was subsequently expelled from the PSOE at its 10th Congress in 1915.

The 10th Congress saw the sharpening of the polarisation between the minoritarian izquierda socialista, the group which was later to form the basis of the Spanish Communist Party, and the pablista leadership, characterised by moderation and pragmatism.[86] The central issue around which the two positions crystallised was the European war which had broken out in 1914. By this stage the minoritarians had been effectively excluded from an official platform. Barred from expressing their views in *El Socialista*, edited by the *pablista* Eduardo Torralba Beci, the minority group was forced to turn to other journals such as *España*, *Adelante* (Valladolid) or *La Justicia Social* (Reus). This last was the mouthpiece of the Catalan syndicalist Andreu Nin, who criticised with particular harshness prevailing Spanish interpretations of Marxism. Joaquín Maurín argued in the same journal that it was precisely because of the rigidity of the PSOE that Barcelona had fallen under the sway of Anarcho-syndicalism. Further criticisms of the organisation of the PSOE came from Antonio Fabra Ribas, a leading member of the Federación Catalana del PSOE. Other groups opposed to the line of Iglesias included the Escuela Nueva collective in Madrid, a group around Oscar Pérez Solís in Valladolid, and sectors of the party in the Basque Country associated with Perezagua. However, the minority group was soundly defeated at the 10th Congress as the National Committee passed a resolution on the European war calling for Spanish neutrality, but with the rider that it wished to see Germany defeated.[87]

Spain did not become involved in the conflict, so the PSOE was neither faced, like the SPD, with the issue of war-credits, nor polarised, like the PSI, by an acrimonious debate over war or neutrality. However, the ideological stance taken by the *pablista* leadership, a reflection, as so often, of that adopted by other European Socialist parties, suggests that the PSOE would anyway have fallen in line with the dominant trend of support for the war. In fact, Spanish neutrality allowed the PSOE to remain distanced from the battles which so damaged the Second International during the First World War. Instead, Spanish Socialism sank ever deeper into a crisis of its own making. The division between the *pablistas* and the minority in 1914 prefigured the later split between supporters of the Leninist Third International and defenders of the Second. That particular struggle, resolved only after three acerbic Extraordinary Congresses held between 1919 and 1921, was exacerbated by the PSOE's own calamitous involvement in an abortive general strike, itself the consequence of disastrous misunderstandings within the Socialist movement, in the summer of 1917. The government-led repression which followed the strike movement, together with the success of the October Revolution in Russia, cemented the polarisation within the PSOE. Traumatised by the consequences of the general strike, the *pablista* leadership definitively rejected revolutionary tactics. The minority group, meanwhile, increasingly convinced of the need to bolshevise the PSOE, left the party after their defeat in the 1921 Congress and formed a Communist Party faithful to Lenin's Third International. Reformist pragmatism was allowed free rein within the Spanish Socialist party until the tragic events of the Second Republic.

Organised Socialism in Spain before the First World War, then, was notable more for its weakness and stagnant theory than for any positive achievements. Faced from its foundation with the formidable handicap of a reactionary state backed by the repressive power of the army and the ideological power of the Catholic Church, the movement's limited appeal was compounded by its dependence for political and theoretical guidance on neighbouring northern European Socialist parties. This dependence was unfortunate. Whereas in northern Europe, France, and the Low Countries, mass Social Democratic parties were tolerated and indeed came to assume an established place in the political spectrum even before the war, a similar situation did not apply in Spain until much later. There, parliamentary democracy remained a façade; the content belied the form. Nonetheless, the PSOE, with few exceptions, was scrupulous in its respect for parliamentary procedures. Legalist and cautious, the Spanish Socialists adhered rigidly to rules designed to exclude them from political influence. What made sense for the SFIO in France, the German SPD or even the British Labour Party, all of which enjoyed genuine involvement to a greater or lesser extent in the official structures of the state, held rather less relevance for the PSOE. Indeed, by 1914 the SFIO had obtained 103 seats in the Chamber of Deputies, while the SPD was the biggest party in the Reichstag with 110 seats, reflecting over four million votes. Even in Sweden, Denmark, Finland, Belgium and Italy, Socialist parties had made impressive electoral advances.[88] The PSOE, meanwhile, attained just 45,000 votes in the 1910 elections, with Pablo Iglesias taking the party's one seat in the Cortes.[89]

Nonetheless, despite the clear lack of genuine democracy in Spain, the PSOE persisted with a legalist line which severely limited its possibilities of growth. The roots of this reformist reticence, married to a revolutionary rhetoric which merely served the interests of the state by providing it with a ready justification for repressing the movement at the slightest provocation, lay in the bizarre ideological inheritance of the Spanish Socialists. Whereas it is probably the case that in most European Socialist movements issues of theory and ideology played a smaller role in their political development than did issues of more direct and immediate relevance to the working class, in Spain ideology was paradoxically of the highest importance in a negative sense. Spanish Socialism before 1914 was marked by the attempt to apply a poorly understood conception of Marxism, mediated by Krausist–Catholic ideological influences, to an even more poorly understood political situation.

2 Reform, revolution and the roots of rupture: the PSOE, 1914–1919

Spain's neutrality during the First World War ensured that this most bloody of struggles aroused little passion amongst the great mass of Spanish citizens. Whereas their European counterparts were profoundly affected by involvement in a conflict which was inescapably to alter the normal course of their lives, the denizens of Spain experienced little immediate alteration to their daily routine following the outbreak of war in 1914.[1] However, it would be mistaken to assume that the war had little impact in the Iberian peninsula. On the contrary, it was instrumental in destabilising the so-called *turno pacífico*, the political system of the Restoration Monarchy, which, since 1875, had maintained both political and economic power in the hands of an agrarian-based reactionary coalition of *latifundistas* and the *haute bourgeoisie*. The economic impact of the war was enormous. Rapid industrial expansion occurred, particularly in northern regions, as Spain took advantage of her neutrality to become a major supplier to the belligerent powers.[2] The dramatic economic boom, however, gave rise to changes of the deepest significance within the existing social and political order. Although short-term benefits to the Spanish economy were spectacular, with a massive rise in the resources of the Bank of Spain, the longer-term impact was highly damaging. Unable and unwilling to respond to pressures for infrastructural modernisation, the ruling oligarchy simply engaged in capital accumulation and conspicuous consumption on a scale unknown since the heyday of Spain's Latin American empire.

There are four direct and linked economic consequences of the First World War which require emphasis here. First, it led to a numerical and political strengthening of two social classes previously noted for their weakness in Spain: the rapid expansion of the urban proletariat in the north of the country was mirrored by the development of a *nouveau riche* industrial bourgeoisie. Textiles, iron and steel, coal and especially the heavy chemicals industry all benefited from the possibilities offered by import substitution. New phosphate and aniline dye factories sprang up in Barcelona, Cáceres, Huelva and along the eastern and southern littorals, while mining concerns in the Basque Country and Asturias enjoyed vastly increased profits. Most dramatically, the previously uncompetitive and languishing Catalan textile industry was boosted by floods of orders for cloth to make military uniforms. For the first time, significant parts of the Spanish economy, particularly in the north of the country, began to exhibit characteristics associated with the industrial capitalist mode of production.[3]

Second, the war-induced boom exacerbated the uneven nature of Spanish economic development. Regional disparities were intensified, with a clear division between the industrial north and the agricultural remainder of the country. In 1914, over 60 per cent of the Spanish labour force worked the land, whilst industrial production accounted for just 20 per cent by the end of the war.[4] Moreover, development remained uneven within the two sectors. Whereas in the Basque Country, war profits were intelligently invested in diversifying the economic structure of the region, in Barcelona little such foresight was evident. With regard to agrarian produce, opportunities for export stimulated considerable increases in the production of wheat, which in turn strengthened the economic position of the Castilian *latifundistas* in particular, as well as acting as a disincentive to much-needed agricultural diversification. The *minifundios* of the north-western provinces remained woefully inefficient, whilst the southern-based *latifundio* estates witnessed few efforts to use war profits in order to modernise agricultural techniques. The region of Valencia, in particular, suffered badly during the war. Its primary export, wine, lost important markets in war-battered France, whilst orange exports were similarly hit.[5]

Third, although the stimulus to northern industrial and manufacturing production provided by the requirements of the belligerent powers failed to alter the continued dominance of agrarian interests in Spain, it did foster significant challenges to the Madrid-based political oligarchy. The expansion of the previously small-scale industrial proletariat, together with the growth of an urban-based bourgeoisie, laid the basis for increasing threats to the complacent hegemony of the reactionary coalition and the *turno* settlement. Most notably, the government's attempt to levy taxes on war profits as part of a wide-ranging economic programme formulated by Santiago Alba, Finance Minister in the Liberal administration of the Conde de Romanones, led to intense resentment in those northern industrial areas which stood to be the worst hit. The ambitious Alba, a disciple of the progressive and idiosyncratic visionary Joaquín Costa, critic of *caciquismo* and advocate of an 'Iron Surgeon' to cure Spain's ills, suffered from his connections with the wheat interests of Old Castile.[6] A centralist deputy for Valladolid, later to be one of the strongest opponents of agrarian reform measures during the Second Republic, Alba incensed the Catalan capitalists by masterminding the so-called Castellana Pact in April 1916, an attempt to undermine regionalist currents which were gaining strength in northeastern Spain. The effect was the opposite of that intended: Francesc Cambó, leader of the Lliga Regionalista which was to be at the centre of the 1917 Assembly Movement of Parliamentarians, was able to utilise Alba's tax proposals to build up impressive anti-Madrid support.[7] The impact of the First World War was thus a major boon to regionalist sentiment.

The fourth and most dramatic impact of the war was the onset of rampant inflation, together with a concomitant decline in labour relations. The price of basic staples such as wheat, corn, barley, rice, chickpeas and potatoes rose by between 70 per cent and 90 per cent between 1914 and 1918, provoking severe unrest amongst those most affected – the working class and the peasantry.[8] Equally damaging for labour relations, however, was the obvious unconcern of factory-owners for the plight of their employees. The industrial boom unleashed in northern Spain exhibited all the callousness associated with the capitalist mode of production at its most unrefined. Conditions of work were appalling, wages derisory, security of employment non-existent. To make matters worse, the entrepreneurial inefficiency of the parvenu bourgeoisie was matched only by the prodigality with which it drained its fatted wallet. Most notably in Barcelona, much new-found wealth was frittered on ostentatious display rather than invested in industry or agricultural modernisation. Such cavalier disregard for the living conditions of those on whose backs the wealth was created could hardly fail to antagonise Spanish workers. Victims of capitalist accumulation at its crudest, the burgeoning Spanish proletariat increasingly responded by flexing its newly acquired and growing industrial muscle. Strikes and labour unrest were to characterise the Spanish economy until the assumption of dictatorial powers by General Primo de Rivera in 1923, the self-proclaimed 'Iron Surgeon' called for by Costa.

Inevitably, the various consequences of the war had deep implications for the Socialist movement. The growth of an urban proletariat, together with increased labour unrest within both industrial and agrarian sectors, required urgent responses by a Socialist leadership anxious to establish hegemony over the Anarchists. Moreover, the PSOE was further influenced by events within the Second International, devastated by nationalist reactions to the outbreak of war within most member parties. Of the Socialist parties directly affected by the conflict, only the Partito Socialista Italiano (PSI) refused to abandon internationalist principles. Indeed, Benito Mussolini, editor of the PSI newspaper *Avanti!* until October 1914, was expelled from the party the following month for his commitment to Italian intervention.[9] In Germany, Rosa Luxemburg and Karl Liebknecht were amongst a small minority in the SPD opposed to voting war credits, supported in Austria by Friedrich Adler and by several exiled Russian Socialists. French Socialists sprang to the defence of their country following the German attack, with Jules Guesde and Marcel

Sembat joining the hated Republican government.[10] The PSOE, already internally divided over its electoral collaboration with the Republicans, was further split by its traditional mimetic dependence on guidance from European partners.

Domestically, the PSOE leadership quickly fell in line with a pro-Allied stance, associated in broad terms with anti-dynastic forces. Indeed, in very general terms, the Spanish *fuerzas vivas* (or establishment) divided between the ruling political oligarchy, which supported Germany, and more progressive liberal groups, mainly Republican, which backed Britain and France.[11] Still very much on the margins of political influence in Spain (the party had just 14,000 members in 1915), and confused by events within European Socialist parties, the PSOE opted to abandon principles in favour of safety through solidarity. The condemnation of the war in *El Socialista* during August 1914 as a conflict made inevitable by the logic of capitalism, gave way by the following month to an *aliadófilo* position based on that of the liberal Republicans, although equally on that of the Section Française de l'Internationale Ouvrière (SFIO). The clearest exposition of this line came in an *El Socialista* editorial of 12 September 1914, reaffirmed in a speech to the Cortes by Pablo Iglesias in November.[12] Rather than risk a return to isolationist stances, the *pablista* leadership followed prevailing trends amongst the more liberal-minded both at home and abroad.

The *pablista* position failed to win unanimous support within the PSOE. In the aftermath of Iglesias' speech, Mariano García Cortés, a portly Andalusian journalist trained as a lawyer, resigned as editor of *El Socialista*. García Cortés was to become one of the strongest critics of the *aliadófilo* position within the party. He was replaced as editor of *El Socialista* by the wiry Eduardo Torralba Beci, still unquestioningly loyal to the PSOE leader.[13] Antonio Fabra Ribas, meanwhile, the Catalan critic of *pablista* dominance, moved in the other direction: he published a book, *El socialismo y el conflicto europeo*, in which he argued that Spain should join a war between imperialism and democracy on the side of the Allies if it had the means to do so.[14] As so often, though, the initial skirmishes in the debate were marked by a lack of intellectual sophistication. As Andreu Nin pointed out, whereas in Germany the ideas of Bernstein were met by reasoned argument in a book by Kautsky, in Spain unpopular ideas provoked insults rather than argument.

Throughout 1915 two clear lines crystallised within the PSOE. The majority line, that of the official leadership, supported by many of the liberal intellectuals who had joined the party after the 1909 Republican–Socialist Conjunction, took a clear stand in support of the Allies. The minority position, associated mainly with García Cortés, Eladio Fernández Egocheaga and José Verdes Montenegro, argued for strict neutrality in a conflict which concerned only capitalists.[15] Supporters of the two positions clashed at the acerbic 10th Congress of the PSOE, held in Madrid between 24 and 31 October, 1915. In fact, there were three main lines of conflict at the Congress: the PSOE's position on the war, the Republican–Socialist Conjunction, and the internal organisation of the party. Delegates tended to align themselves, however, according to the central division between *aliadófilos* and strict neutralists. The first move by the Congress, though, was the expulsion of Facundo Perezagua's Agrupación de Bilbao from the PSOE, the culmination of a bitter struggle in Bilbao between the left-wing miners' leader and Indalecio Prieto, the moderate *pablista*. Perezagua's crime had been to oppose the Republican–Socialist Conjunction, ratified for the March 1914 general elections, and to field independent candidates against the official PSOE slate.[16]

At the Congress, the Conjunction was opposed by Verdes Montenegro, Fabra Ribas and Isidoro Acevedo, erstwhile *pablista*, now editor of *El Aurora Social* in Oviedo.[17] Their principal adversaries were Pablo Iglesias himself, Jaime Vera and a rising star of the Socialist movement, Julián Besteiro, elected vice-president of the party at the Congress. Born in Galicia in 1870, Besteiro had joined the PSOE in 1912, having previously been a member of Unión Republicana and the Radical Party of Alejandro Lerroux. A refined and cultured intellectual, Besteiro's true *métier* was philosophy rather than politics, although he played a leading political role until his death in a Francoist jail in 1940. He hated violence, and espoused an evolutionist view of Socialism, which saw its establishment as the ineluctable consequence of capitalist contradiction. Besteiro was an archetypical representative of the austere asceticism which characterised *pablista* Socialism: moralistic, politically cautious, and fundamentally concerned with the PSOE organisation.[18]

The debate on the Republican–Socialist Conjunction was of a very low theoretical level. Basic issues which lay at the heart of the question, such as the role of electoralism in Socialist strategy, possible participation in power, and the nature and role of Republicanism in Spain, were confronted only in passing. It was decided to continue with the Conjunction by a vote of 3,106 against 2,850. The other debates were of a similarly low standard. On the issue of PSOE organisation, the Catalan Josep Recaséns i Mercadé led calls for the creation of a federal structure with genuine autonomy for regional sections, as opposed to the prevailing dominance within the National Committee of the Agrupación Socialista Madrileña. He was supported by Fabra Ribas and Acevedo, but Iglesias argued that the PSOE's structure was not open to modification, allowing only that regional federations of the party should be entitled to send one delegate to meetings of the National Committee.[19]

The most important issue discussed at the Congress was the position of the PSOE on the war which had broken out in Europe over a year earlier. A working group set up to produce a report, comprised of Jaime Vera, Eduardo Torralba Beci, José Medinabeitia, José Verdes Montenegro and Manuel Vigil, was unable to reach agreement. It was decided to leave Dr Vera, author of the near-legendary *Informe* to the Comisión de Reformas Sociales in 1883, to write the text. The result, like the *Informe*, was a long and confused document, marked this time by a scientistic vocabulary which betrayed Darwinian evolutionist influences.[20] Vera's text concluded with an unambiguous statement of support for the Allies, support for Spanish neutrality and a pointed proposal, aimed at the opponents of the Conjunction with the Republicans, to abandon the isolationism which characterised Spanish Socialism. More than this, though, the final point represented a specific call for reformism:

against the policy of isolationism, we propose a policy of penetration of and struggle within the bourgeois world, into which we should introduce our forces of manoeuvre in order. . .to take advantage of bourgeois capacities and, in particular, to act jointly with all progressive elements, because all progressive action ultimately works in our favour.

Vera's report was supported by Torralba Beci and Medinabeitia; as the latter's rhetorical question put it, 'Were we going to argue with the wise Dr Vera?'.[21]

Vigil and Verdes Montenegro, however, insisted on their right to present individual reports.[22] Like Vera, Manuel Vigil took an *aliadófilo* stance, but presented his views in a far more direct and concise fashion, arguing that Germany must bear specific guilt within the general blame that attached to the capitalist system for the outbreak of the war. Verdes Montenegro took a much more radical stance. While he agreed that the root cause of the war was capitalism, he further insisted that the PSOE should comply with its past pronouncements and condemn the conflict whilst calling on member parties of the Second International to strive for peace. Following this report, an amendment supporting Vera was proposed by Besteiro, Fabra Ribas and Luis Araquistáin. In the debates, Besteiro and Araquistáin were the principal defenders of the Vera position, against the minority line of Verdes Montenegro, Egocheaga and García Cortés. The level of the debate remained uninspired until Araquistáin intervened to provide sparkling support to a lightweight argument made by Besteiro. A widely travelled polemicist and journalist from Santander, Araquistáin had joined the PSOE in 1911. Cultured, indeed almost debonair, he was representative of a group of liberal intellectuals, many with roots in the Krausist-inspired Institución Libre de Enseñenza, who turned to Socialism for its morality more than its Marxism:

The start of my Socialism is this unjust and iniquitous division of things which rules in the world. It is not things in themselves, most of which I would destroy as superfluous and boring, which matter to me, so much as the humiliation represented to my dignity as a man and to the dignity of all others by the rules according to which they are distributed. . .The ends of my Socialism are that there should be a better distribution of goods, not to satisfy desire. . .but rather so that every man can raise himself to a spiritually purer life, to the world of the great questions of ideals.[23]

Twenty years later, when he adopted militant Marxism during the bitter internal struggle of the PSOE in the Second Republic, Araquistáin would utilise his polemical skills to launch an assault on Besteiro which all but ended the professor's political career.[24] In 1915, though, Araquistáin was establishing his reputation within the PSOE as a leading moderate defender of the *aliadófilo* position. He provided the main ammunition for Pablo Iglesias to close the debate on the PSOE's position on the war. *El abuelo*, seriously ill and able to attend the Congress only briefly, rejected Verdes Montenegro's concept of international pacifism, arguing instead that since the war was the fault of Germany, the only people who had betrayed Internationalist principles were the German Socialists.[25] The report by Verdes was rejected by 25 votes to 10, and that of Vigil by 20 to 9; the majority report was therefore automatically adopted, with the Besteiro–Fabra Ribas–Araquistáin amendment included. The PSOE thus published a resolution on the war which called for continued Spanish neutrality, but with the rider that 'we have made clear our sympathies and our wishes that those whose victory we see as beneficial for working people should triumph.'

The 10th Congress had two important implications for the PSOE. First, it underlined the reformist caution which characterised *pablista* Socialism. The rise to prominent positions by figures such as Besteiro and Araquistáin (elected to the National Committee) ensured that evolutionist gradualism would continue to hold sway within the party. Nonetheless, the Congress also demonstrated the existence of a number of opposed currents within the party: advocates of greater organisational flexibility and more radical political postures. Second, though, the 10th Congress confirmed the ideological dependence of the party. The reactions to the war expressed by PSOE leaders were almost entirely secondhand, derived from the manifestos published by neighbouring European Socialist parties. Arguments were poorly elaborated, debate uninspired. More important, they reflected European priorities. The war was analysed almost entirely in terms of Second International orientations. There was no analysis of its impact in Spain, of how the Spanish proletariat and peasantry were being affected by the conflict. Instead, the PSOE loyally played out a debate using borrowed terms. Indeed, it was as if the party had been only peripherally involved in setting the agenda of its own Congress.[26]

It was to be expected that the *pablistas* would make no reference during the 10th Congress to the Zimmerwald Conference which had been held in Switzerland just a month earlier, in September 1915. The stage for Lenin's announcement of the death of the Second International, as well as his call for international social revolution, Zimmerwald had nothing to recommend it to the reformist Spaniards.[27] More surprising, perhaps, was the silence on Zimmerwald by members of the minority group such as García Cortés and Verdes Montenegro. Their opposition to the dominant line within the PSOE, though, was based on what they took to be a principled stance. This did not make them revolutionaries. After all, their proposals were wholly in line with the resolution adopted by the Second International at its Stuttgart Congress in 1907, at which García Cortés had been present as part of the PSOE delegation, and reconfirmed at Copenhagen in 1910 and again at Basle in 1912.[28] The resolution stipulated that:

If an outbreak of war appears imminent, the workers and their parliamentary representatives...must do everything in their power to prevent war breaking out...If war should still break out, they must take all steps to bring it to a speedy conclusion...[29]

Lenin's venomous attacks against 'opportunist, bourgeois, social chauvinists' in the Socialist movement, and his calls for social revolution, were unlikely to receive support from those who were, after all, in practice essentially liberal intellectuals.[30]

   Where Zimmerwald did receive a positive response was amongst some members of the PSOE youth movement, the Federación de Juventudes Socialistas (FJSE), founded a decade earlier by Tomás Meabe. Even though there were no Spanish representatives at the Swiss conference, FJSE members Ramón Lamoneda and Manuel Núñez de Arenas were enthused by the Zimmerwald accords. At the 5th Congress of the FJSE, held in the Madrid Casa del Pueblo at the end of November, they called on the PSOE to adhere to the accords, but were opposed by the president, Andrés Saborit, the centrist editor of *Acción Socialista*.[31] Their proposal was roundly defeated by 18 votes to 2. However, the FJSE Congress marked the opening of the conflict between Lamoneda and Núñez de Arenas on the one hand, and Saborit on the other, which would intensify in bitterness over the following years until the secession of the FJSE from the PSOE in 1921. Radical posturing by FJSE members in late 1915, though, was more of a nuisance than a threat to *pablista* dominance. The Youth Movement remained too small to wield significant influence over the senior organisation.

   By the start of 1916, then, the pro-Allied position had attained hegemony within the Spanish Socialist movement. Concomitantly, even the rhetoric of revolutionary class warfare was increasingly abandoned by a PSOE leadership committed to parliamentary tactics through alliance with the Republicans. Nonetheless, the predominance of the *pablistas* was precarious. Indeed, their victory at the 10th Congress merely prefigured renewed battles with a minoritarian opposition which showed no signs of abandoning its struggle against the *Santa Hermandad* around Iglesias. However, the most significant problem on the horizon for the PSOE leadership was one which had little to do with the debate between neutralism and *aliadofilismo*, but everything to do with the war. The continued economic success engendered by the conflict was matched by rising inflation which in turn was provoking increasingly serious social unrest. As industry developed in the north of the country, so too did use of the strike as an expression of grievance. The number of working days lost in 1916 jumped to 2,415,304 compared to 382,885 the previous year; the number of strikes rose from 169 to 237, of which 71 per cent were directly related to economic demands.[32] In rural areas, the debilitating effect of inflation was exacerbated by the collapse of emigration possibilities during the war. The number of Spanish emigrants fell from 195,000 in 1912 to just 20,000 in 1918. Internal migration to urban centres was therefore intensified, leading inevitably to increased social tension as former agricultural labourers failed to find employment. Between 1910 and 1923 the population of Madrid rose by 170,000 and that of Barcelona by 180,000.[33]

The combination of prices outstripping wage increases, insufficient labour mobility, and brutal working conditions, culminated in a three-year period of uninterrupted social unrest in rural areas, between 1919 and 1921, known as the *trienio bolchevique*. Before then, however, the Spanish body politic was severely rocked by the revolutionary events of 1917. These were essentially urban-based, the result of three basically unrelated protest movements which converged during the summer of 1917 only inasmuch as they were all aimed against the government. The protesters were army officers through the Juntas Militares de Defensa, Catalan industrialists and financiers through the Assembly Movement, and the working class through the PSOE–UGT and the Anarcho-syndicalist CNT. The leaders of this last group not only misinterpreted the aims and aspirations of the other two groups, but also overestimated their own strength and resources. The consequences of the 1917 revolutionary turmoil were to be devastating for the Socialists.

Throughout 1916, the Socialist movement underwent a period of enforced reorganisation. The PSOE and particularly the UGT had been experiencing spectacular, if uneven, expansion since 1910. However, in 1916 the trend started to suffer an alarming reversal. Figures for the whole of Spain showed that the UGT reached a peak of nearly 130,000 members between 1912 and 1914, but had fallen back to under 85,000 by the middle of 1916.[34] In Aragon, to take one local example where the UGT had been enjoying considerable success, membership rose from just 98 in 1910 to

1,144 in 1916, but had crashed to 165 within two years. There was a similar story in the Basque Country, one of the PSOE's early centres of strength, where membership of the Socialist Party fell from a peak of 968 in 1916 after a steady rise in each of the previous six years.[35]

This stagnation in the growth of the PSOE and UGT almost certainly reflected workers' frustration with the characteristic procedures of Spanish Socialism: deliberation and caution rather than confrontation. After a period of relative calm in labour relations, workers were beginning to react to the negative costs of Spain's war-induced economic boom, which had begun to bite by 1916. In the Basque Country, for instance, a strike in the spring of 1916 in the Vizcaya metallurgy industry ended a five-year period of relative harmony, while in Guipúzcoa long and bitter strikes occurred during the summer.[36] While there had been occasional serious strikes in the preceding years – the railway strike of 1912, Rio-Tinto miners in 1913, and above all the frequent strikes organised by the SOMA, the Socialist miners' federation in Asturias[37] – there had been nothing on the scale of the wave of disputes that hit Spanish industry in 1916. The UGT should have been in prime condition to take advantage of the increased size and militancy of the Spanish proletariat. In fact, though, since its leadership comprised the same people who headed the PSOE, the UGT was every bit as cautious and legalistic as the *pablista* party.

Had there been no viable alternative workers' syndical federation, the diffidence of the UGT leadership would not have assumed any particular importance. The local membership would presumably have acted in accordance with its own ends, regardless of official policy. Indeed, to an extent this is exactly what occurred with local leaders such as Perezagua and Egocheaga. As was to happen again during the Second Republic, the reformist parliamentary stances of the PSOE–UGT leadership were often ignored by a membership which sought immediate satisfaction of its grievances. However, in 1916 a viable alternative did exist, and one which was demonstrably more dynamic than the UGT: the Anarcho-syndicalist Confederación Nacional del Trabajo (CNT). The CNT had been formed in Barcelona at the end of 1910, and declared illegal a year later by a Barcelona judge following its involvement in a general strike almost certainly triggered by the government.[38] In 1912 the assassination of the Prime Minister, José Canalejas, brought down vicious repression on the CNT which was forced to live a clandestine existence, in theory organised by a secret National Committee which in practice was unable to meet. The CNT was reorganised in 1915 following its legalisation the previous year by the Liberal administration of the Conde de Romanones.

In spite of the severity of the repression unleashed against the CNT prior to 1914, it managed to rebuild its strength remarkably quickly.[39] In

February 1915, the Anarchists organised an International Congress for Peace, held in the Galician town of El Ferrol. It was contemptuously dismissed by the Socialists; Fabra Ribas, the Catalan *aliadófilo* remarked,

> . . .they can spend their lives building castles in the air. But what they cannot do is make a fool of the Spanish working class in front of outside organisations, nor make insulting remarks about our impotence and ignorance.[40]

Whilst the Congress was hardly an international success, the number of Spanish workers' organisations which sent delegates acted as a powerful stimulus to reconstitute the CNT. Over the summer months of 1915, Catalan Anarchists worked to this end; in October, *La Justicia Social* announced the rebirth of the Anarcho-syndicalist federation. According to Angel Pestaña, the puritanical and widely experienced itinerant worker who was to become one of Spanish Anarchism's leading lights, the CNT had 15,000 members in 1915.[41] In the circumstances, this compared favourably with the UGT's membership, especially since the Socialist union remained poorly embedded in Catalonia. Indeed, the UGT lacked representation altogether in three important Catalan provinces: Lérida, Tarragona and Gerona.[42] This was of the utmost significance, for it was precisely in Catalonia, where the Socialist movement was still under-developed, that the most direct challenges to the Madrid government would arise.

Of equal significance is the fact that the CNT message, promising immediate action, found a ready audience amongst the industrial workers of Barcelona. The workers basically sought effective representation: the CNT appeared more likely to provide it than the UGT. Indeed, it has been shown that in periods when the CNT was subject to repression, particularly between 1920 and 1922 at the hands of the vicious Civil Governor of Barcelona, Severiano Martínez Anido, Catalan workers turned to the Catholic Sindicatos Libres, the so-called 'Yellow Unions', rather than the UGT.[43] Almost since its foundation, the Socialist party had appeared unresponsive to Catalan needs and realities. Both the PSOE and the UGT were based in Madrid, the latter having been moved to the capital in 1898 after its initial establishment ten years earlier in Barcelona under the leadership of Antonio García Quejido. Indeed, there was hardly even any propaganda effort expended in Catalonia by the Socialists. Ironically, and extraordinarily, a party set up primarily by members of the printing profession had failed to establish a single lasting Socialist journal in Barcelona by 1918.[44] There is strong evidence to suggest that the apparent mystery of Anarchist strength in Catalonia finds a large part of its explanation in the simple fact that Catalan workers had little in the way of a viable alternative. The Socialists early ceded control of the workers' movement in Barcelona in order to concentrate on building up their organisation in Madrid. The costs became clear in 1917.

Before then, though, the UGT had made uncharacteristic moves towards *rapprochement* with the CNT. In May 1916, the UGT held its 12th Congress in Madrid. There were two main items on the agenda. First, the economic situation of the working class was discussed. A resolution, proposed by Julián Besteiro, was passed calling on the government to take urgent action to reduce the cost of basic essentials, with the threat of a national one-day general strike should it fail to do so. Second, there was a debate on the question of the relationship between the Socialist union federation and the rapidly expanding CNT.[45] Although various points of view were expressed, there was a general feeling that it would be desirable to seek syndical unity in Spain. These two issues are of fundamental significance. The resolution calling for an *abaratamiento* of the cost of living was pitched in the most reformist and legalistic terms: it was agreed 'to demand [action], once more, from Parliament and the government. . .'; 'to prepare the public for a campaign which has as its end to secure [a response] from Parliament. . .'; to give specific notice of the date of the strike. There was nothing revolutionary here, nothing even particularly threatening to the government. True to their *pablista* heritage, the UGT leaders exercised customary caution.[46]

The second issue of significance concerned the desire for unity with the CNT. Such a desire flew in the face of the Socialists' traditional mistrust of other workers' organisations. Since the foundation of the PSOE in 1879, Pablo Iglesias had always jealously guarded Socialist independence. Indeed, it was not until 1909 that he was prepared to countenance even an electoral alliance with liberal Republican parties. Thus, the call for joint action with the CNT may seem surprising.[47] There are perhaps two main reasons which help explain the Socialist shift. First, as we have seen, a principal concern of the Socialist leaders since 1879 had been to build up an efficient, and ultimately powerful, organisation. Issues of ideology had often seemed to be relegated to second place behind a fundamental concern to maintain intact the structure and coherence of an organisation which had as its basic aim the establishment of hegemony amongst Spanish workers. The growth of the PSOE and UGT in the aftermath of the Republican–Socialist Conjunction, coupled with the state-backed repression of the Anarchist movement following the formation of the CNT in 1911, suggested that by 1914 the Socialist leaders' great ambition was becoming a reality. However, the resurrection of the CNT in 1915 and its immediate success in attracting widespread support among the burgeoning proletariat of Catalonia, represented a serious threat to the Socialists' hopes. The CNT looked capable of establishing itself as a major rival force to the UGT, and even outstripping it. Conscious of this risk, the PSOE–UGT leaders must have realised the potential benefits that would accrue to their organisation should they be able to subsume the still smaller CNT within a united syndical federation in which they would retain hegemony.

Second, though, whereas in the past there had been a major ideological gulf beween the Socialists and the Anarchists, this had now narrowed. The CNT was really an amalgam of Anarchist and Syndicalist strands, with the latter, represented by Angel Pestaña and Salvador Seguí holding the upper hand. Seguí, in particular, shared the Socialist concern with organisation. Known as the Noi del Sucre ('Sugar-boy'), the charming, if volatile, autodidact Seguí had toned down his youthful radicalism to become a profoundly moderate leader.[48] He clashed with the more fundamentalist Anarchists over their impatience to unleash the revolution at every moment. Like the Socialists, he was convinced that the revolution in Spain lay sometime in the future, and that it would come about only after a lengthy period of thorough preparation. Seguí, though, was also well aware of the importance of revolutionary rhetoric. A fiery orator, he often harangued mesmerised audiences in Catalan and demonstrated a remarkable ability to take charge of potentially explosive situations. Together with Pestaña, he ensured that the reconstituted CNT abandoned the more extremist activities associated with the Anarchist movement in Barcelona at the turn of the century, when 'propaganda by deed' was much in evidence. The relative restraint of the new CNT leaders recommended them as allies to the hesitant Socialists.

Discussions between the two federations culminated in the Pact of Zaragoza, signed by the UGT and CNT on 17 July 1916. The latter were represented by Pestaña, Seguí and the local Anarchist, Angel Lacort; the former by Besteiro, Vicente Barrio, the moderate Basque miners' leader, and by Francisco Largo Caballero, a dour former plasterer who had been working his way up the hierarchy of the UGT since joining the union in 1890. Largo was in some respects the Socialist homologue to Seguí. Like the CNT leader, he believed passionately in the virtues of organisation; similarly, he was acutely aware of the need to tailor his message to suit the disposition of a given audience. A Madrid councillor since 1905, and member of the UGT National Committee since 1908, when he became vice-president of the union, Largo had advanced in the Socialist movement through his intense loyalty to Pablo Iglesias. Indeed, *el abuelo* was a major formative influence on this UGT activist who was to play an ever more central role in Spanish politics until Franco's victory in the Civil War. Largo Caballero was the UGT's chief negotiator with the CNT during 1916. He gives only the sketchiest details of the negotiations in his memoirs, but it is likely that the 1916 discussions represented an early example of what was to become a typical feature of Largo's period as leader of the UGT: the attempt to offset threats to the hegemony of the Socialist union by absorption of its rivals.[49]

The aim of the Pact of Zaragoza, which formally allied the UGT and CNT, was to force the government of Romanones to take action on the still rising cost of living. While workers were elated by the signing of the pact, the government was alarmed. Constitutional guarantees were suspended and many trade unionists arrested. The momentum, however, seemed to lie with the workers. Intense propaganda activity culminated in the declaration of a 24-hour general strike on 18 December 1916. Inasmuch as it was widely supported, the strike was a resounding success, the first such success in the history of the Spanish labour movement. It was to be short-lived. The government failed to respond to workers' demands and fell within six months, Romanones having resigned in April and been replaced by Manuel García Prieto.[50] By June, the Conservative Eduardo Dato had taken over, bringing to an end any hopes of governmental concern for workers' interests. In a sense, therefore, the December strike represented a chimerical success.

In fact, the Liberal administration of Romanones did nothing even though it had been kept well informed of UGT–CNT intentions. Julián Besteiro, in particular, had led a number of delegations to see the Prime Minister and the Minister of the Interior, Joaquín Ruiz Jiménez, hoping to persuade the government to obviate the need for a strike.[51] That Romanones chose to do nothing, despite apparently promising action, reflected not so much duplicity as the government's political bankruptcy. The intensification of activity by the labour movement represented just one more in a series of intractable problems which combined by 1917 to render the Liberal administration ineffective. Indeed, more damaging for the government's possibilities of survival than the UGT–CNT initiatives were the discontents developing within the army and amongst Catalan industrialists. Up to a point workers' demands could simply be ignored; that was not true of the providers of Spain's wealth and defence. To the Socialists and the Anarcho-syndicalists, though, it looked as if their pressure had been instrumental in toppling the Liberals. This was to be a very costly misjudgement.

The crisis of 1917, which culminated in August with the savage repression of a Socialist-led general strike, had immensely complex roots. At its most basic, it served to indicate that the Canovite system of the Restoration Monarchy, the so-called *turno pacífico*, had reached the point of political stagnation. That the system was able in the short term to survive the challenges of 1917 was testimony in part to the Machiavellian skills of Eduardo Dato, but more so to the continued repressive power of the state, especially in Catalonia under General Martínez Anido. However, purportedly democratic regimes which rely too heavily on repression often lose legitimacy and hence stability: the *turno* system struggled on for a further six years in the midst of ever-growing challenges before General Miguel Primo de Rivera assumed power in a widely welcomed *pronunciamiento* in September 1923. The crisis of 1917, then, marked the beginning of the end for the Restoration political settlement, an artificial democracy which had as its true aim the defence of agrarian capitalist interests. It was unable to assimilate the challenges posed by the rise of a new industrial proletariat and the growing self-confidence of a Catalan bourgeoisie which was becoming ever more resentful of providing financial support to the Madrid-based political oligarchy.

Two further elements contributed to the growing atmosphere of political breakdown. On the one hand, Spain was becoming ineluctably involved in the war by the twin development of a German submarine blockade which directly affected Spanish shipping, and the entry into the conflict of the United States of America. On the other, discontent in the Spanish military saw the evolution of the Juntas Militares de Defensa, essentially a revolt of military bureaucrats seeking to protect their own professional interests against political ineptitude.[52] The officers involved were deeply affected by the price inflation which was gripping the Spanish economy. Poorly paid and disaffected, the officers sought redress for their grievances through the formation of the Juntas, a sort of mesocratic military version of a trade union. As Juan Antonio Lacomba has suggested, the impact of syndicalism was far-reaching in Spain during the years of the First World War.[53] The first Juntas took shape in early 1916 in Barcelona, centre of syndical dynamism in Spain during the second decade of the twentieth century. Essentially concerned about issues of status, they couched their demands in the fashionable language of 'regenerationism', and posed as figureheads of a national reform movement. Ultimately, it transpired that the Juntas were anything but revolutionary. In 1917, though, while they threatened the governments of Romanones and García Prieto, they looked to many, including the Socialists, like important potential allies.

The First World War accelerated a process that was probably largely inevitable. However, the Liberal administration of Romanones was itself in large measure responsible for unleashing the chain of events which would lead to the 'hot summer' of 1917. In particular, the bill introduced on 3 June 1916 by Santiago Alba, Minister of Finance, announcing a tax on the 'excess' war profits of Catalan industrialists, provoked intense opposition, especially since there was no parallel proposal to tax the wheat profits of Castilian agriculturalists. Alba was forced to withdraw his bill within a week.[54] The incident, though, provided a major boost to the Lliga Regionalista of Francesc Cambó, an ambitious industrialist and financier who was the driving force behind the Assembly Movement. This Movement was an extraordinarily confused amalgam of anti-dynastic Republican forces which came together and quickly fell apart in the summer of 1917.[55] At root, Cambó remained a 'regenerationist' conservative, resistant to social progress which would further the interests of the working class sufficiently to allow them to pose any challenge to bourgeois capitalist accumulation. Nonetheless, in the context of the political stagnation of the Restoration Monarchy, he appeared progressive merely by virtue of his opposition to the Romanones administration.

Cambó spent the early months of 1917 holding meetings with representatives of other parties opposed to the *turno* system and the political dominance of the Madrid-based landed oligarchy. Amongst his many interlocutors were the two mainstays of Republicanism – the Radicals of Alejandro Lerroux, the fiery and ambitious anti-clerical demagogue, and the Reformists of Melquíades Alvarez, a Krausist-influenced modernising democrat whose elitist political commitments were marked by ambiguity.[56] It is of no small significance that both Lerroux and Alvarez would end up on the Right of the political spectrum in the Second Republic. Like Cambó, their opposition to the dynastic *turno pacífico* did not extend beyond the defence of bourgeois interests. In 1917, though, Spanish Republicanism was characterised by confusion. Having entered the electoral alliance with the Socialists partly out of a desire to rationalise the various constituent forces which made up their ranks – Federalists, Centralists, Radicals, Progressives, Possibilists – the Republicans were now once more divided by Lerroux's refusal to remain in the alliance and Alvarez's hesitations over bringing into it his Reformist Party, formed in 1912. The uncertainties of the Republicans during 1917 contributed in no small measure to the collapse of their reformist intentions. Equally, they led to confusion within the Socialist movement.

Space precludes an analysis in minute detail of the events of 1917 which led up to the general strike in August. Instead, the most that can be attempted here is to explain how and why the Socialist movement became involved during 1917 in a series of alliances with ideologically antipathetic groups. Behind the Socialists' activities during 1916 and 1917 lay the fundamental belief that Spain was in the throes of revolutionary change, and that both the Juntas Militares de Defensa and the Catalan industrialists were part and parcel of a wider republican movement seeking to bring down the Restoration Monarchy. There were two major problems in such an assessment. First, it was incorrect: both the Juntas and the industrialists were primordially concerned with particularistic interests, rather than with bringing down the monarchy. Indeed, they could quite happily tolerate a monarchy so long as the ruling government refrained from interfering in their affairs. Second, even had it been accurate, the Socialists remained unclear as to the nature of the revolutionary change in question and their role within it. If, as both the majority *aliadófilos* and the minority neutralists believed, Spain was about to undergo the long overdue bourgeois revolution, then this raised the issue of whether and in what capacity the Socialists should be involved. As would happen again during 1934 with similar consequences, the PSOE leaders had insufficiently developed ideas of what exactly they were fighting for as opposed to what they were fighting against.[58] Beyond the notion of 'revolution', which in practice represented little more than a vague maxim, they had no coherent strategy.

On 5 March 1917, the National Committee of the PSOE convened a meeting of its regional federations, as agreed at the 10th Congress, and issued a strongly worded manifesto against the government's neutralism and passivity. In the light of the German submarine blockade on Spanish shipping, the PSOE executive called on the government to take 'drastic measures'.[59] Against the views of the minoritarians within the party, the PSOE leadership was taking an ever clearer pro-Allied stance on the war. At the same time, the PSOE remained committed to collaboration with the CNT, despite the fundamental disagreements over Spain's position on the war. Thus, on 27 March, UGT and CNT delegates held a meeting in the theatre of the Casa del Pueblo in Madrid. The two union federations signed and jointly published a manifesto, 'To the Spanish Workers and to the Country in General', drawn up by Julián Besteiro.[60] The manifesto made reference to the general strike of the previous December, and noted at some length that the government had done nothing since then to alleviate the privations being suffered by the working class. It ended with the threat to call an indefinite general strike, stating that

the proletarian organisations, in accordance with their leadership, will proceed towards the adoption of all the measures they deem necessary for the success of the general strike, ensuring they are ready for the moment at which it commences.

The signatories included Seguí and Pestaña for the CNT and Largo Caballero, Besteiro, Barrio, Anguiano and Saborit, amongst others, for the National Committee of UGT, together with representatives from Zaragoza, the Levant, the Basque Country, Asturias, Old Castile and Andalusia.[61]

The mood amongst the delegates was buoyant, spirits having been raised by the abdication in Russia of Tsar Nicholas earlier in the month. Although the mass of the Spanish population remained untouched by and uninterested in Russian events, the workers' leaders were encouraged by the news from St Petersburg. However, the Socialists did not see the Ides of March abdication of the Tsar as a harbinger of Socialist revolution; the weight of historical determinism bore down upon them far too heavily to allow such a reading. Socialist revolution was regarded as an impossibility in economically backward countries. As *El Socialista* put it, 'Russia is sufficiently mature for democracy, but not yet for Socialism.'[62] In fact, following the fall of the Tsar, the Socialists were simply strengthened in their *aliadófilo* beliefs now that the Allied powers were no longer compromised by association with an autocratic and despotic regime. Luis Araquistáin published an article in *España* expressing both points:

the liberal revolution has arrived. This revolution gives the allied countries a political unity which they needed. Russia was the dark stain in this immense liberating crusade. With Tsarism eliminated, the new regime is bound to sow confusion in the spirit of many Germans.[63]

However, although the fall of the Tsar was to be welcomed, the possibility of Russian withdrawal from the war provoked alarm amongst Socialist leaders. *El Socialista* carried regular reports from Russia, but no supportive editorial stance was evident.

The strength of *aliadófilo* feeling amongst the PSOE leaders, as well as the measured nature of their response to the fall of the Tsar in Russia, makes the tone of the 27 March manifesto seem surprising in its militancy. There are two probable reasons for the manifesto's revolutionary tenor. In the first place, it reflected accommodation to the desires of both the restless workers and the more militant members of the CNT. The Anarchists had been more positive than the Socialists in their response to the March revolution in Russia, but initial enthusiasm faded rapidly when it was realised that the Tsar had been replaced by a bourgeois Provisional Government. For all the caution of Pestaña and Seguí, the CNT remained at root a revolutionary organisation; it was hardly likely to put its name to anything less than a revolutionary document. Second, the PSOE leaders almost certainly hoped that by adopting a sufficiently threatening tone they might scare the government of Romanones into taking action to avert the necessity actually to call the strike. Such political brinkmanship entailed serious risks for an organisation which was never truly committed to revolution: it not only offered grounds for a governmental crackdown, but also raised false expectations amongst the working class. As Dolores Ibárruri, the young Asturian militant who was later to achieve renown as 'Pasionaria', commented,

We went without sleep, waiting for the call to action at any moment. Time passed, and there was a risk that our revolutionary ardor would subside. The workers were impatient and began to whisper about the leadership, which had hinted at such momentous events to come.[64]

No sooner had the March manifesto been issued than it was declared seditious by the government. Constitutional guarantees were suspended, the Madrid Casa del Pueblo was shut, and several of the signatories to the manifesto were arrested and jailed until 3 April, when public pressure forced their release.[65] The government had by this stage reached the point of exhaustion. Romanones resigned on 19 April, bombarded by criticism from all directions following the sinking by German submarines of the Spanish freighter *San Fulgencia* off the French coast ten days earlier. He was replaced by Manuel García Prieto, his bitter rival for leadership of the faction-ridden Liberal Party. However, the change of prime minister only heightened the sense of crisis which was gripping the entire Spanish nation. García Prieto did take some small steps towards trying to defuse tension. Two days after assuming office, he restored constitutional guarantees, and allowed the Madrid Casa del Pueblo to re-open. However, the action was too little, too late and aimed at the wrong quarter. The most pressing problem for the government was continued discontent within the Juntas Militares de Defensa. An attempt to dissolve the Juntas in May merely resulted in their increased consolidation. By the end of the month there existed a situation of open defiance between the King and the government on the one hand and the military on the other. Mindful of the Russian precedent, in which the defection of the army had been a key factor in the fall of the Tsar, the political estate backed down in the clash of wills when the Juntas published a manifesto on 1 June threatening a full-scale coup.[66]

Within the various opposition groups, meanwhile, activity had been intense. The PSOE, still deeply involved in the war issue, took an ever more explicit pro-Allied stance. The party gave wholehearted support to its counterparts in France and Belgium, as well as rejecting the declarations of the Zimmerwald Conference and its follow-up in Kienthal. Pablo Iglesias, despite being almost constantly ill, repeatedly called for the breaking off of relations with Germany.[67] Nonetheless, the PSOE declined an invitation to participate in a meeting of left Republicans, held on 27 May at the Madrid bull-ring. The speakers at the meeting included Miguel de Unamuno, Melquíades Alvarez and Lerroux.[68] The PSOE National Committee welcomed the resurgence of leftist forces, but stated that it could not join with them until they declared that

given that the Spanish monarchy is not an adequate instrument to serve the national interest either at home or abroad, they show themselves ready to organise sufficient powerful forces *and moral guarantees* to change the regime.[69]

The PSOE position reflected the continued belief in both historical determinism and moral probity – a mixture of Marxist and Krausist influences which remained deeply rooted in the essentially social democratic party.

The stimulus to united action with the other groups in the Assembly

Movement was provided by the Juntas Militares de Defensa. Their 1 June manifesto was taken by the Socialists as the opening salvo of a revolutionary movement which was about to envelope Spain. This much was later recognised by the author of the March manifesto, Julián Besteiro:

Sr (Indalecio) Prieto has said that we proceeded with a certain naivety. I accept that and, what is more, I do not regret it; because you must also bear in mind that many sound elements in the Nation were naive enough to believe that with the manifesto of 1 June the revolution was unleashed.[70]

Four days later, on 5 June, a Coordinating Committee was formed, which brought together Alejandro Lerroux for the Radicals, Melquíades Alvarez for the Reformists, and both Pablo Iglesias and Francisco Largo Caballero for the Socialists. Although the initiative came from the Socialists, the key figure in this process was the Reformist Party leader Melquíades Alvarez, a close personal friend of Pablo Iglesias. Alvarez acted as intermediary between the Republican parties, whose unity discussions had culminated in an abortive Assembly at the end of May, and the Socialists, who had been having serious doubts about the viability of continued association with the fissiparous Republicans.[71] A meeting of the Agrupación Socialista Madrileña at the end of May had agreed with proposals by Besteiro, Largo Caballero and Daniel Anguiano that the Conjunction with the Republicans should be maintained only so long as there existed the possibility of establishing a wide alliance aimed at bringing down the regime.[72] The Socialists therefore now took the initiative in unity moves with other leftist forces, thus becoming the fulcrum of mounting opposition to the Restoration Monarchy. Thus, the PSOE found itself by 1917 in the extraordinary position of having recently abandoned isolationism only to end up collaborating at one and the same time with bourgeois reformists masquerading as radicals and revolutionary Anarchists led by reformists. The result, as will be shown, was to be disastrous confusion.

The 5 June meeting produced an agreement to work for the establishment of a provisional government, to be headed by Alvarez, with the aim of convening a constituent Cortes. This, it was believed, would lead to a bourgeois-democratic revolution. It was further agreed that should the army try to pre-empt such moves through a *pronunciamiento*, a general strike would be declared immediately. In order to prepare for the general strike, a Revolutionary Committee was established, comprised of Alvarez for the Reformists, Lerroux for the Republicans, and Iglesias for the PSOE, although since the Socialist leader was so unwell his place was taken in practice by Besteiro.[73] The CNT was not formally included in the agreements, but did work with the Revolutionary Committee. The entire movement was given added impetus by the resignation of Prime Minister García Prieto on 9 June, brought down by the victory of the Juntas

Militares. It was feared by leftist groups that King Alfonso would offer the government to the hated Antonio Maura, whose call-up of Catalan reservists in 1909 had provoked the Tragic Week in Barcelona. Indeed, the left Republicans' meeting of 27 May in the Madrid bull-ring had been in part a response to a meeting held by Maura earlier in the same month at the same venue, in which he had called for strict Spanish neutrality over the First World War.

The austere, proud and humourless Maura, had been increasingly active in the preceding months. Since abandoning the Conservative Party four years earlier, Maura had allowed an eponymous movement to build up around him. Intensely bitter at having been rejected by Alfonso, Maura remained convinced that he alone could provide the necessary leadership to pull Spain out of its crisis.[74] However, rather than Maura, whom he recognised would be a dangerously explosive choice, the King turned to the Mallorcan politician's greatest rival, Eduardo Dato, his successor as leader of the Conservative Party. Dato was a far less contentious individual than Maura. Nonetheless, his first act was the by now well-worn one of closing the Cortes and suspending constitutional guarantees. The Revolutionary Committee of Lerroux, Alvarez and Iglesias took this as the signal to prepare for the overthrow of the regime. In the meanwhile, however, the closing of the Cortes was precisely the stimulus required for the galvanisation of the Catalan-based Assembly Movement, which having flickered for some months, flared briefly during July 1917. Like most pyrotechnic displays, however, the Assembly Movement proved to be a short-lived spectacle.

The Assembly Movement owed its existence to Francesc Cambó. Following Dato's refusal of his request to re-open the Cortes, the leader of the Lliga Regionalista convened a meeting in Barcelona on 5 July of all Catalan parliamentarians. At the meeting, the request was renewed with support from Radicals and Reformists, but the Prime Minister remained unmoved.[75] Cambó therefore convened a second Barcelona Assembly, for all Spanish parliamentarians, on 19 July. There was tremendous tension in the Catalan capital. The government introduced rigorous censorship in a bid to obstruct the preparation of the Assembly, whilst Cambó made every effort to ensure the widest possible support. He made unsuccessful overtures to both the Juntas Militares de Defensa and to Antonio Maura. However, what seems like an extraordinary misjudgement – neither the military nor Maura were likely to support any movement which was built around Catalanism and co-operated with Socialists – appears less surprising in the light of Cambó's real interests. The leader of the Lliga was no revolutionary; what he sought was simply the restoration of parliamentary procedures in order that the interests of Catalan capitalism should be defended. The Lliga Regionalista was always a party of industrialists, jealous advocates of sectional interests. It was never Cambó's intention to become involved in any revolutionary overthrow of the regime.

Dato was well aware of Cambó's instinctive conservatism. Shrewd and cunning, if rather grey, Dato took a gamble in July 1917 which paid off handsomely. Aware of contemporary events in Russia, he realised the critical importance of placating the army. He therefore moved quickly to meet some of the Juntas Militares' more urgent demands, including the official sanctioning of their statutes.[76] Having quelled the most immediate threat to governmental stability, Dato then benefited from the outbreak of a strike by Valencian railway workers on 19 July, the same day as the second Assembly of Parliamentarians. The origins of the strike movement remain obscure and controversial. There are two favoured explanations. First, it has been suggested that the strike was in response to comments by the Republican deputy Marcelino Domingo, who had told the workers that the Barcelona Assembly was the signal for the general strike.[77] More likely is the second explanation, that Dato provoked the Valencian railway workers into taking precipitate strike action.[78] This would have allowed Dato to realise a double aim: first, he knew that the Socialist leaders were not yet ready to launch the threatened general strike and he therefore hoped to create maximum confusion within their ranks; second, he banked on Cambó having doubts over association with the PSOE and UGT. This is precisely what happened.

The Valencia strike erupted whilst Pablo Iglesias, in Barcelona for the Assembly, was trying to persuade CNT leaders, without much success, to exercise restraint. It was left to Largo Caballero to reason with them at a rather acrimonious secret meeting held at Valvidriera, in the mountains outside Barcelona.[79] Whereas the CNT was ready to launch a revolutionary strike at any moment, the Socialists, cautious as ever, felt the time was not yet ripe: the support of the army, still believed to be an ally, had not yet been secured. The Valencia strike thus came as a severe embarrassment to the Socialists, an indication that their exalted organisational skills had failed them at a crucial moment. Cambó, who had never been persuaded of the viability of strike activity, was already having reservations about the movement he had unleashed even before the Valencia strike occurred.[80] He was finally persuaded to abandon his reforming commitments following the government's response to the Assembly and the continued refusal of the *Junteros* to join with him. Amidst almost farcical scenes, the 19 July Assembly was broken up by the Civil Governor of Barcelona, Leopoldo Matos, after having convened in a restaurant under the guise of being a wedding party. Before its premature end, it had agreed to call for the convocation of a Constituent Cortes. Cambó, though, realised the game was lost when the increasingly confident government chose to ignore the Assembly's demands: the loyalty of the army, the key to the survival of the monarchy, had for the moment been ensured. Cambó and the Lliga remained nominally active in the Assembly movement before withdrawing on 3 November, by which point the entire initiative had been squandered.

The Assembly Movement has been seen as the great missed opportunity of modern Spanish history. In the words of Salvador de Madariaga, the Spanish liberal statesman and man of letters, it

> might have been the true salvation of Spain and, in particular, of the monarchical system, had the Crown been more convinced of the advantages of a parliamentary form of government and had the hot-heads of the labour movement been less convinced of the advantages of revolution.[81]

Madariaga's eagerness to condemn revolutionism within the labour movement, a recurring theme of his highly acclaimed history of Spain, leads him to obscure the fact that the Assembly Movement collapsed less through the actions of any revolutionary hot-heads than through Cambó's return to type when confronted with the prospect of a genuine shift of political power.[82] Contrary to Madariaga's assertion, the Socialists were not seeking to install 'a socialist democratic republic'. Their fundamental aim was the establishment of a bourgeois-democratic republic. Certainly, this was seen as the precursor to Socialist revolution, but the leaders of the PSOE and UGT were anything but revolutionary hot-heads. Instead, their approach to 'revolution' was ultra-cautious, marked by major misgivings at the vital final moments.

The Valencia railworkers strike served as an unwanted catalyst to a rapid escalation of activity within Socialist ranks. Indeed, events quickly overtook the alarmed PSOE and UGT leaders. Following the strike, which ended on the 23 July, the Compañía del Norte refused to re-hire thirty-five members of the local branch of the Sindicato del Norte, which retaliated by calling a strike of all company employees for 10 August. The UGT executive, aware that such a strike would blunt the impact of its own planned general strike, persuaded the local federation to negotiate with the railway company, which in turn was being pressured into conciliation by the Vizconde de Eza, Dato's Development Minister. However, on 9 August, negotiations were abruptly broken off at the insistence of Interior Minister, José Sánchez Guerra, who stated on behalf of the government that he was prepared to 'take on the strike'.[83]

In response, the railworkers voted to call a strike for 13 August. The decision forced the hand of the PSOE and UGT executives, which had met at the end of July to form a strike committee comprised of Besteiro and Saborit for the party, together with Largo Caballero and Anguiano for the union. These four now met to try to halt the tide of events.[84] However, unable to discourage the Valencian railworkers, the strike committee decided to bring forward the date of the general strike to coincide with that of the Sindicato del Norte.[85] By this stage, confusion reigned supreme. Pablo Iglesias sent a message from his sickbed in support of solidarity action, but expressed opposition to giving the strike revolutionary political ends.[86] Had the strike committee not agreed to launch the general strike, then the Valencian strike would have become extended in a sporadic and indisciplined fashion – anathema to the Socialist leaders. The strike committee thus agreed to declare the general strike. According to Besteiro, two reasons lay behind the decision:

first, the evolution of the consciousness, the spirit of the working class, was now complete; the entire working class knew the mission it had to fulfil. . .(second), the elements of the bourgeoisie, who had declared that under this political system it is impossible to live, had given us reason enough to suppose that the most genuine representatives of Spanish capitalism, precisely in those areas where Spanish capitalism has most reality and above all most possibilities, thought like us that Spain cannot prosper under the present system. . .and since we know that capitalism is not the solution to social and economic problems, but also that *without capitalism there is no possibility of Socialism*, we wanted a wide channel for the development of capitalist interests and a wide channel for the development of proletarian claims.[87]

Thus the so-called 'hot-heads of the labour movement' declared the strike most reluctantly, and with the express, if misguided, intention of provoking a bourgeois-democratic rather than Socialist revolution. On 12 August, the strike committee drew up a manifesto, written mainly by Besteiro. Its language was typical of Spanish Socialism, full of references to 'morality' and 'decorum'.[88] More significant, however, was its call for a political rather than a social revolution; indeed, many of its demands were similar to those of the Assembly Movement, a point made with some bitterness by Besteiro the following year in the Cortes debate on the strike. The signal for the commencement of the strike was to be an article by Besteiro, entitled 'Cosas veredes', which was to be published simultaneously in *El Socialista* and the republican daily, *El País*.[89] In the event, things started to go wrong almost immediately. The government sequestered copies of the manifesto and the relevant newspapers in Madrid, thereby ensuring that many areas failed to receive notice or instructions for the strike. The strike was thus rather uneven when it started on 13 August, although it did spread quickly. However, within a couple of days, the police discovered the hiding place of the strike committee: the house of a Socialist couple, José Ortega and Juana Sanabria, at 12, Calle del Desengaño (Disillusion Street).[90] Deprived of its albeit reluctant leadership, which was arrested without even token resistance, the strike all but collapsed within a week. Cambó's Lliga Regionalista, meanwhile, publicly announced that it would not participate in the strike movement, and Radical Party leader Alejandro Lerroux headed across the border to France.

The intensity of strike activity varied considerably according to the area in question. In some areas, particularly Old Castile, it had little impact.[91] In Madrid, though, the strike call was well supported. Tragically for the workers, however, who followed instructions to cheer the soldiers called out by the government to suppress the strike, there was a complete absence of reciprocity. Indeed, at Cuatro Caminos, in the west of the city, shots were fired and several workers killed by soldiers who had seemingly entirely forgotten their own earlier grievances against the government. This pattern was repeated wherever the strike took hold. In Barcelona where the strike was effectively organised by the CNT, the forces of order under Captain General Milans del Bosch were well prepared. The strike received widespread support, but was met with violence and quickly suppressed. It was in the Basque Country and Asturias that the strike achieved its greatest penetration. In the former province, it was led by Indalecio Prieto, the moderate *pablista* who was steadily gaining prominence within the PSOE, and Facundo Perezagua, the miners' leader. Again, even though the strike had begun peacefully, troops were brought in from León to fire upon the workers.[92] However, as would be the case again in 1934, the real centre of the strike was Asturias, where it was headed by Isidoro Acevedo and Manuel Llaneza, with support from Reformist leader Melquíades Alvarez. Once more, an essentially non-violent protest was met by state-sanctioned brutality: soldiers received orders to fire on workers indiscriminately. Indeed, the Military Governor of Oviedo, General Ricardo Burguete, promised to hunt the strikers down 'like wild beasts'.[93] Although the Asturian workers, especially the SOMA of Llaneza, were able to hold out a fortnight longer than their comrades in the rest of Spain, the strike never really stood a chance against the repressive power of the Spanish state.[94] Effectively over in most of Spain by the 18 August, it continued in Asturias only to peter out by the end of the month.

The August 1917 strike had a vitally important double impact on the Socialist movement. First, it traumatised the *pablista* leadership. The ferocity of the government's repression convinced many in the PSOE, particularly Iglesias and Besteiro, that revolutionary activity was best avoided.[95] Twice the Socialists had dallied with anti-governmental risings; twice they had been brutally beaten. From now on, revolution would be looked upon askance. Thus it was that the Bolshevik October Revolution in Russia would meet with a very cool response from the PSOE leadership. Second, though, it provided plentiful ammunition for dissent within Socialist ranks. Militants on the right of the party, such as Indalecio Prieto and Oscar Pérez Solís, from Valladolid, were confirmed in their original scepticism over the whole idea. Others, such as Llaneza, accepted the idea, but criticised its execution. Most significant, though, was the stimulus given to the neutralist anti-*pablistas* within the PSOE, the internationalistic opponents of the party's *aliadófilo* line, who saw in the failure of the strike evidence of craven cowardice within the leadership. Their opposition to the *pablistas* intensified in the following years, culminating in the 1921 schism within the party over the issue of the Third International.

Before then, however, the Socialists faced the more immediate problem of recovery from the repression. The strike committee – Besteiro, Largo, Saborit and Anguiano – were all imprisoned for life after their trial on 29 September. More generally, Socialist militants' freedom of action was severely curtailed. Moreover, there was a sharp decline in membership of the UGT in the immediate aftermath of the strike, with membership figures for 1918 standing at 89,601, a fall of 10,000 from the previous year. Ultimately, however, the events of August 1917 were not so disastrous for the Socialist movement as first seemed likely. Indeed, the scale and brutality of the measures taken by government actually contributed to the downfall of Dato. Although the strike had been defeated, the underlying problems which had led to its being called still remained. By October, the government was again beleaguered by continued crises. Ironically, the greatest threat to Dato now derived from precisely those quarters whose actions had contributed so vitally to his survival in August: the army and the Lliga Regionalista. The Juntas, aware of their centrality to Dato's survival, were able to make new demands of the Prime Minister. Not least, they demanded the execution of the Socialists in the strike committee as well as the continuation of martial law. Neither demand was met. Increasingly dissatisfied with Dato, they withdrew their support altogether in October when constitutional guarantees were restored.[96]

Meanwhile, Cambó's Lliga Regionalista had also been moving rightwards. With the PSOE rendered effectively inactive, Cambó revived the Assembly Movement in order to press for a government of 'national concentration', comprising all willing anti-dynastic forces. Deserted, Dato resigned on 27 October. The Assembly convened three days later, but by this stage Cambó had decided to pitch in his lot with the Madrid oligarchy. Abandoning his colleagues for the second time in two months, he agreed to join a patchwork coalition government, formed on 3 November, under García Prieto. Amongst his new-found ministerial colleagues was the arch-Conservative supporter of Maura, General Juan de la Cierva, who had been responsible for the ferocious repression of Anarchists and Socialists in Barcelona during the Tragic Week of July 1909. La Cierva's appointment to the War Ministry was a sop to the Juntas. Cambó's involvement was the clearest demonstration that the Spanish industrial bourgeoisie remained ready to forego political reform and ally with the reactionary agrarian oligarchy through fear of the working class.

Such fear was only intensified by news from Russia of Lenin's Bolshevik Revolution. However, the success of the October Revolution did not provide PSOE leaders with a much needed lift. Whereas in Europe, the Bolshevik triumph served as the stimulus to a wave of revolutionary movements – the Spartakus uprising in Germany, the Socialist-led factory council movement in the Italian cities of Turin and Milan, the establishment of republics in Hungary and Poland – in Spain, the news found both Socialists and Anarchists in disarray following the events of August. Nonetheless, the Bolshevik triumph, the first successful Socialist revolution, required a response. Rather than unalloyed joy, however, that response was decidedly diffident. Indeed, Pablo Iglesias, weary and old, was filled with barely concealed gloom by Lenin's success. The first reference in *El Socialista* to the fall of Kerensky came on 9 November:

The maximalists have triumphed, the supporters of all or nothing, over those who supported a slower transformation, intelligently prepared. . .

The following day, the paper's editorial was more explicit:

The news we have received from Russia makes us bitter. We sincerely believe, as we have always said, that for the moment the mission of that great country is to devote all its energy to the task of smashing German imperialism. . . If the episodes which we contemplate today with fear and pain give rise to a separate peace, to a desertion from the ranks of the allied peoples in the face of the enemy of all liberty and any claims to popular rights, what will then be left of that proud revolution. . . The ideals which have inspired the authors of this latest movement are lofty and respected. But they are also inopportune, and through being inopportune, perhaps fatal.[97]

The majority in the PSOE remained obsessed by the issue of the First World War. The Bolshevik Revolution was thus seen primarily as a potential impediment to the Allied victory. It was considered to be far less progressive than the March Revolution, and unlikely to survive. Indeed, even in March 1918 Pablo Iglesias wrote that he did not think the 'perturbation' in Russia would last long.[98] Others were even more damning. Eduardo Torralba Beci, the loyal *pablista*, wrote of Lenin and Trotsky in Araquistáin's *España* that

historical reality and social reality will imminently relegate them to a contemplative life in the cells, from where they should never have emerged.[99]

Whilst an initial lack of enthusiasm for the October Revolution was characteristic of several European Socialist parties, few can have been as outspokenly critical as the PSOE. Still fewer can have manifested so little interest over the following months. After the first disparaging reports, references to events in Russia appeared ever more infrequently in *El Socialista* until the end of the First World War. Instead, the PSOE leaders turned their attentions to the more immediate question of the February 1918 general elections in Spain. Once more, Spanish Socialism was marked by a peculiar combination of parochial insular concerns and an almost wholly derivative internationalist outlook. Victims of a rigid Marxist theory which prevented them from accepting the Bolshevik Revolution as a progressive possibility, the PSOE leaders were also unable to apply that theory to the specific conditions in Spain. Despite ample evidence of state repression and corruption, of which they were direct victims, the Socialists remained committed to reformist electoralism. The 1917 essay in revolution merely reconfirmed them in this fundamental belief, as did their showing in the 1918 elections, which they contested in conjunction with the Republicans. Recipients of a widespread sympathy vote, Besteiro (Madrid), Largo Caballero (Barcelona), Saborit (Oviedo) and Anguiano (Valencia) were all elected to the Cortes, and therefore automatically released from jail, along with Pablo Iglesias (Madrid) and Indalecio Prieto (Bilbao). Six deputies and a total of just 173,063 votes in the whole of Spain hardly represented a major triumph, but it did serve to underline the PSOE leaders' commitment to the parliamentary road to Socialism.[100]

However, if the events of 1917, both in Spain and in Russia, reinforced reformism amongst the PSOE's *pablista* leadership, they also provided fuel for the minoritarian dissidents in the party. The divisions which had started to emerge prior to the war, and which crystallised over the issue of Spanish neutrality, now hardened around a new line of fissure: reactions to the Bolshevik Revolution. Denied access to the pages of *El Socialista*, which generally maintained silence on events in Russia, the minoritarians began to coalesce into a coherent anti-*pablista* group during 1918. On the first anniversary of the 1917 general strike, *Nuestra Palabra* commenced publication. Edited by Mariano García Cortés, with support from Ramón Lamoneda, former colleague of Núñez de Arenas in the Escuela Nueva, the journal became the forum of anti-*pablismo* within the PSOE, and brought together most of the figures who would leave the Socialist Party in 1921 to establish a Communist alternative.[101]

The contributors to *Nuestra Palabra* were not united in any formal sense, and indeed there would be several instances of spectacular political shifts before the 1921 schism.[102] However, the journal did bring together two strands within the PSOE – the 'historic' dissidents, such as Verdes Montenegro, Recaséns and Morato, and the Zimmerwald supporters of the FJSE, militants like Lamoneda, Rafael Millá, and César González. In very broad terms these two groups comprised respectively centrist pacifists and leftist revolutionists. They would diverge in 1920, with the more extreme youth leaving to form the first Spanish Communist Party. In 1918, however, they shared a positive evaluation of the principal theme of *Nuestra Palabra*: the Bolshevik Revolution. Despite limited knowledge of what exactly was happening in Russia, a gap which was openly acknowledged, the journal began to organise pro-Bolshevik meetings in the autumn of 1918. *Nuestra Palabra* also maintained contact with the International Socialist Commission (ICS), set up at Zimmerwald and based from early 1917 in Stockholm. The ICS bulletin of 1 September 1918 included a report on the PSOE, presumably based on information provided by *Nuestra Palabra*.[103]

The most significant aspect of *Nuestra Palabra* was that, without engaging in personal attacks on the ailing Iglesias, it formed a focus for those opposed to reformist parliamentary tactics within the PSOE. The division intensified at the party's 11th Congress, held in Madrid between 24 November and 3 December, 1918, but did not reach the point of open confrontation. Instead, the main issue of debate at the Congress concerned the question of whether the Socialists would participate at ministerial level in any future national government. The strongest opposition to such a suggestion came from Julián Besteiro, who had been touring Spain since June, addressing meetings and spreading the message which was to become virtually his leitmotiv: that capitalist democracy must be left to the bourgeoisie.[104] He was opposed by Antonio Fabra Ribas and Andrés Saborit, the Asturian militant who was later to become his most loyal supporter. Besteiro's view prevailed. However, the most significant feature of the Congress was the recognition that the Socialists had paid insufficient attention in previous years to domestic Spanish issues. The feeling was expressed that the PSOE was losing its social orientation, that the minimum demands of the party's programme had been rendered otiose by the passage of time. Preoccupation with the war had left the party seemingly indifferent to Spain's social problems. In particular, the loss of membership in rural Andalusia, where PSOE affiliation had fallen from 9,988 in 1915 to 5,438 three years later, was seen as a reflection of the PSOE's lack of any coherent agrarian policy. A moderate draft programme presented by Fabra Ribas, calling for individual peasant ownership rather than collectivisation, formed the basis of a definitive text, which included more radical amendments by Verdes Montenegro, Largo Caballero and Andrés Ovejero. The overall result was therefore somewhat ambiguous, with maximalist demands serving to hide the continuing influence of reformist aspirations. In short, the PSOE's first systematic agrarian programme was symptomatic of the party's heritage of radical rhetoric masking reformist practice.[105]

Further issues debated at the Congress included the need to expand Socialist propaganda activities, especially in Andalusia and in Catalonia, as well as the perennial issue of the Republican–Socialist Conjunction. Proposals to dissolve it, however, were easily defeated. On international issues, support was expressed for the creation of a League of Nations. Of more immediate significance, it was agreed that Julián Besteiro should travel to Berne as the PSOE representative at the first post-war Congress of the Second International early in 1919. It was unanimously felt that the

International should be resurrected. Equally, however, it was also now felt that the Bolshevik revolution was a positive thing for the international workers' movement, 'the triumph of the revolutionary spirit of the proletariat'. Herein lay the seeds of future conflict. The relative calm which characterised the 11th Congress, the result of general satisfaction on the part of the minoritarians over what they had achieved, was soon to be shattered. In January 1919, Lenin's announcement of the creation of the Third International, Communist rather than Socialist, drove a wedge right into the heart of European Socialist parties. The PSOE was no exception.

3 Socialist schism and the development of organised Communism, 1919–1923

The aftermath of the First World War brought profound political upheaval throughout Europe. The collapse of three major imperial dynasties, Russian, German and Austro-Hungarian, either during or as a result of the war, heralded the redrawing of the European political map at the 1919 Treaty of Versailles. This treaty saw the dismantling of German territories, and led to the establishment of independent republics in Austria, Hungary, Czechoslovakia, Poland and Yugoslavia, as well as of the Weimar regime in Germany. Of equal political significance was the 1917 Bolshevik Revolution. Lenin's triumph served as a stirring stimulus to revolutionary Socialists throughout Europe. Indeed, up until the 1924 Locarno Pact, which ushered in a lustrum of relative peace, revolutionary winds swept westwards from Moscow, whipped up by the events of October 1917. The Bolshevik success did not, of course, exercise a direct causal impact upon all the dramatic transformations which occurred in Europe in its wake. Nonetheless, the establishment of Communist rule in Russia served as the axis of an ideological division which has remained deep-rooted ever since. In many ways, this division was at its most stark in the post-war years. Thus, if Communism as cause lay behind the Spartakus uprising of January 1919 in Germany and Gramsci's Turin-based Factory Council movement in Italy the following year, Communism as curse served equally as a powerful rationale behind the rise of fascism in Europe in the 1920s and 1930s.[1]

In Spain, also, despite non-participation in the war, the struggle between revolutionary and reactionary forces intensified. Whilst the general strike of August 1917 had been easily defeated, it did serve as a precursor to the so-called *trienio bolchevique*, a three-year period between 1919 and 1921 marked by continual labour disturbances, both in Catalonia and most particularly in the predominantly rural southern region of Andalusia.[2] Moreover, Spain continued to suffer from the legacy of her own imperial past, with unrest in her last remaining colonial possession, Morocco, leading to the disastrous and humiliating defeat of Spanish troops at Anual in 1921. Attacked from within and without, the Restoration Monarchy precariously clung on, its Canovite political settlement, the so-called *turno pacífico*, discredited beyond the point of salvation. The six years prior to 1923 witnessed thirteen serious governmental crises and thirty less critical ones.[3] In addition, three important political assassinations – of Eduardo Dato, the Conservative leader, in 1921, CNT leader Salvador Seguí in March 1923, and Juan Soldevila Romero, Cardinal-Archbishop of Zaragoza, three months later – intensified the prevailing atmosphere of crisis until General Miguel Primo de Rivera, the self-styled 'Iron Surgeon', stepped in to establish his dictatorial parenthesis.[4] Thus, although the Iberian peninsula remained excluded from the major European post-war political initiatives, the upheaval it experienced was of no lesser intensity. Indeed, it was largely as a result of economic restructuring in post-war Europe, with the contraction of former export markets no longer geared towards war production and the consequent loss of foreign trade, that Spain experienced major economic crisis and a related breakdown in labour relations. As Raymond Carr has observed, 'between 1918 and 1923 Spain was to be the scene of one of the more savage social conflicts of postwar Europe'.[5]

In many ways it would appear that the stage was set for the PSOE to play a central role in post-1918 Spanish politics. Growing militancy amongst workers and peasants combined with increasing sclerosis within state structures to create conditions in some ways similar to those which prevailed in Russia prior to the fall of the Tsar.[6] Iglesias, of course, was not Lenin, and the PSOE as a whole was decidedly more Menshevik than Bolshevik. Indeed, the initial reaction of Socialist leaders to news of the October Revolution had been one of alarm. Reformist, essentially cautious, and still traumatised by the repression that had followed the August 1917 strike, the PSOE leaders were never likely to grasp the nettle of revolution. The real revolutionaries in Spain were the Anarchists of the CNT. Rather than the PSOE, it was the CNT which dominated anti-governmental initiatives within the workers' movement, its dynamism given added impetus by the success of a strike in February 1919 at La Canadiense, an Anglo-Canadian hydroelectric company that supplied power to Barcelona. The strike lasted over a month, and was brought to an end only by the internment of nearly 3,000 workers in the Montjuich Prison and the proclamation of a state of war in the province of Barcelona by General Milans del Bosch.[7] Nonetheless, the terms of the settlement forced on the company represented an almost total victory for the strikers. Ultimately, however, it could be argued that the triumph was counter-productive: spurred on by the success at La Canadiense, CNT extremists forced a general strike in March. The repression this time was intense, with martial law declared immediately and the CNT subjected to a twin-pronged attack by the state and by employers, who were increasingly drawn to the use of lock-out tactics.

The important point, however, is that the CNT was taking the lead in the workers' struggle against inflation and exploitation. This much was reflected in its membership figures: in Catalonia, the CNT had grown from 107,096 members at the end of 1918 to 345,000 a year later, and to 714,028 throughout the whole of Spain.[8] Moreover, the Anarcho-syndicalist federation was beginning to make serious inroads into areas traditionally associated with Socialism, such as Asturias and Vizcaya. Whilst the PSOE and UGT also experienced an increase in membership, it was on nothing like the same scale. By 1919, the PSOE boasted just over 42,000 members.[9] This was a considerable increase compared to the previous year, although the rise in Vizcaya and Asturias was proportionately far smaller than that in the rest of Spain.[10] More indicative from the point of view of a comparison with the CNT, however, was the growth of the UGT. The Socialist union in fact doubled its membership between 1918 and 1920, reaching a peak of 211,000 affiliates, but, significantly, it was expanding at a far slower rate than its Anarchist rival. Whilst the growth of the Socialist movement was indicative of increased confidence and worsening conditions of employment amongst the Spanish labouring masses, the even greater growth enjoyed by the Anarchists reflected their more dynamic approach.[11] If the Socialist leaders were to wrest the initiative from the CNT, therefore, it was vital that they should demonstrate to Spanish workers and peasants a readiness to challenge the state in their defence. Not only did they fail to do so, but they did not even make the effort.

Instead, quite remarkably, the PSOE between 1919 and 1923 sank into a phase of self-absorption during which it surrendered the political initiative almost entirely to the CNT. Far from deriving renewed vitality from a more numerous and more politically conscious membership, the Socialist leaders allowed themselves to become immersed in a mire of internal debate over the question of whether or not to join Lenin's Communist International (also known as the Comintern or Third International). In the midst of an unprecedented period of revolutionary potential, both in Spain and in Europe, the PSOE effectively withdrew from active political involvement. Of course, the announcement in January 1919 of the creation of the Comintern, and more especially the elaboration of the 21 Conditions of membership the following year, exacerbated divisions in all European Socialist parties between reformist social democrats and advocates of revolution.[12] In France a majority of the SFIO opted at its Tours Congress in December 1920 to join the new International, becoming first the Section Française de l'Internationale Communiste (SFIC) and then the Parti Communiste Français (PCF) in October 1921.[13] Earlier that same year in Italy, the PSI, already a member of the Communist International, also split during its acrimonious Congress in the Teatro Goldoni at Leghorn on 20 January. With a majority of delegates expressing reservations about the 21

Conditions, the left wing marched out to form the Partito Comunista Italiano (PCI) the following day in the Teatro San Marco, with Amadeo Bordiga and Antonio Gramsci amongst its leading lights.[14] In Germany, meanwhile, the SPD had split as early as 1917, with the formation of the Unabhängige Sozialdemokratische Partei Deutschlands (USPD), the left wing of which later joined the Kommunistische Partei Deutschlands (KPD), itself formed in December 1918 as an outgrowth of the Spartakist League of Luxemburg and Liebknecht.[15]

It is arguable that the creation of the Comintern ultimately severely weakened the international workers' movement by generating unrealistic expectations and enforcing division in nearly all Socialist parties.[16] However, in no party other than the Spanish did the division between defenders of the Second International and advocates of joining the Third taken on quite such all-consuming importance. Whereas the German, Italian and French Socialist parties maintained an active, indeed central, presence in the politics of their respective nations, the PSOE sank back into the isolationist wilderness which had characterised its development prior to the establishment of the Republican–Socialist Conjunction in 1909. Indeed, as if to emphasise the party's retreat into self-contemplation, the Conjunction was dissolved at the PSOE's December 1919 Congress, the first of three Extraordinary Congresses convened to debate the issue of the Communist International.[17] The history of the PSOE between 1919 and 1923, then, is very much one of internal wranglings within the context of minimal national political influence and a falling membership after 1920. As might be expected, the level of theoretical debate within the party remained uninspired throughout these years.

Lenin's invitation, broadcast by Trotsky in January 1919, to thirty-nine member parties of the Second International to abandon that body in favour of a new, purged International, met with a cool response amongst Spanish Socialists. The PSOE leaders, with their lengthy tradition of legalist parliamentary struggle, were reformist in temperament if not often in rhetoric. Having been initially hostile to the Bolshevik Revolution, they remained hesitant over aligning themselves with a movement about which they still knew little. Even the most outspoken supporters of the Russian Communists, the group associated with the journal *Nuestra Palabra*, regarded Lenin's call as potentially schismatic and refused to publish it, even though it appeared in the resolutely *pablista* party newspaper, *El Socialista*.[18] The Socialists, in keeping with their emphasis on loyalty and discipline, sought the reconstruction of the Second International. To this end, Julián Besteiro attended the Berne Conference of the remnants of that organisation as the PSOE delegate in February 1919, whilst Francisco Largo Caballero represented the UGT at a parallel international trade union conference. Remarkably, Besteiro sided with leftist factions in

Berne, defending the 'dictatorship of the proletariat' against Hjalmar Branting, the Swedish Socialist leader who had been a strong supporter of the Allies during the war and was one of the prime movers behind the idea of resurrecting the Second International.[19] Besteiro later explained his seemingly contradictory stance by pointing out that it was only at Berne that he first started to give serious thought to the issue, and that

proletarian dictatorship was a necessity in Russia, since the choice was between Socialist dictatorship or anarchy, and that decision was not one that allowed for doubts. By the same token, I judged that the attempt to obtain the same results in the European nations was bound to fail.[20]

There is more than a touch of wisdom after the event in Besteiro's words. In fact, ideological equivocation was to become particularly marked amongst PSOE leaders between 1919 and 1923. In broad terms, three main currents developed within the party in the aftermath of the First World War. First, there was the dominant centrist group, best represented by Iglesias, Besteiro and Largo Caballero. Somewhat right-leaning and concerned principally with the PSOE organisation, these reformist social democrats clung to their radical self-image. Besteiro, in particular, expressed a somewhat paradoxical commitment to Marxist revolution. Influenced by German positivism and the Spanish variant of Krausism, the Madrid-born philosophy don attempted to merge a determinist vision of Marxism with voluntarist moralism. The result was a bizarre syncretism, characterised by contradictory stances. Thus, for instance, Besteiro consistently rejected ministerial participation by the PSOE because 'we want total and exclusive power for the working classes [sic]', yet also rejected the necessarily revolutionary implications that such a position entailed.[21] Instead, he increasingly lauded the British Fabians as being the most faithful to the ideas of Marx and Engels.[22] Torn between revolutionary goals and a fear of their consequences, Besteiro sought refuge in a quietist faith in fatalism which allowed him to claim Marxist credentials whilst avoiding having to submit them for inspection. Hence the seemingly contradictory position adopted at Berne: the dictatorship of the proletariat was acceptable only at a distance.

At root, Besteiro saw his position as analogous to that of Karl Kautsky, whom he admired, yet he behaved like Eduard Bernstein, whom he ignored. Indeed, Bernstein's ideas, for all their influence in France, made little impact upon PSOE leaders. Although *Die Voraussetzungen des Sozialismus* (1899), the principal work of what came to be known as revisionism, was translated into Spanish in 1911, Bernstein's thought failed to penetrate Socialist ranks except in isolated instances such as that of Rafael Delorme, a journalist who had written for *El Socialista* in its early years, but did not remain long in the PSOE.[23] Nonetheless, for all the revolutionary Marxist self-image and the lack of acknowledgement by Spanish Socialists of Bernstein's ideas, they continued to collaborate in municipal, provincial and national level legislatures, as well as participating in effectively moribund state agencies such as the Institute of Social Reforms, an outgrowth of the Comisión de Reformas Sociales originally set up in 1883 by the Liberal government of Moret.[24] This failure to relate their political practice to the theory from which it was allegedly derived remained the most significant characteristic of the centre-right, or *pablista*, Spanish Socialist leaders. Convinced that Marxist laws of historical development were immutable, they never appreciated the importance of analysing the specificity of the socio-political and economic situation in Spain. In truth, there was no self-reflexive relation between theory and practice in the PSOE, because the former was reduced to the level of mere phraseology, an exercise in revolutionary linguistics. The latter, meanwhile, simply amounted to an attempt to gain ever greater pockets of influence in all levels of the state administration in readiness for the inevitable triumph of Socialism. Unable to apply Marxist theory, they simply tried to follow prevailing fashions in the major European Socialist parties. It is for this reason that they were effectively paralysed during the post-war crisis of the Second International.

The second main group in the PSOE, although far smaller, consisted of what could be termed principled pragmatists. Associated mainly with figures like Indalecio Prieto and Remigio Cabello, the leading Socialist in Valladolid, these were reformists who eschewed any attempt to justify their political activity by reference to Marxist theory. Prieto, brilliant as a Socialist tribune in the Cortes, and one of the most respected of Spain's politicians prior to the Civil War, was happy to confess that he had never found the time to read Marx.[25] Prieto was concerned above all else with practicalities. He remained committed throughout his political career to establishing alliances with the Republicans, with whom he maintained very close relations, because he was convinced that the Socialists on their own lacked sufficient strength to win a parliamentary majority in order to govern.[26] A massive man, both metaphorically and physically, Prieto was never seduced by any Marxist Muse. In an article published in *El Sitio* (Bilbao) in early 1921, he stated

I am a Socialist as a liberal. That is to say, I am Socialist only in so far as I believe that Socialism represents the highest level of efficiency of liberalism and the most effective support there can be for liberty.[27]

Also belonging to this second group was Fernando de los Ríos, a professor at the University of Granada, who joined the PSOE from the Reformist Party in 1919. Unlike his friend Prieto, De los Ríos was deeply committed to the study of political theory. Like many of his new colleagues, he was strongly influenced by Krausism, having been educated at the Institución Libre de Enseñanza. De los Ríos was intensely moralistic, an ethical humanist who rejected Marxism on the grounds that it was mechanistic and teleological. For him, the motor force of history was not the class struggle, but ideals of justice, liberty and human plenitude. His Socialism derived from the belief that capitalism was anti-humanist in that it negated the essence of man by giving material matter predominance over people. This view was similar in some respects to the idea of reification in Gyorgy Lukács' *History and Class Consciousness* (1923). It was juxtaposed to a Marxism seen through the lenses of the Second International with its overtly reductionist economistic interpretation.[28] The major political work by De los Ríos, published in 1926, was entitled *El sentido humanista del socialismo* (The humanist sense of socialism), in which these themes were fully developed.[29] A rather dapper aesthete, De los Ríos soon achieved prominence within the PSOE and was to be a leading figure in the debates over the party's relationship to the Comintern.

The third group in the PSOE was made up of the leftist opponents to *pablismo* who had been gradually gaining strength and momentum since before the First World War. Grouped mainly around the journal *Nuestra Palabra*, these defenders of the Bolshevik Revolution formed the nucleus of the faction which would leave the PSOE in 1921 to form a Communist Party following the definitive rejection of the Comintern by the *pablistas*. Collectively known as the *terceristas* (Thirdists), the principal figures in the group included Mariano García Cortés, editor of *Nuestra Palabra*, Manuel Núñez de Arenas, founder of the Escuela Nueva, Ramón Lamoneda, one of its leading pupils, and César and Virginia González. The most outspoken *tercerista*, however, the former railway clerk Daniel Anguiano, was unconnected with either *Nuestra Palabra* or the Escuela Nueva. Anguiano, who had been secretary to Pablo Iglesias prior to becoming head of the Railworkers' Federation, had become Socialist deputy for Valencia in 1918.[30] The least revered of the Socialist leaders, he had been deeply influenced in a revolutionary direction by his meeting with Leon Trotsky in 1916 during the latter's brief sojourn in Madrid's Model Prison whilst *en route* to New York after his expulsion from France.[31] Anguiano had never penetrated the *Santa Hermandad* (Holy Brotherhood) around Iglesias, and despite attaining an executive position within the UGT, wielded little real influence in the Socialist movement. His revolutionism, like that of many of the *terceristas*, remained idealistic, a sincere but unspecific commitment to a vague paradisiacal future. Straightforwardly seduced by the success of Bolshevism, the *terceristas* were, in fact, no more equipped than their *pablista* opponents to use Marxist theory as a guide to analysing revolutionary possibilities in Spain.[32]

The ideological uncertainties and ambiguities prevalent within the

Spanish Socialist movement were reflected, as will be seen, in the confusions which characterised the protracted debate on the issue of the
Comintern. Also of fundamental importance to that debate, however, was
the changing relationship between the PSOE and the UGT executives.
Prior to the First World War, leaders of the political party had also tended
to be leaders of the union. Thus, figures like Iglesias, García Quejido,
Largo Caballero and Besteiro held high executive posts in both the PSOE
and the UGT; indeed, Iglesias, as would Besteiro later, simultaneously
held the presidency of both bodies. However, by 1919 an increasing
number of PSOE executive members did not hold executive posts within
the UGT, although the reverse did not tend to hold true. The most
prominent examples were Prieto and De los Ríos, both principally party
politicians rather than union activists, who held executive posts only in the
PSOE. Equally significant, the majority of the *terceristas* were PSOE
members who did not enjoy significant influence within the UGT. The
leaders of the UGT, meanwhile, who were also on the PSOE executive,
were precisely those *pablistas* like Iglesias himself, Besteiro and Largo
Caballero, who were not only supporters of the Second International, but
also fundamentally interested in the traditional Socialist emphasis on
organisation and discipline. Thus, to some degree, the debate over affiliation to the Comintern became also an organisational struggle by joint
PSOE–UGT leaders to maintain their united leadership in the Socialist
movement. Ultimately they would succeed, but only at the cost of a highly
damaging schism within the movement, a significant loss of membership in
the PSOE, and almost total political paralysis.

In large measure, the political paralysis was inevitable. Put in rather
schematic terms, there was a double *desfase*, or lack of synchrony, within
the Socialist movement. On the one hand, the UGT was beginning to
swamp the PSOE in terms of membership: by 1920, the PSOE accounted
for just 26.3 per cent of Socialist affiliation as opposed to the UGT's 73.7
per cent. On the other, there was a major mismatch between the stances of
the UGT leadership and the increasingly militant desires of its rank and
file. Over 70 per cent of the growth of the union federation since 1918 had
taken place in the rural southern regions of Andalusia, Estremadura and
the Levant.[33] It was in these regions, where landless peasants had to endure
the most appalling living conditions, that mass social unrest broke out
during the *trienio bolchevique*.[34] Little concerned with the complexities of
Internationalist affiliation, these peasants simply sought effective redress
of their grievances. In this regard, the *terceristas*, with their commitment to
revolution, probably reflected more accurately than the essentially reformist UGT–PSOE leaders the increasingly militant mood of the new UGT
members. However, the main strength of the *terceristas* lay in the PSOE
rather than the UGT; moreover, their political base lay precisely in the

traditional areas of Socialist strength, Madrid, Asturias and Vizcaya, which had seen a much slower rate of growth in membership than southern regions. There, not only did they confront the problem of a limited constituency of potential support, but also it was in these areas that reformist defenders of the Second International, especially Largo Caballero, Besteiro and Prieto, enjoyed their main support. Whereas Madrid, Asturias and the Basque Country accounted for just 16.6 per cent of PSOE strength in 1920, over 50 per cent of the UGT membership was based in these three regions. Thus, although the *terceristas* were able to build up support within the PSOE, this was of little use whilst the leadership of the UGT remained the virtual fiefdom of the *pablistas*. Hence there was virtual stalemate until the *terceristas* decided to abandon the Socialist movement in 1921, to be followed out of the PSOE, if not into the Communist Party, by several thousand rank-and-file militants.[35]

The continued caution of the *pablista* leadership in the face of the increasing radicalism of the Spanish labour force was confirmed by the PSOE's rather lacklustre participation in the general elections of July 1919. A low-key campaign resulted in six PSOE deputies, the same ones as in 1918, being returned to the Cortes, but with a slightly reduced overall vote.[36] However, the tide of events, both nationally and internationally, ensured that sympathy for social democratic reformism and for the Second International diminished amongst many leading activists within the Socialist movement in the remaining months of 1919. In Spain, the economic recession that followed the end of the First World War, was biting ever more deeply. The recession, a product of a fall in exports of raw materials and manufactured goods, deteriorated steadily to reach its nadir in 1921. By April of that year, 140 factories in Catalonia had closed with the loss of 20,000 jobs. In Vizcaya, the mining sector was hit by post-war recession in the British iron and steel industry, its main consumer. By 1921 exports of iron ore from Bilbao had crashed to less than one tenth of their 1899 volume. This collapse was in turn transmitted to the shipping sector, and to the domestic coal industry in Asturias, where declining demand led to a fall in output.[37] The loss of jobs in all sectors of the economy was matched by a chronic inflation which hit hardest in the rural south of the country. Indeed, the brutality of daily life endured by the landless peasants was exacerbated to a horrific level.[38] It was within such a context that the CNT was able to make such massive advances with its promises of immediate, radical action, made known through its major emphasis on propaganda efforts which far outstripped anything of which the Socialists were capable.

However, it was developments outside Spain which did most to erode support for the Second International within the PSOE. In particular, the Treaty of Versailles caused major disappointment. After the almost unreserved support given to the Allies during the First World War in the belief that their victory would establish the basis for the progress of Socialism, the harsh terms of the treaty were a cruel blow. Eduardo Torralba Beci, the most loyal of *pablistas*, wrote rather bitterly in *El Socialista* that Versailles was not

the peace of the peoples, the peace of right and reconciliation. . .but an iniquitous and dangerous peace, a capitalist and imperialist settlement that opens up a terrifying vision of new wars.[39]

Thereafter, Torralba increasingly distanced himself from the legalist gradualism which had been so dominant within the PSOE, and looked approvingly to the Comintern. In this, he was representative of several intellectuals in the PSOE whose faith in the ideals of the Second International was shattered by the now obviously erroneous interpretation it had put on the war. Erstwhile *aliadófilo* moderates like Andrés Ovejero, Juan José Morato and Luis Araquistáin gradually turned to Bolshevism during the summer of 1919.[40]

The rise in support for the Comintern in the aftermath of the Versailles Treaty intensified the struggle between *pablista* UGT–PSOE leaders and more radical militants. In the influential Agrupación Socialista Madrileña (ASM), control was wrested from the hands of Besteiro by Mariano García Cortés and César González, elected President and Secretary respectively at the start of 1919. This gave rise to tension between the National Committee of the PSOE and its Madrid section.[41] In early September 1919 the ASM voted overwhelmingly in favour of the Comintern and called for the dissolution of the Republican–Socialist Conjunction. The Madrid section of the Federación de Juventudes Socialistas de España (FJSE) was similarly won over to the cause of Bolshevism, against the more cautious stance of its Asturian-based president, Andrés Saborit. In the café of the Madrid Casa del Pueblo, Ramón Merino Gracia, a leading FJSE militant, set up a 'Bolshevik buffet' (*ágape bolchevique*) which reached a wide audience.[42] The FJSE, increasingly dominated by the Madrid section, had little patience with the prevarications of both its senior organisation and of the Second International, which had postponed any decisions on reconstitution until its Geneva Conference, scheduled for January 1920. Towards the end of 1919, Saborit was deposed as editor of the FJSE journal, *Renovación*. According to Juan Andrade, one of the leaders of the Madrid group, the deputy for Oviedo irritated them with his 'mediocrity, crudeness and arrogance'.[43] Ultimately, in 1920 the FJSE would abandon the PSOE to become the first organised Communist Party in Spain.

In the meanwhile, the PSOE leaders made preparations for an Extraordinary Congress, to open on 10 December 1919, aimed at resolving the party's position with respect to the Comintern. For the next two years, this single issue would dominate the Spanish Socialist movement virtually to the exclusion of all other considerations. At the December Congress, the views of the *pablista* leadership prevailed, despite the growth in support for the *tercerista* line in the preceding months.[44] In fact, for all the disagreements, the Congress was marked by typical PSOE organisational discipline. However, it also demonstrated quite clearly that the *pablistas* remained committed to parliamentary gradualism. Julián Besteiro, by now *de facto* leader of the party in view of the ever-worsening health of Iglesias, presented a motion during the debate on the Comintern, backed by Saborit and Francisco Núñez Tomás, which repeated the themes he had expressed in Berne at the start of the year. After exalting the Bolshevik regime and defending the dictatorship of the proletariat, he qualified his remarks with the observation that the Russian example was not necessarily transferable:

Like the Russian maximalists, the Partido Socialista Español believes that the dictatorship of the proletariat is an indispensable condition for the triumph of Socialism. It should not be believed, however, that the dictatorship of the proletariat must necessarily take the same form in all countries... The Executive Commission proposes to the Congress that, far from contributing to the weakening of existing international organisations, our party should procure their strengthening...therefore, it should agree to maintain its membership of the Second International, which constitutes the most powerful Socialist organisation in existence today, whose decisions, if its potency is not imprudently weakened, can exercise an effective influence on the development of world events in this historically critical moment.[45]

With masterly casuistry, Besteiro argued that the form of the dictatorship of the proletariat had to vary according to the degree of development in a given country: in Spain, since the aim of the Socialist revolution must be the establishment of a bourgeois parliamentary democracy, the dictatorship of the proletariat could take the form of workers' domination within a powerful parliament.[46]

The Besteiro motion was followed by a provocative speech from Prieto which was dismissively contemptuous of the entire issue of the Comintern, and of its supporters. The Vizcayan leader was particularly scornful of an early pro-Comintern speech made by Andrés Ovejero, a Madrid professor, describing it as 'Byzantinism and literary dilettantism in the Madrid style'. Down to earth as ever, Prieto concluded with the comment,

I share all of the Russian revolutionary creed; but I say, is it the case that in the ideas of Lenin and Trotsky there is something superior to the ideas of Socialism? NO! That is an almighty blasphemy which must not be allowed to pass the lips of any Socialist.[47]

Also dismissive of the *terceristas* was Oscar Pérez Solís, the Valladolid Socialist who within eighteen months would become one of their most fervent supporters. Together with Antonio Fabra Ribas, he submitted a straightforward resolution in favour of remaining in the Second International. The Catalan Fabra was in fact another whose position was extraordinarily inconsistent. A long-standing critic of the *pablistas* and editor, alongside Andreu Nin, of *La Internacional*, a pro-Bolshevik journal set up in 1919, Fabra was nonetheless opposed to any splits in the PSOE. By the following year he had become effective editor of *El Socialista* in place of the extremely ill Iglesias. The Solís–Fabra resolution was opposed by the *terceristas* Anguiano, Verdes Montenegro, García Cortés, and Ovejero. However, a compromise amendment was proposed by the Asturian Socialist leader, Isidoro Acevedo, long-standing friend of Pablo Iglesias. Acevedo's amendment proposed that the PSOE remain in the Second International pending the outcome of that body's Geneva Congress. If it should prove impossible to establish the union of all Socialist parties on account of the intransigence of members of the Second International, then the PSOE should join the Comintern.[48]

The Acevedo amendment was accepted and the Solís–Fabra resolution was passed by a narrow majority.[49] It amounted to nothing more than a vacillating compromise which deferred resolution of the issue, and ensured that the Socialist movement would in the short term remain politically hamstrung. This much was recognised by the FJSE, which agreed at its own 5th Congress, held immediately after the PSOE's, to affiliate immediately to the Comintern.[50] To add to the Socialists' worries, the CNT also decided on adherence to the new International at a coterminous congress, also held – for maximum provocation value – in Madrid. Furthermore, the CNT, in which the moderating influence of Angel Pestaña and Salvador Seguí was coming under ever greater challenge, firmly rejected repeated overtures made by Largo Caballero, most recently in a letter of 19 September, for unification with the UGT.[51] The CNT decision to join the Comintern, extraordinary though it seems in the light of subsequent developments, reflected the level of confusion that reigned within the CNT. On the one hand, an unresolved tension between Anarchists and Syndicalists led to problems of self-definition; on the other, events in Russia were poorly understood. Many CNT delegates genuinely saw themselves as Bolsheviks.[52] The decision to spurn Largo's suggestions of unity reflected the confidence of the Anarcho-syndicalist federation, which was outstripping the UGT in terms of membership by a ratio of more than three to one. With no small degree of *Schadenfreude*, CNT delegates like Manuel Buenacasa and Enrique Valero were able to turn the tables on Largo Caballero and demand that the UGT accept absorption within the larger federation.[53]

Thus, as 1920 dawned, the self-styled Marxist leaders of the PSOE had revealed the distance between their supposedly revolutionary theory and decidedly reformist practice with a temporising compromise which betokened intensified divisions within the Socialist movement. The Anarcho-syndicalists of the CNT, meanwhile, had opted to align themselves with the Russian Bolsheviks whom they mistakenly saw as Anarchist soulmates. However, the interest generated within the Iberian workers' movement by the new regime in Russia, for all its confusions, was not reciprocated by the Communist International. Like its predecessors, the Comintern showed scant concern over events in Spain. Its first representative in the Iberian peninsula, Michael Borodin, in fact arrived there almost by chance. *En route* back to Moscow from an unsuccessful mission to become Soviet ambassador in Mexico, and in the company of the Indian, M. N. Roy, as well as a Mexican known simply as Ramírez, he was told to stop briefly in Spain and discover what he could.[54] Borodin spoke no Spanish, and relied on Ramírez to act as interpreter in a series of meetings with such *terceristas* as Anguiano, Lamoneda, García Cortés, Núñez de Arenas, and the FJSE radical Merino Gracia. Significantly, Borodin did not consult with the mainstream *pablista* leaders of the PSOE. In line with the Comintern tactic of sowing discord within Social Democratic parties, Borodin presumably saw his best chance as lying with the more radical *terceristas*. If this was the case, he achieved quick, though hardly important, results.

In April 1920, impatient with the PSOE–UGT leadership and with the problems of the Second International, which had postponed its Geneva Congress to July, the Madrid-dominated Executive Committee of the FJSE decided to reconstitute the Youth Organisation as the Partido Comunista Español (PCE).[55] The new party failed to make a significant impact on the regional federations of the FJSE, attracting perhaps a fifth of their 5–6,000 members. Known as the 'partido de los cien niños' (party of a hundred children), the PCE included amongst its ranks Ramón Merino Gracia, Dolores Ibárruri, as well as Luis Portela and Juan Andrade, both of whom would join the Partido Obrero de Unificación Marxista (POUM) when this was formed in 1935. Andrade, who became editor of *El Comunista*, the new journal set up to replace *Renovación*, was the leading figure in the rather exiguous PCE.[56] With support in Asturias from its former leader, Andrés Saborit, the FJSE was able to rebuild its organisation almost immediately; the new PCE, meanwhile, adopted the violently anti-parliamentary stances so contemptuously dismissed by Lenin in his *Left Wing Communism. An Infantile Disorder*. If such stances did have a certain logic in the context of Spanish electoral corruption, they stood little chance of making an independent impact whilst the CNT remained powerful. The first schism from the PSOE, then, was more of a nuisance than a major blow. Indeed, had the impatient FJSE members bided their time, they could have joined forces with the growing number of *terceristas* who remained in the PSOE and caused a far greater impact within the party.

As it was, the PSOE convened a second Extraordinary Congress for June 1920, and opened the pages of *El Socialista* to debate on the issue of the Comintern. The balance of opinion within the party was clearly moving in favour of affiliation to the new International, in spite of the embarrassment caused by the arrest of Daniel Anguiano and Julián Besteiro, *en route* to the Rotterdam Conference of the Action Committee of the Second International, by Dutch police in March 1920. Anguiano was discovered to be carrying a letter, written in English (apparently by Ramírez), asking the Comintern for financial assistance to spread propaganda in Spain. Besteiro, allowed to continue to the conference whilst Anguiano was held in custody and then sent back to Spain, was horrified.[57] At the PSOE Congress, which opened in the third week of June, Besteiro lamented the behaviour of the *terceristas*:

The extremists are compromising the moral concept of the Party, since through the imprudence of several of them people have been made to believe that money is received and asked for from abroad in order to make the revolution. What is becoming of the immaculate morality of the Partido Socialista Obrero Español?. . . It is vital to respect and save the honour of Spanish Socialism.[58]

However, for all the efforts of the *pablista* heavyweights, the result of the June Congress was virtually a foregone conclusion. Indeed, the combination of increased labour unrest in Spain, the state's repressive response, and disappointment over the Versailles Treaty had turned the question less into one of whether than of how to join the Comintern.

The main debate at the Congress centred on whether to agree on unconditional entry, as proposed by García Cortés, Anguiano, and company, or to attach a number of conditions to membership. This latter proposal was argued most effectively by Fernando de los Ríos, the law don from Granada who had joined the PSOE the previous year. With support from Acevedo, De los Ríos called for adherence to the Comintern, but under three conditions: that PSOE autonomy be maintained, that it be allowed to revise the doctrine of the Comintern at its own congresses, and that there be no expulsions from the party.[59] He was opposed by García Cortés, who argued that it was 'rather grotesque' to demand PSOE autonomy in view of the limited number of party members who possessed deep knowledge of Marxist doctrines.[60] With Besteiro and Largo Caballero bitter and outnumbered, the *terceristas* were bound to win the day. However, a violent rumpus in the Congress hall, provoked by infiltrators from the new PCE, re-instilled the traditional PSOE spirit of discipline and compromise. The pro-Comintern majority was persuaded to demand 'immediate' rather than 'unconditional' entry, and the De los Ríos conditions were duly incorporated into the final resolution.[61] It was further agreed to send two delegates, Fernando de los Ríos and Daniel Anguiano, to Moscow in order to negotiate Spanish membership and report on events in Russia. Significantly, Pablo Iglesias – once more absent through illness – was still able to wield sufficient influence by proxy to ensure the addition of a further commitment by the PSOE to continue its participation in municipal councils, provincial assemblies and the Cortes. Indeed, the sense of ambiguity this entailed was underlined by the re-election of Besteiro and Largo Caballero to the Executive Committee with personal votes that far outnumbered those in favour of joining the Comintern.[62] Both, however, resigned on the rather unconvincing grounds that the number of *terceristas* also elected would make it impossible for them to work with their new colleagues on the committee.

Besteiro and Largo were, of course, well aware that they retained dominant influence within the UGT. Their control was ensured through a paid and permanent union bureaucracy which militated against both flexibility and democratic decision-making. Indeed, it is no small irony that the UGT was in fact organised along lines in many ways similar to those which would become familiar throughout the post-Lenin Communist world as democratic centralism. Nonetheless, the two union oligarchs, for all the revolutionary references in their rhetoric, remained above all gradualist syndical corporativists in the sense that they believed in the steady impregnation of society with areas of socialist influence. Besteiro made much of the identity between revolution and evolution:

The difference between revolution and evolution does not exist in Socialism. Every instance of the development of the class struggle against the capitalist regime is revolutionary. . . The proletariat makes the revolution with its every act.[63]

It is likely that Besteiro and Largo were fairly sanguine about their chances of influencing the UGT in an anti-Comintern direction at its 14th Congress which opened immediately after the PSOE Congress in June 1920. It therefore came as little surprise that, despite the militant mood of the rank-and-file UGT membership, the Congress voted overwhelmingly in favour of remaining in the Amsterdam International, the syndical counterpart of the Second International.[64] Moreover, the new Executive Committee elected at the Congress was entirely dominated by *pablistas*.[65] Largo Caballero underlined this dominance with the statement at the end of the Congress that the UGT would not again be drawn into a political strike like that of 1917: revolution would come about *only* through evolution.[66] Thus, by mid-1920 there existed for the first time in the history of the Spanish Socialist movement a clear division between the Executives of the PSOE and of the UGT. Numerical advantage in terms of membership would alone have made the eventual establishment of hegemony by the latter likely; the fact that the UGT was also the stronghold of figures of the authority of Iglesias, Besteiro and Largo Caballero made it certain. Thus, the victory of the *terceristas* at the PSOE Congress turned out to be not only conditional, but also pyrrhic.

In the meanwhile, however, the Socialist movement remained somewhat distanced from events on the wider political stage. The division between the PSOE and UGT in fact heralded a bizarre period of confusion within the Spanish Left. Following the Socialists' June Congresses, the CNT engaged in an unexpected volte-face and proposed a pact with the UGT in September 1920.[67] This development was in response to the almost complete breakdown of law and order in Barcelona, a breakdown which threatened to bring down intensified repression on the CNT and was already rendering its decisions largely ineffective.[68] *Pistolerismo*, or gunlaw, was rife. It was a tactic employed both by the CNT and by the state-backed Catholic Sindicatos Libres, which came into being in 1919.[69] With the city of Barcelona in turmoil, the Madrid-based dynastic oligarchy was showing ever greater signs of crumbling, giving rise to the attendant danger of a knee-jerk military repression being unleashed in an attempt to shore up the Restoration Monarchy. Between January and May 1920, José Maestre Laborde, Count Salvatierra, was civil governor of Barcelona. An austere figure, he moved quickly against the CNT, closing down workers' centres. The repression of the CNT by Count Salvatierra, though, was as nothing compared to that of General Severiano Martínez Anido, appointed civil governor in November 1920. Martínez Anido would rule Barcelona as 'a personal satrapy', using methods of extreme brutality to control and effectively destroy the CNT.[70]

Between May and November, though, Barcelona was under the control of two somewhat more moderate civil governors, Julio Amado and Carlos Bas, who actually tried to negotiate with CNT leader Salvador Seguí in an attempt to restore order.[71] This seemingly schizophrenic policy of appointments to the governorship of the Catalan capital reflected both the shortage of ideas and the political chaos that reigned in Madrid. Essentially, Madrid ministries wavered between attempts at negotiation with moderate CNT leaders and, when these failed (usually owing to the intransigence of employers), reversion to repression. The trouble in Barcelona, together with continued and increasing unrest in the rural south of the country, led King Alfonso XIII to juggle ever more recklessly with his prime ministerial appointments. In the three years between December 1919 and December 1922 there were ten changes of government, the one that survived longest being that of the Conservative Eduardo Dato, from May 1920 to March 1921.[72] Desperate to preserve the fiction that he presided over a democracy, however, Alfonso allowed periodic, though somewhat meaningless, elections to take place. Indeed, elections and changes of government bore little obvious mutual relationship: the King remained ultimate arbiter. Nonetheless, following those of 1918 and 1919, new general elections were convoked for December 1920. As had regularly been the case since 1917 a state of exception was in force. This did not prevent the PSOE from dutifully presenting candidates for election, although this time on its own rather than in alliance with the Republicans.

The Socialist position had by this stage become hopelessly confused. The PSOE Executive Committee was dominated by ostensibly revolutionary *terceristas* who nonetheless backed the participation in general elections of Socialist candidates like Largo Caballero and Besteiro, leading figures in the reformist UGT, which in turn had recently signed a pact with the anti-electoral CNT. Unsurprisingly, the electoral campaign was marked by extraordinary contradictions. The new PSOE executive on the one hand was critically dismissive of the possibilities of achieving reform through parliamentary activity in the Cortes, and on the other tried to enlist the widest possible electoral support, including that of CNT members.[73] The UGT reformists, meanwhile, dusted down and donned their revolutionary uniforms: Largo made reference to open hostility between the bourgeoisie and the proletariat, the proximity of revolution throughout Europe, and common membership of the Comintern by the PSOE and CNT, whilst Besteiro called on Lenin's arguments against ultra-leftist anti-parliamentarianism in his defence.[74] The CNT, singularly unimpressed, angrily broke off its pact with the UGT on the eve of the elections, disgusted by the lack of support from the Socialist union for its general strike call on 12 December. It is hardly surprising that the PSOE vote plummeted to 56,489 compared with 106,774 the previous year, leading to the loss of two deputies out of six.[75] The very high abstention rate at the elections (40 per cent overall and more than 50 per cent in Madrid) was concentrated within working-class districts, suggesting that for all the radicalism of the rhetoric, Socialist candidates in the Spanish capital at least were elected on the strength of middle-class support.[76] The overall picture of Spanish Socialism as 1920 drew to a close, then, was one of almost total disconcertion.

The sense of confusion was intensified on 15 January 1921 following a PSOE National Committee meeting to discuss the conflicting reports on their mission in Russia by Daniel Anguiano and Fernando de los Ríos. The two Socialists had returned to Spain at the start of the year after an eventful six months abroad.[77] To their eternal embarrassment, they had arrived in Moscow bearing the PSOE resolution with its three conditions of membership only weeks after the Second Congress of the Comintern had instituted Lenin's own rather more stringent and, of course, exclusive 21 Conditions. The Comintern Executive Committee's reply to the PSOE resolution took the Spaniards severely to task:

This resolution denotes the lack of clarity which exists in your Party with respect to the most essential questions of the international workers' movement, questions whose solution should determine the tactics of all proletarian parties in the current period... world revolution, dictatorship of the proletariat and the power of the Soviets... Losing sight completely of the world revolution, it is necessarily impossible for you to understand the character and meaning of the Communist International. You depict it as some kind of club aimed at 'uniting the social forces which aspire to live with the same ideal'. No, comrades, the Communist International is not that: it is a fighting organisation, it is the army of the world proletariat...[78]

De los Ríos defended his non-Marxist position with tenacity, arguing against the Comintern leader Bukharin that there was no scientific basis for asserting that capitalism was in its final phase.[79] The impression created by De los Ríos must have been extraordinary: almost aristocratic in manner and bearing, the sartorially immaculate academic could list the Sorbonne, the London School of Economics and the German universities of Jena and Berlin amongst the centres of study he had attended. Appointed in 1911 at the age of 32 to the chair of political theory in the University of Granada, De los Ríos was possessed of a refined intellect and immensely wide cultural interests. Neither revolutionary nor Marxist, he felt no need to make rhetorical obeisance in the direction of the Russian experiment.[80] Indeed, he returned from Russia even more convinced that the PSOE should not join the Comintern.

Anguiano, on the other hand was favourably impressed by what he saw. Neither he nor De los Ríos, however, was able to persuade the PSOE National Committee of their views. Since the Comintern's own report was also rejected, it was decided to call a further Extraordinary Congress for April 1921 in order to resolve the issue definitively.[81] The indecision was costing both the PSOE and the workers' movement dear. With Severiano Martínez Anido recently installed as civil governor in Barcelona, and the CNT beginning to show signs of collapse under the weight of state repression, it was vital for the Socialists to offer a coherent front. This they were unable to do whilst the leadership of the movement remained divided between *terceristas* in the PSOE and parliamentary gradualists in the UGT. Indeed, the longer the workers' movement remained exposed to the twin pressures of repression and internal division, the greater were the monarchical state's chances of survival. The relative success of repressive measures, however, led to the undermining of more moderate CNT leaders like Seguí and Pestaña, and triggered off a counterpoint of escalating violence between the state and extremist 'pure' Anarchists. The opening months of 1921 witnessed massive scale terrorism in the Catalan capital, often the work of immigrants from other Spanish regions. It was met by an equally violent response from Martínez Anido: a law of forcible repatriation was introduced, by which non-Catalan militants could be returned to their point of origin. In addition, the notorious *ley de fugas* was established. This latter measure amounted to a shoot-on-sight policy, given official authority through the formula, 'shot while trying to escape'.[82] CNT extremists sought revenge. On 8 March, Prime Minister Eduardo Dato was assassinated by Anarchists in the centre of Madrid, provoking yet another governmental crisis and still greater repression of the CNT.

It was in an atmosphere of generalised crisis, then, that the third PSOE Extraordinary Congress opened in early April 1921. The Congress would be marked by the re-establishment of *pablista* hegemony, serious schism and deep acrimony. The *pablistas* had been making intensive efforts during the preceding months to countermand the continued revolutionary drift of the Socialist rank and file, particularly in Asturias and Vizcaya, and ensure that the regional delegates chosen to attend the Congress would be sympathetic to their viewpoint. Pablo Iglesias, in addition to corresponding with regional leaders, had published a series of four articles in *El Socialista* prior to the congress. He utilised his considerable and unmatched authority within the Socialist movement to argue against acceptance of the Comintern's 21 Conditions, but also to make a strong plea against division within the PSOE.[83] His concern that entry to the Communist International would lead to the expulsion of reformists like himself, was clearly demonstrated in an anxious letter to Enrique de Francisco, founder of the Paperworkers' Union of the Basque–Navarre Region, and later to become PSOE deputy for Guipúzcoa during the Second Republic:

It is not going well, but we have to keep on working vigorously until the end, for we could win or we could be expelled... I am delighted that you can come to the Congress. You do not know how tormented I feel over lacking the energy to go to meetings and do other tasks.[84]

In the event, De Francisco failed to attend the Congress, the Basque Socialists having mandated instead the Comintern supporters Perezagua and Pérez Solís, a recent but totally committed convert to the cause. It is likely that there was considerable double-dealing over the election of regional delegates, as well as falsification of membership figures.[85]

At the Congress itself, there was a strong feeling of mutual hostility and recrimination between *pablistas* and *terceristas*.[86] The principal speakers against the Comintern were Fernando de los Ríos, Julián Besteiro, and Francisco Largo Caballero. They were opposed by Daniel Anguiano, Virginia González, and Roberto Alvarez, whilst Andrés Saborit took a rather ambivalent stance. There were also brief pro-Comintern interventions from Isidoro Acevedo and Ramón Lamoneda, and a letter was read from Pablo Iglesias, absent through illness, expressing his unwavering opposition to PSOE membership of the new organisation. The debate opened with reports by De los Ríos and Anguiano on their impressions of the Bolshevik regime in Russia, the former laying emphasis on the lack of liberty and the latter replying that this was inevitable. In fact, though, Anguiano's speech was somewhat ambiguous: in spite of supporting the 21 Conditions, he criticised the dominance of the Communist Party in Russia. Largo Caballero, who had recaptured the presidency of the Agrupación Socialista Madrileña from García Cortés a few weeks earlier, then made an effective speech in which he played on the possibility of the expulsion of those who voted against the Comintern should the Congress eventually decide to join it. The issue of expulsions was highly emotive; some of Largo's remarks, though, were astonishingly disingenuous:

I have always been characterised in the organisation as a reformist, and I am not ashamed of that; I would be ashamed of making revolutionary declarations and then in practice behaving like an opportunist... To consider that those of us who have spent thirty or forty years in the Party, and have been in that time the object of derision and mockery by many of you, is to forget that we were the founders of the Party and that we have dedicated the efforts and enthusiasms of our whole life to it.[87]

Acevedo, the Asturian delegate and erstwhile *pablista*, rebutted Largo's remarks with the observation that Zinoviev had said nothing about expulsions and that the differences between the two positions at the PSOE Congress merely revolved around tactics.

However, it was Besteiro who introduced a genuinely acerbic note to the proceedings with a scathing attack on the *terceristas*, effectively accusing them of dishonesty:

You do not dare to adopt a truly Communist position. The Russian Communists have one virtue above all others: they do not lie... You may be very revolutionary, but while you discuss this business of the Third International all our revolutionary activities are held in abeyance. The logical thing, if you want to join the Third International, is to go and join the Communist Party. But you do not do that, because in reality the Communists do not want you. According to documents we have all been able to read, the Communist Party does not want you because it believes you to be insincere... The only revolutionary manifestations you can offer are insults. You say that we are Conservatives, evolutionists, reformists, that we are going to the Congress (Cortes) to collaborate with the bourgeoisie. When you make these claims you do it knowing that they are false.[88]

Understandably, the *tercerista* delegates were deeply offended at the tone of Besteiro's remarks. However, Largo Caballero then pulled off something of a procedural coup by winning a motion which imposed a restriction on the scope of the debate and limited the right of Executive members to speak.[89] Ramón Lamoneda, the final speaker in the debate before De los Ríos and Anguiano summed up, remarked that the 21 Conditions were not the obstacle, since the opponents of entry to the

Comintern had equally been opponents prior to their elaboration.[90] Whilst this was true of leading *pablistas* like Besteiro and Largo, it was less so with people like Luis Araquistáin, who in fact would abandon the PSOE altogether after the Congress, rejoining only in 1929, and Andrés Ovejero, who also left the party in disgust. Nonetheless, it was with some degree of bitterness that Lamoneda accused Pablo Iglesias of using unfounded fear tactics in suggesting that acceptance of the 21 Conditions would necessarily lead to the PSOE being declared illegal. He maintained that it was the *pablistas* who had introduced the issue of expulsions and concluded with the gloomy prediction that a split in the party appeared inevitable.[91]

The vote confirmed Lamoneda's view. By a majority of 2,603 out of a total of 14,833, affiliation to the Comintern was rejected. In accordance with a prior arrangement, the *terceristas*, led by the veteran anti-*pablista* Antonio García Quejido, immediately abandoned the PSOE to set up a second Spanish Communist Party.[92] It is likely that the vote was not strictly above board. During the Congress, the credentials of various delegates had been called into question, particularly those of César González, father of Virginia, whose pro-Comintern mandate from the Federation of Spanish Socialist Groups in France was called into question by Antonio Fabra Ribas. He was successfully defended, however, by Torralba Beci. The credentials of the delegate from Toledo were also called into question, leading to the withdrawal in protest from the Ccongress of one Domingo Alonso. Later, a telegram was read from forty Socialists in Baracaldo, opposing their delegate's pro-Comintern vote on the grounds that only a quarter of their membership had supported the Bolshevik International. In addition, Oscar Pérez Solís demanded an explanation of restrictions that were being imposed on entry to the Casa del Pueblo, to which Largo Caballero replied that they were necessary in order to keep out rowdy elements, by which he was obviously referring to supporters of the Comintern.[93] Pablo Iglesias expressed his own doubts over the veracity of delegates' mandates in a letter to Enrique de Francisco, revealing of his bitterness towards the *terceristas*, sent immediately after the Congress had finished:

I was very sorry that you did not come to the Congress, if only because you would have been able to see close up some *terceristas* and been able to appreciate what they are capable of, although you already know it and will have seen it in the press. . . They stopped at nothing. . . The Workers' Centre in Alcira, which voted not even for Republicans, but actually for monarchists, is listed as enrolled in the Party with no end of affiliates, and their delegate, who, according to what I have been told, is a real 'gem' (*alhaja*), voted *representing 2,000*. Take that away from the 6,000 votes they got and plenty more acquired in a dodgy manner, and there would have been very little support for the *terceristas*. Asturias gave them, if I'm not mistaken, 1,300 votes, for which they should thank Acevedo, whose behaviour would shock even those who are not shocked by anything. . . As you do not know what happened in Fitero, I will tell you. They got your letter, and were all set to mandate you, but a co-religionist from Bilbao arrived, went mad about the Third International, they discussed it for three days, and then opted for it; but there was a clever chap who pointed out that they still owed their subscription (to the PSOE) and were not in a position to pay it, so they did not elect a delegate.[94]

It is impossible to ascertain with any degree of accuracy to what extent behind-the-scenes deals affected the composition of delegates at the Congress. What is not open to dispute, however, is that throughout the entire struggle between *pablistas* and *terceristas* both sides used tactics which called into question the supposedly incorruptible moral probity of Spanish Socialism. When all was said and done, Socialist leaders like Pablo Iglesias and Francisco Largo Caballero were never likely to relinquish the party with which they had become so closely identified without employing every means at their disposal to prevent such an eventuality. These ranged from deliberately emotive appeals, based around the patriarchal authority of *el abuelo*, to local-level pressure of dubious constitutional legality. If the *terceristas* had Asturias and the Basque Country in their control, the *pablistas* retained the dominant influence in the Spanish capital, Valencia and in the massive southern region of Andalusia, where the post-war growth of both the PSOE and especially the UGT had been greatest. It is almost certainly the case that a majority of rank-and-file militants in the PSOE were in favour of joining the Comintern. Certainly, the decline in membership of the party would suggest as much, falling from 45,477 at the start of the year to 23,010 immediately after the 1921 Congress.[95]

The UGT, on the other hand, remained steady in terms of membership, hovering around the quarter-million mark until the creation of the Second Republic in 1931 triggered spectacular growth. The implication of this is not necessarily that rank-and-file UGT members were less radical or revolutionary than were their counterparts in the PSOE.[96] Indeed, it is likely, especially in the intensely conflict-ridden region of Andalusia, that UGT members were every bit as militant as activists in the PSOE. There are two probable reasons for the lack of a decline in UGT membership following the 1921 schism in the PSOE. First, at a local level the reasons for membership of the two organisations were likely to be different. Militancy in a political party like the PSOE implied some form of long-term political vision, with Socialism as its end; membership of the UGT, on the other hand, would more likely correspond to immediate aspirations, such as the defence of workers' interests, or protection against employers. Macro-level political theory was hardly likely to be uppermost in the minds of landless peasants and exploited industrial workers. In other words, membership of the UGT, unlike that of the PSOE, did not *necessarily* imply a commitment to the establishment of Socialism as opposed to an alteration of prevailing circumstances. Thus, whereas the protracted debates over PSOE affiliation to the Comintern could both call into question the efficacy of the party as a vehicle for social change, and disappoint more militant rank-and-file activists in terms of the final decision, they did not carry the same implications for the UGT.

This, of course, helps to explain the apparent mystery of Anarchist strength in Spain: just as in Barcelona, workers primarily sought *effective* representation, so in Andalusia the landless peasants paid their dues to the organisation which looked like it could do most to defend them.[97] Juan Díaz del Moral cites the case of a syndicalist society in Carcabuey which replaced an article in its statutes calling for apoliticism with another announcing adhesion to the PSOE following the resolution by the local Socialist leader of a problem involving the civil governor. Antonio Calero, meanwhile, has reported that conversations with Andalusian militants of this era revealed little perceived difference between the purpose of membership of the UGT and the CNT.[98] It is unsurprising, therefore, that the CNT should have enjoyed such an advantage over the UGT, since the latter only really began to consider the importance of the agrarian question after the First World War. Furthermore, here is perhaps the most obvious example of how the Socialist leaders' theoretical dependence, with its rigidly Marxist conviction that revolution was inevitable but impossible until after the establishment of bourgeois democracy, cost the movement massively in terms both of flexibility and efficacy. Only with the establishment of the landworkers' federation, the Federación Nacional de Trabajadores de la Tierra (FNTT) in 1930 would the UGT begin to build the infrastructure for a genuinely effective presence in rural areas.[99]

The second reason for the relative stability of UGT membership compared to that of the PSOE concerns the organisational structure of the two bodies. Membership of the UGT was usually via the collective affiliation of a local federation, that is to say that workers joined a particular local-based union which then decided whether or not to affiliate to the UGT. This gave rise to the possibility, as in the case of the local federation in Carcabuey, of easy manipulation by the local leadership of national-level affiliation. It is precisely through the establishment of a loyal local-level bureaucracy that UGT leaders like Iglesias, Largo Caballero and Besteiro were able to retain such dominance within the union. In the case of the PSOE, on the other hand, there was far less collective affiliation. Indeed, in the main areas of *tercerista* support, Asturias and Vizcaya, affiliation was strictly on an individual level, whereas in Madrid, where the *pablistas* managed to maintain hegemony despite the efforts of the FJSE and the militants in the ASM, there were two collective members for every one direct affiliate.[100] This assisted the manipulation of block votes at congresses by *pablistas*, but also gave rise to the desertion of the PSOE by militant individual members in Asturias and Vizcaya following the 1921 Extraordinary Congress. Thus, in Vizcaya membership of the PSOE fell from 1,478 affiliates in 1921 to just 698 in 1923. In Asturias, meanwhile, the situation was somewhat complicated by the leadership of the radical miners' union, the Sindicato de los Obreros Mineros de Asturias (SOMA), by the confirmed *pablista*, Manuel Llaneza. Following the 1921 Congress, both the SOMA and the Asturian Socialist Federation would experience dramatic falls in membership, the former collapsing from 20,000 in 1921 to 7,500 the following year.[101]

The 1921 Extraordinary Congress then, saw the re-establishment of *pablista* hegemony in the PSOE, and therefore in the Socialist movement as a whole. It was achieved, however, only at the cost of a highly damaging schism and considerable loss of membership in the PSOE and in certain regional strongholds of UGT support. Moreover, the Socialist leaders were sufficiently traumatised by the entire conflict over membership of the Comintern as to collapse in its aftermath into a kind of self-contemplative stasis. Thus, for instance, a proposal in June 1921 by Marcelino Domingo, the former Republican deputy, to rebuild an alliance of anti-dynastic parliamentary groups was rejected because it would include groups which had criticised the PSOE.[102] In an ironic manner, though, Spanish Socialism, and the UGT in particular, benefited from its quietest isolation in the thirty months that lay between the Extraordinary Congress of April 1921 and the assumption of political power by General Primo de Rivera in September 1923. It was during this period that repression of anti-state initiatives by the working class and peasantry was at its harshest as the Restoration Monarchy desperately tried to stave off the crisis unleashed by the disastrous defeat of Spanish troops by Abd-el-Krim at the Moroccan town of Anual in July 1921. The reclusive stance of the Socialist movement, and its strict respect for parliamentary legality during the debate on responsibility for the Anual fiasco, saved it from the more extreme examples of state repression.[103] Indeed, Socialist moderation in this period was to be of major importance in recommending the UGT to Primo de Rivera as a potential ally in his attempt to cauterise Spain's ills.

The second Spanish Communist Party, the Partido Comunista Obrero Español (PCOE), founded on 13 April 1921, was thus born at a most unpropitious moment. The revolutionary wave which had threatened to swamp Spain since the end of the First World War was on the ebb; years of successive reversals for the workers' movement, both in Spain and in Europe, had blunted the revolutionary aspirations of leaders and members alike. The new party was not only small, with a maximum membership of 5,000 in 1921, but was immediately subjected to attack from the even more exiguous existing Communist Party, the PCE. Between April and November 1921, the political efficacy of both was hampered by their mutual recrimination and reluctance to comply with Comintern instructions over unification.[104] Furthermore, the growing CNT disillusion with Bolshevism made Anarchist initiatives with the new Communist parties unlikely. An indication of how the fabric of revolution in Spain was starting to unravel came during July 1921, when the PCE, PCOE and the CNT all independently sent representatives to Moscow. Ramón Merino Gracia (PCE), and Eduardo Torralba Beci (PCOE) attended the Third Congress of the Comintern, whilst Joaquín Maurín and Andreu Nin, Catalan syndicalists who fourteen years later would form the POUM, were the CNT representatives at the simultaneously staged founding Congress of the Red International Labour Union (RILU, or Profintern). Merino Gracia and Torralba Beci represented insufficient members to make a real impact, and were in any case hindered by their constant efforts to upstage each other, while Nin and Maurín were soon to break with the increasingly troubled CNT.[105]

Unity between the PCE and PCOE eventually had to be imposed by the Comintern, its agent Antonio Graziadei arriving in Madrid in early November 1921 to oversee negotiations. Graziadei's arrival, however, coincided with a period of severe state repression: *El Comunista* had been suspended, and most of the PCE's Executive Committee was in jail as a result of protests over the Moroccan war. He was therefore able to see only one representative from each party, Gonzalo Sanz for the PCE and Manuel Núñez de Arenas for the PCOE. The agreement that was hammered out favoured the PCE, giving them nine members in a new National Committee as opposed to six members from the PCOE. The united party journal, meanwhile, was to be *Claridad*, although this was later renamed *La Antorcha*, edited by Juan Andrade, a future collaborator with Nin and Maurín in the POUM.[106] Immediately after the First Congress of the new united party, the Partido Comunista de España (PCE), in March 1922, five of the nine original PCE members began to identify with the six leaders who had come from the PCOE. The other four, including Andrade, set up a faction within the new PCE, known as the Oposición Comunista Española, which would later be expelled from the party and would form the basis, in 1930, of the first Trotskyist group in Spain.[107]

The continued internal struggles of the PCE, together with state repression, rendered the party largely irrelevant within the wider Spanish political process. It achieved national notice only briefly, in November 1922, under the most unfortunate of circumstances. At the 15th Congress of the UGT, being held in the Madrid Casa del Pueblo, the attendance of a number of PCE members, exacerbated an already tense atmosphere. Angered by the re-confirmed dominance of the *pablista* tendency within the Socialist movement, which ensured that the PCE members would not be allowed representation as Communists on UGT committees, as well as by the exclusion of pro-Communist workers by armed guards placed on the doors by Largo Caballero, the PCE militants who had managed to get inside the Casa del Pueblo became increasingly restless.[108] In a moment of extreme confusion, FJSE member Manuel González Portilla was shot dead. The police moved in and arrested several of the PCE members present, including Núñez de Arenas, Mariano García Cortés and Virginia González, although no one was brought to trial for the murder.[109] The incident was a major blow to the PCE's hopes of winning influence among the Spanish working class. Indeed, the party remained constantly on the verge of collapse until the Primo de Rivera coup forced it underground.

Whilst the PCE was discredited and repressed, the CNT was forced ever more onto the defensive, devastated by a combination of internal division and effective state action. Pro-Comintern Comités Sindicalistas Revolucionarios (CSR), set up in late 1922 by Joaquín Maurín, drew ever further from the CNT leadership, increasingly in the hands of extremists. The dominance of the extremists in a largely broken movement was confirmed by the assassination of Salvador Seguí on 10 March 1923.[110] This in turn provided the rationale for still further state repression, as did the murder at the hands of an Anarchist of the Cardinal-Archbishop of Zaragoza three months later. By the summer of 1923, the political fabric of the country seemed totally unravelled. Further general elections in late April, the fifth in six years, had been marked by record rates of abstention and had simply heightened the impression of a political power vacuum.[111] It was in this context that General Miguel Primo de Rivera staged his *pronunciamiento* in support of the monarchy. Six years of uninterrupted labour unrest, especially in Barcelona and Andalusia, the loss of much of the monarchy's legitimacy and most of its credibility following the continued suspension of constitutional rights, brutal repression of the workers' movement, and the Moroccan disaster, as well as a general feeling of stagnation, contributed to Primo de Rivera's September 1923 coup being widely welcomed. The Socialists, severely weakened following their protracted internal struggles, were neither ready nor inclined to launch an offensive against the re-establishment of military rule after a gap of nearly fifty years. Indeed, contrary to all expectations, the UGT was soon to be actively collaborating with the General.

4 Dealing with a Dictator: organised Socialism, 1923–1931

On 13 September 1923, General Miguel Primo de Rivera assumed political power in Spain through a *coup d'état* organised with the connivance of King Alfonso XIII.[1] His regime survived just six years, the popular enthusiasm with which he was initially received having long since dissipated when finally he was obliged to resign, a broken man, in January 1930. The precise nature of his regime remains a matter of some controversy.[2] However, it is undeniable that Primo was given assistance of inestimable value by the willing co-operation of the Socialist movement, after only the briefest initial hesitancy, in his plans for the re-organisation of labour relations along fashionably corporativist lines. The Socialists abandoned all opposition to Primo by 22 September 1923 with the publication of a note by the PSOE Executive Committee calling on all Socialists and their sympathisers to refrain from extra-legal action which might provoke a violent response from the Dictatorship.[3] By their participation in undemocratic state structures, the Spanish Socialists allowed the new regime scope to retain some degree of popular legitimacy despite its ban on party political activity, rigorous repression of the Anarcho-syndicalist CNT and the Communist PCE, establishment of a military Directory and a single party, and the imposition of press censorship. However, it is an ironic paradox of Spanish Socialism that collaboration with the Dictatorship of Primo de Rivera can be seen not only as the most undistinguished episode of its history, but also as a period vital to the PSOE's ability to play the central role in the establishment of the Second Republic. Through collaboration with the Dictator, the Socialists did not merely avoid proscription, they were also able to build up their forces in a manner not open to rival groups. Thus, when the Second Republic was eventually declared in April 1931, the PSOE had established itself, *faute de mieux*, as the most coherently organised political force in Spanish politics.

It is perhaps because of this development, a prime example of the unintended consequences of political action, that right-wing historians of Spanish Socialism have subsequently tended to underplay the cordial relations between Primo de Rivera and the Socialist movement.[4] Primo's labour policy inadvertently paved the way for the dominant role of the

PSOE in the establishment of the Second Republic. Furthermore, the PSOE's participation in Primo's plans gave the lie to the picture, painted by Francoist propagandists, of a Socialist movement made up of irredeemably revolutionary Marxist extremists, infiltrated by Communism.[5] Similarly, however, historians sympathetic to Socialism have also tended to underplay the mutual understanding manifested between the PSOE–UGT and Primo. Although a number of self-justificatory works were published by Socialist leaders in the first years of the Republic, little attention has been devoted since then to the issue of collaboration with the Dictatorship.[6] In fact, virtually the only detailed accounts of collaboration have come from Marxists like Joaquín Maurín or Juan Andrade, and, more recently, liberal historians such as Shlomo Ben-Ami and José Andrés-Gallego. They have been able to establish an orthodoxy, still unchallenged, that Socialist collaboration represented little more than naked opportunism, a thinly disguised attempt to ensure the survival of Socialist organisations whilst their more leftist rivals suffered state persecution.[7]

Whilst opportunism most certainly played a major part in the decision of the Socialists to collaborate with Primo, it is overly reductionist to grant exclusive causal weight to this one factor. Before a proper assessment can be made of the Socialists' role during the Dictatorship, there are at least three further factors which should be considered. First, if it is true that Primo's coup met with no demonstrations of opposition from the PSOE or UGT, it is equally the case that Republican resistance was conspicuous by its absence. Melquíades Alvarez, leader of the Reformist Party, remained silent on the take-over, a first indication perhaps of his subsequent shift to the right of the political spectrum.[8] However, the Junta Nacional Republicana, headed by the Radical Party leader, Alejandro Lerroux, also failed to react, being internally divided and caught unawares by Primo's assumption of power. Only in 1926 would Republican forces begin to respond to the Dictatorship, through the formation of the Alianza Republicana.[9] Moreover, it was not just Socialists and Republicans who refrained from manifestations of protest in September 1923; on the contrary, Primo de Rivera was widely welcomed. In the words of Manuel Azaña, whose creation of Acción Republicana in 1925 served as the stimulus behind the Alianza, and who was to be President of the Second Republic,

It is not only baseness, or cowardice, or selfish desires, or class hatred, or anti-liberal fanaticism in the opinion that supports the Directory; no. Honourable people, those who form the 'neutral mass', have received with rejoicing this clean sweep (*escobazo*). The reason is that the country just could not stand any more, and being paralysed, being incapable of moving on its own, it hopes that the military will achieve the miracle of national salvation.[10]

Thus it was that the calls to resistance by both the CNT and the PCE received a most limited popular response, even in those areas where Anarchist strength was greatest. The CNT and PCE suffered the further blow of seeing their invitation to the Socialists to set up a committee of action against the Dictatorship brusquely rejected.[11] As Manuel Suárez Cortina has suggested,

the implantation of the Dictatorship of Primo de Rivera had the blessing, or at least the consent, of a great part of the Leftist just as much as the Rightist press, of the politicians, and undoubtedly of the King himself.[12]

Indeed, even amongst the politicised working class and peasantry, if Primo's seizure of power failed to win their blessing, it did at least receive their tacit acceptance inasmuch as they declined to respond to the exhortations of the CNT and PCE. In large measure, this lack of protest – among rank-and-file militants just as much as Azaña's 'neutral masses' – derived, as the Republican leader stated, from weariness. Six years of struggle marked by repeated defeats, above all in Barcelona, where the CNT still bore the scars of the brutal repression unleashed by General Martínez Anido between 1920 and 1922, had left many members of the working class and peasantry disheartened. They no longer had the stomach for the fight; at the very least, they needed a period of recuperation. For others, including José Ortega y Gasset, the liberal essayist and philosopher, Primo seemed to embody the regenerationist hope associated principally with Joaquín Costa (whose call for an 'Iron Surgeon' the Dictator sought to answer) and the so-called 'generation of 1898'.[13] Regenerationism held a particularly strong appeal amongst the liberal intellectuals who dominated the leadership of the Socialist and Republican movements. First mooted in the aftermath of the Cuban disaster of 1898, regeneration became something of a national watchword in the early years of the twentieth century:

At the turn of the century regeneration was a theme essayed by all, from the cardinal archbishop of Valladolid to Blasco Ibañez, the Republican novelist, from professors to poets, from heirs of the sober tradition of Jovellanos to political quacks, from Catalan nationalists to Castilian patriots. . . All were regenerationists of a kind. 'The Regenerator', wrote a satirist, 'a tonic for weak nations. Recommended by the best doctors, apostles and saviours.'[14]

Whilst Costa, the intensely patriotic and workaholic polymath and visionary, was the leading light of regenerationist sentiment, his ideas found a strong echo amongst the Krausist-inspired intellectuals of the Institución Libre de Enseñanza (ILE), originally set up in 1876.[15] These progressive liberals were heirs to the peculiar Spanish intellectual tradition of self-contemplation, the obsession with Spain as a 'problem', characteristic of the work of so many Iberian philosopher politicians, if not kings.[16]

The ILE, so deeply imbued with the Krausist spirit of harmony and rational humanism, was the alma mater of a generation of leading anti-dynastic politicians, including Melquíades Alvarez, Manuel Azaña, and above all the Socialists Julián Besteiro and Fernando de los Ríos.[17] Their primordial concern in regard to politics was to inject morality into a corrupt and discredited system, to rebuild state structures on a more principled and democratic basis, to 'regenerate' the nation. Some of these concerns were shared, on a rhetorical level at least, in a most unlikely quarter: the Juntas Militares de Defensa, which had played such an instrumental role in the crisis of 1917. The leading figures within the Juntas made frequent reference to regenerationist imperatives, above all to the need to sanitise Spanish politics, to rescue the Constitution from the incompetence of the dynastic politicians of the *turno* system.[18] In spite of the disappointments of 1917, many reformists were still ready to allow Primo de Rivera the chance to prove himself a regenerationist 'Iron Surgeon' come to rescue Spain. After six years in which the political system of the *turno pacífico* had become utterly discredited, Primo was widely welcomed as a potential saviour of the nation. Ultimately, of course, the Dictator turned out to be more bogus god than authentic mammon.[19] In the immediate aftermath of his assumption of power, however, he was genuinely seen by many as possessing regenerationist potential, an improvement at the very least on the thoroughly discredited *turno* system.

The second point in regard to the lack of Socialist protest over Primo de Rivera's coup is that the *pablista* leadership of the movement remained deeply traumatised over the repression unleashed on the PSOE following the strike movement of August 1917. Furthermore, it was easy for Socialist leaders to imagine that their movement would suffer similar treatment to that meted out to the Anarchists by the likes of Count Salvatierra and General Martínez Anido should they adopt a more confrontational stance. Primo de Rivera was, after all, a military man. The Socialist leaders were perfectly aware that, even should they wish to oppose the *pronunciamiento*, their movement lacked the strength and support to resist the new Dictator. The Executives of both the PSOE and the UGT warned their members to avoid initiatives from

well-intentioned but impatient people or by those who want to throw the proletariat into sterile movements which can only serve as a pretext for repression.[20]

Whether arrived at through prudence or cowardice, the Socialist leaders' assessment of the likely response to anti-Primo protest was undeniably well-founded. Thus, what little protest did emerge was restricted to rather anaemic comments in *El Socialista*. For instance, the party newspaper responded to the implication in the liberal daily *El Sol* (which early decided to support Primo on the grounds that he promised 'the rectification of past injustices') that the Socialists shared its view on the Dictatorship with the terse comment:

The Socialist Party and the Unión General de Trabajadores do not see any sign in the action of the military Directory of a desire to rectify any fundamental injustice. They believe it to be a movement. . .Therefore, they do not regard it with sympathy, nor do they place any hope at all in it.[21]

Such indignant protestations, however, were belied by the decision, taken in the immediate aftermath of the *pronunciamiento*, to continue participating in official state bodies.[22]

The third factor to be considered is one which is absolutely central to the very essence of *pablista* Socialism. It has been a constant theme of this study that the Socialist leaders consistently misinterpreted, or failed to interpret at all, the given socio-political situation in which they were operating. Instead, victims of a rigidly deterministic interpretation of Marxism which posited an ineluctable stagist development towards Socialism, the PSOE leaders remained convinced that Spain was yet to experience a bourgeois revolution. Until this took place, it was pointless to think in terms of the Socialist revolution. Of no figure was this more true than Julián Besteiro, the most influential theorist in the Socialist movement, who was to become leader of both the PSOE and the UGT when Pablo Iglesias, *el abuelo*, died on 9 December 1925. Besteiro clung with unquestioning faith to a teleological view, highly reminiscent of the early Kautsky, of the revolutionary process as an organic necessity of the evolution of capitalism.[23] His belief in the inevitability of social progress was linked to a rejection of violence and a commitment to the maintenance of the workers' struggle within the bounds of state-defined official legality. Socialism would come about in the fullness of time, but only at its pre-ordained moment which would follow the bourgeois revolution, in turn a necessary historical stage yet to arrive in Spain.

The most remarkable feature of the Socialist response to Primo's *pronunciamiento*, and one which cannot be overemphasised, is the total absence of any attempt to analyse the nature of the new regime. Just as the declaration of the First Republic in 1873 had provoked no reaction from the members of the Socialist Federation in Madrid (who were to form the basis of the PSOE at the end of that decade), so the coming of the Primo Dictatorship elicited no theoretical debate as to its significance. As Alfonso XIII remained on the throne, the new regime was seen simply as a reinforcement of the existing monarchy and therefore not requiring any particular theoretical attention. No parallels were drawn, for instance, between Primo de Rivera's takeover and the assumption of power in Italy by Mussolini the previous October.[24] Indeed, the rise of the Italian Fascist Party and Mussolini's March on Rome had received virtually no attention in the Spanish Socialist press, obsessed as it was with internal party matters in the aftermath of the 1921 schism. Of course, there was no equivalent in Spain to Mussolini's fascist movement, but one searches Socialist publications in vain for *any* theoretical or comparative analyses of Primo's *pronunciamiento*. Concepts such as Bonapartism were apparently foreign to the Spanish Socialists in more than just a geographical sense.

Interestingly, one of the most incisive Marxist analyses applicable to the Primo de Rivera Dictatorship was developed by the leading leftist victim of Mussolini's fascist regime, Antonio Gramsci. His concept of Caesarism, elaborated in his Prison Notebooks of 1932, was of particular relevance to the situation in Spain in the early 1920s:

Caesarism can be said to express a situation in which the forces in conflict balance each other in a catastrophic manner; that is to say, they balance each other in such a way that a continuation of the conflict can only terminate in their reciprocal destruction. When the progressive force A struggles with the reactionary force B, not only may A defeat B or B defeat A, but it may happen that neither A nor B defeats the other – that they bleed each other mutually and then a third force C intervenes from outside, subjugating what is left of both A and B.[25]

In broad terms, this may be said to describe the route by which Primo assumed power after the stalemate in Spain between the forces of progress and reaction represented by the struggles of 1917 to 1923. Gramsci further argued that the Caesar figure might, according to specific circumstances, favour either progressive or reactionary forces, and did not necessarily even have to take the form of a heroic individual.[26] In the Spanish case, Primo aspired to the status of hero, but failed to favour reactionary forces sufficiently to retain their support.

However, there was no Gramsci in the Spanish Socialist movement. On the contrary, the PSOE's leading theorist, Julián Besteiro, could hardly have been further removed, in both ideological and political terms, from the activist Sardinian revolutionary. The Madrid professor was perhaps the most deeply influenced of all the Socialist leaders by Krausist education at the ILE; indeed, in 1924 he was awarded a grant by the ILE's Junta de Ampliación de Estudios e Investigaciones Científicas to travel to England and study the Workers' Educational Association.[27] Somewhat ironically, Besteiro's faith in a crudely Marxist evolutionary model was actually reinforced by political events in England during his seven-month stay there.[28] He hailed the electoral success of the Labour Party at the end of 1923 as clear-cut evidence of the inevitable progress of the labour movement, as well as confirmation of Marx's belief that England, as the most industrially developed European nation, would be the most likely site for the implantation of Socialism.

During his stay in England, Besteiro wrote fourteen articles on British political affairs for the liberal republican newspaper, *El Liberal*, all of which were also printed in *El Socialista*.[29] The most important of these, 'El modelo inglés', was published in the special 1 May edition of the Socialist newspaper. In it, he stated:

Of course, the Socialist ideal is not easy to understand (*concebir*), because it is not founded on primary and elementary concepts, but rather is the product of a long and complex mental elaboration, which finds fertile ground only when certain economic conditions have been produced, which, in turn, are the product of great processes of civilisation... There can be no seriously Socialist and revolutionary spirit for whom the Russian revolution and the English revolution (especially the latter as more perfectly and more genuinely Socialist) does not offer a vast field of study and meditation.[30]

Besteiro also warned, however, against attempting to transplant revolutionary models through 'superstitious faith':

From a genuinely internationalist point of view...a social Revolution is perfectly conceivable without workers' and soldiers' Councils, just as it is without the 'speaker's' wig and Sunday best trousers.[31]

Others in the Socialist movement were no less fulsome in their eulogies of the British Labour Party's success. Manuel Cordero, a UGT bureaucrat who was to be in the early years of the Second Republic one of the strongest defenders of collaboration with Primo, hailed the British election results as confirmation of Marx's prophecies. After drawing an ideological parallel between Lenin and MacDonald, Cordero manifested some degree of conceptual confusion over Marxist categories when he asked rhetorically,

How could Socialist ideas take root in feudal Russia, with some peasants accustomed to living in a slave regime, in the same way as they could in England with more than a century of liberal and parliamentary life?... The victory of the English workers must have repercussions in Spain, strengthening the forces of the Socialist Party.[32]

Antonio Fabra Ribas, the Catalan Socialist who had been so uncertain over how to react to the Comintern, also now found encouragement in the 'transcendence' of the Labour Party's success.[33] *El Socialista*, meanwhile, lauded the Labour Party's achievement in its editorial columns, describing it as the most significant event in Europe since the Russian and German revolutions in 1917 and 1919.[34]

As so often, it was Indalecio Prieto who introduced an element of down-to-earth realism into the issue. The Basque leader pointed out that the British Constitution and the general level of political education in the country allowed the Labour Party a freedom of manoeuvre which would be impossible for the Socialist movement in Spain under Alfonso XIII. Never one to mince words, Prieto stated,

When the reflection of Communism in Russia began to dazzle in the Spanish

Socialist camp, we hastened to react against the senseless urge to imitate it. Spain is not Russia, we said then. But nor is Spain England, we say now.[35]

Another who warned against drawing parallels between Britain and Spain was Gabriel Alomar Villalonga, a Catalan republican who was to join Manuel Azaña's party, Acción Republicana, in the Second Republic. In an article in *La Libertad*, reprinted in *El Socialista*, Alomar wrote of the Socialists' role:

The experiment of English labourism (which is not Socialism) has got nothing to do with the hypothetical reconstructive and governmental mission of Socialism in Spain. Without wishing to give the word Revolution any catastrophic sense, it is undeniable that the supposed function of our Socialism ought to be revolutionary.[36]

Alomar's point was fundamental. The inescapable difference between the British Labour movement and the Spanish Socialists was that the latter, even if only tenuously on occasion, held to a radical Marxist self-image. For all their reformist practices and ultra-cautious hesitation, the *pablista* leaders of the PSOE and UGT, with few exceptions, still saw themselves as Marxist Socialists. More importantly, they were committed to the replacement of the monarchy with a republic, an imperative stage *en route* to the Socialist revolution. In Britain, the Labour Party held no anti-monarchist brief. Marxism was the preserve of marginal groups on the Left, of the Communist Party (formerly the SDF, then the British Socialist Party), Sylvia Pankhurst's Workers' Socialist Federation, or the 'proletarian philosophers' of the Socialist Labour Party; in Spain, no matter how rigidly conceived, it was the guiding impulse behind the mainstream Socialist movement.[37] In tactical terms, there may have been on occasion little to distinguish the activities of the PSOE–UGT from the British Labour Party; in practical terms, however, the vastly different social, political and economic situation in the two countries, together with the different final ends of the two organisations, rendered such coincidences meaningless. As Prieto so rightly said, Spain was not England.

However, perhaps the most significant impact of events in England on the Spanish Socialist movement was less ideological than organisational. Francisco Largo Caballero, the ascetic UGT leader, saw in the structure of the Labour Party, with its organic link to the trade union movement, a potential model for the Spanish Socialist organisation. He developed this theme throughout 1924, and used it as the principal line of justification for the acceptance by PSOE and UGT members of official posts in the Primo de Rivera regime. Luis Araquistáin, who had left the PSOE in 1921 but would return to play the role of ideological guru to Largo during the Second Republic, wrote in *El Sol* on 30 March 1924:

Few external events are destined, it would seem, to exercise in Spain such a profound influence as the coming to Power of British labourism. . . Men like Largo

Caballero and Fabra Ribas, in recent speeches and declarations, have felt moved to take up the teachings of victorious English labourism, and modify the structures of its Spanish equivalent.[38]

Araquistáin was referring to Largo's desire to extend the political role of the UGT by creating a united UGT–PSOE Committee, but without formally fusing the two bodies. As will be seen, this was to be a major theme of Largo's thought throughout the Dictatorship. In his memoirs, which concentrate on the events of 1917, 1930 and 1934 in an attempt to present himself as a revolutionary leader, Largo Caballero deliberately underplays his role in UGT collaboration with Primo.[39] In fact, though, he was to be the central protagonist in Socialist debates over participation in state bodies throughout the Dictatorship.

Primo's first formal approach to the Socialists was made in late September 1923 to Manuel Llaneza, the moderate Asturian miners' leader who had been at the centre of disputes in the SOMA during the crisis over affiliation to the Comintern.[40] Llaneza was invited to Madrid for 'discussions' about problems in the mining industry. He attended after consultations with the Executive Committee of the SOMA, and reported to the UGT Executive immediately after his meeting with the Dictator on 2 October. Primo de Rivera at this stage had no clearly elaborated labour policy beyond that of smashing the power of the CNT, a crucial step in his aim to save the monarchy by restoring social order to Spain.[41] He looked to enlist the participation of the Socialist leaders in his intended 'brief parenthesis in the constitutional life of Spain' fundamentally because they had shown themselves since 1917 to be reasonable and responsible, thoroughly chastened by their dalliance with revolution. Moreover, the historical hostility between the two workers' organisations suggested that Socialist leaders would not be unduly distressed at the repression of their Anarcho-syndicalist rivals. So it was to prove.

The meeting with Llaneza was intended to prepare the ground for a series of far-reaching measures which would inevitably involve the Socialist movement. Already the PSOE Executive had abandoned all pretence at protest by issuing the instruction that

provincial deputies and Socialist councillors, as well as those coreligionists who hold representative posts, should continue in their posts. . .within legal channels, without giving the slightest pretext to resolutions which. . .would prejudice the interests of the proletariat and of the country in general.[42]

On 1 October 1923, the official state *Gaceta* announced the decision to dismiss all local town councillors and replace them with 'associate members', who would in fact be the same people.[43] The PSOE Executive expressed its acceptance of the change on 3 October, and recommended that Socialist councillors, of whom there were forty-six, continue in their renamed posts.[44] However, the plans of the new Military Directory went beyond mere cosmetic changes, and required the active participation of the Socialists. The most significant change, masterminded by Labour Minister Eduardo Aunós, was the establishment of a corporative system of labour relations.[45]

In June 1924 the Instituto de Reformas Sociales (IRS), a body unique in Europe, was abolished and replaced by a Consejo de Trabajo.[46] The IRS had functioned since the late nineteenth century as an independent investigative and advisory body, reporting to governments on strikes and labour conditions as well as acting on occasion as a negotiating body in disputes. The new Consejo de Trabajo had none of the IRS's independence. Nonetheless, four members of the UGT – Largo Caballero, Manuel Núñez Tomás, Lucio Martínez Gil and Santiago Pérez Ynfante – were co-opted onto it without protest. It was not until the Consejo de Estado, a consultative body supposedly intended to assist the Military Directory oversee a return to 'normality', was established on 13 September 1924 that serious division occurred amongst leaders of the Socialist movement.[47] Primo de Rivera invited the Consejo de Trabajo to nominate a representative to serve as a State Councillor on the new body; the designation of Francisco Largo Caballero as that representative, however, caused great controversy. The UGT Executive Committee, in line with the majority current of opinion within the Socialist movement, ratified Largo's nomination in late September.[48] However, the decision was strongly opposed by PSOE members Teodomiro Menéndez, Fernando de los Ríos and, above all, Indalecio Prieto. The basic line of division between the two factions defined the terms of the debate which would continue throughout the Dictatorship.

The arguments marshalled by the majority group in favour of participation in the Consejo de Estado were essentially, if not totally, pragmatic. Most forcefully defended by the Executive triumvirate of Besteiro, Largo and Saborit (who between them held the offices of president, vice-president and secretary in both the PSOE and the UGT), their position had two main strands. First, it was argued that Socialist gains which had been made so slowly and at such cost over the previous decades should not be squandered by acting in such a way as to provoke the Dictator into taking repressive measures against the movement. This was a view defended with remarkable tenacity by Pablo Iglesias on his deathbed. Repeatedly, the so-called grandfather of Spanish Socialism called in his last months for continued Socialist activity, since 'workers' political abstentionism is the wall which best safeguards the privileges of the bourgeoisie'.[49] The primary objective of Socialist leaders in the wake of Primo's coup had been to maintain their organisation intact and functioning, particularly in view of the decline in membership of the PSOE following the 1921 schism, against the potential threat represented by the new regime. For this reason, the Executives of the PSOE and UGT had both immediately counselled caution.[50]

Second, it was implicit that since the Socialists perceived no real difference between the Dictatorship and the previous regime – on account of their assessment that power was still exercised by the same fraction of the political oligarchy – the tactics employed previously retained their validity.[51] This was an effective, if specious, argument in defence of the familiar *pablista* theme that revolution was the inevitable organic result of the evolution of capitalism. Largo Caballero had made his position clear in this regard within days of Primo's *pronunciamiento*, arguing that 'the most revolutionary thing to be done is to make the workers' organisation stronger'.[52] Such sentiments were no more than a continuation of the line initially developed systematically in response to the arguments of those Socialists in favour of joining the Third International. A series of articles in *El Socialista* during 1920 and 1921 had outlined Largo's basic view that all progressive advances were equivalent to revolutionary acts.[53] However, the most sophisticated exponent of this argument was Julián Besteiro. The successor to *el abuelo* had long advocated the view that Socialism would come about as the inevitable outgrowth of capitalism; he abandoned all vestige of violent revolution in his political outlook during his time in England in 1924. Indeed, in early 1925 Besteiro argued that the Dictatorship was more favourable to the workers' cause than the old regime had been.[54]

At root, the view of both Besteiro and Largo amounted to *'hay que estar dentro'* (you must be on the inside); in other words, the Socialists could best defend the interests of the working class and peasantry if they attained positions of influence within the state. Thus, the form of the state mattered less than the continued existence and operation of the Socialist organisation within it. Such an outlook has been described as 'worker corporativism'; in fact, it is probably more accurately seen as the reverse side of the coin of 'accidentalism', the political philosophy derived from the writings of Leo XIII and associated most closely with Catholic monarchists in both France and Spain.[55] Where the accidentalists 'accepted' democratic regimes the better to be able to challenge them from within, so the Socialists in the Besteiro–Largo camp advocated participation in the Dictatorship in order to defend the social advances which would speed its inevitable downfall. The position had a certain coherence, but was balanced precariously on a very thin tightrope between legitimate (if rather ineffective) defence of workers' interests and rank opportunism.

It was precisely the possibilities afforded their rivals to level damaging charges of opportunism against the Socialists that played a major part in the opposition of Prieto, De los Ríos and Menéndez to the majority line.[56]

Prieto, in particular, was utterly opposed to any collaboration with the Dictatorship. In an angry letter to the PSOE National Committee, a copy of which he also sent to De los Ríos, the Basque leader expressed his views on the nomination of Largo Caballero to serve on the Consejo de Estado:

From the moment that the Directory came to Power I have maintained the opinion, reiterated verbally and in writing before this Committee, that a very marked distancing of the men in our Party from the military figures who hold Power was indispensable, even going so far to this end as to withdraw from official organisms all representative functions carried out by our members. . .

What will now happen, by granting advice from a consultative Body as high as the Consejo de Estado and through a man of the significance and merit of Largo Caballero to a dictatorial and arbitrary power such as that exercised by the Directory, in my opinion amounts to increasing, with very serious damage to the prestige of the Socialist Party, the mistake of collaboration. . .[57]

De los Ríos supported his colleague with another letter to the National Committee in which he again stressed the damage caused to the PSOE's prestige by collaboration with Primo.[58] On 17 October, the PSOE National Committee met to discuss the two letters, but refused to convene a meeting of the Executive on the grounds that it was incompetent to act in a matter which was the sole concern of the UGT. This was an extra-ordinarily disingenuous pronouncement: of the eleven members on the PSOE Executive, eight were also on the Executive of the UGT. Nonetheless, on 25 October 1924, Largo Caballero duly took possession of his new position as Councillor of State, although he later made much of his refusal to wear formal dress at the official opening of the Consejo de Estado, attending instead in a lounge suit.[59] Prieto was not placated by this gesture of sartorial rebellion, and resigned from the PSOE Executive.

The formal grounds of Prieto's resignation were that, in accepting the nomination of Largo as a representative on the Consejo de Estado, the UGT had gone against an earlier decision taken by the PSOE National Committee on 9 January 1924. According to that decision, Socialists would accept official posts only if they were allowed full freedom to choose their own representatives and if no other workers' organisation was offered equal representation. In a rather technical and very bitter exchange, Prieto alleged that Largo Caballero had in fact been nomi-nated by the King as head of state, whilst the National Committee retorted that his nomination was fully in line with earlier decisions.[60] However, arguments over internal constitutional legality failed to mask a more fundamental division within the Socialist leadership over the nature of relations with the Dictatorship.[61] Largo's participation in the Consejo de Estado was just the first in a series of moves which greatly increased the political activity of the UGT. Socialists were soon to be participating alongside employers and state representatives on such official bodies as the Consejo de Administración y de la Información Telegráfica, the Consejo Interventor de Cuentas de España and the Junta de Abastos.[62] They did withdraw, though, from the Junta de Subsistencias when it was placed under the charge of Primo's Minister of the Interior, the notorious General Martínez Anido, whilst the participation of Catholic syndicates led to a withdrawal from the Consejo de Economía Nacional.[63]

The greater political role acquired by the UGT under the Dictatorship suited Largo Caballero's interests perfectly. The trauma of the struggles which had culminated in the 1921 schism had convinced Largo of the need to alter the nature of the relationship between the PSOE and UGT in order to ensure that the leadership of the two bodies remained united. Thus, despite the close coincidence of membership in the two Executives, Largo advocated the establishment of some form of official pact between the party and the union, whilst still wishing to avoid any formal fusion. In February 1924, in a speech at the Madrid Casa del Pueblo, Largo proposed co-ordination between the PSOE and UGT 'by means of a Committee, with representatives of both organisations charged with fixing at all moments the lines of conduct for the struggle'.[64] Largo's view, repeated in various speeches during March, was misinterpreted by Antonio Fabra Ribas, who understood him to be calling for the creation of a single organisation. Fabra, it will be remembered, was highly enthused by the success of the British Labour Party, and envisaged the creation of a similar organisation in Spain. In order to avoid confusion, Largo clarified his view in a speech in the UGT stronghold of Asturias:

There is no fusion, no; the UGT will continue to be as autonomous as it has been up to now, and it will fight its own syndical battles, for which it will be responsible, with the party lending it support as it has done up to now and going further when the union asks and it suits both. But no fusion, nor dependence of one organisation on the other; imposition, enslavement, dictatorship, still less. Just an agreement, a coincidence of opinions, a pact in order to make improvements for workers easier and more positive...[65]

If the evolutionist view outlined earlier is granted any coherent internal logic – leaving aside the question of its specific relevance to Spain – then, equally, Largo's proposals for a closer relationship between the UGT and PSOE made sense in the prevailing circumstances. Since the normal political activities of the PSOE had been drastically curtailed, whilst those of the UGT had been greatly increased, it was an obvious move to extend the political competence of the union body. In practice, of course, there was little difference in terms of the leadership of the two bodies, so such a move would in reality represent a means of restoring to the PSOE some of its political capacity.[66] That said, it must be acknowledged that Largo's fundamental concern was the well-being of the UGT. He outlined his views on the role of the union in a book published in January 1925, in which he further developed the themes adumbrated in his speeches of the previous year on the nature of the relationship between the UGT and PSOE.[67] Largo also laid stress on his belief that the UGT must be represented 'in the places where matters relating directly or indirectly to workers' interests are dealt with'.[68]

The principal theme of Largo's book was that the UGT must adopt a more political role, although he rejected any suggestion that a new party should be created:

That would mean introducing into the proletariat a suicidal division. The political party of the working class is and ought to be the Socialist Party. What the General Union ought to do is co-operate and collaborate with that party in everything they coincide over, but retain intact its autonomy, as it has up to now. . .[69]

To coordinate this rather vague unity, Largo called for a Joint Committee (Comité Mixto), already agreed upon in principle for election purposes by the National Committees of the PSOE and UGT.[70] The aims of all this included: the creation of a genuinely civilian parliamentary regime; legislation to reduce illiteracy; the right of free association and freedom of the press; religious freedom; social legislation so that peasants should 'not lack the means to live'; democratisation of industry, with participation of the workforce in its organisation and running; the establishment of a society in which men would be equal 'at the starting point in life's struggle' and in which exploitation could not exist.[71] The aspirations were certainly revolutionary in the context of Spain under the military Dictatorship of General Primo de Rivera, but were hardly the stuff of Marxist maximalism. Indeed, they were pitched in terms which remained scrupulously within the bounds of reformist legislation. Of course, it is impossible to tell how far, if at all, Largo tailored his message to avoid the censor's blue pencil.[72]

Nonetheless, it cannot be denied that the establishment by Eduardo Aunós in November 1926 of a fully corporative organisation, the Organización Corporativo Nacional (OCN), to deal with labour conflicts and social legislation fitted in well with Largo's plans.[73] Indeed, the very structure of the UGT lent itself to participation in a corporative framework, based as it was on small-scale urban concerns which were federated to particular associations within the UGT.[74] Thus, when Aunós created the urban-based *comités paritarios*, joint committees of workers and employers, as part of the OCN, the Socialists became their most fervent defenders. In fact, the *comités* were widely seen as being biased in favour of labour; indeed, the French Socialist and director of the International Labour Organisaton, Albert Thomas, praised them for stimulating trade union activity.[75] By the same token, the *comités* were hated by the employers, who went so far as to dub Aunós the 'White Lenin'. All the employers' demands with regard to the composition of the *comités*, delivered through the Asociación de Estudios Sociales y Económicos, were rejected by Aunós.[76] Thus, it is hardly surprising that the UGT should have been keen to participate in the *comités*. Not only did they ensure the UGT a genuine voice in matters which affected the urban labour force, but also allowed the Socialist union to seek to extend its domination of labour representation in Spain. In particular, UGT leaders were anxious to counter the growth of the Catholic Sindicatos Libres, centred principally in Catalonia.

Indeed, one of the principal justifications used by Besteiro and Largo for Socialist participation in official state bodies during the Dictatorship was that it not only allowed the UGT to defend earlier gains, but also to increase its influence.[77] However, it is far from clear whether this was unambiguously the case. Membership figures for both the UGT and the PSOE suggest that the Dictatorship represented a period of stagnation for the two organisations. In Catalonia, former CNT members tended to join the Sindicatos Libres rather than the UGT.[78] The UGT, of course, had always been weak in Catalonia. However, in Asturias, a traditional stronghold, there was a notable decline in membership, particularly in the SOMA.[79] In 1927, the SOMA would stage a strike against the wishes of its moderate *pablista* leader, Manuel Llaneza, an indication of dissatisfaction with the tactics being employed by the UGT. In Aragon, also, PSOE membership fell in the years of the Dictatorship.[80] Moreover, Socialist penetration in rural areas was limited, particularly since political pressure brought to bear by Catholic organisations such as the Confederación Nacional Católico-Agraria succeeded in delaying the establishment of *comités paritarios* outside urban centres.[81] Indeed, figures suggest that the rural strength of the UGT actually declined during the Dictatorship, affiliation in rural sectors falling from 31 per cent of total UGT membership in July 1922 to just 24 per cent in April 1928.[82] Overall membership of the PSOE stood at 9,089 in 1923, rising to just 12,757 by the end of 1929; the UGT, meanwhile, rose by less than 7 per cent, from 210,617 in 1923 to 225,000 in 1929.[83] The real take-off in membership of the PSOE and UGT came only after the Socialist organisations started collaborating actively with Republican forces towards the end of 1930.[84] Thus, although the Socialists were able to maintain their numerical position through participation in the Dictatorship, there is little evidence to suggest that they extended their influence amongst the working class or, more particularly, the peasantry. The vital point, however, was that they maintained organisational cohesion whilst other anti-monarchical forces were either forced underground (Anarchists and Communists) or marginalised from the political process (Republicans). It was this fact which left the Socialists in the strongest position when Alfonso XIII finally fell in 1931.

The process by which the Socialists gradually abandoned Primo de Rivera and moved towards collaboration with Republican forces in the late 1920s was far from smooth. That they did so at all represented a triumph for Indalecio Prieto and Fernando de los Ríos, both of whom had maintained their trenchant opposition to collaboration throughout the entire period. Their ideas eventually came to hold sway in the PSOE and UGT for two basic and inter-related reasons. First, by 1927 it was clear that Primo intended to establish his rule on a more permanent basis, rather than to restore a parliamentary democracy, thus undermining one of the justifications used to defend Socialist participation. Second, by the following year it became clear that Primo's ship of state had begun to take on water, and as it became increasingly obvious that the regime would not long be able to remain afloat, Largo Caballero was persuaded that it would be a prudent move to man the lifeboats. Only Julián Besteiro, the curiously doctrinaire reformist, remained committed to collaboration.

The definitive indication of Primo's changed intentions came with the formal convocation on 13 September 1927, the fourth anniversary of his *coup d'état*, of a National Assembly. Its promulgation had been rumoured for over a year, ever since the Dictator's signal success in resolving the Moroccan problem in 1925.[85] The Assembly eventually took the form of a non-elective, consultative body, designed to draft a Constitution which would return Spain to 'normality'. Primo offered posts on the new body to six Socialists, including Largo Caballero, an obvious choice, Llaneza, in recognition of his moderate stances as leader of the Asturian miners, and – more surprisingly – Fernando de los Ríos, presumably looking to co-opt him into the regime's ruling elite.[86] Largo was prepared in principle to accept the UGT's participation in the Assembly, provided this could be done 'in a dignified manner'.[87] However, the National Committee had decided as early as August 1926 that an extraordinary congress should be convened to discuss the matter once an official announcement was made, but that in all circumstances the UGT should refuse participation if it were not allowed free choice of its own representatives. It was further agreed to consult local sections of the UGT in order to ascertain an accurate picture of national opinion about participation in the Assembly.[88] Thus, when official notification of the National Assembly appeared in the state *Gaceta* in September 1927, it was already known that a majority in the UGT was opposed to participation; moreover, there was no mention of free election of the Socialist representatives. Nonetheless, according to Eduardo Aunós, Socialist leaders made efforts between 13 September and the UGT Congress of 7 October to see if there was any possibility of arriving at a formula which would allow participation in the Assembly.[89]

The terms by which the National Assembly was constituted ensured that the Extraordinary Congresses of the UGT and PSOE, held respectively on 7 and 8 October 1927, would automatically reject Socialist participation in Primo's latest institution.[90] Thus, the Assembly opened on 10 October without Socialist participation. From this point on, the Socialist movement increasingly distanced itself from the Primo Dictatorship, now seen to have abandoned its expressed commitment to a return to constitutional normality. Largo Caballero and Besteiro, however, remained the dominant figures within the Socialist movement and continued to seek ways of ensuring a continued high profile for the UGT. Meanwhile, their two main rivals, Prieto and De los Ríos, began to assume a growing importance within the movement, even though they were roundly defeated at the 12th Congress of the PSOE in 1928. This Congress, held between 29 June and 4 July, revealed in stark form the division which had crystallised in the heart of the Socialist movement since the 1923 *pronunciamiento*.

The main debate at the Congress centred on the question of Socialist collaboration with the Dictatorship.[91] The principal opponents to the majority line were Prieto, Teodomiro Menéndez and Gabriel Morón, an Andalusian journalist and former agricultural labourer who would publish in 1929 a bitter attack on the Socialists' failure to oppose Primo.[92] Fernando de los Ríos, Prieto's closest collaborator, was in Latin America.[93] In a sense, the Congress became transformed into an inquiry into, and vote of confidence on, the activities of the PSOE during the previous five years. Also at issue, though, was the question of Socialist co-operation with Republican forces. On the more immediate issue of collaboration with the Dictatorship, Prieto and Menéndez based their opposition to the majority line on the view that, by accepting political posts, the party had conferred legitimacy on the source from which those posts derived. This did not, however, imply that they were opposed to *pablista* gradualism. As Menéndez stated,

We Socialists are evolutionists and we accept, therefore, participation in public bodies, acting in them only so long as the governmental situation guarantees the political liberty of the citizens.[94]

Unequivocally in favour of a republic, they not only opposed collaboration, but also called on the Socialists to unite with other liberal republican forces aiming to bring down the Dictatorship. On their own, argued Prieto, the Socialists would be unable to overthrow Primo. This stance earned them the rather unlikely sobriquet of 'revolutionaries' from the Minister of Labour, Eduardo Aunós.[95]

Largo and Besteiro shared their opponents' commitment to the establishment of a republic, but differed over the means to achieve it. The latter defended the PSOE's activity on well-worn grounds:

we will move by ever more progressive stages to the establishment of our ideal. . .
Our task is not a matter of one day, nor of a generation, for our ideals are so wide-
ranging that, without neglecting the problems that reality is constantly posing, they
will take a long time in achieving the tangible nature to which we aspire.[96]

Largo, meanwhile, agreed with Prieto that the Socialists on their own
lacked the strength to aspire to power, but maintained that collaboration
with bourgeois parties, no matter how anti-monarchical, would imply a
loss of Socialist autonomy. However, the bulk of his lengthy speech at the
Congress was spent repudiating the call by Menéndez for a withdrawal of
Socialists from official state bodies. Largo argued that even if the PSOE
agreed on this proposal, it would not be binding on the UGT; moreover,
the PSOE as such, as opposed to the UGT, did not actually have any
representatives on official state bodies. Thus, if PSOE members acting in
their capacity as UGT representatives were obliged to resign as a result of a
Congress decision, they could always be replaced by other UGT members.
This was a technically correct, if highly specious, argument. Largo knew
that none of the Socialist leaders would countenance the split in the
movement that such an eventuality would entail. He also knew, of course,
that he still had the backing of the Congress, even if there were signs that
support for the Prieto–Menéndez position was growing. In the event, the
'continuationist' line won easily: the Congress approved the 'overall
conduct' of the Executive and National Committees by 5,388 votes to 740;
backed continued participation in the Consejo de Estado by a similar
margin; and elected Besteiro, Largo and Saborit to the leading positions on
the Executive Committee.[97] However, a special committee set up to
examine the party's tactics rejected various aspects of collaboration by six
votes to four.[98]

Two months later, again in Madrid, the UGT held its 16th Congress.
The themes discussed were the same as those at the PSOE Congress, but
the absence of Prieto, who was not a member of the UGT, together with
the convincing victory of the majority line in July, ensured that the tone of
the UGT meeting was less conflictive. The activities of the UGT were
approved by a massive majority, and the elections to the Executive
Committee reconfirmed the dominance of the Largo–Besteiro–Saborit
line, with the three supporters of continued collaboration again taking the
top Executive positions.[99] Indeed, it would seem that Besteiro, now
formally installed as leader of both the PSOE and UGT, must have been in
a position of some considerable power and influence. In fact, his authority
within the Socialist movement began to decline almost immediately.
Besteiro was never able to dominate the movement in the same manner as
his predecessor, Pablo Iglesias, who had died in December 1925. Although
the Madrid philosopher remained a central figure within Spanish Socialism
for the rest of his life, which ended in 1940 in one of Franco's jails, he never

commanded the authority or respect of *el abuelo*. Somewhat ironically his arch-rival throughout the Second Republic was to be Largo Caballero, who in 1929 began to move away from the collaborationist stance so closely associated with Besteiro towards the position of Prieto and De los Ríos.

The first indication of Largo's changing views came in August 1929 at a UGT National Committee meeting convened to discuss a new offer from Primo de Rivera. The Dictator, anxious to shore up the widely boycotted National Assembly, had finally agreed to Socialist demands: on 26 July, a Royal Decree announced the recomposition of the Assembly, which was now to include five freely elected posts for the UGT.[100] However, the tide of opinion in the Socialist movement had turned. At its 11 August meeting, the UGT National Committee roundly rejected Primo's offer, with Largo Caballero its most committed opponent. However, the argument he used to justify his position was weak. Largo maintained that the UGT's rejection of the original offer in 1927 had not made specific mention of the non-election of Socialist representatives. Therefore, it followed that the issue of free elections was subsidiary to the main objection (which was not specified) and that to accept the new offer would be to go against previous UGT directives.[101]

Of the principal members on the UGT Executive, only Besteiro maintained a consistent position. He pointed out that his own rejection of the 1927 offer had been based exclusively on the lack of free choice in electing representatives and that, since this objection had now been met, there were no grounds for refusing to participate in the newly constituted Assembly. Despite his sincerity, Besteiro received the backing only of Enrique de Santiago. Andrés Saborit, the third member of the Executive troika, followed Largo's lead, thereby ensuring that Besteiro's proposal was decisively defeated. There can be no doubt that the UGT decision was a serious blow to Primo. The Dictator refused the Socialists leave to publish a manifesto explaining their decision, and expressed his 'sincere regret' at their refusal to join the Assembly:

I expected something different from the comprehension and equanimity of the men who represent Socialism.[102]

The deprivation of Socialist collaboration, one of his strongest claims to legitimacy, merely added to the Dictator's growing sense of isolation. He managed to hold on to power for a few months, but his fall was now virtually inevitable.

The UGT National Committee meeting of August 1929 clearly raises the twin questions of why Largo changed his position whilst Besteiro did not. Largo's revised assessment of the Socialists' role in the Primo regime has usually been seen as the result of opportunism, just as his decision to collaborate in the first place has equally been seen as opportunistic. There are two main strands to this argument. First, it has been suggested that Largo wished to avoid the political isolation of the Socialist movement that would derive from being left as the only significant social or political group in Spain still supporting Primo.[103] By 1929 the Dictator was almost bereft of backers, the heady days of glory which had followed Moroccan success long since past. The stability of the Dictatorship had been severely damaged by a combination of intractable problems. Most crucially, disaffection within the armed forces had undermined one of the regime's principal pillars of support. Primo's clumsy attempts to impose much-needed institutional reform on the army had created a groundswell of resentment among the artillery corps, which remained immensely bitter over the Dictator's attempts in 1926 to alter strict promotion procedures.[104] In January 1929 there was even an attempted *pronunciamiento* against the Dictator, led in Valencia by the seventy-year-old Conservative, José Sánchez Guerra. The rebellion quickly became something of a fiasco. However, its very outbreak served as an ominous warning to both King and Dictator, reinforced shortly thereafter by a military tribunal's acquittal of the conspirator.[105]

Whilst discontent in the army posed the most telling threat to Primo's regime, a host of other right-leaning groups had also begun to distance themselves from the regime. Employers had never been happy with corporatist labour legislation; they were increasingly joined in their mistrust by landowners, bankers and the Church. The Catholic Church was frustrated both by the failure of the Sindicatos Libres to become firmly established in Spain, and by its failure to regain control over all levels of education. The issue of education was highly contentious: it was very precious not only to the Church, which fervently sought to re-establish its pre-eminence, but also to free-thinking Liberals, especially those associated with the Institución Libre de Enseñanza. Indeed, next to army unrest, disaffection in the academic world posed one of Primo's most serious problems. Extraordinary as it seems to Anglo-Saxon eyes, a proposal in 1928 to allow private Catholic colleges to grant degrees commensurate with those of state universities provoked widescale and sometimes violent demonstrations. Student demonstrators clashed with police in several university centres. Not only students were involved; leading academic figures like the Socialist Fernando de los Ríos, Ramón Menéndez Pidal and the exiled Miguel de Unamuno lent their support to the protests.[106]

To add to these problems, influential quarters within the financial world had begun by 1929 to manifest discontent with the Dictatorship. Economic growth, assisted by questionable budgeting techniques, had served as one of Primo's main sources of legitimacy since coming to power. By 1929, though, it was on the wane. A poor harvest in 1928 coincided with a deteriorating trade balance, and a net export of capital. In turn, this led to a depreciation of the peseta, for which the financial world blamed the Dictatorship's monetary policies.[107] Although the full impact of the world economic depression would not hit Spain until after the declaration of the Second Republic, already by 1929 economic difficulties were building up and crisis was looming on the horizon. Thus, as the decade drew to a close, Primo found himself almost devoid of support. It is within this context, then, that Largo Caballero decided to disassociate himself from the Dictatorship: supposedly just an opportunistic move which followed prevailing trends.[108]

The second strand to the argument over Largo's opportunism lays emphasis on pressure from the UGT membership, which has to be seen in conjunction with his concern to protect the interests of the union and its affiliates.[109] Thus, as the rank and file started to become more militant as Primo's popularity declined, so Largo began to strike attitudes which reflected his members' desires. In late 1927, Asturian miners in the SOMA, always the most radical sector of the Socialist union, had staged a strike over job losses in the industry.[110] The strike was called despite the opposition of the SOMA's moderate *pablista* leaders, Manuel Llaneza and Ramón González Peña. However, the strike itself, together with the evidence presented to the PSOE 12th Congress of local level unrest in those areas worst affected by poor working conditions, cannot have been lost on Largo. Although he remained committed to the idea of a corporatist structure in labour relations, Largo now came to realise that continued association with the Dictatorship would cost the Socialists dear.[111] Accordingly, he cautiously began to distance himself from Primo.

It is undoubtedly the case that Largo's political activities were usually determined by what he judged to be in the best interests of the UGT. Moreover, there is an important sense in which the Socialists' collaboration must be seen as opportunistic in that their long-term ideals were blurred, if not rejected, in favour of short-term benefit. However, the line dividing opportunism from prudence is sometimes a thin one, moreover, it is usually drawn on the basis of a highly normative distinction. If Largo's move into the opposition camp was opportunistic, the charge could equally be levelled against virtually all other social and political groups in Spain which had initially welcomed the Dictator, only to turn against him when his regime failed to live up to expectations. This is not to try to construct an elaborate apologia for Largo, rather, it is simply to suggest that his action in distancing himself from Primo made clear logical sense. Continued collaboration with a regime which was crumbling would undoubtedly have left the Socialist movement in a distinctly uncomfortable position when the fall finally came. To suggest, as does Ben-Ami, that Largo's decision was based on wholly political grounds is hardly open to dispute; to argue further, however, that he sought 'in the process, the acquisition of the merit for, and the highly reputable halo of, having contributed to the breakdown of his regime' is rather more questionable.[112]

Largo's shift of position was comprehensible, then, if not wholly creditable. More significant in many ways was Besteiro's constancy. Like Louis XVIII's courtiers, Besteiro had forgotten nothing and learnt nothing. He clung to his political position with an inflexibility which betokened not so much honourable probity as tunnel vision. Unlike Largo, the Madrid philosophy don remained unmoved by changing political circumstances. Just as Primo's assumption of power in 1923 had prompted no analysis, so the impending collapse of his regime was seemingly a matter of political indifference. For Besteiro there was one indelible truth, inscribed in the tablets of deterministic Marxism. Spain must pass through a bourgeois revolution; that revolution must be sponsored by the bourgeoisie alone; the role of the Socialists in the meanwhile was to defend the interests of the working class until the historical moment of their own revolution arrived. Certainly they should support the bourgeois revolution, but the exercise of political power should be avoided at all costs since this belonged properly to the bourgeoisie. Such a theoretical schema amounted to a recipe for political quietism: all the Socialists could do was to maintain their organisation and await the inevitable revolution. Thus, Besteiro manifested his sympathy for a bourgeois-democratic republic rather than the monarchy Primo's regime was attempting to save, but resisted the idea that the Socialists should take the initiative in bringing about that republic. Put simply, it was not their job to do so. Besteiro, however, rarely put things simply:

Our tactic is not one of uprisings, from which one expects, as if by magic, the total redemption of Humanity; our main tactic is continuous, methodical work amongst the working masses through their ranks and organisations and by this tactic, through calm and stormy times, whatever freedoms we are allowed, even deprived of all freedoms, we advance like the waters of a flood no dyke can contain, which demolish, devastate and smash any obstacle in their path, until they completely cover the dead fields of capitalist domination and carry the warmth of life and humanity to every corner, even into the darkest, farthest places on earth.[113]

Besteiro's position offers a vivid example of how his unquestioning dependence on rigid conceptions of Marxist orthodoxy militated against engaging in theoretical analysis of changing socio-political situations, and also undermined the flexibility of his response to such changes.

It is noteworthy that the two most committed Socialist opponents of collaboration with Primo, and proponents of collaboration with Republican forces, were precisely those PSOE leaders who did not identify themselves as Marxist: Indalecio Prieto and Fernando de los Ríos.

Unconstrained by the shackles of determinist theory, Prieto in particular was free to establish a dialogue with Republican groups which would be of immense significance to the PSOE's future political role. If Largo Caballero, who made only rhetorical obeisance to Marxist formulations, realised belatedly the true importance of Republican opposition to the Dictatorship, Prieto had long been convinced of the need for Socialists to be closely involved in any anti-Primo initiatives such opposition might sponsor. The pertinence of his assessment acquired a stark clarity with the resignation of Primo de Rivera on 28 January 1930. Although Alfonso XIII appointed General Dámaso Berenguer to replace Primo, the new Dictator's hold on power was tenuous indeed. Berenguer's so-called *dictablanda* lasted just over a year before the general resigned in February 1931, opening the way to the establishment of the Second Republic two months later.[114] That the Socialists were able to play a leading role in that Republic was in large measure due to their having maintained organisational cohesion throughout the Primo Dictatorship. However, that they received the blessing of Republican forces in playing that role was due to the efforts of Prieto and De los Ríos during 1930. The two main opponents within the Socialist movement of collaboration with the Dictatorship were also the principal architects of the alliance with the Republicans which played such a major role in the fall of the monarchy.

The official Socialist line, however, had throughout 1930 remained hostile to collaboration with Republican forces. When Primo fell, the immediate concern of Socialist union leaders was to preserve the labour legislation of his Dictatorship. The Socialist leadership did not modify its political line of evolutionary struggle through legal channels.[115] Despite the upsurge in social unrest during 1930, evidenced by strikes in Andalusia, Valencia, Bilbao, Catalonia and Galicia, the UGT shunned official participation in such protests. It was left to the CNT and PCE, emerging from six years of enforced inactivity, to provide the political initiative for the strike moves. The Socialists preferred to have disputes resolved through the *comités paritarios*, the major achievement in terms of labour legislation of the Primo Dictatorship. Indeed, the wave of summer strikes in 1930 was condemned by *El Socialista*:

This senseless movement has the unfortunate virtue of strengthening reaction and of weakening the democratic, Republican and Socialist forces. . .Therefore we shall not collaborate in that unfortunate task. . .[116]

If the activities of the CNT and PCE were dismissed as senseless and dangerous, those of the Republicans were seen as lacking 'seriousness'. Republican forces were seen – by Besteiro and Largo Caballero, above all – as being too divided, too riven by personalistic disputes for the Socialists to be able to collaborate with them.[117] With a haughty self-regard so characteristic of Spanish Socialism, all other groups opposed to the monarchy were denied real significance.

Thus it was that the activities of Prieto and De los Ríos in establishing contact with Republican forces went against official Socialist policy.[118] However, Prieto had maintained close ties with Manuel Azaña, the prime mover of the Republican revival, who kept him informed of developments. It is true that the Republican forces were divided throughout the Dictatorship, but Azaña instilled a coherence and sense of purpose through the creation of the Alianza Republicana which was to be vital in provoking the fall of the monarchy.[119] On 17 August 1930, Republican leaders held a meeting in San Sebastián, attended by Prieto and De los Ríos in an unofficial personal capacity. From the meeting arose the Pact of San Sebastián, a key moment in the establishment of the Republic, together with a Republican revolutionary committee and the future Republican provisional government.[120] The action of the two Socialists was criticised by Besteiro and his followers, and their transmission of the Republicans' request that the PSOE join their initiative met with a cool response at a meeting of the party's National Committee on 16 September.[121] However, Prieto and De los Ríos were more closely in tune with the desires of local sections of the Socialist movement than was the leader of the UGT and PSOE. In Asturias, the Socialist Federation expressed its readiness to make alliances with any anti-monarchical party which sought to establish a republic.[122] The Granada federation also expressed its commitment to alliances, while the Madrid, Bilbao and Granada branches of the FJSE, the Socialist Youth Movement, all supported moves towards collaboration with Republican forces. Increasingly, the Besteiro position was being undermined.

On 4 October 1930, the PSOE Executive agreed to endorse the Pact of San Sebastián. From that point on, the Socialist leadership found itself bound up in a series of events which quickly assumed their own momentum. The 17 October saw the PSOE and UGT Executives approve total support for the revolutionary movement against the monarchy; three days later the PSOE Executive met again to discuss precise details of its role in the projected revolutionary coup. At this second meeting, Largo Caballero also brought up the issue of whether the Socialists should accept ministerial posts in the provisional government. As was to be expected, Besteiro was strongly opposed. However, he was now in a small minority – an indication of his declining influence within the movement.[123] Three Socialists – Largo Caballero, Prieto and De los Ríos – were designated ministerial posts, thus setting the seal on Socialist involvement in the movement to overthrow the monarchy. The array of forces now lined up against Alfonso made his survival virtually impossible. Before the monarchy fell, however, there was one more scene in the drama still to be played out.

The revolutionary movement agreed upon in October was finally set for mid-December. According to the arrangements of the revolutionary committee, the UGT was to support a military coup with a general strike. However, the premature rising of two captains, Galán and García Hernández, at Jaca on 12 December – three days before the agreed date – disrupted preparations. The movement went ahead as planned, but collapsed rapidly. Galán and García were executed on the 14 December. Later on the same day, virtually the entire provisional government was arrested. Crucially, on the following day the Socialists failed to strike in Madrid, the most critical centre of the proposed rising. Despite a disciplined response to strike calls in the rest of Spain, the movement collapsed. Largo Caballero and De los Ríos, who had escaped arrest the previous day, duly gave themselves up to the authorities.[124] Subsequent debates over responsibility for the failure of the December rising would lead to bitter confrontation within the Socialist movement.[125] A more immediate consequence was the further undermining of Besteiro's position. By this stage the Socialists had come too far to pull out. Despite the efforts of Besteiro and Saborit to engineer a Socialist withdrawal from the revolutionary committee, a joint meeting of the PSOE and UGT National Committees on 22 February 1931 reconfirmed the commitment to co-operation. Besteiro immediately resigned in what must be judged a rather forlorn and quixotic gesture, although his action gave added strength to the suspicion, which was never proven, that he had sabotaged the December strike.[126] Whatever the truth of the matter, the Madrid intellectual was thereafter ever more obviously forced to cede real influence within the Socialist movement to Largo Caballero and Prieto.

The failure of the December movement ultimately turned out to be of little significance. General Berenguer's government was hamstrung by concerted opposition, and the call for elections became irresistible. Berenguer resigned in February; municipal elections were called for 12 April. The anti-monarchist vote in the elections was so overwhelming that Alfonso found himself obliged to retire from the throne, perhaps the single most gracious act of a wholly undistinguished reign. The Second Republic was declared on 14 April, the long-awaited triumph of Socialist and Republican forces. The PSOE and UGT, by virtue of their activities during the Primo de Rivera Dictatorship, were the most coherently organised political organisations in Spain and enjoyed the largest membership.[127] However, the tensions between the various factions in the movement which had developed throughout the Dictatorship would erupt in the most damaging manner during the Republic. The much-vaunted organisational cohesion of Spanish Socialism was unable to prevent a split within the movement which has been seen by many as a primary catalyst of the Spanish Civil War.

5 Marxist mistakes: misinterpreting the Second Republic, 1931–1934

When the Second Republic came into being on 14 April 1931, it seemed reasonable to assume that its main source of support would derive from the PSOE and its union body, the UGT. Their collaboration with the Dictatorship of Primo de Rivera had left them as the most viable and coherent political organisations within the post-Primo political panorama. Moreover, the Socialists had accepted three central ministries, Labour, Economy and Justice, in the new Provisional Government.[1] However, even though the PSOE was the best organised political force in the new regime, in practice its intervention in major issues of state – relations with the Church, reform of the Armed Forces, foreign and financial policy – was to be only marginal.[2] Instead, the leading role in legislation was left to the various Republican forces which made up the first government of the Second Republic in collaboration with the Socialists. The PSOE saw its position in terms of offering support to the Republic rather than of taking political initiatives. As an editorial in *El Socialista* explained on 26 April, the Republic did not represent *their* revolution; as soon as they had played their part in consolidating the new regime they would return to their task of organising the working class in order to challenge the bourgeoisie.[3] Such an outlook highlighted the conceptual confusion which existed within the Socialist movement over the relationship between Socialism and democracy. While the Republic was welcomed as the long-awaited bourgeois revolution and deemed to be in need of Socialist support in order to ensure its survival, it was also ultimately an obstacle which needed to be overcome.

In fact, the establishment of the Second Republic was to exacerbate within the Socialist Party serious tensions already visible during the previous regime. These tensions would culminate in the 'radicalisation' of an important sector of the PSOE, and its participation in the abortive insurrectionary general strike of October 1934. In order to understand this process, it is important to lay emphasis on two fundamental elements, endogenous and exogenous, of the PSOE's relationship to the Republic. First, at an endogenous level, the divisions which developed within the party between 1931 and 1934 fully acquire meaning only in the light of internal theoretical debates over the historical significance of the Republic. The debates were unsophisticated, to be sure, but nonetheless served as the basis of the confrontation between moderate or 'centrist' elements, which saw the task of the PSOE as one of support for the Republic, and 'radical' elements, which soon came to reject the Republic as a bourgeois harbinger of fascism. Second, at an exogenous level, the PSOE's position as an early linchpin of the Republic reinforced the party's traditional mistrust of, even hostility towards, other workers' organisations in Spain. Thus, while the Socialists were prepared to collaborate with Republicans in what they saw as the latter's historic mission of making a bourgeois revolution, they rejected any joint action with other leftist groups in order to progress beyond the Republic. However, the same process which led to the notorious 'radicalisation' also produced the first chinks in the PSOE's isolationist armour. By 1934, when disillusion with the Republic had set in, more radical sectors of the PSOE had accepted in principle united action with other workers' organisations. The practice, though, as would be evidenced in the October risings, betrayed residual jealousy of any threats to the party's hegemony on the Left.[4]

In political terms, such threats were seen as deriving principally from the Anarchists of the CNT. In terms of theory, though, the PSOE's position as the principal interpreter of Marxist orthodoxy was challenged by the growth during the Second Republic of a number of groups, mainly in Catalonia, also claiming to derive political action from Marxist postulates. The most important among these groups were the Partido Comunista de España (PCE), rigidly dependent on the Third International, the Bloc Obrer i Camperol (BOC) of Joaquín Maurín, and the Trotskyist Izquierda Comunista Española (ICE). Common to all of them was the realisation, sooner or later, that on their own not only were they powerless to lead the Socialist revolution, but also vulnerable to attack by reactionary forces. In the Spanish round of the world struggle between fascism and Socialism, only some form of alliance strategy could defend the bourgeois republic against extremists on the Right and ensure victory for the forces of progress.

Essentially, the central debate amongst Spanish Marxists during the Second Republic became polarised around two issues: the form and shape that such an alliance should take, and also, more importantly, its purpose. In regard to the first issue, the key lay with the PSOE in a double sense: its overall political strength on the one hand, and the struggles for dominance within the party on the other, were crucial to the political possibilities of Spain's other Marxist groups. The fact that the PSOE had always jealously guarded its independence from other workers' organisations, frequently shunning any form of collaboration with them, meant that revolutionary aspirations of other Marxist groups such as the BOC and ICE would ultimately remain of limited political significance. Only when disillusion with the reforming possibilities of the Republic set in, and certain sectors of the PSOE began to look to more radical measures following the Right's electoral victory in 1933, would the chance arise for other workers' groups to collaborate with the Socialists and thereby establish a significant political presence.

In regard to the second issue, disagreement hinged on whether Marxist groups should simply defend the Second Republic against rightist attacks, or whether they should stage their own anti-Republican revolution. At root, the debate centred on the question of whether Spain was ripe for the transition to Socialism. During the so-called *bienio negro* (1933–5), a loose radical alliance, or rather commonality of purpose, extending from the Caballeristas in the PSOE to the revolutionary Marxists of the BOC and ICE, gradually came into being. The shared aim was the revolutionary overthrow of the Republic and the establishment of a Socialist regime. Crucially, however, the Caballeristas never achieved complete domination within the PSOE, which, despite the uprising of October 1934, never became a fully-fledged revolutionary Marxist organisation. It was precisely because of the continued political hegemony on the Left enjoyed by the essentially reformist Socialist movement that the more radical organisations were obliged to seek continued collaboration in order to maintain a political presence.

Ultimately, the question of the form of transition to Socialism would become irrelevant once Franco gained the political initiative during the civil war of 1936–9. What is striking, though, is that during the course of the Republic all the Spanish Marxists misread the prevailing socio-economic situation, a vital factor in their failure to evolve an entirely coherent strategy for socialist transformation. This much was reflected in the fact that when genuine unity on the Left was finally achieved in the Popular Front of 1936, its creation owed more at a practical level to the Republican leader, Manuel Azaña, and his moderate Socialist collaborator, Indalecio Prieto, than to the pronouncements or efforts of any Spanish Marxists.

There is a fitting symmetry to the fact that Prieto was the main PSOE architect of the Popular Front. Prieto, who was to become the key opponent to Francisco Largo Caballero in the struggle for control over the PSOE during the Second Republic, had also been the main protagonist, alongside Fernando de los Ríos, of the Socialists' *rapprochement* with the Republicans during 1930.[5] Prieto made no claims to Marxist faith. He declared himself a Socialist on the grounds that 'Socialism is liberalism taken to its most effective limit, and the most effective support possible for liberty.'[6] His attitude to theory was that it should not be allowed to impinge on the practical requirements of political activity. Indeed, it has been argued that there was little to distinguish the views of Prieto from those of his Republican friend, Manuel Azaña: both sought the establishment of a liberal, parliamentary, democratic republic which would dislodge from power the representatives of the Restoration Monarchy's political oligarchy, and introduce greater social justice to society.[7] Prieto never called for full-blooded Socialist revolution.

De los Ríos, meanwhile, a humanist social democrat above all else, also saw Socialism in Spain as the executor of the unfinished programme of the liberal revolution.[8] A constant theme in the writings of De los Ríos since the mid-1920s had been the need for the Socialists to collaborate in the implantation of a liberal republic which would provide the only platform upon which Socialism could be constructed. On their own, argued De los Ríos, the middle classes would be unable to carry through the uncompleted democratic revolution in Spain. Thus the PSOE must assist them in establishing formal bourgeois democracy, as an essential precursor to Socialism. This Socialism, though, would be brought about not through revolutionary upheaval, but through a series of social reforms.[9] For De los Ríos, the proclamation of the Republic represented a major step towards the long-overdue bourgeois revolution. In this assessment, he enjoyed the backing of all sectors within the PSOE. Indeed, the decision to collaborate with the Republic, originally taken in October 1930, found perhaps its strongest supporter in Francisco Largo Caballero, later to be the leading light of the leftist elements within the party.

While the PSOE would be riven in the following five years by acrimonious debate over the nature and extent of collaboration, in April 1931 all factions were agreed on one thing: the new Republic was bourgeois-democratic. Moreover, with the exception of Julián Besteiro, the moderate Marxist professor of logic, all the Socialist leaders were convinced that, as the main organised political force in Spain, the PSOE had a responsibility – often pitched in moral terms – to act as the Republic's major source of consolidation, sustenance and defence.[10] This was a constant theme of the party newspaper, *El Socialista*, in the first months of the new regime. Antonio Fabra Ribas, the paper's long-serving Catalan editor, encapsulated the dominant view in the following statement: 'the PSOE and UGT are the bedrock on which the new regime must be built'.[11] Luis Araquistáin, who had rejoined the PSOE in 1931 after a ten-year lapse and who was later to provide the theoretical underpinning for Largo Caballero's leftist stance, argued that the role of the UGT in the new regime was to control social conflict by dissuading its members from imitating the irresponsible strike tactics of the Anarcho-syndicalists.[12] Largo Caballero himself, in an interview granted to the journal *Crisol* shortly after taking office as Minister of Labour, commented on the discipline and seriousness of the proletarian classes [*sic*] which must be at all times the Republic's firmest support.[13]

Restraint and reasonableness, the very hallmarks of Spanish Socialism, were emphasised by the leading figures in the PSOE and UGT. The need to support the Republic went unquestioned.

However, what none of the Socialist leaders appreciated was that their analysis of the historic moment of the Second Republic was untenable, a fact which was to have a profound and damaging effect on both the PSOE and the Republic itself. Central to Socialist assumptions was the idea that the new Republican leaders represented the progressive bourgeoisie, while the landed oligarchy which had held sway over Spanish political life throughout the Restoration Monarchy (1875–1931) was seen as a feudal remnant. This was poor Marxism. In the first place, the various Republican elements which made up their representation in the government were not only far from homogeneous, but also comprised mainly intellectual individualists.[14] While Manuel Azaña, Marcelino Domingo and, perhaps to a lesser extent, Alvaro de Albornoz and Diego Martínez Barrio stood for progressive liberalism, Niceto Alcalá-Zamora and Miguel Maura, respectively Prime Minister and Minister of the Interior in the first months of the Republic, were clearly conservative. Alejandro Lerroux, meanwhile, the ambitious and demagogic leader of the Radical Party appointed Foreign Minister in the new Republic, had long since abandoned his revolutionary rhetoric of the early years of the century. Within six months, Lerroux would become one of the PSOE's most bitter opponents.[15] The disparate nature and make-up of the Republican–Socialist coalition should have given the lie to the easy assumption that the Republican representatives of the new regime stood unambiguously for progress and liberalism.

Second, the landed oligarchy had ceased to be feudal in any meaningful sense some hundred years earlier when it started its process of co-opting the commercial bourgeoisie. This bourgeoisie was numerically small, unevenly spread and politically weak, to be sure, but took advantage of the disentailment of Church lands in the 1830s and 1850s in order to buy its way into a 'reactionary coalition' with the landed oligarchy, thereby forfeiting its claim to rule in return for the provision of political stability in which to make money. For all its inefficiency, Spain by the 1930s had long been an agrarian capitalist society.[16] The PSOE Marxists were guilty of reducing bourgeois revolution to its democratic political aspects, thereby ignoring the changes in relations of production which had taken place during the previous century. This fundamental misunderstanding was to influence not just the PSOE, but also all other Marxist groups in Spain during the Second Republic. It was based on a number of misconceptions: first, bourgeois revolution was identified exclusively with *industrial* capitalism and bourgeois democracy; second, latifundism and *caciquismo* were identified with feudalism, leading to the denial of any possibility that the 1876 Constitution could have been liberal; third, Spanish socio-political development was consistently and inappropriately compared with the French model.[17]

The shortcomings of the PSOE's analysis of the relation of class forces in Spain were soon revealed. There was no numerically significant or politically powerful dynamic bourgeoisie in the Second Republic pressing for progressive social change.[18] Instead, the Socialists were confronted by a landed oligarchy which, far from being a politically bankrupt feudal remnant, organised quickly and effectively as a reactionary conservative bloc in order to impede as far as possible the moderate reforms of the Republican–Socialist coalition government.[19] Such resistance had not been anticipated; the representatives of the fallen *turno* system had been expected to follow their patron, Alfonso XIII, into political oblivion. Their failure to do so upset the calculations of the reformist Socialists; the resultant confusion within PSOE ranks led directly to highly damaging splits within the party and to the collapse of the electoral alliance with the Republicans. In turn, this allowed rightist forces to win the elections of November 1933. Thereafter, divisions within the PSOE intensified, the so-called 'radicalisation' of Largo Caballero and his supporters being opposed by the moderate sectors associated with Prieto, De los Ríos and Besteiro.

Throughout the first two years of the Republic the weakness of the Socialists' theoretical postulates was reflected in much of their literary production. Rather than analysis of the new regime, there emerged a clear sense of attempted self-justification, both in relation to the PSOE's role during the Primo Dictatorship and its ministerial collaboration with the new Republican regime. An oft-repeated theme, expressed in evolutionist terms, was that the PSOE would remain in government only so long as it was necessary to consolidate the Republic while Spain passed through the ineluctable bourgeois-democratic stage *en route* to Socialism. Three works in particular, *Los socialistas y la revolución* by Manuel Cordero, *Nosotros los marxistas* by Antonio Ramos Oliveira, and Enrique de Santiago's *La UGT ante la revolución*, all published in 1932, adopted a markedly defensive tone in expounding this line.[20] Cordero, a UGT bureaucrat renowned for accumulating sinecures and whose personal gains under the Dictatorship may have influenced his views, was perhaps the most explicit:

The improvement of the moral and material living conditions of the workers has to be brought about through successive stages. . .in accordance with the evolution of the bourgeois economy and the moral level of the working masses, and at the end of this evolution capitalism will be overcome.[21]

Ironically, perhaps, Cordero made much of morality. At the Paris conference of the Socialist International in August 1933 he was to explain the rise of Hitler to power in terms of it being a transitory phenomenon reflecting a moral crisis in Germany. De Santiago, a supporter of Besteiro and fellow defender of the ethical element of *pablista* orthodoxy, suggested that only the Socialists could offer a responsible lead in the workers' movement. Like Cordero, De Santiago called for gradual reforms within the parameters of bourgeois legality.[22]

Antonio Ramos Oliveira was considerably more accomplished as a theorist than his two syndical colleagues. His main concern in *Nosotros los marxistas* was to defend the role of the PSOE under the Primo Dictatorship and to reclaim the party's Marxist heritage from Communist critics, particularly Joaquín Maurín.[23] A young but widely travelled journalist, Ramos used his experience in Europe to lend a veneer of erudition to what was essentially a rather rambling restatement of the gradualist road so long favoured by the PSOE. Claiming that Lenin's success in Russia represented an opportunistic distortion of Marxism, Ramos insisted that the PSOE was acting in accordance with Marx's own views by collaborating with the Republic. Only through gradual reforms could the dominant classes be displaced from power; only through the Republic could such reforms be enacted. The Republic was thus seen as a kind of capitalist antechamber to Socialism in which the working class could be educated in the need to await the proper moment for the transition. However, such sentiments, argued Ramos, should not be expressed too openly for fear of provoking an immediate adverse reaction from the bourgeoisie.[24] While *Nosotros los marxistas* lacked any analysis of the relations of production and distribution of power under the Second Republic, it did mark an advance on the more simplistic formulae of Cordero and De Santiago.[25]

In any case, the primary purpose of the work was polemical. Ramos was concerned not only to rebut the criticisms of the non-Socialist Left, but also to defend the PSOE leadership against dissenters within the party. In particular, he criticised Gabriel Morón, a militant union leader based in Córdoba, who in 1929 had published an attack on the PSOE's failure to play the role of catalyst since 1923 to the struggle against Primo de Rivera.[26] In that work, even Morón had stressed the need for the PSOE to act as a bulwark of democracy, taking up the torch dropped by the Republican and Liberal Parties. However, in a new book, also published in 1932, Morón argued that reformist, gradualist tactics were meaningless in the context of the Republic, since the new regime was inevitably implicated in what he called a worldwide bourgeois offensive against Socialism.[27] Another who opposed the dominant view within the Socialist movement was Javier Bueno, an Asturian militant who was to become editor of the mineworkers' journal *Avance* in July 1933 and convert it into an important mouthpiece for radicalism.[28] In June 1931 Bueno had published a book, probably of limited impact, which called on Socialists to 'break the chains' and seize the opportunity presented by the end of capitalism.[29]

Critics such as Morón and Bueno notwithstanding, there was widespread agreement within the PSOE and UGT over the need to support the Republic as the setting for the Spanish bourgeoisie's historic mission. However, there was no unanimity as to the form such support should take. The main debate in the party centred on the issue of whether or not the Socialists should accept ministerial posts in the new Republic's first government.[30] An Extraordinary Congress of the PSOE, convened in July 1931 to resolve the party's position, ratified the ministerial appointments of De los Ríos, Prieto and Largo Caballero. The opposition to this decision was led by Julián Besteiro, who had been president of both the PSOE and the UGT until his resignation in February 1931 over the party's actual participation in the Comité Revolucionario and proposed participation in government. Besteiro, who still had strong backing in the UGT, enjoyed the support of leading union bureaucrats such as Andrés Saborit, Trifón Gómez, Lucio Martínez Gil, and Manuel Muiño. These figures, the first three of whom had resigned from the UGT in solidarity with Besteiro, saw themselves as the natural inheritors of the mantle of *pablismo*, marked by an overarching concern with syndical organisation as an end in itself, an emphasis on moral dignity, and a highly cautious approach to political involvement. Indeed, in March 1930, Besteiro had written in the Madrid newspaper *El Sol*, 'the proletarian revolution must be essentially spiritual'.[31]

Besteiro's position within the PSOE and UGT had been severely weakened by the various resignations. However, freed from his leadership duties, he was able to concentrate more attention on theoretical activity, the main fruits of which would start to ripen after the Asturian rising of October 1934. In the meanwhile, Besteiro remained true to his *pablista* roots. Claiming to represent Marxist purism, the professor in fact merged reformist quietism with a highly schematic view of the PSOE's role redolent of the party's founder, Pablo Iglesias: 'On the question of the Socialist Party exercising power, I am in favour of all or nothing.'[32] Besteiro saw his task as one of countering the voluntarist and dogmatic distortions of Marxism he detected amongst his rivals; against their views, he proposed a strictly intellectual and scientist vision. Revolution was seen as the consequence of a higher cultural level and greater self-consciousness amongst the masses. Only when the PSOE was properly prepared could the revolution be launched. Such views demonstrated the continuing influence of Besteiro's Krausist inheritance; indeed, in line with the guiding precepts of the Krausist-inspired Institución Libre de Enseñanza (ILE), where he had held the Chair of Psychology, Logic and Moral Philosophy at the end of the previous century, Besteiro placed major emphasis on scientific induction and human rationality. During the course of the Republic he was to re-establish a close relationship with the ILE.[33]

Besteiro's incorporation into the PSOE had derived from an intellectual evolution which led him to regard Marxism as a science and equate its methods with those of the natural sciences. However, his understanding of Marxism was marked by a tension between both positivist and neo-Kantian influences which resulted in his rejection of dialectical material-ism.[34] Instead, his intellectualist vision of Marxism was more compatible with a rigid economic determinism which held that revolution would come about as an inevitable result of the higher cultural level amongst workers consequent upon infrastructural developments. In line with this, Besteiro saw the gradualist programme of the British Labour Party, and particularly Fabian Socialism, as the most faithful European approximation to the ideas of Marx and Engels.[35] In fact, there was a marked similarity between Besteiro's ideas and the programme followed by the SPD in Germany in the 1890s.[36] Revolutionary practice was reduced in Besteiro's scheme to a subsidiary position within an essentially passive and reformist evolutionist outlook. Revolution was inevitable; the form it would take depended entirely on the reaction of opponents to the inexorable march of Socialism. In a speech in the Cortes on 6 October 1931, Besteiro stated that the Russian revolutionary model was inapplicable to Spain, but warned that should the bourgeoisie attempt to stand in the way of historical inevit-ability then a bloody revolution would result.[37] Bloodshed could be avoided, however, through the progressive impregnation of bourgeois politics with Socialist content. This perspective placed major emphasis on the role of intellectuals, both as scientific interpreters of reality and as educators of the working class.

It is perhaps surprising, then, given the seeming similarities between Besteiro's views and those of reformist gradualists such as Cordero and Ramos Oliveira, that the former PSOE President should have been so vehement in his rejection of Socialist participation in government. However, Besteiro insisted that the Socialist Party, rather than accept ministerial posts, should concentrate instead on ensuring that the organisa-tion was in the best condition to take advantage of the day on which the reforms enacted by an increasingly socialised bourgeoisie would induce the Socialist takeover of power. This takeover, though, would have to be on the basis of democratic Socialism. Besteiro, along with many of the Spanish reformist Socialist leaders, was horrified by the notion of a dictatorship of the proletariat, arguing that it ran counter to the democratic import of Marxism.[38] In this, as in his appeal to historical inevitability, Besteiro manifested an affinity with the thought of Karl Kautsky, the German Marxist who had become increasingly disillusioned with the Bolshevik experiment in Russia since the end of the First World War.[39] However, both Kautsky and, by extension, Besteiro misrepresented the thought of Marx on this issue.[40] In Kautsky's case, his arguments have to be seen in the context of his long and bitter polemic with Lenin and Rosa Luxemburg; in Besteiro's, the eclectic provenance of his theory, so strongly influenced by Krausism, Kautsky and British Labourism, facilitated his gravitation towards an interpretation of Marx which eschewed violence.[41]

Nonetheless, for all Besteiro's convictions, he remained out of line in 1931 with the majority view expressed at the PSOE Extraordinary Congress on the issue of ministerial collaboration. The majority position was perhaps most forcefully expressed by Remigio Cabello, Besteiro's successor as President of the PSOE. Cabello emphasised the need for the party to act as the bedrock of the Republic.[42] However, the main spokesperson for the collaborationist position against Besteiro was Indalecio Prieto, Minister of Finance in the Republican–Socialist government. Prieto's position, which won majority support, was that the PSOE should maintain its presence in the government at least until the new Republican Constitution had been formally approved and a President elected, whereupon another Extraordinary Congress should be called to review the position. Should this prove impossible, the issue would be resolved by the Executive Commission of the PSOE in collaboration with its parliamentary minority group.[43] In fact, the whole question of ministerial participation was revived at the respective National Congresses of the PSOE and UGT, held in October 1932.

At the PSOE Congress, its thirteenth and the last to be held before the Civil War, the central themes revolved around a discussion of the party's involvement in the December 1930 strike movement fiasco, and its tactics during the Republic. The debate on the December strike was cut short after fierce mutual recrimination between Largo Caballero and Saborit. This left as the main issue to be discussed the question of whether the PSOE should withdraw its collaboration with the government.[44] However, as José Manuel Macarro has argued, the lack of any penetrative analysis of the prevailing political and socio-economic situation in Spain during the preceding eighteen months led to confusions in the level of discussion at the Congress.[45] Thus, whether or not to remain in government was not discussed in terms of questioning the PSOE's moderation; the Republic was seen as a given which the Socialists had to support, and so the debate remained trapped within the parameters of how best to do so. In vain one searches for a coherent political project aimed at disarticulating capitalism.[46] Instead, once more, the prevailing theme of the Congress was the PSOE's need to continue in government in order to consolidate the Republic. Indeed, Prieto, the leading exponent of this view, argued that it was anyhow impossible to bring about Socialism in Spain, given the political, economic and social situation in the country.[47] Prieto's support came from unlikely quarters. While De los Ríos was an obvious backer, and at this stage Largo Caballero still retained faith in the reforming possibilities of the Republic, few would have expected Margarita Nelken, later to be a fellow-traveller of the Communists, to lend her approval.[48] Even more unlikely, though, was the backing of Julián Besteiro. He justified this extraordinary volte-face on the grounds that 'if the Socialist ministers leave the government, the political equilibrium of the Republic will be broken, the life of the Cortes will be considerably shortened and premature elections could be too dangerous an adventure'.[49] Again, the stability of the Republic was seen as sacrosanct.

The Socialists' position hinged entirely on the success of their reformist aspirations in consolidating what they saw as the bourgeois-democratic revolution. Such aspirations, though, faced two major and related problems. First, as has been shown, the proclamation of the Republic did not represent, as the PSOE leaders thought, a bourgeois-democratic revolution. Apart from anything else, the Republican leaders understandably did not interpret their own role within the framework of a Marxist perspective which posited their inevitable political demise. More importantly, the various forces of the Right which had constituted the reactionary coalition were not feudal remnants about to be swept ineluctably into the dustbin of history. Instead, they would mobilise from the first day of the Republic in defence of their interests.[50] In very general terms, the Right developed two broad responses to the Republic: on the one hand, a legalist tactic known as 'accidentalism', which was based on the view that the form of a regime – monarchical or Republican – mattered less than its social function; on the other, 'catastrophism', which was based on outright opposition to the Republic and sought its immediate and violent overthrow. The former position was associated principally with Acción Popular (later the Confederación Española de Derechas Autónomas, CEDA); the latter with the Carlists, Alfonsine monarchists and after October 1933 the fascist Falange Española.[51]

Second, therefore, in the face of alternative perspectives within the government itself over the role of the Republic, as well as of opposition from the Right, Socialist hopes for reform were always likely to be unrealistically optimistic. And so it proved. Although PSOE proposals for reform were guardedly moderate, *latifundistas* and leading industrialists saw them as a dangerous challenge to their own position.[52] Rightist hostility to the Republic had been early revealed, with a large-scale flight of capital from the country reported by Prieto at the first meeting of ministers. Indeed, even before the Republic had been established, followers of General Primo de Rivera had been taking measures to impede the progress of liberalism and Republicanism, with aristocrats, landowners, bankers and industrialists contributing funds to support the propagation of authoritarian ideas.[53] It was never likely that even the most modest attempts at reform would meet anything other than hostility and obstructionism.

However, the Socialists faced two further problems. Promises of reform had awoken great expectations amongst the peasant masses, victims for so long of oppressive conditions of employment. Their aspirations were not likely to be satisfied by limited reforms which remained strictly within the framework of bourgeois legality. At the same time, though, what reforms were enacted took place within the context of a deepening world economic crisis. The Republic suffered the misfortune of having been born in the wake of twin economic disadvantages: on the one hand, Spain was still paying the price of economic mismanagement under Primo de Rivera; on the other, that price was severely inflated by the knock-on effects of a world depression.[54] Thus it was vital that the Socialists should develop a coherent analysis both of relations of production and the class nature of the new republic, and, on the basis of this, a viable strategy for agrarian reform. As has been shown, the former was lacking and this made the latter almost inevitably inadequate. By falling back on an evolutionist perspective which saw the historical emergence of Socialism as inescapable, the Socialist leaders abrogated the need to develop a more sophisticated understanding of the nature of the Republic and the role of the state within it.

Such theoretical niceties, however, were of no concern to the tens of thousands of peasants and members of the working class who had been flooding into the PSOE and UGT in the hope of seeing them institute radical reform through the Republic. The PSOE had rocketed from under 10,000 members in 1928 to over 75,000 in 1932, while the UGT had also grown vertiginously, rising from just over 200,000 to more than a million members in the same period.[55] The highest proportion of these new affiliates to the UGT had joined the Federación Nacional de Trabajadores de la Tierra (FNTT), the landworkers' federation which had been established in 1930.[56] The 17th Congress of the UGT, which opened in Madrid on 14 October 1932, therefore assumed great importance. It was to represent a surprising, albeit temporary, triumph for Besteiro, who was elected President on the basis of votes controlled by his old supporter Lucio Martínez Gil, head of the FNTT. In addition, by vindicating the Executive of December 1930 over its role in the attempted general strike, the Congress provoked the resignation of Largo Caballero, who saw in the decision implicit criticism of his own actions at the time.[57] Much more importantly, though, the Congress ratified the gradualist reformist policies of the leadership, whether this was comprised of Besteiristas or supporters of Largo, Prieto and De los Ríos.

It is the central tragedy of the PSOE during the Republic that it was unable to elaborate and put into practice a policy of agrarian reform relevant to the needs of the Spanish peasantry.[58] This is in no sense to decry the genuine efforts of Francisco Largo Caballero, as Minister of Labour between 1931 and 1933, to legislate measures aimed at alleviating the brutality of daily peasant life; nor is it to underestimate the obstructive hostility to such reforms by the Right. Caballero acted to guarantee better wages and protect peasants against arbitrary dismissal. In April 1931, the Decree of Municipal Boundaries prevented the hiring of outside labour while there remained unemployed local labourers in a given municipality. The following month, arbitration committees, known as *jurados mixtos*, were established, a mechanism aimed at formalising the rights of the landless *braceros*. One such right was the eight-hour day, established by decree on 1 July 1931. Finally, a decree of obligatory cultivation (*laboreo forzoso*) obliged owners to keep working their land.[59] These measures were, of course, important. However, they failed to hit at the real roots of the agrarian problem. Instead, by attempting to ameliorate rather than fundamentally restructure, they left unchallenged the southern power base of landed interests. Part of the reason for the spectacular growth of the FNTT had been the expectation of far-reaching reform; as such expectations were dashed, the leadership found it increasingly difficult to temper its members' indignation and unilateral violent interventions against owners.

In a sense, Largo was a victim of the particular Marxist heritage of the PSOE. From its foundation in 1879, the Socialist Party had adhered to schematic interpretations of Marxist orthodoxy, initially articulated in the form of a simplistic and simply incorrect assertion that Spanish society was divided between a reactionary bourgeoisie and a revolutionary proletariat.[60] This interpretation gave way in the early years of the twentieth century to the equally erroneous, if marginally more sophisticated, view that Spanish society was in fact on the verge of a bourgeois-democratic revolution which would lay the foundations of an inevitable Socialist revolutionary takeover. The important point, which can hardly be over-stressed, is that these analyses were derivative and based on the misguided and ultimately damaging view that Spain must both develop in line with the idealised French model, and – more importantly – pass through a phase of capitalism which was seen exclusively in terms of industrial development. It was this latter perception which was to be highly costly. Within the PSOE, agrarian issues had always been underplayed by a leadership which not only analysed Spanish socio-economic development in terms of a supposed industrial dynamic, but had traditionally been based in urban centres like Madrid, Bilbao and Oviedo, far removed from the daily reality of life in the agrarian south and northwest of the country. Consequently, remedies proposed for the agrarian problem were pitched in terms derived from urban industrial experiences: wage arbitration and legislation on working hours. While such measures were undoubtedly necessary, they did not strike at the root of the agrarian problem, nor did they satisfy the aspirations of the landless peasants.[61]

The shortcomings of the Socialists' agrarian reform proposals were exacerbated by the paucity of their analysis of the class structure and relations of production within the Republic. Thus, they not only misjudged the potential reaction of the Right, but failed to appreciate that their reforms were in any case largely unenforceable. The state machinery to ensure that the new decrees were enacted simply did not exist.[62] This was an absolutely fundamental point, for it showed in dramatic relief how the Socialists had failed to engage in adequate analysis of the nature of the Republic. Much of the agrarian legislation was ignored with impunity by *latifundista* landlords. There was little the government could do. Indeed, the problem was exacerbated by the fact that the Socialist ministers failed to receive the full backing of their Republican partners in the government. In short, Socialist aspirations had little hope of success.

It might be argued that the Socialists were in fact putting into practice policies similar to those recommended by the Austro-Marxists Rudolf Hilferding, Otto Bauer and Karl Renner. Whilst there is no evidence to suggest that this was being done consciously, it is certainly the case that the Spanish Socialists shared an outlook superficially similar to that of the Austro-Marxists in that they aimed to occupy the space between Bernsteinian revisionism and Bolshevik revolutionism.[63] However, although the Austro-Marxists, in particular Renner, emphasised the importance of winning reforms through the constructive extension of welfare provisions and the rational organisation of the economy under a regime of public ownership, these ideas rested upon a much more sophisticated understanding of the role of the state than existed in Spain. For the Austro-Marxists, building on Hilferding's analysis of structural changes in the capitalist economy, the breakdown of capitalism would come about through state penetration of the economy which would steadily advance towards direct state management. Thus, Socialist society would be gradually constructed after the conquest of political power by a working-class party – 'slow revolution' in Bauer's terms.

The Spanish Socialists had an altogether different perspective: gradual reforms were intended to hasten the moment at which a Socialist revolution would overthrow the capitalist system. For them the problem was one of first establishing the *laissez-faire* capitalism they associated with the bourgeois-democratic revolution. For the Austro-Marxists, capitalism had already moved well beyond this stage to that of finance capitalism and imperialism, thereby obviating the need for a 'destructive' revolution. Ironically, while of the PSOE leaders Julián Besteiro was the closest to the Austro-Marxists in terms of his analysis of the actual mechanism of the transition to Socialism, his essential political quietism meant that he was the most removed from them in terms of how to engineer that mechanism. Prieto, Largo Caballero and De los Ríos, meanwhile, shared the Austro-Marxists' perspective on legislation through the Republic, but on the basis of an entirely different understanding of the nature of state power.[64]

The Spanish Socialists might usefully have explored Otto Bauer's concept of an 'equilibrium between class forces', developed to explain the class structure in both the Hapsburg Empire and the Republic which followed it. According to this view, there existed an almost equal division between the working class in Vienna and a few other industrial areas, and the peasantry in the rest of the country, thereby creating a situation in which the state developed an important degree of autonomy, opening possibilities for influence in one direction or another by contending political forces.[65] The analogy with Spain, which was predominantly agricultural, but with burgeoning industrial bases in Barcelona, Bilbao and – to a lesser extent – Madrid, is clear to see. However, although there is evidence that some works by Bauer were known, no works by Renner were translated, while the only study by Hilferding available in Spanish was a twenty-four page pamphlet published in 1928.[66] As had been the case so often in the previous fifty years, Spanish Socialism suffered from its narrow horizons.

The subtleties of Austro-Marxist theoretical analysis, however, were far from the forefront of Socialist concerns in the first years of the Republic. Instead, immediate practical concerns associated with Rightist resistance to reform were leading to rather more basic debates. During the course of 1933 dramatic changes were to occur within the PSOE. As disillusionment set in with a Republic which had failed to live up to cherished expectations, so began the so-called 'radicalisation' of the party. In reality, this was a radicalisation of just certain influential sectors of the PSOE. Nonetheless, it was to have an impact both on the PSOE and on the course of the Republic whose magnitude it would be difficult to exaggerate.[67] As a direct consequence of divisions within the party, the Socialists contested the general elections of November 1933 on their own, despite an electoral law, formulated with PSOE participation, which favoured coalitions. This decision enabled the Right to score a convincing victory and was a vital step on the road to the attempted insurrectionary general strike of October 1934. One man has been seen as instrumental in this process: Francisco Largo Caballero. However, Largo was as much instrumental*ised* as instrumental, as much victim as protagonist. Convinced by his experience as Minister of Labour that gradual reform through the Republic was ineffective against the entrenched reactionary Right, Largo took up the banner of revolution. As a result he was feted – and fated – as the heroic leader of the peasant and working-class masses, culminating in his being dubbed the 'Spanish Lenin'. In fact, though, once Largo began to mouth Marxist maximalism, rather like the sorcerer's apprentice he released forces which quickly moved beyond his control.

Throughout the first months of 1933 there had been a rapid deterioration in the political stability of the Republic. In January of that year, twenty-four people were killed at Casas Viejas, in the province of Cádiz, as the government acted with brutal alacrity to crush a revolutionary strike called by the CNT.[68] The incident had a devastating effect on the morale of the Republican–Socialist coalition, and allowed the Right to delight in disingenuously indignant condemnation of the Republic as unjust and barbaric. Most important, though, it represented a severe blow to Largo Caballero. Although Prime Minister Azaña received the brunt of the blame for the government security forces' over-reaction, the incident at Casas Viejas served to underline that Socialist-led agrarian reform measures failed to satisfy the demands of southern landworkers while the Anarchists' ever more insistent calls for revolution struck a chord with them. Since the end of 1932, the CNT had been increasingly vociferous in its condemnations of the Republic, regularly issuing statements pregnant with menace. To mark the new year, the latest Anarchist journal, *CNT*, announced:

Workers: Bear in mind that the instruments of production are invincible weapons. A sickle can be used for something other than to reap, and a hoe can serve to dig the grave for all that has outlived its time.[69]

Since the CNT clearly retained considerable support while membership of the UGT was showing the first signs of what would become a serious fall during 1933, the FNTT leadership came under increasing pressure to adopt more radical stances.[70]

This pressure was intensified in February 1933, following the formation of the Confederación Española de Derechas Autónomas (CEDA), a right-wing Catholic authoritarian coalition led by José María Gil Robles. The CEDA, which had grown out of myriad rightist groups, would engage during the next three years in a counterpoint with the left-wing elements of the PSOE marked by the spiralling extremism of its rhetoric.[71] On the very day of the CEDA's launch, Gil Robles warned prophetically:

We are faced with a social revolution. In the political panorama of Europe I can see only the formation of Marxist and anti-Marxist groups. This is what is happening in Germany and in Spain also. This is the great battle which we must fight this year.[72]

The following month Hitler assumed power. For many in the Socialist Party, the CEDA looked ominously like a potential Spanish counterpart to Hitler's National Socialists.

Indeed, the collapse of the Weimar Republic triggered amongst certain sectors of the Socialist movement a sharp decline of faith in the ability of

Republican bourgeois democracy to act as a guarantee against the rise of fascism. *El Socialista* started to issue warnings full of foreboding:

> We do not renounce, as we have already said, the paths of democracy. It is others who might oblige us to renounce them by making them impracticable.[73]

Although Juan-Simeón Vidarte, elected vice-secretary of the PSOE at its 13th Congress in 1932, has claimed that there was little discussion in Spain of the rise of Hitler and its possible repercussions, since January *El Socialista* had been devoting space to the fascist threat in Europe.[74] Luis Araquistáin, Spanish ambassador in Berlin from February 1932 to May 1933, published two articles in the PSOE newspaper which gave the first intimations of his move to the left. Arguing that the PSOE had failed in government not through the excessive application of Socialist measures, but rather through its failure to be Socialist enough, Araquistáin drew the conclusion that the party now had to ready itself to move beyond the ambit of Republicanism and prepare for the implantation of Socialism.[75] In early 1933, however, Araquistáin had still not embraced the Marxist outlook he was to adopt as the chief ideologue behind Largo Caballero's radical stance. Instead, his analysis betrayed the continuing influence of ILE-inspired regenerationist currents. The crisis of Socialism, suggested Araquistáin, was both tactical and, above all, psychological.[76]

Within the Socialist movement, events in Germany had their greatest impact on the PSOE youth federation, the Federación de Juventudes Socialistas de España (FJSE). Although usually the most militant sector of the party, the FJSE had in fact supported the PSOE leadership from the outset of the Republic.[77] However, since its 4th Congress in February 1932, the organisation had been adopting progressively more radical stances. The Congress elected a moderate Executive, with José Castro as President and Mariano Rojo, Andrés Saborit's brother-in-law, as Secretary, but an important appointment was that of Santiago Carrillo as Minutes Secretary. Carrillo, backed by José Laín Entralgo and Segundo Serrano Poncela, was to be the driving force behind the markedly leftist line of the FJSE journal, *Renovación*. In the 18 March 1933 issue, Carrillo wrote an article entitled 'El poder para el proletariado' – Power to the proletariat – while Serrano Poncela warned that Socialism could not be achieved through bourgeois democracy.[78] As the year wore on, Carrillo would become increasingly explicit. In September he wrote in *El Obrero* (El Ferrol):

> That is the error of some brother parties, attempting to maintain democracy above their struggles with the bourgeois class. . . We should take from democracy what it contains that is good. But there is a moment – when the objective circumstances of

the revolution come about – when bourgeois democracy awaits the powerful (*enérgica*) hand that will bury it.[79]

By the time of the 1933 elections, in November, Carrillo was talking in terms of the definitive collapse of democracy, a line echoed by his comrades Serrano Poncela and Carlos Hernández Zancajo. These FJSE radicals used the pages of *Renovación* to expound consistently a line not dissimilar to that of the more extreme right-wing elements in Spain: the rejection of democracy and parliamentarism in favour of an authoritarian state – in this case, a dictatorship of the proletariat.[80]

The FJSE represented an important component element of the PSOE. While precise figures for membership during the Second Republic do not exist, 50,000 was mentioned at the 4th Congress in 1932.[81] Beyond sheer numerical weight, however, the FJSE enjoyed additional standing as a vital source of recruitment to the Socialist Party, and also as a main source of future leaders. The national leadership of the PSOE could therefore ill afford to ignore its youth federation. In August 1933 the FJSE organised a Summer School at Torrelodones, near Madrid, at which Largo Caballero, Besteiro and Prieto all spoke. It was to prove highly significant as the first occasion on which direct public confrontation between the major PSOE leaders over their assessment of the Republic was manifested. Before then, though, after two years in which he had kept a relatively low profile in terms of public pronouncements, Largo chose the occasion of a speech at the Cine Pardiñas on 23 July, also to the FJSE, to give the first intimations of his move to the left.[82] His disillusionment with the Republic had come about as a result of a number of factors: the resistance of the Right to his labour legislation; the obvious weakness of the *jurados mixtos*; the decline in membership of the UGT; the hostility of the CNT; the political offensive of the Radical Party; the growing combativeness of landowners and the propertied classes. His speech at the Cine Pardiñas, however, was primarily aimed at rebutting Besteiro's continued criticisms of Socialist ministerial participation.

Largo cited in his defence the criticism levelled at Kautsky by Engels over the SPD's 1891 Erfurt Programme.[83] This was clearly a calculated response to the fact that Besteiro had just written the prologue to a translation of the Erfurt Programme by Francisco Ayala, though it is likely that the significance was lost on his audience.[84] Engels, he reminded them, had repudiated Kautsky over his readiness to seek reforms under the Bismarck regime; a minimum requirement for the use of state institutions against the bourgeoisie was the existence of a democratic republic. However, since in Spain a democratic republic did exist, then the PSOE was justified in collaborating with it to improve the position of the working class. After two years, though, Largo had come to realise the hopelessness of trying to use the institutions of the Republic against the reactionary Right:

> I have always had the reputation of being conservative and reformist. The people who have accused me of it have got things confused. To be interventionist in a capitalist regime does not mean being either conservative or reformist. No, no; I've been an interventionist all my life... Let me tell you that since I've been in government, through observations that I've made of what bourgeois politics means, if it were possible I would come out much more of a red than when I went in. Much more![85]

From this point on, Largo was to adopt an ever more revolutionary rhetoric until confronted with genuine revolution in the Civil War. Julián Besteiro, meanwhile, had written in his prologue that the Erfurt Programme explained 'the fundamental principles of the Marxist idea'. Kautsky was praised effusively as a defender of Marxist orthodoxy against 'reformist opportunism', a clear reference to the PSOE's ministerial collaboration with the Republic. Three days after Largo's talk at the Cine Pardiñas, Besteiro expressed his disagreement with his rival during a speech delivered to the congress of the Sindicato Nacional Ferroviario. In fact, this was just the latest shot in what had been an increasingly bitter series of exchanges between the two Socialist leaders, which had really started with Besteiro's lecture at the Teatro María Guerrero in Madrid, on 26 March 1933, to mark the fiftieth anniversary of Marx's death. In that lecture, entitled 'Marxism and the current political situation', Besteiro attacked both collaborationists and those who were calling for wholescale withdrawal of the PSOE from government. As he had at the 13th Congress of the PSOE in 1932, Besteiro placed major emphasis on maintaining the stability of the Republic, a position he would hold until July 1933 when he reverted, like a needle stuck in a groove, to his earlier call for no PSOE participation in government.[86]

   Thus, the scene was set for confrontation at the Torrelodones Summer School. Besteiro was the first to speak, on 5 August, on 'Los caminos del socialismo' – routes to Socialism.[87] In a wide-ranging and rather professorial speech, the UGT President criticised both collaborationism and the growing bolshevisation within the Youth movement. He made only a brief reference to fascism, arguing that Hitler had triumphed on account of genuine popular support and that the collapse of the Weimar Republic was of no relevance to the situation in Spain. This cavalier dismissal of the fascist threat notwithstanding, Besteiro did raise some important points. The underlying theme of his lecture was that the PSOE, because of its historical development, had a particular organisational structure which determined its modes of political analysis and action. These were geared, in the best *pablista* tradition, towards gradualism and reformism. For the

PSOE realistically to propound revolution, it would have to change its structure radically. Certainly, the more leftist elements within the PSOE had not given any intimation that their demands implied any such changes; nor, pointed out Besteiro, had they really thought about how the other leftist parties would react to the PSOE seeking to monopolise political power.[88] Once again, Besteiro's approach amounted to quietism: on a global level, the bourgeoisie should be left to complete its task in accordance with historical necessity, while on a more particularistic level, the PSOE could act only in accordance with its given structure. The role of human agency seemingly found no place in Besteiro's schema.

The following day, 6 August, Indalecio Prieto spoke at Torrelodones. Of the three major PSOE leaders, Prieto was the least concerned to support his position by reference to doctrinal Marxism. Instead, he showed himself above all to be a highly shrewd political pragmatist. His speech, on 'The political and parliamentary panorama', stressed that the PSOE was in no position to take power. As he had done at the party's 13th Congress the previous October, Prieto pointed out that the prevailing socio-economic and political situation in Spain precluded any hopes of establishing Socialism:

I sincerely believe that if the possession of power in the present circumstances, right now – because I cannot foresee tomorrow's – were in our hands, it would be a grave misfortune for the Socialist Party. Our kingdom, in relation to Spain, is not of this moment.

For Prieto, the PSOE must continue to act as a bulwark of the Republic against attacks from the Right. Revolution was not a realistic option: Spain in 1933 was hardly comparable to Russia in 1917. Essentially, Prieto's line consisted of stressing that the Republic had come about as a result of a coalition in which the PSOE and UGT, although they were the major elements, must continue to work in collaboration with the Republicans.

Neither Prieto nor Besteiro left a favourable impression on their audience. The FJSE organisers, of whom Santiago Carrillo was secretary, had also hoped to hear a more revolutionary message. In response, therefore, Largo Caballero, who had not originally been scheduled to attend the summer school, was invited to talk on 7 August. Largo, never one to forego the opportunity of delivering a popular message, used the occasion to develop some of the ideas first elaborated a fortnight earlier at the Cine Pardiñas.[89] Again, an explicit call to revolution was avoided. However, Largo warned that should it prove impossible to move towards Socialism through legal means then it would be necessary to seek other methods:

We have two roads: the legal struggle and the illegal struggle. We say that we prefer the legal struggle, that we want to triumph using the legal struggle. . . . What we must think of is that if the moment arrives, with all its drawbacks, we have to face up to it as and how we can. Legally through Parliament? Legally through Parliament. And if they don't allow us? Ah! well then we'd have to use other methods.[90]

Such statements were calculated to fire the enthusiasm of the FJSE members, particularly since much of Largo's speech was spent cataloguing obstacles to Socialist transformation through a bourgeois republic. It should be stressed that at this stage, Largo Caballero remained in favour of parliamentary legality.

Indeed, it is likely that beyond currying favour with radical militants within the Socialist movement, Largo also hoped that his threatening references to possible revolution would discourage the Republicans from expelling the PSOE from the ruling coalition. Since the incident at Casas Viejas, the government had been under increasing pressure from both within and without. While the Radical Party leader Lerroux engaged in obstructionist tactics aimed at provoking a crisis which he hoped would see him installed as premier, militants on the Left and the Right of the political spectrum progressively raised the stakes in what for the moment remained rhetorical bids of violence. Throughout the summer of 1933 Azaña's government remained effectively paralysed. To add to its difficulties, it had become clear that the President, Niceto Alcalá-Zamora, had lost confidence in his Prime Minister. Hamstrung by mounting attacks from all quarters, the Republican–Socialist coalition could do little but play out time until something gave way. On 11 September, Alejandro Lerroux's wish was fulfilled as Alcalá-Zamora asked him to form a government. Lerroux's first act was to refuse to invite the Socialists to serve in his Cabinet, thereby effectively expelling them from power. However, unable to form his own majority, he was forced to rule with the Cortes closed. Thus he was able with remarkable speed to set about dismantling much of the reformist legislation enacted by the Socialists.[91] Inevitably, this polarised Left and Right still further, with many PSOE militants now convinced that Lerroux was opening the door to embryonic fascism in the shape of José María Gil Robles and the CEDA. The general elections, called for November 1933, were thus to assume a critical importance for the stability and future of the Second Republic.

For José Manuel Macarro, the expulsion of the Socialists from government must be seen as crucial to the radicalisation of the Caballeristas and the FJSE.[92] Once out of government, the PSOE lost its only real strategy. Conditioned by its entire history to engage in moderate reformism, the party now adopted a revolutionary stance quite foreign to its traditions. The result, according to Macarro, was that the PSOE entered a world of ideology for which it had no relevant preparation.[93] The argument is attractive, but places too much emphasis on Largo Caballero himself.

Certainly there is a strong case to be made that Largo's definitive shift to revolutionism, or rather his cross-over from the legal to the violent road to revolution, occurred as a result of the departure of PSOE ministers from government in September 1933.[94] However, the rhetoric that Largo now increasingly adopted merely brought him into line with currents within the PSOE which had been germinating for some time. He did not foster these currents. What is certainly the case, though, is that by virtue of his prominence, both as President of the PSOE and as former Minister, Largo was able to give an impetus to the more radical elements within the FJSE and the FNTT which would otherwise have been lacking. Once he had decided to go down the revolutionary road, Largo – together with his under-secretary at the Ministry of Labour, Luis Araquistáin – quickly became the central focus of the most leftist elements within the PSOE.

For some, none more so than Gabriel Mario de Coca, this was sufficient for Largo to be deserving of vilification as the villain of the Republican peace. Mario de Coca, an *El Socialista* journalist and faithful follower of Besteiro, published in 1936 a sustained and hard-hitting attack on Largo. The very title, of Engelsian inspiration, was expressive of his intention: *Anti-Caballero*.[95] Mario de Coca maintained that while Besteiro had remained faithful to the traditions of Spanish Socialism, Largo had fallen victim to a Bolshevik fever which had seduced him into leading the Socialist organisations down the disastrous path to attempted insurrection in October 1934. It is an interpretation which has enjoyed a remarkably widespread and long-lasting currency; only recently have a number of scholars begun to challenge its overt reductionism. Although there remains controversy over the origins and chronology of the PSOE's so-called radicalisation, any adequate attempt to analyse it must start by rejecting personalistic arguments. This is not to argue that personalities were unimportant: clearly, the mutual antipathy between Prieto and Largo Caballero, for instance, introduced added bitterness to their confrontations. Rather, it is simply to state that the actions of individual personalities have to be seen in a far wider context than that of the internal dynamics of the PSOE. Nonetheless, these internal dynamics should not be underplayed. Ultimately, the radicalisation of the PSOE represented one, temporary, response to a complex series of pressures.

On 29 October 1933, Araquistáin, who had been ambassador in Berlin until the previous May, gave a talk in Madrid on the collapse of German Socialism, at the invitation of the FJSE.[96] That same day José Antonio Primo de Rivera, son of the dictator Miguel, founded the Falange Española, an explicitly fascist organisation. The polarisation of Spanish politics was becoming daily more evident. Araquistáin's speech had a dual purpose: on the one hand, he elaborated clearly the change in line which would later be associated with the 'bolshevising' wing of the PSOE; on the other, he attempted to formulate a theoretical justification for this shift. There existed a genuine problem in this respect. As Besteiro had warned at Torrelodones, the PSOE as a political organisation was geared towards reformist gradualism. Moreover, for two years the Spanish proletariat had been used to hearing the PSOE leadership insist that its principal role was that of acting as a bastion of support for the Republic. However, unlike Besteiro, Araquistáin did not reject the importance of fascism in Germany as a warning to Spain. Instead, in a somewhat eclectic speech, he outlined the choice facing Spanish workers as one between Socialist or bourgeois dictatorship, or in other words, a dictatorship of the proletariat or fascism. Although the former ambassador made explicit reference to Marxist ideas, these were interspersed with a voluntarist vision more redolent of Nietzsche, with appeals to a 'will to power' and a 'will to rule'. His analysis of the rise of German fascism stressed the importance of myths in mobilising support for Hitler. Most important, though, Araquistáin drew from the German experience the conclusion that workers' unity was necessary: the threat of fascism could best be met by the combined resistance of Socialists and Communists. This represented a fundamental challenge to the traditional isolationist stance of the PSOE *vis-à-vis* other workers' organisations.

By the end of the summer of 1933, then, Araquistáin and Largo Caballero had embarked definitively on a course which would lead them irrevocably to confrontation – both with the Right and with more centrist elements within the PSOE. The most immediate result of their new-found radicalism was that the PSOE entered the 1933 elections on its own, a decision taken after consultations with the local *agrupaciones* and *federaciones* of the party. Indalecio Prieto saw the decision as disastrous. Convinced that the PSOE's only chance of success lay in continued collaboration with the Republicans, Prieto repeatedly insisted on the by now familiar theme that the Socialists must shore up the Republic in order that the Left could play its proper role. Moreover, Prieto was concerned about the possible impact of granting the vote to women.[97] Nonetheless, in the prevailing atmosphere of ever deepening political tension, it was always likely that party militants would view moderation with suspicion. Hence, the PSOE rejected an electoral alliance with the Republicans. This contributed in no small measure to its being soundly defeated in the elections, held on 16 November 1933. Victory went instead to the Right, with Alejandro Lerroux's Radical Party (now unashamedly aligned with the forces of reaction) forming a government which enjoyed the backing of the CEDA.[98] For the more leftist elements in the Socialist Party the results served to confirm the threat of creeping fascism. Out of power and no longer even numerically the major party in the Republic, there was little now to halt the PSOE's headlong march towards Marxist maximalism.

In early 1934, Largo Caballero published *Discursos a los trabajadores*. With a prologue by Araquistáin, the book brought together in one volume all of Largo's speeches made between July 1933, when he spoke at the Cine Pardiñas, and January 1934. It signalled his definitive distancing from parliamentary legality as a means to achieving Socialism. From this point forward, Largo would repeatedly call for the imposition of a dictatorship of the proletariat in Spain, aimed at dismantling the power of the financial and agrarian oligarchy. For all the revolutionary rhetoric, however, Araquistáin still referred in his prologue to Largo's 'ethical passion, (and) action for justice, for the good of others'.[99] Fundamentally, Largo Caballero would always remain a union bureaucrat rather than the 'Spanish Lenin'.

Nonetheless, as 1934 drew on and class conflict intensified in Spain, the stance taken by the PSOE President served as an important spur to the more genuinely radical elements in the FJSE. Equally important, it would lessen the distance between a large section of the PSOE and the other Marxist political groups in Spain – principally the Communist Party and the dissident Marxist groups in Catalonia, the Bloc Obrer i Camperol (BOC) and the Izquierda Comunista Española (ICE). It is worth devoting some attention to these other groups in order to underline how their fortunes were inextricably bound to those of the Caballeristas within the PSOE. Indeed, it was only with the post-1933 emergence of the Caballeristas as a distinct radical group within the PSOE that revolutionary Marxist groups began to escape from their isolation. The so-called radicalisation of the PSOE allowed them the point of entry they had been seeking to the national political stage.

The PCE in particular, although its revolutionism was circumscribed by the Comintern's dictates, would have reason to be immensely grateful to the Caballeristas. Up until 1934 it had always been a tiny party marginal to developments in Spanish political life. With only 800 members when the monarchy fell, the PCE was further hampered by its dependence upon Comintern directives. This was later acknowledged by Fernando Claudín, at the time a leading figure in the Communist youth movement, the Unión de Juventudes Comunistas (UJC):

We Spanish Communists had the same experience as the nineteenth-century Liberals: we had no ideas of our own, developed on the basis of an analysis of Spanish society. Instead of using Marxism as an aid to the particularity of the Spanish revolution, we used the Spanish revolution to serve the particular kind of Marxism which had been valid for the Russian revolution.[100]

Like the Second International, the Comintern had displayed no particular interest in Spain. Thus, when the Republic was declared, the Communists found themselves taken by surprise and without specific instructions. They therefore improvised on the basis of the 'ultra-left' line then in force, though in consultation with the Comintern representatives Jules Humbert-Droz and Octave Rabaté, and were roundly condemned for doing so by the Executive Committee of the Comintern (ECCI) when it finally turned its attention, a month later, to events in Spain. In an open letter to the Central Committee of the PCE on 21 May 1931, the ECCI harshly criticised the leadership for having failed to appreciate the bourgeois-democratic nature of the revolution and the role that the Communists should have played.[101]

In a manner similar to the Socialists, if for different reasons, the Comintern allowed pre-determined theoretical formulations to impede its analysis of the Spanish Republic. For the PSOE, Spain had to follow the French model of development; for the Comintern, it was the analysis developed by Lenin at the turn of the century for Russia which was sacrosanct. Again, it was held that Spain was going through the bourgeois democratic preliminary stage to the Socialist, proletarian revolution. According to Comintern directives,

The Communist Party should under no circumstances make pacts or alliances even of a temporary nature with other political forces... In no way should it defend or support the Republican government... It should unleash and develop direct action by the masses...fight as the revolutionary vanguard and guide of the masses, against all attempts to re-establish the monarchy, against all counter-revolutionary plots, taking advantage of such occasions to arm the working masses and conquer new positions for the proletariat and the peasantry.[102]

Thus, when the PCE leadership rallied to the defence of the Republic following General José Sanjurjo's abortive *pronunciamiento* of August 1932 in Seville, the Comintern, in line with its ultra-leftist policy, now attacked the Spanish Communists for 'opportunism'.[103] On the very day of Sanjurjo's coup, the headlines of *Mundo Obrero*, the PCE newspaper, had read: 'The Azaña government is the centre of fascist Counter-revolution.' José Bullejos, the PCE secretary-general, immediately realised the absurdity of such a claim. Taking a lead from the workers in Seville who had actively resisted Sanjurjo by launching a general strike, Bullejos issued a slogan calling for the 'revolutionary defence of the Republic'. The ensuing debate between the PCE and the Comintern led to the ousting of Bullejos, as well as Manuel Adame, Etelvino Vega and Gabriel León Trilla from the Spanish party leadership.[104]

In the Comintern-nominated replacement team, the most important figures were the new secretary-general, José Díaz, and the secretary of agitation and propaganda, Jesús Hernández. Both of them were loyally to implement the Comintern's directives.[105] Humbert-Droz, meanwhile, was replaced by Victorio Codovilla as Comintern representative. Codovilla, like Palmiro Togliatti during the Civil War, was to play a major role in defining PCE policy. In the aftermath of the *Sanjurjada*, however, this policy simply amounted to a continuation of the call for a United Front from below of the working class, a tactic first elaborated in 1921 and reformulated in sectarian guise at the Fifth Congress of the Comintern in 1924. For the Comintern, following Lenin's lead, the Republic in Spain was irremediably bourgeois and must therefore be opposed by the workers, who could expect nothing from it. The PCE hoped to win influence through the establishment of a United Front. However, the party's tiny size meant that its calls for working-class unity had consistently gone unheeded. Indeed, the PCE was to remain a marginal party until after the rising of October 1934 for which it sought to claim the credit by capitalising on Largo Caballero's reluctance to admit Socialist involvement.

Similarly, the Catalan Marxist organisations were generally unsuccessful in their struggle to establish a wider political presence during the first *bienio*. The rise of fascism, though, and in particular Hitler's accession to power in 1933, signalled the start of a widespread recognition within the Spanish Marxist Left that some form of effective alliance strategy was vital if Spain was to avoid the fate of Italy and Germany. The most important result of this was to be the formation of the Alianza obrera in 1933 by Maurín, leader of the Catalan-based BOC.[106] Indeed, Catalonia during the years of the Second Republic was the centre of probably the most advanced indigenous Marxism ever known in Spain. This was perhaps ironic given that Catalonia was also the main area of strength of Anarcho-syndicalism, and it was precisely this fact which had been a major contributory factor to the slow growth of the Marxist PSOE in its first decades. In the 1920s, however, there had started to emerge in Catalonia a group of Marxist politicians who were to assume an increasingly important profile until the advent of the Negrín government in May 1937. Principal amongst them were Maurín[107] and Andreu Nin,[108] leader of the ICE.

The idea behind the Alianza obrera, according to Maurín, was the overcoming of the divisions which had split the workers' movement in Spain and led to its loss of self-confidence. Maurín's central thesis was that a democratic revolution led by the bourgeoisie would be impossible in Spain; in order to succeed it must be headed by the working class. In a significant advance on the conceptions of both the Socialists and Communists, Maurín recognised that Spain was a capitalist society, in which a basic division existed between the bourgeoisie and the proletariat. The bourgeoisie, though, had failed to carry out the political tasks of its particular revolution, even though it had become the dominant class. Thus, according to Maurín, democratic revolution remained on the agenda; however, since the bourgeoisie had passed the stage at which it could act as a progressive force, the coming revolution would therefore have to be Socialist. In short, Spain must carry through a democratic-Socialist revolution or fall into the grip of counter-revolution and fascism.[109] However, Maurín's insistence that there were *only* two classes in Spain was a gross over-simplification, and it led him to misjudge the nature of Republicanism. Thus, Manuel Azaña was seen as playing a counter-revolutionary role, the perfect representative of the industrial bourgeoisie. Against the forces of the bourgeoisie, the BOC must create a workers' front to defeat counter-revolution. The Alianza obrera, with its intention to serve as a means of unifying the workers' movement within a central organisation, was therefore perceived in terms of being the realisation of what Moscow and the PCE had been talking about for some years but had been unable to bring about.[110]

At first the PSOE had rejected the Alianza, but in the aftermath of the November elections Maurín's organisation was seen as offering the possibility of establishing Socialist dominance in areas where the PSOE and UGT were weak.[111] Despite the growth in revolutionary fervour on the Left as 1934 progressed, however, the Alianza obrera failed in any significant sense to get off the ground. The main obstacle to its success lay in the fact that the PSOE remained both divided and equivocal over united action with other workers' organisations. Since a National Committee meeting of September 1933, at which several regional representatives had spoken of the need to break with Republicanism, the PSOE had started to manifest a clear division between a revolutionary wing, associated principally with the Caballeristas and the FJSE, and a centrist wing, represented by Indalecio Prieto and Fernando de los Ríos. Nonetheless, confusion within the two wings remained. A proposal that same month to allow PSOE participation in a possible government headed by Felipe Sánchez Román, head of the conservative Partido Nacional Republicano, found favour with Largo Caballero and De los Ríos, but was strongly opposed by Prieto and Pascual Tomás, normally a supporter of Largo.[112] Again, although both Prieto and De los Ríos would subsequently speak of the need for revolution, theirs was a wholly defensive conception aimed at maintaining intact the Republic. Only Julián Besteiro manifested a clear consistency by counselling inaction. While he remained head of the UGT, Besteiro retained considerable influence within the Socialist movement. However, his failure to adapt his assessment of the Republic following the November elections seriously undermined his position. Whereas Prieto and De los Ríos called for united action with the UGT in defence of the Republic against the threats posed by Lerroux, Besteiro remained sceptical. Whilst accepting defensive action in principle, the UGT leader questioned both the nature of its preparation and its objectives.

The differences between Prieto and Besteiro came to a head in December

1933 at a joint meeting of the PSOE and UGT Executives, convened to discuss the appointment by Lerroux of senior military figures like General Goded to key administrative posts. Whereas Besteiro maintained that the UGT should hold fire until some serious event precipitated a response, Prieto argued that such events had already occurred. Subsequently, after unsuccessful efforts to elaborate a joint programme, the two leaders each put forward a series of proposals for consideration by the PSOE and UGT Executives. Prieto offered a far-reaching series of measures which included agrarian reform as a priority as well as plans to dissolve religious orders, the army and the hated Civil Guard.[113] Besteiro, in contrast, produced a proposal which clearly derived its inspiration from the experiences of the Primo de Rivera Dictatorship. He called for the creation of a national corporative assembly (initially consultative but with provision for its conversion into a legislative body) to administer an ambitious programme of nationalisation and socialisation. The proposal was idealistic and impractical: the self-styled Marxist professor envisaged a period of several years to enact measures which depended on taking immediate control of the commanding heights of the Spanish industrial and financial world. No mention was made of how to respond to Rightist resistance.[114] Besteiro's plans were defeated heavily at a meeting of the Executive Commission of the PSOE on 17 January 1934, and of the National Committee of the UGT on 27 January. This latter result left him with little option but to resign as UGT President.[115]

Instead of Besteiro's plan, the UGT National Committee meeting approved a five-point proposal drawn up by Largo Caballero. This included a call for the organisation of a 'frankly revolutionary movement' in order to take power and implement Prieto's ten-point plan.[116] At the same meeting, Largo Caballero was elected to replace Besteiro as leader of the UGT. This represented a significant boost to the revolutionist position within the Socialist movement, for it now meant that the PSOE, UGT and the FJSE were all led by like-minded militants, increasingly ready to issue calls for revolutionary action. Henceforth, throughout the spring and summer months of 1934, the PSOE and UGT would be marked by an air of confidence and self-belief in their role as catalysts to the socialist future. From February 1934, the two organisations adopted a twin-pronged policy: on the one hand, normal activity through the legal channels of the Republic; on the other, semi-clandestine preparations for a revolutionary movement against what was seen as the growing fascist menace in Spain. To this latter end, a revolutionary *comisión mixta*, comprising Juan-Simeón Vidarte and Enrique de Francisco for the PSOE, Pascual Tomás and Díaz Alor for the UGT, Carlos Hernández Zancajo and Santiago Carrillo for the FJSE, and Largo Caballero in his capacity as President of both the PSOE and UGT, had been set up at the start of February.[117] The basic aim of the *comisión mixta* was to ensure that in any joint insurrectionary action with other workers' organisations, the PSOE would be the dominant partner. Although the PSOE had now moved away from its isolationist stance towards other workers' groups, it was still far from being ready to accept any form of alliance on anything but its own terms.

In February 1934, Largo Caballero travelled to Barcelona to negotiate an agreement with the Catalan leaders of the Alianza obrera.[118] In an interview granted to *Adelante*, the BOC periodical edited by Joaquín Maurín, Largo outlined his view of the political situation. Laying emphasis on how Lerroux depended on the backing of Gil Robles and the CEDA to continue in power, he warned

This situation has no other solution than either a right-wing dictatorship – and the workers' movement will make that impossible – or else a workers' dictatorship. The working class must prepare itself for the violent seizure of political and economic Power.[119]

Such a seizure of power, however, must take place only under the leadership of the PSOE and UGT. When Maurín and Andreu Nin proposed the formation of a new national organisation to direct preparations for a revolutionary general strike, this was firmly rejected by the Socialist leader. Indeed, Largo's real interest seemed exclusively, and typically, to revolve around the maintenance of the PSOE and UGT as the organisational fulcrum of the working class. Like Pablo Iglesias before him, Largo was perfectly willing to mouth Marxist rhetoric so long as this did not impinge on the Socialists' national bureaucratic imperialism over the workers' movement.[120]

However, just as in the days of Iglesias' hegemony, there existed groups within the PSOE much more concerned with developing party policy in line with what they saw as Marxist orthodoxy. To this end, the FJSE launched at its 5th Congress in April 1934 the journal *Espartaco*, justified in terms almost identical to those used by Antonio García Quejido in 1901 to announce *La Nueva Era*:

It is necessary to focus once and for all on. . .the creation of a theoretical journal – monthly – in which young Socialists can find a Marxist perspective on the various problems posed by political and social life. The education in general of the militants – in the party as a whole just as much as in the FJSE – suffers, with a few exceptions, from this grave defect. Our party, in contrast to the Russian or other large European parties, lacks theorists. . .[121]

Espartaco was to be edited and written by Santiago Carrillo and Carlos Hernández Zancajo, also elected Secretary-General and President respectively of the FJSE at its 5th Congress.[122] Indeed, the 5th Congress saw the rout of the Besteiristas from the Executive. Also voted onto the Executive Committee were Segundo Serrano Poncela, José Laín Entralgo, Alfredo

Cabello and Federico Melchor, all of whom were to contribute to the three issues of *Espartaco*.[123] Born in unpropitious circumstances, with heavy censorship of the left-wing press a regular occurrence, *Espartaco* had ambitious aims. Proclaiming its links to the revolutionary German socialism of Karl Liebknecht and Rosa Luxemburg, the journal sought to identify the centrists of the PSOE with 'accommodating and yielding German social democracy'.

Espartaco represented a clear attempt to forge links with other Marxist forces in Spain. Its very title was confusingly similar to *Joven Espartaco*, the theoretical journal of the Juventud Comunista Ibérica (JCI), the youth movement of the Trotskyist Izquierda Comunista Española (ICE). The pages of the journal were opened not just to radical Socialists like Margarita Nelken, Julio Alvarez del Vayo and Carlos de Baraibar, but also to Francisco García Lavid, one of the founding members of the Spanish branch of the Trotskyist Communist Opposition, and members of the ICE. The central theme of *Espartaco* concerned the need for the PSOE to adopt a military revolutionary strategy; its watchwords were 'preparation, discipline, daring'. Indeed, the call to 'cleanse' the Socialist movement of reformism and eliminate all traces of evolutionism bordered on the obsessional.[124] While *Espartaco* necessarily had only a limited impact, being forced to close as part of the widespread repression of the Left following the October insurrection, it did represent an important step on the road to the FJSE leaving the PSOE. It was to be another two years before the FJSE seceded from the Socialist party to join forces with the Communist youth movement, the UJC, but the two organisations did hold joint meetings on 26 and 30 July 1934. Representing the FJSE were Carrillo, Laín Entralgo and Serrano Poncela, while the UJC sent Jesús Rozado, Trifón Medrado and Fernando Claudín.[125] The meetings achieved little, other than to demonstrate the gulf that existed between the two groups. While the FJSE, and Carrillo in particular, objected to the UJC's calls for the formation of Soviets in Spain, the Communist youth leaders rejected utterly the suggestion that the PCE should join the Alianza obrera. The main disagreement, however, centred on their respective assessment of the peasant strike of June.

The peasants' general strike of June 1934 was to be of great significance in the Socialists' preparations for insurrection; once more, the bifurcation between revolutionary rhetoric and reformist practice which had marked the Socialist movement since its foundations was made evident. The situation in the southern countryside had been growing desperate since the Radical–CEDA election victory in November 1933, with all restraints on landlords lifted.[126] The reforming legislation of the Republican–Socialist coalition government did not have to be repealed by the new government; it was simply ignored by landowners and *caciques*. Peasants with known

Socialist or Anarchist affiliation were refused work, and wages were slashed. In several regions, particularly Badajoz in Estremadura and Granada in Andalusia, there were reports of near starvation and physical attacks on members of the Socialist landworkers' federation, the FNTT.[127] In the light of this situation, the FNTT naturally found it difficult to counsel moderation to its members. After months of restraint, it was decided to call a strike – although strictly within the legal provisions of giving ten days' notice. However, despite the elimination of the Besteiristas from the executive of the UGT, the FNTT was refused support by the new Caballerista executive, which had warned against calling a general strike. Essentially, the UGT was worried about possible repercussions: the lessons of 1909 and 1917 still weighed heavily on an organisation which had always been ready to sublimate ideals to simple survival.[128] Despite his radical pronouncements since the previous summer, Largo Caballero made it clear that the FNTT should not expect sympathetic action from industrial workers. In addition, the joint PSOE–UGT committee, created at the start of the year with a view to preparing a revolutionary movement, issued the message that the peasants' strike did not figure within plans for such a movement.

Thus, when the strike was eventually called, it lacked co-ordination. Hardly revolutionary in their aspirations, the strikers achieved only limited success.[129] There was great disparity between different regions in the intensity of the strike – only in Jaén, Málaga and Seville did it attain significant backing and manage to keep going for up to a fortnight. Nonetheless, the government reprisals, led by the Radical Party's reactionary Minister of the Interior, Rafael Salazar Alonso, were severe. Salazar Alonso was determined to use the strike as a pretext for smashing the FNTT. With CEDA backing, he declared the strike a 'revolutionary conflict' and responded accordingly: any public references in defence of the strike were made illegal; *El Obrero de la Tierra*, the FNTT newspaper, was banned; mass arrests of left-wing sympathisers took place, including even four Socialist deputies; workers' centres were closed down; whole town councils in the areas where the strike had penetrated deepest were disbanded and replaced by government appointees.[130] The strikers' main hope – disrupting the harvest – was dashed by the use of the army and the importation of outside labour under Civil Guard protection.

The failure of the peasants' strike provoked sharp debate within the Spanish Left. In particular, the repressive measures introduced by Salazar Alonso lent credence to the view that the Radical Party, through its readiness to act in accordance with the CEDA's wishes, represented the thin end of the wedge of fascism in Spain. For the FJSE, both the strike and the government's response confirmed their belief that all attention must now be devoted to full-scale preparations for a revolutionary takeover of power. The UJC, meanwhile, saw the role of the UGT in the strike as further proof of the Socialists' irremediable reformism. However, it was within the Alianza obrera that debate was sharpest. The UGT's failure to back the peasants so disgusted Manuel Fernández Grandizo, the ICE representative in the recently formed Socialist-dominated Madrid Alianza obrera, that he resigned.[131] In a bitter article published in *Comunismo*, José Luis Arenillas, a doctor who would be executed by Francoist forces in 1938, denounced the Socialists for their defence of capitalism, and, quoting Trotsky, compared the role of the PSOE to that of the Jesuits within the Catholic Church:

The true Christian doctrine, such as it was conceived by the masses and by popular conscience, is separated from official Catholicism by an abyss as great as that which exists between the theories of Marx (which represent the highest level of revolutionary thought and feeling) and the remains of the rampant sentimentalism which inspires the bourgeois thought of the Socialist leaders.[132]

Arenillas accused the PSOE of adopting revolutionism not through genuine concern for the fate of the working class, but rather through fear that its organisational structure was jeopardised by the rise of fascism. This was palpably an unjustifiable slur. Reformist perhaps, even pusillanimous, but the PSOE was hardly hypocritically insincere.

Nonetheless, there does remain a problem in explaining the Socialists' attitude towards the peasant strike. It could, of course, be argued that the reluctance of Largo Caballero to support the peasants has an easy explanation: caught in a genuine dilemma between pressure from the FNTT and his own reformist instincts, the latter won out for fear of defeat in a full-scale confrontation.[133] However, if reformist rejection of confrontation had become the indelible hallmark of the Socialist movement, this accounts neither for the revolutionary preparations made throughout 1934, nor the decision to take on the government in spite of overwhelming odds in October.[134] If October was the right moment, why not June? It can hardly be maintained that the political situation in Spain deteriorated so much in the intervening three months as to make revolution unavoidable. Nor can the immediate catalyst of the October rising, the appointment of three CEDA ministers, be given causal rather than descriptive weight. In a sense the strike was a disaster waiting to happen. Instead, in light of the virtual silence on the issue in the various volumes of Largo's memoirs, it can only be assumed that the Socialist leader did not think the peasant issue sufficiently explosive a spark to ignite a nationwide revolutionary general strike. This would be consistent with the PSOE's and UGT's historic underplaying of the agrarian question in Spain. In the Socialists' conception, if there was to be an insurrectionary strike, it would be led by the industrial proletariat – the true gravediggers of capitalism. The entire edifice of the PSOE's analysis of the Republic had been built on the assumption that it represented the first stage on the inexorable road to industrial capitalism through bourgeois revolution. The agrarian dimension in such an analysis was conspicuous through its absence.[135]

However, Largo and the PSOE were not alone in underestimating the importance of the landless wage-earning peasantry as an independent social force in Spain. The Trotskyist former member of the Communist Party, Luis García Palacios, had complained while in the PCE:

Our party lacks an agrarian policy. It has neither a good nor a bad one: plainly and simply, it does not have one, and never has had.[136]

Independent policy initiatives in the PCE were, of course, frowned upon by the Comintern, as demonstrated by the expulsion of Bullejos when he dared to contradict the Moscow line in 1932. Thus, since the Comintern itself placed little emphasis on agrarian issues in Spain, being more concerned with events in Germany and Italy, it was never likely that the PCE would develop a coherent approach to one of the most pressing issues in Spanish politics. Instead, the PCE was reduced to an echolalic repetition of calls for a United Front of the working class to lead a workers' and peasants' revolution against the landowners and the bourgeoisie. Comintern directives paid little attention to the role of the peasantry, seeing it as little more than a supportive appendage to the proletariat in the inevitable Socialist revolution.

The situation was somewhat different amongst the Catalan Marxist groups, which enjoyed greater independence with regard to theory. Nonetheless, the ICE was still heavily influenced by its mentor, Leon Trotsky. The Soviet dissident recognised the importance of the peasantry, but saw it in undifferentiated terms – simply part of Spain's feudal inheritance, marked by localism and reactionary influences.[137] For Trotsky, Spain had to be understood in terms of combined and uneven development; the peasantry had a vital role to play, but only as part of the permanent revolution which was not yet on the political agenda. Thus, there was no specific policy aimed at the peasantry, other than to try to inculcate it with the need to follow the lead of the proletariat.[138] An indication of the low importance attached to the landless peasantry as an autonomous social force is the fact that the ICE journal *Comunismo* carried just three articles on agrarian matters, all of them referring to the reforms of the Republican–Socialist coalition government, in its thirty-eight issues between 1931 and 1934.

Maurín's BOC had a line similar to that of Trotsky, without, however, explicitly embracing the concept of permanent revolution. For Maurín, there was no chance of a successful proletarian revolution without peasant backing, nor any possibility of an independent peasant revolution divorced from the industrial proletarian masses. However, in his view, the Spanish peasantry lacked leadership: the PSOE was acting as an agent of the bourgeoisie by promising agrarian reform in order to stem revolutionary initiatives among the peasantry; the Anarcho-syndicalists had no appreciation of the importance of the peasant movement; the Stalinists of the PCE had seen everything in the Spanish revolution – including Soviets – except agrarian revolution. Maurín pointed out that changes in the world economy, with increased competition from Asia, Africa, Algeria, the United States and Italy undermining Spanish agricultural production, meant that a simple division of land such as would be normally associated with bourgeois revolution would be insufficient in Spain. Only in Galicia, Catalonia and the Levant would this be of any immediate benefit. In the rest of the country, particularly Castile and Andalusia, the peasants, localist in outlook for the most part, would continue with the prevailing system of monoculture, leading to inevitable economic ruin. It would be as useful, he argued, as receiving as an inheritance a fan shop in Siberia. The only solution, therefore, was a Russian-style bourgeois revolution in the countryside, followed immediately by Socialist revolution:

Agrarian revolution and industrial revolution are two faces of the same coin. The one cannot exist without the other. We are entering full-scale social revolution.[139]

Maurín's conception was thus closer to Lenin's than to Trotsky's.[140] In this view, although the peasantry was still basically seen as an essentially undifferentiated mass to be instrumentalised, deprived of the capacity to engage in autonomous collective initiatives, it had a fundamental revolutionary role to play. Maurín derived from the Russian experience the basic lesson that the peasantry was a principal actor in the bourgeois revolution against the ruling autocracy. Nonetheless, while in the nine issues published between 1930 and 1931 of *La Nueva Era*, the theoretical journal of the BOC, there were articles on topics as diverse as Marxism and art, literature and the Mexican revolution, Gandhi, the tragedy of Mark Twain, and the theatre, and by authors ranging from Marx himself to Engels, Lenin, Plekhanov and Trotsky, there was not a single piece on the peasantry or the agrarian issue in Spain or anywhere else.[141]

The defeat of the peasants' general strike and the subsequent reprisals by the CEDA-backed Radical government in the summer of 1934 had two principal effects on the Spanish Left. First, it confirmed the view that the Right in Spain was determined to introduce a fascist-style corporatist state. Second, and related to this, it underlined the need for united action against such a possibility. However, the only organisation capable of providing the basis for such united action was Maurín's less than solid Alianza obrera. Aware of the Left's conviction that he represented a fascist threat, José María Gil Robles set about playing on such fears by engaging in deliberately provocative actions. After the peasants' strike, the CEDA turned its attention to Catalonia, where the existence of the autonomous Generalitat, particularly as it was under the control of the moderate left Republican Esquerra, offended its sense of Spanish unity. The independence of the Generalitat was called into question in June 1934 by a Constitutional Tribunal ruling in favour of a complaint by the right-wing Lliga Regionalista, supported by the CEDA, against agrarian reform measures introduced by the Esquerra.[142] Thereafter, in September the extremist CEDA youth movement, the Juventud de Acción Popular (JAP), held a mass rally at Covadonga in Asturias, a site chosen for its symbolism as the starting point of the reconquest of Spain from the Moors. The JAP had for some time been engaging in a verbal maximalism which more than matched that of the FJSE; its rallies were closely modelled on the Nazi example. Thus, as summer turned into autumn in the Spain of 1934, political emotions were running dangerously high. Events came to a head in early October. At the end of September, Gil Robles had provoked a government crisis by withdrawing his support from the minority Radical administration. In the new cabinet, drawn up by Lerroux at the start of October, three ministerial posts were given to members of the CEDA. All Republican forces in Spain were unanimous in denouncing the move as a direct attack on the Republic.

The Socialists took the CEDA's entry into government as a signal for action. On 4 October, the UGT called a general strike – the supposed culmination of its preparations since February for revolution. In the event, the strike was almost inevitably a failure.[143] In most parts of Spain it was quickly crushed by the prompt action of the government in declaring martial law. Only in Barcelona, where the Esquerra offered brief resistance, and in Asturias, where the bravery of the local miners turned the strike into an insurrectionary uprising lasting a fortnight, was there any degree of success. Ultimately, of course, the strike never stood a chance against the repressive power of the state. However, an important factor which contributed to the strike's collapse and made the state's task easier was the underlying attitude of the Socialists. For all the talk of united action by the Left, the Socialists still wished to dominate any combined moves. Unwilling to cede its traditional hegemony, the PSOE rendered the Alianza obrera necessarily ineffective. Of the other Marxist groups, the BOC and the ICE were too small to challenge the PSOE's dominance, except in Catalonia where they faced the alternative challenge of the Anarchists. The PCE remained largely irrelevant at this stage, having opened relations with the Socialists and solicited entry to the Alianza obrera only after the Comintern changed its line in the summer of 1934, following Stalin's decision to seek a *rapprochement* with the western democracies.

Thus, there was little genuine unity on the Spanish Left. Moreover, the strike was very poorly planned. Differences within the PSOE meant that there was no agreement even as to the programme of the strike. For the FJSE and other leftists, it represented the initiation of a full-scale Socialist revolution; for Prieto and the centrists in the party, the aim of the strike was to force Alcalá-Zamora to reconsider, and invite the Socialists back into a coalition government with the Republicans; for the Catalan sections of the party, the strike was in defence of the Catalan statute. Largo Caballero's position remains somewhat murky, although there is little to suggest that the revolutionary *élan* of his rhetoric was ever truly genuine. One thing, however, did emerge clearly from the October strike. The example of Asturias provided a pointed lesson for the Left: crucially, the key to the relative success of the insurrection there was the participation of the CNT in an effective Alianza obrera. Without the CNT, the Asturian rising would have been as short-lived and as easily defeated as those in Madrid and Barcelona. It was this which reinforced and finally drove home the point now understood by all Spanish Marxists: revolution depended on united action. The problem surrounded both the form of action and the form of union.

6 Marxism marginalised: the PSOE and the creation of the Popular Front, 1934–1936

In broad terms, the Socialist-led insurrectionary strike movement of October 1934 was a failure throughout all of Spain, collapsing rapidly everywhere except in Asturias, where it was brutally suppressed by Moorish troops led by General Francisco Franco.[1] It would be difficult, though, to exaggerate the significance for the Left within the Republic, and ultimately for the Republic itself, of the events of October 1934. While the immediate aftermath of the abortive rising saw the trial and imprisonment of several Socialist leaders, as well as of the Republican leader, Manuel Azaña Díaz, the longer-term repercussions were profound and far-reaching. Most obviously, the fact that only in Asturias had there been any hint of success underlined the importance of genuine united action. That the Asturian mine-workers had been able to hold out for two weeks was obviously a reflection of their courage and commitment; however, it was also due in large measure to the presence of the CNT within a local Alianza obrera which approximated more closely than most to Joaquín Maurín's original conception.[2] Moreover, the widespread imprisonment of workers' leaders, together with the call by CEDA ministers for the execution of Asturian miners' leaders Belarmino Tomás and Ramón González Peña, provided the Left with a powerful cause around which to unite.[3] The commutation of any death sentences became an immediate and urgent aim, while the call for the release and pardon of all those involved in the October rising was to become a central plank of leftist politics throughout 1935.

Nonetheless, despite the fact that October 1934 served as a clear demonstration of the importance of united initiatives, one of its most telling consequences was to be a bitter and highly damaging split within the PSOE. Francisco Largo Caballero and Indalecio Prieto, the two leading figures within the Socialist movement, drew radically opposed conclusions from the disastrous insurrectionary strike movement. The former was persuaded that the failure of October 1934 derived from the fact that the PSOE had not been revolutionary enough, and that it should therefore be 'bolshevised'; the latter, having supported the revolutionary line with some misgivings, was now more than ever convinced of the need to regain political power at the ballot box through a coalition with the Republicans.

146

Caballero's assessment, while never given practical shape, was ultimately to lead to the wholesale loss of the FJSE to the Communist Party (PCE). Indeed, the 'radical' postures adopted by Largo Caballero while in prison allowed the PCE to assume a significance within Republican politics wholly out of proportion to its real mass support. It would be mistaken, however, to credit the Communists with the creation of the Popular Front, despite the repeated claims to the contrary by the PCE itself and by Francoist propagandists.[4] Instead, the consummation in early 1936 of the electoral coalition which went by the title of 'Frente Popular' represented a tactical triumph for Prieto and his main Republican collaborator, Azaña.[5]

It is perhaps the central paradox of Spanish Marxism during the Second Republic that the period of its greatest fruitfulness in terms of theory, from October 1934 to the outbreak of the Civil War in July 1936, should coincide with its effective abandonment as the guiding principle behind the political line of the PSOE. While the October rising certainly acted as a catalyst for intense productivity by Spanish Marxist theorists, the eventual formation of the Popular Front coalition, and the PSOE's presence within it, owed little to Marxist theoretical formulations. This marginalisation of Marxism as a guiding principle is made the more ironic by the fact that since the PSOE's foundation in 1879, and most particularly during the first years of the Second Republic, its leaders had consistently relied on their, albeit distorted, conceptions of Marxist orthodoxy to inform the party's political practice.[6] In the aftermath of October 1934, however, the self-styled Marxist militants within the party, be they Caballeristas or members of the FJSE, were increasingly isolated from the executive nerve centres of the PSOE. Prietista moderates, of course, enjoyed the considerable advantage that many of their radical rivals, such as Largo Caballero himself, Amaro del Rosal, Santiago Carrillo, and Carlos Hernández Zancajo, were in prison as a result of the October rising. Prieto, on the other hand, had managed – hidden in the capacious boot of a car driven by the Republic's air attaché in Rome, Ignacio Hidalgo de Cisneros – to escape to France, from where he was able to coordinate the recapture of the party from supporters of Caballero.[7]

The struggle between Prieto and Largo Caballero for control of the PSOE following the October uprising has often been explained in terms of their deep mutual animosity.[8] While it is true that there was little love lost between the two Socialist leaders, disagreements between them reflected issues far more fundamental than those of personal feelings. A rather more sophisticated recent analysis has emphasised a longer-term basic division within the Socialist movement between '*corporativistas obreros*' and '*reformadores políticos*', or worker corporativists and political reformists, whose origins can be traced back to 1923.[9] According to this approach (associated principally with Santos Juliá), worker corporativists, identified most obviously with Largo Caballero, placed major emphasis on the consolidation and growth of workers' organisations, their presence in official state bodies, their capacity to negotiate, and such like. The political form of the regime mattered less to them than the freedom of operation enjoyed by the workers' union representatives. Thus, the worker corporativists within the Socialist movement had accepted in 1926 the offer of UGT representation within Primo de Rivera's Organización Corporativa Nacional, despite the provenance of the offer from an anti-democratic dictator. Indeed, their rejection of the Dictatorship, so the argument goes, came only after 1928 when it was felt that the gains made under Primo were under threat as his popularity waned and his regime began to totter.

The political reformists, on the other hand, who were best represented by Indalecio Prieto and Fernando de los Ríos, identified Socialism with democratic liberties. Where the worker corporativists saw in the Second Republic the opportunity to consolidate definitively the role of the UGT in labour relations with the state, the political reformists were guided simply by their liberalism and their faith in democracy as an instrument of social transformation. It has even been argued that the Republican leader, Manuel Azaña, expressed more effectively than Prieto what the latter desired: a liberal, parliamentary, democratic Republic which would serve as the instrument of the transformation of society towards greater social justice.[10] Common to Azaña and Prieto was the view that the working class had to play a subordinate role in the new regime. Its proper function was seen as being one of support for the Republicans in their historic mission of completing the long-overdue bourgeois revolution in Spain. The only real difference between Prieto and Azaña was that the former remained committed at a rhetorical level to the ultimate establishment of a Socialist regime, although this had no effective practical implications.

Despite their differences, at the outset of the Republic (while the coalition government concentrated on carrying through basic and urgent reforms) the worker corporativists and political reformists within the Socialist movement were broadly in alliance. However, once the government had enacted its initial reforming measures, according to Juliá, the political reformists were left without a programme, thereby ceding hegemony within the Socialist movement to the corporativists. With a parliamentary democracy established and basic liberties secured, all that was left for the reformists to do was to wait for the inevitable turn of the wheel of history which would bring about Socialism. The worker corporativists, on the other hand, were able to continue with their aim of consolidating the position of the UGT within the Republic, albeit in line with the *pablista* tradition of hesitant moderation. However, the obstructionism of rightist forces during the first *bienio*, aided and abetted by Lerroux's ever more conservative Radical Party, forced the worker corporativists to revise their political programme. As disillusionment with the reforming possibilities of the Republic set in, so the argument continues, the corporativists began to question the viability of their tactics. Following the 1933 general elections, which the Socialists and Republicans contested independently rather than in alliance and which ushered into power a reactionary rightist coalition government committed to disarticulating the reforms of the previous two years, Largo Caballero and his corporativist colleagues abandoned legal moderation in favour of a revolutionary stance. Behind this shift lay the fear that the UGT would no longer enjoy its privileged position in relation to the Republic under a right-wing government. The political reformists, meanwhile, were somewhat reluctantly swept along by the wave of revolutionary rhetoric which was to culminate in the disastrous October rising.

Ironically, one result of the abortive insurrection was to be a reversal of the respective strength within the Socialist movement of the worker corporativists and political reformists. Where the former found themselves committed to a revolutionism wholly out of tune with their *pablista* legacy of cautious circumspection, the latter were able to re-embark on the well-trodden path towards alliance with the Republicans. Thus, concludes Juliá's argument, hegemony within the Socialist movement returned to the true heirs of reformist moderation, the Prietistas.[11] Indeed, it is held that so strong was this tradition that the revolutionism of Largo Caballero was, in fact, never really genuine, being instead a rhetorical device designed to dissuade the Right from carrying through its more extremist policies. The position of Julián Besteiro, meanwhile, is reduced to one of barely secondary importance: a worker corporativist during the Primo Dictatorship, the Marxist professor split with Largo in 1930 over the issue of Socialist ministerial participation in a future Republic. Increasingly isolated from real executive influence during the first *bienio* of the Republic, Besteiro did enjoy a brief renaissance after October 1934 as a '*corporativista retraído*', or born-again corporativist, only to return to isolationist obscurity as Largo Caballero and Prieto dominated the contest for control of the PSOE and UGT throughout 1935.[12]

There is much to be said for this schema which posits a basic division between worker corporativists and political reformists within the Spanish Socialist movement. In heuristic terms, it emphasises the importance of examining differences between the ideas and aims of PSOE and UGT leaders. Moreover, it also underlines essential continuities within the Socialist movement, rather than seeing the Second Republic as representing some kind of clean break or hiatus in the movement's development. However, while welcome as a significant advance on previous analyses of the Socialist movement during the Republic, the new approach contains a number of problems. First, precisely because of the stress on continuities, there is a tendency to see the two positions – worker corporativist and political reformist – as rather more coherent and clearly delineated than they actually were. In fact, one of the striking features of the Spanish Socialist movement since its inception is the sheer lack of coherence and consistency in the positions held by many of its leading figures: from Pablo Iglesias, who shifted from rigidly isolationist rhetorical radicalism to reformist collaboration with both Anarchists and Republicans; through Oscar Pérez Solís, whose roller-coaster political trajectory took him from moderate Socialist to founder member of the Communist Party only to end up fighting for Franco in the Civil War, and Luis Araquistáin, who evolved from regenerationist Republicanism to maximalist Marxism before returning to the safer shores of parliamentary Socialism; to Francisco Largo Caballero and Julián Besteiro themselves, who spent much of the decade prior to the Civil War trading not just insults, but also the leadership of the PSOE and UGT.

A second drawback to the division beween worker corporativists and political reformists, related to the first, is that it helps clarify an exceedingly complex situation only at the expense of over-simplification. Thus, the importance of Julián Besteiro and his followers, people like Andrés Saborit, Trifón Gómez, and Lucio Martínez Gil, in the period 1931 to 1934 is underplayed; equally, the role of the FJSE in acting as a spur to the radicalisation of the PSOE, particularly after October 1934, receives no consideration whatsoever. Neither group fits comfortably into the categories defined by Juliá – the Besteiristas can be seen as incorporating elements of both worker corporativism and political reformism, while the FJSE represented a more revolutionary stance which stands outside the schema altogether.

Third, the schema fails to account satisfactorily for Indalecio Prieto's support for revolutionary initiatives during 1934: the logic of a political reformism committed to the maintenance of parliamentary democracy as an ultimate ideal should have precluded revolutionary adventurism, on the grounds of unpredictability alone. If, however, it is argued that Prieto went along with revolutionism merely out of a highly developed sense of party loyalty, then a further problem arises, one which highlights the major drawback to the worker corporativist–political reformist approach.[13] If it is held that Prieto played his part in preparations for revolution out of his sense of discipline, then the necessary implication is that these preparations must have been genuine – otherwise, there would have been no point to Prieto's participation.[14] If, however, it is held instead that neither Prieto nor Largo Caballero were genuine in their preparations, because neither the worker corporativists nor the political reformists were truly revolutionary, then this fails to explain satisfactorily two issues. First, how and why did the Socialists become involved in the October rising; second, and more important, why did the worker corporativists rather than the political reformists go down the path of revolutionary maximalism after October 1934? There is nothing in the previous experience of either group to suggest that one rather than the other should have been more susceptible to radicalisation; indeed, within the confines of the characteristic caution of both groups, worker corporativism appears even further removed than political reformism from revolutionary adventurism.

This underlines the principal problem to the approach: 'worker corporativism' and 'political reformism' are descriptive rather than analytic characterisations. While they help elucidate important long-term currents within the Spanish Socialist movement, they fail to account adequately for the movement's development during the Second Republic. One main reason for the lack of explanatory power in the worker corporativist–political reformist division is that it underplays the importance and nature of Marxist theory within the Spanish Socialist movement. Although it has become a commonplace to disparage the level and sophistication of Spanish Marxist theory, this should not be allowed to obscure the fact that in general the Spanish Socialists attempted to act in accordance with their admittedly limited conceptions of Marxist orthodoxy.[15] While no one would argue that such conceptions were anything other than unsophisticated, not to say simplistic, the interest of the PSOE's Marxist formulations during the Second Republic lies not so much in their intrinsic theoretical qualities as in the results they fostered. In any case, the level of Marxist theoretical debate in Spain during the 1930s reflected a more generalised poverty of analysis within the European Left as a whole during the historical moment of fascism. The subtleties of approach now recognised in Thalheimer, Gramsci and Trotsky not only went largely unappreciated when originally adumbrated in the 1920s, but had by the 1930s been swamped by an official Comintern line of ineffable, though sadly ineffective, simplicity.[16]

Essentially, there developed within the European Marxist movement of the 1930s two separate orthodoxies: the first, associated with the Comintern, saw the rise of fascism as the dying spasm of monopoly capitalism prior to the birth of Socialism; the second, prevalent within Social Democratic parties, held that fascism was a temporary historical aberration on the ineluctable evolutionary road to Socialism. Not only were both approaches somewhat lacking in analytical penetration, they also became prey to opportunistic reformulation. As is well known, the revolutionary leftism of the Comintern's Third Period gave way in 1934 to an alliance-seeking reformism which would culminate in the Popular Front strategy; leading Social Democratic parties, meanwhile, abandoned reformism after the Dollfuss coup of March 1933. If so sophisticated a Marxist as Otto Bauer should embrace revolutionism when deprived of the possibilities of parliamentary practice, it is hardly to be wondered at that much lesser figures like Largo Caballero should follow a similar course when faced with what was believed to be a similar threat.[17]

Thus, while the specific details of Marxist theory in Spain were notable for their naivety, the general pattern of developments on the Marxist Left mirrored that in other European nations such as Austria and, more particularly, Germany. The major difference was the relative weakness of the Communist Party in Spain. However, one of the most telling results of the 'radicalisation' of the Caballeristas was that it brought the PCE into the mainstream of Spanish politics. More specifically, it will be seen that, contrary to most available interpretations, Largo Caballero played a central and vital role in ensuring the presence of the PCE in the Popular Front electoral coalition. This in turn led to the last-minute forced acceptance of the Popular Front by those dissident Marxist groups which had been most critical of the concept: the Catalan-based Bloc Obrer i Camperol (BOC) and Izquierda Comunista Española (ICE), which united in late 1935 to form the Partido Obrero de Unificación Marxista (POUM). Like their dissident counterparts in the rest of Europe (Thalheimer, Trotsky, Tasca) the most perspicacious amongst the Spanish Marxists, above all Maurín, found themselves marginalised from positions of political power or influence.

The central issue which was to dominate leftist politics in Spain after October 1934 and throughout all of 1935, was the question of alliance strategies. While Prieto set about with Azaña trying to reconstruct the 1931 Republican–Socialist alliance to defend Republican democracy, Largo Caballero, in a bid to avoid surrendering Socialist hegemony on the Left, retreated into a Garbo-like rejection of all approaches from Communists or Republicans. It fell to the FJSE to try to build bridges between the Socialist Left and the various other Spanish Marxist groups. There thus developed a twin struggle over the direction of leftist politics in the Second Republic: first, within the PSOE between the Prietistas and the Caballeristas, with the latter both supported and surpassed in radical commitment by the Youth Movement; second, between the PSOE–UGT as a whole and the other Marxist parties.

If Prieto and Caballero were bitterly divided over control of the PSOE and the UGT, they were united in their desire to maintain the hegemony of the Socialist bodies within the Left as a whole, and therefore in their suspicion of the Alianza obrera. In particular, the Socialist leaders were opposed to the formation of an Alianza obrera nacional, proposed repeatedly throughout 1935 by Joaquín Maurín, leader of the BOC.[18] This in turn, however, created further tensions within the Socialist movement between its leaders and local level militants anxious to become involved in united initiatives: for example, Socialist militants in Valencia supported a call by the local Alianza obrera in March 1935 for the creation of a national coordinating committee, claiming that the lack of such a body had been responsible for the defeat of the October rising.[19] In Zaragoza, the radical Youth Movement, committed to the creation of a Partido Marxista Unificado, clashed with both Prieto and Largo, while in Alicante, the Prietista deputy, Manuel González Ramos, was to be expelled from the PSOE by local militants opposed to his moderate stances.[20]

The main reason for the hostility of the Socialist leadership to the idea of a national level coordinating committee derived from the fear that such an organisation would threaten PSOE dominance within the workers' movement, a criticism expressed with some bitterness by Andreu Nin in *La Batalla*.[21] In particular, the reaction of the Communist Party to the events of October 1934 had confirmed Socialist leaders' suspicions that other workers' organisations intended to usurp their position. In contrast to the dominant view within the PSOE that the workers' movement should rebuild its strength before launching any further initiatives, PCE leaders called for more strikes in order to maintain morale and to demonstrate to the bourgeoisie that its victory had been ephemeral. The Communist journal *Bandera Roja*, for instance, gave prominence to this view in December 1934, while in January of the following year, the Buro Político of the PCE published a resolution under the title *Los combates de octubre*, a full-scale attack on reformism in the PSOE. In particular, the Socialists were criticised for underestimating the importance of the peasantry and accused of lacking the capacity to lead the revolution, a task for which the PCE, naturally, was uniquely suited.[22] The PCE's resolution also called for the creation of Alianzas obreras y campesinas, 'created on the basis of the widest democratic criterion', in direct opposition to *La Batalla*'s proposal for an Alianza obrera nacional. The distinction, it must be said, was a subtle one.[23]

Los combates de octubre was just one of a series of publications by the PCE aimed at persuading PSOE militants that responsibility for the defeat of October 1934 lay with a Socialist leadership which lacked both revolutionary theory and tactics. Certainly, Largo Caballero seemed set on helping the Communists convey this impression. An extraordinary miscalculation by the Socialist leader allowed the PCE to usurp much of the glory for Asturias. Fearful of potential CEDA reaction, Caballero strenuously denied during his trial any participation in the 1934 rising. Such a move was politically exceptionally naive, a point certainly not missed by the Communists:

The Socialist leaders, and particularly Largo Caballero, whom Jose Díaz went to visit in prison, rejected the PCE's proposal that both parties should together assume responsibility for the October movement. The Communist Party therefore decided to assume this responsibility publicly, thereby winning great prestige amongst the Socialist militants and amongst the working masses in general. . .[24]

PCE leaders hoped to take advantage of the PSOE's discomfiture following the Asturias uprising to attract its rival's members into the Communist Party. To this end, the PCE placed major emphasis on the establishment of a *'ligazón orgánica'*, or 'organic bond', with the Socialist Party. Unlike the French Communists, whose proposal in May 1934 to form a *front unique* against fascism was extended to include Republican parties, the PCE concentrated its efforts exclusively on the Socialists as the major political grouping of the Left.[25] As early as the end of October 1934, the Buro Político issued instructions to PCE provincial committees to work for unity of action with the PSOE in the form of formal agreements, or what amounted to a United Front from above. The policy of 'frente único por la base', or United Front from below, was suspended, if not abandoned, as the PCE expended major effort on a propaganda campaign aimed at PSOE leaders. A barrage of proposals was proffered: the establishment and strengthening of *comités de enlace* (liaison committees) and Alianzas obreras y campesinas; the creation of joint workers' commit-tees at factory, farm and local district level; the unification of Socialist and Communist union bodies; the convoking of mass meetings and issuing of manifestos. All met with firm rejection from the Socialist leadership.[26]

The PCE's commitment to the creation of a 'frente obrero' with the Socialist Party obeyed Communist International directives, delivered by the Comintern's Italian-born Argentine representative in Spain, Victorio Codovilla, following the dramatic shift in Stalin's foreign policy during the summer of 1934.[27] The reasons behind the shift are well known: briefly, by mid-1934 it had become obvious to the Soviet leader that Hitler's accession to power the previous September represented a major defeat both of the German Communist Party (KPD) and of the Comintern's isolationist policy during its so-called Third Period, most closely associated with the KPD in its relations with the SPD since 1928. Faced with the reality of the spread of fascism in Europe, together with grass-roots pressure for a united front from Communists in those countries which looked vulnerable to further fascist advances – most notably France – Stalin reversed his foreign policy orientation. In the field of international diplomacy, he sought to foment closer ties with the bourgeois democracies, Britain and France. The Comintern, meanwhile, in order to assist this diplomatic initiative, instruc-ted European Communist parties to abandon the sectarian line of the Third Period, by which Social Democratic parties had been excoriated as 'social fascist'. Instead, 'like scene-shifting in the theatre before which people sit in open-mouthed surprise', in the words of Léon Blum, the Comintern announced through *Pravda* on 23 May 1934, a new united front policy.[28] According to the new policy, Communists should work both for a *united* front with Social Democratic parties in defence of the working class, and for a *popular* front with bourgeois parties so long as these were not actively opposed to the Soviet Union.[29]

In Spain, the emphasis placed by the PCE on the united front, or 'frente obrero', with the PSOE led it to underplay the second strand of the Comintern's sudden switch in policy. Whereas the French Communists under Maurice Thorez duly extended the policy originally associated with the maverick Jacques Doriot to encompass the Radical-Socialists, PCE leaders believed that the 'popular bloc' or 'concentration' would come about only through the extension of the Alianzas obreras.[30] Thus, leftist Republican groupings in Spain, such as Azaña's Izquierda Republicana and the Catalan Esquerra, were ignored by a Communist Party which insisted on promoting the idea of Alianzas obreras y campesinas as a central plank in its bid to foment the *ligazón orgánica* with the PSOE.

It is true, though, that in December 1934 a *comité de enlace* was established, involving representatives of the PCE and PSOE as well as their respective union bodies, the UGT and CGTU. However, as José Díaz, the Communist secretary-general, observed, the lack of willingness on the part of the Socialist representatives to engage in genuine co-operative action left the *comité* largely ineffective.[31] While the establishment of the *comité de enlace* was followed by an expansion in the number of local Alianzas obreras, the Socialists remained deliberately obstructive. The Executives of both the PSOE and the UGT refused to grant the *comité* any executive power, and attempted to limit its scope for action. In February 1935, Juan-Simeón Vidarte, the Prietista party secretary responsible for negotiating the formation of the *comité de enlace* with the PCE, suggested that it should be suspended, but the PSOE Executive responded with the suggestion that it should meet only when 'absolutely indispensable'.[32]

It was a similar story with the PCE proposal for the creation of Alianzas obreras. During the first months of 1935, the Executive Commission of the UGT told local sections that the mission for which the original Alianza obrera had been created was over, and that any unity policy should be entrusted to local *comités de enlace*. In fact, there was some confusion as to what the actual difference was between the two entities. In Madrid, for example, the Executive Commission of the influential Agrupación Socialista Madrileña (ASM) entered into correspondence with the Executive of the PSOE over whether it was dealing with a *comité central de alianza*, a *comité central de enlace* or a *comité central pro-presos* (prisoners' aid).[33] Such problems, however, were often skirted around by the simple expedient of refusing to reply to any letters sent by the CGTU soliciting unification, or calling for the creation of *comités de fábrica*, and so on. Indeed, no clearer demonstration of the Socialists' antipathy to united action exists than the agreement by the Executives of the PSOE and UGT in early 1935 that party members should 'abstain from intervening in any actions organised by other elements, be they Communists, syndicalists or Republicans'. This agreement provoked a bitter argument with the UGT in the Basque Country, which declared itself 'stupefied' by the Executives' position, and by their 'lack of resolve'.[34] Nonetheless, the policy adopted by the PSOE and UGT was effective inasmuch as it disrupted Communist plans to win over converts through a policy of infiltration.

The positions adopted by both the Socialists and the Communists follow an obvious logic. As a large party, the PSOE wished to maintain its traditional independence to formulate policies without reference to outside bodies; the policy of Alianzas obreras, on the other hand, was the only realistic option open to those small parties lacking significant influence amongst the working class. By establishing formal links with the main workers' party and its union movement, they hoped to acquire through the back door, as it were, an influence over the direction of proletarian politics in the Second Republic. However, the Socialist policy of non-response to PCE proposals left the Communists in a difficult situation: without sufficient influence to deal directly with the Republican parties, they were also unable to force the PSOE to respond to their initiatives. The Communist policy of creating a *ligazón orgánica* had thus run into a solid brick wall of Socialist intransigence; not until late 1935 would Largo Caballero allow in the demolition experts when he realised belatedly that the wall threatened to encircle him.

In the meantime, however, whereas the Caballeristas were rigid in their rejection of all alliances, the moderate sector of the PSOE, headed by Prieto, followed a more flexible course. The Vizcayan leader took full advantage of the opportunity presented by Largo's incarceration and intransigence to seize the political initiative from his arch rival. In this, he was greatly assisted by Manuel Azaña, the Republican leader who had been released from prison on 28 December 1934, following the declaration by the Supreme Tribunal that there was no evidence to implicate him in the Catalan rising of October.[35] Since the previous month, Azaña and Prieto had been in contact by letter. It was the leader of Izquierda Republicana who first proposed, after his release, the need 'to arrange (*combinar*) a tactic which allows us to await the formation of a political force powerful enough to win the first battle we are faced with'.[36] Indeed, it could be argued that the real initiative for the recreation of the Republican–Socialist coalition of 1931 came above all from Azaña.[37] It was Azaña who made the running in early 1935 by contacting various friends in the Socialist movement with his proposal for a common tactic. One such friend was

Fernando de los Ríos, the moderate intellectual deputy from Granada, who had drifted away somewhat from the limelight of leadership since the disastrous general elections of November 1933. Now, however, with Largo Caballero in prison, De los Ríos was ready to resume his role as outspoken defender of moderate reformism.

In March 1935, De los Ríos presented to the Executive Committee of the PSOE a circular on tactics, to be sent to the local *agrupaciones*. The circular contained sections from a letter sent to the PSOE Executive by Prieto, at the invitation of Juan-Simeón Vidarte, which spoke of the need to reach an alliance with the Republicans.[38] Shortly afterwards, a further circular was issued, written by Vidarte, vice-secretary general of the PSOE. This circular, known as the 'Circular Vidarte', contained elements taken from both Prieto's letter and the De los Ríos proposal, and has been claimed by its author as the genesis of the Popular Front.[39] The claim is exaggerated, but the 'Circular Vidarte' did receive widespread publicity and was the real starting point in earnest of the centrist campaign to resurrect the 1931 alliance with the Republicans. As a result of the circulars and the manner in which they were presented, the jailed Socialists sent a letter of protest, signed by Caballero, De Francisco, Carrillo and Zancajo amongst others, to the Executive of the PSOE. The only effect it had was to provoke the resignation of Fernando de los Ríos, whose call for a meeting of the PSOE National Committee was vetoed by Caballero. Thus ended the brief and rather bitter return to political prominence of the refined intellectual from Granada.[40]

The intensity of centrist activity in the Spring of 1935 was stimulated by the strong expectation of a general election in the near future. The always unsettled government of the Radical leader Alejandro Lerroux, supported by the three CEDA ministers whose appointment had provoked the October rising, had by March 1935 run into crisis. Towards the end of that month, the Cortes debated the death sentences passed by the military tribunals on the Socialist deputies, Ramón González Peña and Teodomiro Menéndez Fernández, for their participation in the Asturian rising. While Lerroux responded favourably to calls by the Spanish President, Niceto Alcalá-Zamora, for the death sentences to be commuted, Gil Robles, the CEDA leader was adamant that the sentences should be carried out. On 29 March, when the seven Radical cabinet members voted in favour of commutation, the ministers of the CEDA, the Agrarian Party and the Liberal Democrats all resigned. Gil Robles hoped to utilise the governmental crisis in support of his own aims of achieving power; the moderate Socialists saw it as opening a possible route for their return to government.[41] In the event, both were to be frustrated. Alcalá-Zamora did not trust Gil Robles sufficiently to invite him to form a government; nor, however, did he wish to call fresh elections. Thus, after various abortive attempts had been made at creating a new ministry acceptable to the various rightist groups jostling for power, Alcalá-Zamora suspended the Cortes and once more entrusted the job of ruling the country to Alejandro Lerroux.[42]

However, as the summer of 1935 approached, the prevailing atmosphere of governmental instability intensified. The prospect of an election lent added urgency to the task of re-creating the Republican–Socialist coalition. To this end, Prieto stepped up his efforts to promote an alliance with Azaña. On 14 April, the fourth anniversary of the declaration of the Republic, Prieto published a major article in *El Liberal*, 'On the electoral struggle. The extent and conditions of the leftist coalition'. In it, the pragmatic Socialist leader underlined his belief in the need for an electoral alliance, and heaped damning criticism on the PSOE's decision to contest the 1933 election on its own. Later in the month, he issued a call for the start of pro-alliance negotiations. Indeed, the Prietista sector of the Socialist movement enjoyed during the first half of 1935 a virtual monopoly of public visibility on the Left. Of the leading figures in the PSOE, Fernando de los Ríos and Juan-Simeón Vidarte had escaped imprisonment after the October rising. In addition, the leader of the Socialist minority in the Cortes and Secretary of the Agrupación Socialista Madrileña, Ramón Lamoneda, was a supporter of Prieto.[43] Moreover, since publication of *El Socialista* had been suspended by government decree since October 1934, the most progressive wide-circulation newspaper available in Spain was the aptly titled Bilbao-based *El Liberal*, the pages of which were open to Prieto, but not to his opponents.[44] Between 22 and 26 May, Prieto published a series of five articles in *El Liberal*, later issued by Publicaciones Indice as *Del momento: posiciones socialistas*.[45] The articles developed the themes outlined in his earlier article of 14 April. Essentially, Prieto's position remained unchanged from that expressed in his speech to the FJSE summer school at Torrelodones in 1933: social revolution was not on the political agenda, and the PSOE should concentrate on rebuilding its alliance with the Republicans. To do so, it was necessary to combat the growing leftism within the party – both the revolutionism of Caballero and the calls for bolshevisation from the Youth movement. Indeed, the third article in the series had the explicit title, 'Circumscribing ourselves to revolutionary action could equal suicide'.[46]

One significant result of Prieto's stance had been to assist Julián Besteiro in his attempt to recapture some of the ground lost to Largo Caballero during the previous year. Since April 1934, Besteiro had relied largely on the uninfluential Madrid journal *Tiempos Nuevos*, edited by his faithful follower Andrés Saborit, to maintain a rather limited public presence within the PSOE. In the aftermath of the October débâcle, however, he was able to stage something of a comeback. In early 1935, Besteiro had been elected to membership of the prestigious Academy of Political and Moral Sciences, and he chose to give his inaugural lecture, on 28 April, on the topic, 'Marxism and anti-Marxism'.[47] In an arcane, magniloquent and quite extraordinarily long speech, the professor offered a spirited, if unconvincing, defence of the view that Marx opposed the idea of the dictatorship of the proletariat. Essentially, the speech was a sustained statement of his familiar thesis that evolution equalled revolution, and that the true heirs to the mantle of Marxism were democratic socialists. Indeed, in support of his assertion that Socialism was penetrating virtually all aspects of bourgeois society, Besteiro pointed to Mussolini's Socialist background and to the fact that Hitler, 'that strange personality, a mixture of secondary qualities of Wotan, Hercules and the Archangel St Michael', had to 'baptise' his party National-Socialist.[48] In addition, Besteiro outlined his view of how fascism was a 'new form of romanticism', similar to Anarchism in that it was a protest against the entire existing order. More persuasive was his observation that fascism served the interests of the bourgeoisie financially whilst attacking it politically. In fact, though, Besteiro's comments on fascism were simply a prologue to his central theme of juxtaposing the 'intelligent Socialism' represented by British Labourism, Swedish Social Democracy and the American New Deal with the damaging distortion of Marxism that was the dictatorship of the proletariat.[49] The lecture, more than one hundred pages long in its printed form, can have had little impact amongst Socialist militants when it was published. Its importance lay in the fact that Besteiro was able to use a respected tribune to support Prieto, albeit not explicitly, in his struggle against Largo Caballero for control of the PSOE.

Nonetheless, despite the growing momentum of centrist currents, the radical sectors of the PSOE were hardly languishing. Although they remained in prison, leaders such as Largo Caballero and Santiago Carrillo were able to maintain regular contact with the outside world largely through the laxity of the governor of the Modelo Prison, a certain Señor Elorza, who was happy to turn a blind eye to the political activity of his charges.[50] The FJSE in particular had been active in its calls for greater radicalism within the PSOE. In early 1935, the FJSE published the pamphlet *Octubre: segunda etapa*, written by the imprisoned Carrillo, Carlos Hernández Zancajo and Amaro del Rosal.[51] The pamphlet, a fiery tract which called for the bolshevisation of the PSOE, concluded with a series of unrealistic demands which reflected, above all else, youthful radicalism.[52] It concluded with a declaration of the FJSE's unity and strength, and an expression of unquestioning faith in Largo Caballero, the 'leader and initiator of the revolutionary resurgence' within the PSOE. Largo's response was an expression of annoyance with Carrillo at the publication of the pamphlet without permission; FJSE members in Oviedo prison, meanwhile, in the very heartland of the Asturian rising, expressed their dissent in the clearest terms:

Bolshevise the Party? And what does that mean, comrades? Perhaps you mean to imply that our Party should adopt the tactics of the Third International? Yes? Ah, well in that case our reply is categorical: NEVER![53]

However, the publication of *Octubre: segunda etapa* and the articles in *El Liberal* by Prieto marked the start of a war of words within the PSOE which, while notable for the sheer quantity produced, was to generate rather more heat than light. Although the revolutionists had the better lines, the reformists were to produce a more convincing screenplay.

Open hostility between the two sectors was declared with the publication of Carlos de Baraibar's *Las falsas 'posiciones socialistas' de Indalecio Prieto*.[54] Baraibar, an old rival of Prieto who hailed from the Basque province of Alava, had come to socialism through his ardent nationalism. A leading writer on the eve of the Republic for the liberal Madrid daily, *El Sol*, Baraibar had been appointed Director General of Labour under Largo Caballero and remained loyal to the dour workers' leader thereafter.[55] *Las falsas 'posiciones socialistas'* aimed to demonstrate the lack of doctrinal support for Prieto's position, as well as to offer a full résumé of the policies supported by the Caballeristas. The central argument of the book was that the democratic revolution headed by the petty bourgeoisie in Spain had reached the point of stagnation; however, Prieto's position, according to Baraibar, consisted in making Socialism the cornerstone of that democratic revolution. Such a stance could only operate against the interests of the working class. Instead, it was necessary for the PSOE to go down the path opened up by the October rising, and to avoid forming a coalition with the Republicans. The PSOE had to play a Leninist role, and rid itself of the 'corrupting cancer' of the centrist threat which was personified by Prieto. The language employed by Baraibar was highly personalistic, and marked the start of a degeneration of the debate to a level of vitriol which at times obscured the importance of the issues in question.

The Prietista reply to Baraibar, delivered in kind was not long in coming. Publicaciones Indice produced *Por hoy y por mañana* by Antonio Gascón and Victoria Priego, a direct, if rather ineffective, response to Baraibar's attacks on Prieto. More important was Indice's *Documentos socialistas*, a collection of letters by leading centrists, including Prieto himself, as well as Ramón González Peña, the Asturian deputy whose death sentence had been commuted, Toribio Echevarría, Amador Fernández and Alejandro Jaume.[56] The support for Prieto from these Asturian mine-workers' leaders was of immense propaganda value to the centrists. While the Caballeristas and the FJSE, in particular, made much of how the Asturian rising of October 1934 represented a heroic example to be followed, the heroes' leaders themselves expressed public support for the thesis that such 'infantile' revolutionism should be abandoned in favour of constructing a wide electoral coalition.[57] This could only have been the source of some embarrassment to the more revolutionary elements within the Socialist movement.

Any such embarrassment was hardly in evidence, however, in an article by Luis Araquistáin, published in the May edition of his theoretical journal, *Leviatán*. Concerned that Julián Besteiro's speech of the previous month at the Academy of Political and Moral Sciences heralded a renewed challenge to Largo's leadership of the UGT, Araquistáin set about dismantling the distinguished professor's arguments. Titled 'El profesor Besteiro o el marxismo en la Academia', the *Leviatán* article was the first in a merciless and devastating series ridiculing the former president of the PSOE and UGT. The sarcasm of the title – the Academy had never before elected a declared Socialist – set the tone of Araquistáin's approach. Essentially, Besteiro was accused of simply following in the tradition of Fabian Socialism, which had nothing to do with Marxism, and was irrelevant to the divided Spain of the 1930s:

Of Marxism, he says virtually nothing until you have skipped through a mere hundred, large format, pages of the pamphlet. Instead he talks of everything else, both human and divine; of 'the case of Roosevelt', of 'Collaboration with the bourgeoisie', of 'Democratisation of the epic genre', of 'Revisionism and how to overcome it' (the criticism coming before the doctrine criticised), of 'The principal objections to the Marxist idea' (the cart still in front of the horse), of 'the reaction against the *Aufklaerung*' (which always used to be translated as the Enlightenment, although Besteiro now seems to think it is untranslatable), of '*behaviourism*' (and not *behaviourisme*, because it is an English rather than a French word), of '*Wertphilosophie*' and a thousand other things which one supposes must be impregnated by Marxist doctrine; but if the reader does not know beforehand what Marxism is, he will come away from his copious and multicoloured reading in more or less the same state as a virgin from a whorehouse.[58]

So effective was the attack that Besteiro was virtually forced out of the running for the leadership of the PSOE, returning to political prominence only through involvement in the Casado coup against the Negrín government in the dying days of the Civil War.

Araquistáin was a curious figure. A moderate reformist who was resolutely opposed to the Third International in the 1920s, he was later to be accused by Prieto of being directly responsible for the radicalisation of Largo Caballero during the Second Republic.[59] This, however, attributes too great an influence to Araquistáin, whose importance lay less in any Svengali-type hold over Caballero than in his role as articulator of the theoretical underpinnings to the revolutionary current within the PSOE. The main vehicle for this task was the journal *Leviatán*, founded in May

1934 and widely recognised as the most important Marxist journal ever to have been published in Spain.[60] If important as a journal of ideas, though, *Leviatán*, with its principal aim of theorising fascism both in Spain and abroad, was probably not particularly influential amongst Socialist militants, whose concerns were more immediate and less rarified.[61] Indeed, its often abstract content saved the journal from governmental proscription after the October rising. In fact it might be argued that *Leviatán* has enjoyed a rather inflated reputation, particularly in recent years, largely on account of the lack of any alternative forum in Spain devoted to developing Marxist theory. Nonetheless, the journal did serve an important purpose in acting as a bridgehead between the radical sectors of the PSOE and the dissident Marxist groups mainly based in Catalonia, the Bloc Obrer i Camperol (BOC) and Izquierda Comunista Española (ICE).

In the meantime, though, the Besteiro camp attempted a riposte to Araquistáin's attack. On 15 June 1935, the first issue of the journal *Democracia* appeared. Edited by Andrés Saborit, Besteiro's most loyal supporter, with collaboration from José Castro and Mariano Rojo, *Democracia* stood for the recreation of the PSOE in its traditional image – a party of few members, but with stability and strict discipline. In the first issue, Saborit stated, 'We are the living expression of a strong desire which beats in the breast of the UGT and the PSOE to return to its traditional and glorious tactics.'[62] In a sense, *Democracia* was a highly apposite vehicle for the Besteiro faction: several of its collaborators were political 'has-beens'. Manual Muiño was a former deputy; Lucio Martínez Gil a former secretary of the FNTT, and Esteban Martínez Hervás its former president; Trifón Gómez was former secretary of the Sindicato Nacional Ferroviario; Celestino García was a former deputy and councillor; and Mariano Rojo was a former deputy, a former provincial deputy and a former secretary of the FJSE.[63] Besteiro himself, of course, was a former leader of both the PSOE and the UGT.

Andrés Saborit remained editor of *Democracia* throughout all of its twenty-seven issues. He firmly believed that Socialist principles had been betrayed by the radical stance of the Caballeristas, asserting in the second issue of the journal that they had 'no moral authority' behind them. The emphasis on moral superiority, so redolent of *pablismo*, was a constant feature of *Democracia*. Also prominent was a glorification of the PSOE's past, amounting in effect to the view that the party's route forward lay behind it.[64] In political terms, *Democracia* stood for a modification of traditional Socialist isolationism by backing the Republican initiative to defend democracy; indeed, the third issue of the journal carried Prieto's 14 April article, 'Ante la contienda electoral'. The corollary of this position was a rejection of all alliances with other workers' groups, perhaps a rather unlikely point of contact between Saborit and the Caballeristas. In fact, though, the editorial line of *Democracia* was that there existed no ideological disputes within the PSOE:

There are no real ideological tendencies amongst us. There remain, survive, remnants of personalistic tendencies, of extreme bourgeois bad manners.[65]

Essentially, *Democracia* was little more than a vehicle for Besteiro's struggle, articulated mainly by Saborit, against Largo Caballero.[66] Its polemics with *Claridad*, the Caballerista journal set up in July 1935, assumed such a degree of bitterness that in December, following the reappearance of *El Socialista*, the PSOE National Committee urged both papers to cease publication. *Democracia* did so, but was replaced by *Los Marxistas*, edited by Gabriel Mario de Coca, a fervent supporter of Besteiro. Only two issues of *Los Marxistas* appeared, presenting Besteiro as an 'inextinguishable light' against the 'shameful bolshevisation' being encouraged by Caballero. Mario de Coca's attacks on the jailed Socialist leader were to reach their apogee in March 1936, with the publication of *Anti-Caballero*, a sustained defence of Besteiro against the 'bolshevising menace'.[67]

Meanwhile, however, the Caballeristas took up the cudgels through the pages of *Claridad*. Edited by Carlos de Baraibar, *Claridad* became the principal mouthpiece for the Socialist Left. The first issue carried a long article by Enrique de Francisco, originally submitted to *El Liberal*, criticising Prieto, who was attacked on the rather flimsy grounds of having broken party rules by making public a private discussion in his *Posiciones socialistas*. A further series of articles, under the title 'Against vanity and arrogance', was directed against the Asturian Socialists.[68] *Claridad*, however, was to become, alongside *Leviatán*, an important motor force in the establishment of meaningful contacts between the Socialist Left and other Spanish Marxist groups. Its theoretical position, expressed most clearly by Baraibar, Araquistáin, Rodolfo Llopis and Julio Alvarez del Vayo, was constructed around four basic constants.

First, and central to the *Claridad* line, was the view that the proletariat must take political power through the establishment of its own dictatorship. The relationship between the bourgeoisie and the proletariat was seen in bipolar terms, its resolution able to come about only through confrontation. In the words of Rodolfo Llopis, the deputy for Alicante,

The state has to be conquered. Correct. But let no one be deceived. We are not dealing with a partial conquest of political power, but rather the complete and total domination of power by the proletariat.[69]

Luis Araquistáin looked to the works of Lenin for doctrinal support for the imposition of a dictatorship of the proletariat, while Baraibar spoke of the 'necessity for the proletariat to take possession of the bourgeois state and destroy it immediately in order to substitute its *own* State'.[70] Second, and following on from the call for a dictatorship of the proletariat, there was a total rejection of parliamentary democracy, seen as an instrument proper to the bourgeoisie. This view found confirmation for the left Socialists in the experience of the first *bienio*, during which all the moderate reforms proposed by the PSOE met with harsh resistance from the Right. Third, there were consistent calls for the purging of the reformist sectors from the party. Largo Caballero, in a series of interviews conducted by Santiago Carrillo and published in *Claridad* between 23 November and 21 December 1935, spoke of the need for a radical restructuring of the PSOE. Largo was merely confirming statements made in October, which amounted to a call for democratic centralism.[71] Fourth, and most important, there emerged calls, particularly from FJSE members, for the unification of the proletariat. This was of the greatest significance, as it marked the move away from isolationist rejection of other Marxist groups. While the Youth Movement had in fact been open to such a development for some time, for Largo Caballero to support such calls represented a fundamental change in stance.

Despite repeated rejection since October 1934 of all unity initiatives from the PCE, towards the end of the following year Largo not only lent tacit support to such initiatives – in particular the unification of the UGT and the CGTU – but actually insisted on the inclusion of the Communists in any electoral front involving the PSOE. Four main reasons can be adduced for this change. First, and most obviously, Largo was anxious to avoid political marginalisation should Prieto succeed, as seemed increasingly likely, in reformulating the Republican–Socialist electoral alliance with Azaña. Since the end of May, the leader of Izquierda Republicana had been giving a series of open-air lectures, known as the 'Discursos en campo abierto', which culminated in a triumphant speech at the Campo de Comillas, near Madrid, on 20 October.[72] Over 400,000 people thronged to hear Azaña call for the defence of the Republic and the re-establishment of the reforming legislation of the first *bienio*, above all agrarian reform – the 'spinal column' of the regime. Aware that a large proportion of his audience was Socialist, Azaña in characteristic manner alluded metaphorically to the need for any alliance with the PSOE to be based on strict respect for the Republic and its Constitution. The rapturous reception he received sounded a clear warning to the revolutionists that the tide of popular sentiment was not moving in their favour. Largo was forced to accept that Azaña, and therefore by implication Prieto, had caught the mood of the masses.[73]

The second reason for the Caballerista shift, and also for the popularity of the Azaña–Prieto message, was that in the summer and autumn of 1935 the Radical–CEDA government of Lerroux increasingly looked to be reaching the point of terminal crisis. An election was clearly possible at any moment. Indeed, Azaña exploited the difficulties of the government with precisely such an end in view. Throughout much of the summer, important areas of Spain had been under martial law. In September, his government damaged by the withdrawal of the Agrarian Party, Lerroux was forced to cede the premiership to Joaquín Chapaprieta, the independent deputy for Alicante. Early the following month, however, Lerroux – now foreign minister – was further damaged by rumours of a major scandal involving his nephew and adoptive son, Aurelio. In 1934, Aurelio Lerroux was one of a group of leading Radicals who had agreed to support Juan Pich y Pon, soon to be appointed governor of Catalonia, in a shady financial venture involving permission (which was subsequently withdrawn) to introduce a new type of roulette wheel to Spanish gaming houses. Known as the *straperlo*, after its inventors, Daniel Strauss, a Dutch impresario of Mexican nationality, and, according to the source used, either one or two others (Perl, Perlo, Perlowitz or Pérez and López) the roulette wheel was to bring about a dramatic decline in the fortunes of Alejandro Lerroux and the Radical Party.[74] The precise details of the deal are vague, but it is clear that Azaña was sufficiently appraised of the situation to allow him to threaten a revelation of the scandal in his Comillas speech should Lerroux not do so himself.[75] Lerroux was inevitably obliged to resign from the government, leaving the Radical–CEDA coalition broken in pieces. Thus, between November 1935 and January 1936, when Alcalá-Zamora was finally forced to call new elections, Spanish government remained effectively without direction. Largo Caballero could ill afford to allow Azaña and Prieto to step into the breach without a response; hence the need to move away from confrontation towards accommodation.

The third main reason for Largo's changed assessment is more nebulous. It is commonly asserted, though rather unlikely, that Largo 'discovered' Marxism while in jail.[76] It is certainly the case, however, that his Socialist comrades in the Modelo prison were mainly more radical members of the FJSE, like Carrillo, Hernández Zancajo and Del Rosal. As against Largo's instinctive caution, they espoused a no-holds-barred revolutionism which inevitably must have had some impact upon the ageing and rather humourless labour leader. The revolutionary enthusiasm of the FJSE members in a sense represented the other side of the collaborationist coin to that of the moderates: where Prieto looked to Azaña and the Republicans, they turned to the Marxists of the PCE, BOC and ICE. Conversations between the FJSE and the Communist Youth Movement, the Unión de Juventudes Comunistas (UJC), had started as early as October 1934. Little is known about the precise details of these conversations, which would ultimately lead to the unification of the two movements under Communist hegemony in April 1936.[77] However, the urge towards unity cannot have been lost on Largo.

The final influence on Largo Caballero, and perhaps the most important one, was the announcement by Georgii Dimitrov at the 7th Congress of the Communist International, held between July and August 1935, of the Popular Front strategy. Clearly, the official adoption of a policy which to some extent was already being carried out – José Díaz, the PCE secretary-general had issued an appeal on 2 June in Madrid for the creation of a 'Popular anti-fascist concentration' – left Largo in a difficult position.[78] Suddenly, there loomed the prospect of an anti-fascist electoral coalition involving all groups other than his own; worse, the new PCE line placed the Communists firmly in the Prieto camp. Largo's response was typical: in order to avoid political marginalisation, he adopted the well-worn tactic of stealing his opponents' thunder. Where previously he had opposed all unification initiatives from the PCE, he now became a firm advocate of their inclusion in any joint agreement with the Republicans. *Claridad* adopted a line supportive of the 7th Congress of the Comintern, with Alvarez del Vayo leading the way. This was an astute move, for in reality neither Prieto, and still less Azaña, actually wanted to deal with the Communists. The Republican leader had written to Prieto in April, stating

Where can we, or you, go with the Communists? The coalition with the Socialists, for a task to be carried out by Republicans in power, is legitimate, normal and desirable... With the Communists it is not the same. Moreover, electorally, without bringing us any appreciable number of votes, they will frighten the electorate and distort, to our disadvantage, the nature of the coalition.[79]

Thus, when the Executive Commission of the PSOE met in the Modelo prison on 16 November to discuss Manuel Azaña's formal invitation, sent two days earlier, to participate in an electoral coalition of the parties of the Left, Largo not only accepted with alacrity, but suggested that the invitation be extended to the PCE also.[80] Indeed, Largo pressured the Executives of the PSOE, the UGT and the FJSE to reach an extensive syndical and political agreement with the PCE, in the belief that this would balance the favoured relationship that Prieto enjoyed through Azaña with the Republicans. Far from being an obstacle whose resistance to the formation of the Popular Front coalition had to be broken down by the Comintern representative, Jacques Duclos, Largo was an enthusiastic, if tardy, supporter of the idea. To demonstrate this new-found conviction, the UGT now responded favourably, after months of rigidity, to a proposal from the Communist union body, the CGTU, for unification.[81] Unsurprisingly, the merger was not universally welcomed: dissent was expressed in the Prietista bastion of Vizcaya, while the moderate UGT president, Anastasio de Gracia, also had strong reservations.[82]

Nonetheless, Largo's insistence on the PCE's inclusion in the Popular Front coalition, which contradicts the conventional wisdom on his supposed intransigence, allowed that coalition to assume a wider ambit than had been in the original intentions of either Prieto or Azaña. At the same time, however, it highlighted the extent to which considerations of theory were relegated to a secondary role behind political pragmatism in Largo's schema. In particular, it gave rise to the bizarre situation of a latterly bolshevised leader of an essentially reformist political movement preaching revolution, yet insisting on the presence of a genuinely Bolshevik party in an expressly reformist electoral coalition. In a sense, pragmatism became the driving force behind the politics of the entire Marxist Left towards the end of 1935 and start of 1936: all the various self-defined revolutionary Marxist groups would ultimately seek entry to the Popular Front coalition, reflecting their acute appreciation of the centrality to their political prospects of preventing the Right from holding on to power. Equally, however, involvement in the moderate coalition obliged them to engage in often tortuous exercises in theoretical gymnastics.

Of the Marxist groups in question, it was the PCE which was able to marshal the most coherent justification at the level of theory for its entry into the Popular Front coalition. Indeed, the PCE had first suggested the idea of an inter-class bloc to halt fascism as early as March 1933, although the suggestion was somewhat limited by the constraints of Third Period class versus class sectarianism. It was really only after the June 1935 call for a *bloque popular antifascista*, but more especially the 7th Congress of the Comintern in August, that the PCE was in a position to attempt to tailor its theory to the prevailing political situation in Spain. Unfortunately, although the Communist Party's vision of the Popular Front elaborated after the Comintern congress had the virtue of theoretical clarity and practical coherence, it had the defect that its theoretical clarity remained dependent on Comintern directives and was therefore inappropriate to the Spanish situation, while its practical coherence effectively amounted to capitulating before the proposals for unity put forward by Manuel Azaña.

The basis of these proposals was contained in a Republican declaration of April 1935 which had listed the minimum conditions for political co-operation in Spain.[83] Essentially moderate, the seven-point declaration constituted the outline of what was eventually to be the Popular Front programme: it called for the re-establishment of Constitutional guarantees, the release of those imprisoned as a result of the October 1934 rising, the legalisation of trade union activity, the prevention of torture of political prisoners, an end to discrimination against left-wing and liberal civil servants, the reinstatement in their jobs of workers dismissed after the October rising, and the reconstitution of town councils overthrown by the government. In order to make its theory match such a programme, the PCE was obliged to adapt its stagist conception of the revolution: it now spoke of the first stage, the bourgeois-democratic, being divided into two sub-stages. The first of these would be restricted to the enactment of the Popular Front programme, while the second would see the completion of the bourgeois-democratic stage, prior to moving on to the Socialist stage. This Procrustean approach was inevitable, given, in the words of Fernando Claudín,

the Comintern's belief that it possessed the absolute truth of Marxism: that the proletarian revolution could now be led only by the Comintern; that the Soviet model was essential for every country; that the 'Marxist-Leninist party' had to be structured and to work on the lines of the type of party created by the Comintern; that the Comintern had the only correct theory of the Spanish revolution; that the policy of the Popular Front was as suitable for Spain as for France or Italy; that a 'Marxist-Leninist' party had to consider Trotskyism the most pernicious of all heresies. . .[84]

In fact, by late 1935 Trotskyism in Spain was not so much pernicious as penurious. The principal Trotskyist organisation, the ICE, faced the problem of being based almost exclusively in Catalonia, where it was just one among a welter of leftist groups, including, most obviously, the Anarcho-syndicalist CNT, but also other non-Stalinist communist groups such as Maurín's BOC as well as strong Republican forces like the Esquerra Republicana. Moreover, in the aftermath of October 1934, its leader Andreu Nin had fallen out with his mentor and former employer, Leon Trotsky, over the relationship between the ICE and the PSOE. The exiled Russian leader instructed his former secretary Nin that the ICE should infiltrate the PSOE in order to strengthen the Socialists' revolutionary credentials.[85] This was deemed especially opportune as Largo Caballero and the increasingly radical Youth movement, the FJSE, appeared to hold sway in the party. In Trotsky's view, the Spanish revolution was under the hegemony of the bourgeoisie and petty bourgeoisie, and the task for communists in Spain, therefore, was to win over the masses for the coming proletarian revolution.[86]

Nin, however, was afraid that the PSOE was too powerful and that his own grouping would simply be subsumed by a party which had always shown itself at moments of truth to be thoroughly reformist. He therefore drew closer politically to Maurín, whose views on the centrality of the struggle between the bourgeoisie and proletariat he shared and who was also a long-standing friend. By doing so, it is arguable that he committed a crucial political error by opening the way for the PCE to steal a march on the Catalan Marxists. As has already been argued, the revolutionary Marxist groups were dependent on the PSOE if they were to have a future political presence, since on their own they lacked sufficient support – hence Maurín's advocacy of the Alianza obrera. However, Nin's refusal to foment formal ties with the PSOE allowed in the Communists, who were to win over the FJSE in early 1936. Had the BOC and the ICE entered the PSOE and strengthened its left wing, the appeal of the Comintern to the Socialist Youth movement might well have been reduced. As it was, the PCE coup in early 1936 turned out to be a significant step on its march towards establishing its own political hegemony over the Left during the Civil War.[87]

Throughout 1935, Nin increasingly distanced himself from Trotsky, leaving the ICE virtually rudderless in the choppy seas of Catalan politics. Moreover, the ban on its journal, *Comunismo*, after the October rising left the ICE without an effective propaganda organ, further contributing to its growing sense of political isolation. Nin therefore turned to his Catalan counterpart in the BOC, Joaquín Maurín, with whom he joined forces on 25 September 1935, to form the Partido Obrero de Unificación Marxista (POUM). The POUM has often mistakenly been designated as Trotskyist; in point of fact, the POUM quickly joined the London Bureau of Revolutionary Socialist Parties, much to Trotsky's disgust.[88] Indeed, far from being an explicitly Trotskyist organisation, the POUM in a sense represented the eclipse of Trotskyism in Spain.

Of the new organisation's two constituent groups, Maurín's BOC was clearly dominant.[89] Maurín remained convinced that the specific form of proletarian power in Spain could be organised only through the Alianza obrera, given that the Alianza was designed to represent the entire proletariat through the fusing of all its political and syndical organisations into one body. The Alianza was therefore not just an instrument designed to bring about a united workers' front, but equally an instrument for the taking and exercising of power. The formation of the POUM was the closest that Maurín would come to the realisation of his long-cherished dream of the Spanish proletariat united in one organisation. He had hoped, as evidenced in a polemic conducted with the FJSE leader, Santiago Carrillo, in August and September 1935, to persuade the left Socialists and the PCE to join the new formation. Such a hope, though, was never realistic: the PCE would always be bound by Comintern directives, while a mainly Catalan-based organisation was never likely to appeal to the FJSE and the Caballeristas with their strongholds in the Agrupación Socialista Madrileña. Instead, the POUM was condemned from its birth to a marginal role in Spanish politics. For all its protestations of the need for an Alianza obrera, the POUM was able to do little except repeat its calls virtually *ad nauseam* and condemn the moves towards a Popular Front. Indeed, it could be argued that like Nin and the ICE, Maurín's refusal to entertain the idea of taking the BOC into the PSOE in order to help resolve that party's dilemma, expressed by Carrillo in terms of 'the elimination of one or the other, either Marxists or reformists', significantly eased the path to the later unification of the FJSE and the Unión de Juventudes Comunistas (UJC).[90] Ultimately, the POUM would be forced to seek somewhat humiliating last-minute entry to the Popular Front.

In the meanwhile, the Caballerista wing of the PSOE appeared caught in a conundrum of its own. Its theoretical confusion was reflected in two polemical debates between Largo's first lieutenant, Luis Araquistáin, and Vicente Uribe, the editor of the Communist journal, *Mundo Obrero*. Conducted in August 1935 and March 1936 through the pages of *Leviatán* and *Claridad* on the one hand, and the Communist *Pueblo* on the other, the arguments centred on the nature of the revolution required in Spain. Whereas Uribe argued, in line with the Comintern analysis, that the Popular Front must aim to consolidate the bourgeois-democratic phase of a two-stage revolution, Araquistáin maintained that there existed no possibility of consolidating the Republic: 'The historic dilemma is fascism or Socialism, and only violence will decide it.'[91] Largo, as has been shown, continued to call for a purging of the reformists from the party. In short, the left Socialists appeared to be arguing that the Popular Front coalition was at one and the same time both necessary and irrelevant.[92]

Such confusion should not be seen as altogether surprising. The already rather restricted theoretical formulations of the left Socialists were inevitably exacerbated by further restrictions immanent to Marxism. Principal among these is the imprecision which lies at the heart of the relationship between Marxism and democracy. Marxist discourse up to the 1930s – indeed, up until the 1970s when 'Eurocommunism' attempted to define a 'Third Way' to Socialism – remained trapped within the parameters of a seemingly immutable division between 'reformism' and 'revolution'.[93] For the PSOE bolshevisers, this dichotomy allowed of a fatefully simplistic interpretation: since reformism had failed in Spain during the Second Republic, as evidenced by the failures of the Left during the first *bienio* and the rise of the Right thereafter, then the only logical path left to achieve Socialism was through revolution. Conveniently, the Right in the shape of José María Gil Robles and the CEDA gave every indication throughout 1935 of wishing to confirm the equally simplistic assertion that the choice in Spain lay between Socialism and fascism. Theoretical sophistication was neither required nor offered: the choice was straightforward and stark. However, there was a great gulf between rhetoric and reality, and whereas it made sense within the limited terms of Caballerista maximalism to call for revolution, it was never likely that this would be translated into actual practice. The PSOE as an organisation was simply not geared towards revolutionary adventurism. This much was demonstrated by the entry of the Caballeristas into a Popular Front coalition which was in reality the creation of Manual Azaña and Indalecio Prieto.

Indeed, events in Spain during the twilight weeks of 1935 followed a seemingly inexorable course towards the formal constitution of the

Popular Front electoral coalition. The final collapse of the Radical–CEDA coalition in November 1935, and the knowledge that a general election was inevitable, lent an added urgency to the negotiations between the Republicans and the Left over the details of the Popular Front agreement. Within the PSOE, the struggle between Largo Caballero and Prieto reached a new pitch of intensity as each tried to assert his own control over the Socialist electoral platform. Largo, who had consistently since May acted to postpone any meeting of the National Committee of the PSOE or UGT, now relaxed his opposition. At the National Committee meeting of the UGT on 11 December, Largo led the call for electoral co-operation with the Republicans, and argued that nationalisation of the land and the Bank must be made a central plank of any Popular Front manifesto. He also suggested that the Socialist programme should be submitted to the PCE and CGTU for approval prior to being forwarded to the Republicans. This provoked the ire of Prieto, who was able to gain revenge at the National Committee meeting of the PSOE, held on 16 December, by obliging Largo to resign over the issue of the relationship between the party's Executive and the parliamentary minority;[94] for the first time since 1920, the PSOE and UGT had what amounted to entirely independent leaderships. Largo's resignation from the PSOE Executive left Prieto a clear path in his negotiations with Azaña, thereby ensuring that the final content of the Popular Front manifesto would be decidedly moderate.[95] Largo, in the meanwhile, utilised his continued control of the UGT to move still closer to the Communists, attempting to ensure that the PCE would be present in the Popular Front *comité electoral*. Azaña's refusal to accept this led to Largo's abstaining from the *comité*, strengthening still further Prieto's position.[96]

In mid-December 1935, the Republicans decided that they would negotiate only with the PSOE. Largo responded by threatening that if the PCE were not allowed to sign the pact, then the UGT would refuse as well. On 4 January 1936, the Republicans agreed to negotiate with the UGT; the following day Largo proposed that the PSOE be allowed to act in the name of the other leftist groups. After further tension and disagreement over the presence of the Communists, the electoral pact was finally signed on 15 January 1936. The signatories were Amos Salvador for Azaña's Izquierda Republicana; Bernardo Giner de los Ríos for Unión Republicana; Manuel Cordero and Juan-Siméon Vidarte for the PSOE; Francisco Largo Caballero for the UGT; José Cazorla for the FJSE; Vicente Uribe for the PCE; Angel Pestaña for the tiny Partido Sindicalista; and Juan Andrade for the POUM.[97] The details of the pact, which rejected nationalisation of the land and of the Bank, as well as workers' control, represented a near total triumph for the Republicans. Equally, the results of the elections of 16 February, although highly disputed, again confirmed the validity of the

assessment shared by Azaña and Prieto over the importance of collaboration and moderation. Despite a small increase in the number of votes
received by the Right, overall victory went to the Popular Front coalition.
Significantly, it has been pointed out that 'in each slate in each province the
most moderate groups won the most votes'.[98]

Nonetheless, the spring of 1936 confirmed what the Asturian rising of
October 1934 and its aftermath had already suggested: that the antagon-
isms of Spanish society which had been endemic throughout the nineteenth
century – confrontations between landowners and peasants, Catholics and
anti-clericals, regionalists and centralists, especially military ones, and
between industrial workers and employers – were now beyond any
conceivable peaceful compromise. Immediately the election results were
known, exuberant workers set about reaping revenge for the starvation and
wage-cuts of the *bienio negro* and for the brutal repression which had
followed the Asturian rising. Ricardo Zabalza, the dynamic secretary-
general of the FNTT, urged the prompt return to their lands of lease-
holders expelled in 1935, and the re-establishment of the *jurados mixtos*.[99]
However, economic circumstances ensured that these reforms, which were
essential to alleviate the misery of the landless peasants, could not be
absorbed by the owners without a significant redistribution of rural
wealth. Throughout March the FNTT encouraged its members to take the
law into their own hands, particularly where they had been the victims of
eviction. In Salamanca and Toledo there were small-scale invasions of
estates. However, only in Badajoz were there mass land-seizures. Indeed,
after a bitter clash between peasants and the Civil Guard in Yeste
(Albacete), in which seventeen peasants were killed, as many wounded,
and fifty FNTT members arrested, it was remarkable that the FNTT
managed to maintain the discipline of its members at all.[100]

The reaction of the Right to the victory of the Popular Front was abrupt.
The middle and upper classes began to feel that the 'red' violence they had
long been expecting was about to inundate society. The CEDA's failure to
secure electoral success meant the end of legalism. Many began to look for
more militant leadership and turned from Gil Robles to José Calvo Sotelo,
the extremist leader of the monarchist group Renovación Española.[101]
However, once convinced that the legal road to corporativism was
blocked, Gil Robles did everything possible to help those who were
committed to violence. Indeed, as Preston has shown, he had already made
two crucial contributions to the success of the 1936 rising – the creation of
mass right-wing militancy, and the undermining of Socialist faith in the
possibilities of bourgeois democracy.[102] It could be argued that the Right's
reaction to the Popular Front election victory was hardly surprising –
landowners saw the prospect of accelerated land reform, employers
dreaded the return of the *jurados mixtos*, the Church feared the enforce-

ment of the anti-clerical clauses of the Constitution and army officers realised that now there would be no redress for Azaña's reforms and no way of preventing the promotion of Republican officers.[103] However, the virulence of the CEDA election campaign, with its brutal rhetoric of the Jewish–Masonic–Communist conspiracy poised to enslave Spain, had already shown that the Right was poorly prepared for either moderation or compromise. The consequent abandonment of legalism was starkly demonstrated by the startling rise of the Falange Española, which cashed in on middle-class disillusionment with the CEDA's failed tactic. The CEDA's youth movement, the Juventud de Acción Popular (JAP), went over to the Falange *en masse*, attracted by its code of violence. The Falangists soon emulated and even outstripped the Anarchists with their terrorist squads, bombings and assassinations.[104]

Thus, despite evidence of a generalised desire for moderation amongst the Spanish electorate in the February elections, political degeneration soon set in. The counterpoint of violence between Left and Right, both real and rhetorical, daily made the possibilities of political stability more remote. In large measure, the activities of the Right were a conscious attempt to create an atmosphere of disorder which would justify the implantation of a regime of authority. They helped to ensure the escalation of a spiral of mindless violence which rendered rational discussion impossible. In the midst of the conflict stood the new government, weak and effectively paralysed. By an arrangement made prior to the elections, only Republicans sat in the Cabinet.[105] Although Azaña, as Prime Minister, produced a programme which catered for speedier agrarian reform, the main tenor of the government was one of moderation and caution; as Azaña said, 'we want no dangerous innovations. We want peace and order.' Before he could implement his plans, however, there occurred a constitutional crisis in which the President, Niceto Alcalá-Zamora, virtually bereft of support, was deposed.[106] Azaña was elected in his place. In many ways, this was a severe blow for the Republic, since Azaña was one of the few men of sufficient stature and influence to be able to maintain control in such troubled times. His elevation to the presidency removed him from direct political involvement. Moreover, the new Prime Minister, Santiago Casares Quiroga, a victim of tuberculosis, was not the man to provide strong or effective leadership.

A more positive choice as Prime Minister would have been Indalecio Prieto. Indeed, on 11 May, immediately after assuming the Presidency, Azaña had asked the moderate Socialist leader to form a government. In turn, Prieto elaborated a series of measures designed to restore order and implement a series of reforms which would undermine the power of the Right.[107] However, Prieto harboured few illusions that his nomination would be accepted by the PSOE parliamentary minority, headed by Largo

Caballero. On 12 May the Vizcayan leader's suggestion to his party that the PSOE recommend a broad Popular Front government was defeated by the counter-proposal of Julio Alvarez del Vayo, a close supporter of Largo at the time, that there should be an all-Republican cabinet.[108] Prieto accepted defeat virtually without argument. Giving in to one of his bouts of fatalistic pessimism, he believed that his own party would not support him and that in any case Azaña did not really want him as Prime Minister. In fact, the PSOE Executive and National Committee were solidly behind him, and there is no evidence that Azaña was less than sincere in his request. Nonetheless, when Juan-Simeón Vidarte, the party secretary, urged him to form a government in the confidence that when the crunch came Largo would not vote against him in the Cortes, Prieto replied bitterly, '*Que se vaya Caballero a la mierda*' (Caballero can go to hell).[109]

The Socialists were becoming increasingly divided. In essence, the division was between the followers of Prieto, who was prepared to collaborate with the government, and the supporters of Largo Caballero, who was not. As such, the central conflict remained the same as it had been when the Republic was established in 1931. In other words, the relationship between Socialism and democracy remained ambiguous. Where Prieto's horizons extended only to the consolidation of the Republic and its government, Largo envisaged the short-term assumption of exclusive power by the Socialists. This would come about in one of two ways: either the PSOE would take power constitutionally as soon as the government's promised reforms had been enacted, or else through revolution, should the military stage a coup.[110] Prieto's failure to become Prime Minister was a tragedy for the Republic and for Spain. Prieto realised, as did few others, that attempts at revolutionary social change would only enrage the middle classes and drive them to fascism and armed counter-revolution. Instead, Prieto was convinced that the answer was to calm things down, to strengthen the government by the inclusion of Socialists, and then for the Socialists to introduce legislation to make 'the power of the working class indestructible'.[111] However, Prieto's power in the PSOE was more than matched by Largo's in the UGT.

While Prieto counselled caution, Largo Caballero did exactly the reverse. Intoxicated by Communist flattery, the so-called 'Spanish Lenin' toured Spain, prophesying the inevitable triumph of the coming revolution to crowds of cheering workers. In March 1936, his grip on the Socialist movement had been considerably strengthened. Early in the month Caballeristas had won all the leading seats in the Agrupación Socialista Madrileña, the strongest section in the party. Then, on 16 March, he was elected president of the PSOE parliamentary minority. With the UGT playing a far more political role than ever before, the Caballerista grip on the movement appeared unshakeable.[112] Largo, however, then made a bad error which would weaken both his own position and that of the PSOE as a whole. Julio Alvarez del Vayo, the pro-Communist PSOE deputy for Madrid and vice-president of the ASM, had arranged with the Comintern agent, Victorio Codovilla, for the unification of the Socialist and Communist youth movements. The creation of the Juventudes Socialistas Unificadas (JSU) in April 1936 seemed to fulfil part of Largo's ambition to unify the working class under PSOE hegemony. In reality, though, it simply meant the loss of 40,000 young Socialists to the PCE.[113] Nonetheless, the full implications of the merger for the strength of the Socialist movement would not become apparent until some months later when the majority of the FJSE leadership, headed by Santiago Carrillo, actually joined the PCE itself.[114]

In the meantime, Largo continued to engage in revolutionary rhetoric which served to undermine the Republic, since the government had no control over apparent Socialist radicalism, yet suffered the right-wing opprobrium it stimulated. It will always remain debatable whether Largo Caballero was ever genuine in his revolutionary pronouncements. Essentially a pragmatist concerned to further the interests of his UGT members, Largo tended to 'lead from behind'. For all the rhetoric, the only real weapon available to the Left in early 1936, the revolutionary general strike, was neither used nor even prepared. Indeed, when genuine proposals for revolution were made in April by the POUM leader, Joaquín Maurín, they were abruptly rejected by the Caballeristas in the Socialist movement.[115] Ultimately, Largo's conception of revolution was passive, dependent on responding to events rather than initiating them.[116] In this, Largo was wholly representative of the traditional procedures of Spanish Socialism. Revolution was bandied as a threat, but one which it was hoped to avoid having to translate into reality. Such tactics, as Prieto appreciated, were always likely to lead to an escalation of extremist rhetorical bids between Left and Right. By mid-1936 the stakes in this particular game of bluff had been raised beyond the Socialists' ability to pay. When General Franco finally rose against the Republic on 17 July, it was not the PSOE or UGT which unleashed a revolutionary response, but rather the true purveyors of revolution in Spain – the Anarchists of the CNT, supported by the dissident Communists of the POUM.

Conclusion

The central feature which has emerged from this study is that from its foundation in 1879, the PSOE was always marked by a profound ideological ambiguity. This ambiguity centred on the nature of the relationship between Socialism and democracy. Essentially, the PSOE Marxists never worked out clearly either the aims or the methods of their struggle. Most critically, the concept of revolution was never formally elaborated; instead, it was referred to in only the most unspecific terms as the inevitable precursor to an equally inevitable Socialist future. This left the PSOE operating within a vague hinterland between a grudging gradualist, parliamentary legalism and occasional essays at a revolutionary overthrow of the state, most notably in 1917 and 1934. Neither approach was founded upon a coherently developed Marxist analysis of the socio-political and economic situation in Spain at any given moment. Thus it was that there emerged such a consistent pattern of division and failure within the PSOE. Indeed, the 'radicalisation' of the PSOE during the Republic, far from representing a new phase within the development of the party, actually represented a logical culmination of tensions which had always existed within its heart.

In part, the PSOE's ideological ambiguity reflected divisions over the aims, goal and methods of revolution which are immanent to Marxism itself, and which retain their significance even today. The debates over 'Eurocommunism' in the 1970s and 1980s can be seen as simply the latest in a long line of attempts to confront the question of the relationship between parliamentary democracy and Socialism. In essence, there are three basic Marxist approaches to the issue of revolutionary strategy and tactics: the minority seizure of power prior to changing society; the seizure of power by workers after they have become a majority; and the reformist transformation of society from within. As so often with Marxism, the origins of these divisions can be traced back to the multiplicity of available interpretations of the views of Marx and Engels themselves. *All* Marxist political groups have had to confront these issues; indeed, they can be seen as central to the division between the Mensheviks and Bolsheviks in early twentieth-century Russia and the subsequent split within the international Socialist movement between Communism and social democracy.

However, precisely because these divisions must be seen as immanent to Marxism, they fail on their own to explain the poverty of the Spanish variant. Instead, the present study has sought answers in specific Spanish factors. Two were principal amongst these: first, the dependence of the early Spanish Marxists on their French neighbours, particularly Jules Guesde, Gabriel Deville and Paul Lafargue, for an introduction to the Marxist canon. This led to the early implantation of a distorted, mechanistic interpretation of Marxist thought, devoid of the subtleties and richness characteristic of the original works by Marx himself. Second, however, this already distorted view of Marxism was further mediated by the twin intellectual influences of an all-pervasive Catholicism, and of Krausism, an obscure yet remarkably influential moralist philosophy which permeated the world-view of several leading liberal intellectuals in Spain. Together, these two influences militated against the elaboration of a coherent Marxist identity within the movement and contributed to its tendency towards conceptual confusion. Equally, they exacerbated the split between revolutionary rhetoric and reformist practice which became so characteristic of the Spanish Socialist movement.

Moreover, these handicaps were worsened by the context within which the Spanish Socialist movement emerged. Unlike their contemporaries in France, from whom in large measure they derived their ideological identity, the first Spanish Socialists were faced by a repressive state in which, under the Restoration Monarchy (1875–1931), political power remained in the hands of a narrowly class-based reactionary oligarchy. The basic aim of this oligarchy was to guard against all threats to the landed interest. From this simple fact derived the central tragedy of Spanish Socialism. On the one hand, the leaders of the Socialist movement never analysed and therefore never fully understood the nature and function of the Spanish state. On the other, and as a consequence, they failed to appreciate the crucial significance of the agrarian question in Spain. Indeed, the predominance of agricultural production rendered meaningless their oft-expressed fatalistic prediction of revolution led by the industrial proletariat. Similarly, the electoral corruption of the Restoration Monarchy made a nonsense, at least prior to the twentieth century, of the Socialists' scrupulously legalistic participation in the charades which went by the name of general elections.

Instead of expending major effort on responding to landworkers' needs and establishing a presence within rural areas, the Spanish Socialist movement under the domination of its founding father, Pablo Iglesias, devoted attention to the establishment of a Madrid-based bureaucratic organisation. In so doing it helped cede the political initiative to the Anarchist movement both in rural areas and in the nascent industrial heartland around Barcelona. Indeed, as if to compensate for the inadequacies of its theoretical insights, the PSOE retreated into a kind of *pablista* organisational ghetto characterised by an overarching concern with issues of party structure. Moreover, the PSOE guarded its organisational independence jealously: joint initiatives with other workers' groups were generally shunned. On those few occasions when the Socialists ventured into joint activity with the Anarchists, as happened briefly between 1917 and 1923 and again during the Second Republic, the *pablista* party sought to dominate the partnership. This attempt to maintain predominance within the Spanish workers' movement in fact reached its apogee during the Republic, and was a central factor in the divisions which so damaged the Left between 1931 and 1936. Moves towards united action with other workers' organisations were acceptable to the Socialists only so long as they were established on the PSOE's or UGT's own terms.

The Socialists found it easier to contemplate collaboration with Republican groups, especially after the Conjunction of 1909 which marked the end of the PSOE's initial period of totally intransigent isolationism. However, collaboration with the Republicans, justified in terms of helping the latter in their historic mission of completing the bourgeois revolution, pulled the PSOE ever more firmly in the direction of reformist parliamentary tactics. It is the main argument of this study that ultimately the PSOE was a Marxist organisation only in the sense of rhetorical self-definition and delusion. Moreover, it was *never* a revolutionary organisation. This was shown starkly in August 1917 and October 1934. On both occasions the PSOE leadership found itself drawn reluctantly into ill-judged revolutionary initiatives for which it was not suited either organisationally or temperamentally. The result in each case was heavy defeat by the state, followed by repression and internal splits. In both 1920–1 and 1936–7 significant sectors of the Youth Movement, dismayed at the leadership's lack of revolutionary resolve, seceded to join forces with the Communists.

It is thus evident that a consistent pattern of tension emerged within the Socialist movement at key moments of political crisis, notably 1917–23 and 1931–6. This can hardly be overstressed. The so-called 'radicalisation' of the PSOE after 1933, about which so much has been written and to which so much has been ascribed, reflected in many aspects the earlier divisions within the party. On each occasion the PSOE was severely damaged by a bitter struggle between majority reformists and minority revolutionists; on each occasion the reformists ultimately retained control of the Socialist organisation only at the cost of a significant loss of membership. However, a central argument of this study is that on each occasion the divisions were intensified by the fact that neither the reformists nor the revolutionists were able to provide a coherent theoretical underpinning to their position. In the final analysis, revolutionism and reformism within the Socialist movement were simply abstractions, poorly articulated and divorced from political reality. Marxism was mouthed, but it was never understood. Of course, all Marxists face acute problems when stubborn reality refuses to conform to predetermined theoretical schemata; in the case of the Marxists in the PSOE before the Civil War these problems were aggravated by their poor grasp of both theory and reality.

Finally, it should be said that it has never been the intention of this study to make the implicit argument that better theory would have led automatically to better, or more successful, political practice. Instead, it is merely contended in this regard that good theory is probably a necessary, but certainly not on its own sufficient, condition for successful action. That much can be seen by contrasting the fortunes of the Spanish Socialists with their counterparts in both Germany and Italy, where greater theoretical sophistication was of limited value in the struggle against fascism. The concomitant to this position, though, is that bad theory generally leads to disaster. Both points can be seen most clearly in Spain by contrasting the fortunes of the PSOE with those of their rivals in the BOC and the ICE. Under the leadership of Joaquín Maurín and Andreu Nin, these two groups, which merged in 1935 to form the POUM, were the source of the most advanced and sophisticated Marxism known in Spain up to that point. However, their sophistication served little purpose while they remained unable to command sufficient support to translate theory into practice. For this reason, like the Communists, the Catalan-based Marxists were ultimately forced during the Republic to bow to the imperious force of *Realpolitik*.

The logic of that force led ultimately to the creation of the Popular Front alliance, an essentially defensive front which aimed to save Spain from fascism. An expressly reformist formation, it was sponsored principally by Manual Azaña and Indalecio Prieto, the two outstanding non-Marxist leaders on the Spanish Left. For all the subtlety of their analyses of the political situation in Spain, Marxists like Maurín and Nin found themselves obliged to join a reformist alliance which represented the negation of all they claimed to stand for. Equally, the less sophisticated Marxists of the PSOE's 'radical' wing were also obliged to tailor their maximalist claims according to political circumstance. The Popular Front itself, of course, can be seen as representing the final triumph of the reformists within the PSOE. It also represented the effective formal abandonment of Marxism within the Spanish Socialist movement.

Notes

1 Decaffeinated Marxists: the PSOE, 1879–1914

1 The idea that the Socialists must bear major responsibility for the collapse of the Second Republic was first given academic 'respectability' by Salvador de Madariaga, *Spain* (London, 1942), p. 455. It still enjoys currency, as evidenced by the publication of Julio Merino, *Los socialistas rompen las urnas, 1933* (Barcelona, 1986).
2 See Richard A.H. Robinson, *The Origins of Franco's Spain* (Newton Abbot, 1970), Paul Preston, *The Coming of the Spanish Civil War* (London, 1978); Santos Juliá, 'Segunda República: por otro objeto de investigación', in Manuel Tuñón de Lara *et al.*, *Historiografía española contemporánea* (Madrid, 1980); Carolyn P. Boyd, ' "Responsibilities" and the Second Spanish Republic' in *European History Quarterly*, **14** (1984), pp. 151–82. For a fuller consideration of these debates, see chapters 5 and 6 below.
3 In Spanish, *descafeinado* has come to mean a weak version of an original item.
4 Luis Araquistáin, *El pensamiento español contemporáneo* (Buenos Aires, 1962), p. 98.
5 See, for instance, Anselmo Lorenzo, *El proletariado militante* (Madrid, 1974; first published in two volumes, 1901 and 1923), pp. 38–44. The story of Fanelli's arrival in Spain has become virtually a cliché, even though it is unlikely that one man – who did not even speak Spanish – can have had such a pronounced influence. For an alternative approach to the early implantation of Anarchism in Spain, see George Esenwein, 'Anarchist ideology and the Spanish working-class movement (1880–1900): with special reference to the ideas of Ricardo Mella' (Unpublished PhD thesis, University of London, 1986).
6 See Pierre Vilar, *Spain. A Brief History* (Exeter, 1977), pp. 76–80; J. Vicens Vives *et al.*, *Historia de España y América* (Barcelona, 1972; 5 vols.), vol. V, p. 327.
7 Madariaga, *Spain*, p. 15: 'By temperament and psychology the Andalusian tends to the philosophical anarchy of Kropotkin; environment and experience tempt him to follow the violent path of Bakunin.'; see also, pp. 118–19, 125. In similar vein, George Hills, *Spain* (London, 1970), pp. 107–8 and M. Cantarero del Castillo, *Tragedia del socialismo español* (Barcelona, 1971), pp. 48–54.
8 Virtually nothing exists in English on the Spanish Socialist movement before 1914. Most of the general histories have just a few lines; the most detailed studies remain Gerald Brenan, *The Spanish Labyrinth* (Cambridge, 2nd edn, 1950), pp. 215–21, now somewhat out of date though still important; and the

somewhat superficial account by Stanley Payne, *The Spanish Revolution* (London, 1970), pp. 62–8. A recent, synthetic account is Paul Heywood, 'The labour movement in Spain before 1914' in Dick Geary (ed.), *Labour and Socialist Movements in Europe before 1914* (London, 1989), pp. 231–65. In Spanish, far greater quantity has not always been matched by quality, although a number of important monographic studies have started to appear in recent years. Reference to these will be made in the remainder of this chapter. The historiography of the Spanish labour movement still lags behind that of other European countries, although that situation is now changing in relation to the Second Republic and the Civil War. Nonetheless, for the early period there remain basic questions to be answered. As Tomás Jiménez Araya has commented, 'the introduction of Marxism is still a question not even satisfactorily posed by Spanish historiography', 'La introducción del marxismo en España: el Informe a la Comisión de Reformas Sociales de Jaime Vera', in *Anales de Economía*, 15 (July–September 1972), p. 107. For this reason, the present chapter concentrates on rather basic, though still fundamental, issues: ideology, organisation and leadership, for example.

9 The analysis here is based on Barrington Moore Jr., *The Social Origins of Dictatorship and Democracy* (London, 1967), chapter 8, pp. 433–52, and also on Paul Preston's 'Spain', in Stuart Woolf (ed.), *Fascism in Europe* (London, 1981), pp. 329–51. On the issue of bourgeois revolution in Spain, see especially Juan Sisinio Pérez Garzón, 'La revolución burguesa en España: los inicios de un debate científico, 1966–1979' in Tuñón de Lara (ed.), *Historiografía española*, pp. 91–138; see also, Alberto Gil Novales (ed.), *La revolución burguesa en España* (Madrid, 1985).

10 For political and historical details, see Raymond Carr, *Spain, 1808–1975* (Oxford, 1982), pp. 257–346; on the economic background, see Gabriel Tortella, 'La economía española a finales del siglo XIX y principios del siglo XX' in José Luis García Delgado (ed.), *La España de la Restauración* (Madrid, 1985), pp. 133–52; Jordi Nadal, 'The failure of the Industrial Revolution in Spain, 1830–1914' in Carlo M. Cipolla (ed.), *The Fontana Economic History of Europe* (Glasgow, 1973) vol. 4 (2), pp. 532–626.

11 See Miguel Artola, 'El sistema político de la Restauración' in García Delgado (ed.), *La España de la Restauración*, pp. 11–20; Robert W. Kern, *Liberals, Reformers and Caciques in Restoration Spain, 1875–1909* (Albuquerque, 1974), pp. 40–53.

12 On *caciquismo* see Joaquín Costa, *Oligarquía y caciquismo* (2 vols., Madrid, 1975); Joaquín Romera Maura, '*Caciquismo* as a political system' in Ernest Gellner and John Waterbury (eds.), *Patrons and Clients* (London, 1977), pp. 53–62; José Varela Ortega, 'Los amigos políticos: funcionamiento del sistema caciquista' in *Revista de Occidente*, 127 (October 1973); José Varela Ortega, *Los amigos políticos* (Madrid, 1977).

13 Raymond Carr, *The Spanish Tragedy* (London, 1977), pp. 9–10.

14 Karl Marx, 'On the Jewish question', *Early Writings* (Harmondsworth, 1975), p. 232.

15 Juan José Morato, *El Partido Socialista Obrero* (Madrid, 1976; first published 1918) gives the figure of 40 founding members (p. 78), while Juan José Castillo,

in the intro. to Jaime Vera, *Ciencia y proletariado (Escritos escogidos de Jaime Vera)* (Madrid, 1973) mentions 25 (p. 16). Antonio Elorza, 'Los primeros programas del PSOE, 1879–8' in *Estudios de Historia Social*, 8–9 (January–June 1979), p. 144, mentions 37. Carlos M. Rama, *La crisis española del siglo XX* (Mexico, 2nd edn, 1962), pp. 86–7, has an altogether different version, stating that the PSOE was founded in 1878 through the intervention of Paul Lafargue.

16 The Federación Regional Española, formally constituted on 24 January 1869, was the Spanish branch of the First International. See Jacques Maurice, 'Sobre la penetración del marxismo en España' in *Estudios de Historia Social*, 8–9 (January–June 1979).

17 See Jean-Louis Guereña, 'Contribución a la biografía de José Mesa: De "La Emancipación" a "L'Egalité" (1873–77)' in *Estudios de Historia Social*, 8–9 (January–June 1979); Morato, *Partido Socialista*, pp. 60ff.

18 *La Emancipación*, no. 63, 24 August 1872.

19 See Antonio Elorza, 'Primeros programas', p. 144. Of the founder members of the Socialist Party (between 25 and 40 people), apparently at least twenty were typographers, and there were six 'intellectuals'. See Morato, *Partido Socialista*, p. 79. See also on the Asociación General del Arte de Imprimir the recently republished Juan José Morato, *La cuna de un gigante* (Madrid, 1984; first published 1925).

20 Other, less important, groups were formed in Barcelona and Guadalajara – the first under José Pamias, José Caparo and Ramón Arrufat, and the second under Julián Fernández Alonso. See Morato, *Partido Socialista*, pp. 85ff.

21 Morato, *Partido Socialista*, p. 86.

22 See Elorza, 'Primeros programas', pp. 145ff.

23 The full text can be found in *Estudios de Historia Social* 8–9 (January–June 1979), pp. 164–77, where it is compared with the 1879 programme, the 1881 and 1882 programmes of the PSOE, the 1882 programme of the French Socialist Party, and the 1888 programme of the PSOE.

24 I thus locate the origins of the diremption between revolutionary rhetoric and reformist practice as occurring much earlier than suggested by Tuñón de Lara, who argues that its roots were established in the mid-1890s. See Manuel Tuñón de Lara, 'Sobre la historia del pensamiento socialista entre 1900 y 1931' in Albert Balcells (ed.), *Teoría y práctica del movimiento obrero en España (1900–1936)* (Valencia, 1977), p. 20.

25 *El Obrero* (Barcelona), 180, 2 May 1884.

26 On the Comisión, see Angel Marvaud, *La cuestión social en España* (Madrid, 1975; first published, 1910), pp. 246ff. On the PSOE's responses, see Antonio Padilla Bolívar, *Pablo Iglesias y el parlamentarismo restauracionista* (Barcelona, 1976), pp. 43–51; *Anthropos* (Monographic issue on Pablo Iglesias) 45–7 (1985), pp. 2–58.

27 Juan José Castillo, introduction to Vera, *Ciencia*, p. 21; Juan José Morato, 'Jaime Vera y el socialismo', quoted in J.J. Castillo, *ibid.*; in fact Morato went rather further than this, suggesting that Jaime Vera was 'one of the most prodigious brains not only of Spain, but of the world' (*Partido Socialista*, p. 81), and that 'when the *Informe* of this good and wise man has been published in all the cultured languages, it will be seen that this document must be placed

alongside no less than the *Communist Manifesto* and *Capital*,' *ibid.*, p. 97. Others have been similarly eulogistic: 'The document. . .is a substantial piece which condenses the essential elements of the Marxist idea, and which stands comparison with the Manifesto of 1848' (Luis Gómez Llorente, *Aproximación a la historia del socialismo español* (Madrid, 1971), p. 91); 'one of the strongest minds of Spain' (Amaro del Rosal, *Historia de la UGT de España 1901–1939* (2 vols., Barcelona, 1977), vol. i, p. 114); the *Informe* is 'a key report in the definition of hispanic Marxism, and one which constitutes one of the most important documents in the history of Spanish Socialist thought' (Antoni Jutglar, *Ideologías y clases en la España contemporánea (1874–1931)*, (Madrid, 2 vols., 1969), vol. ii, p. 197); 'the first Marxist text of importance in the history of Spanish Socialism' (Manuel Pérez Ledesma, *Pensamiento socialista español a comienzos de siglo* (Madrid, 1974), p. 32), although in a review of Emilio Lamo de Espinosa, *Filosofía y política en Julián Besteiro* (Madrid, 1973), Pérez Ledesma criticised the author for repeating unfounded clichés in exalting Vera (review in *Sistema* 9 (1974), p. 154); 'Dr Jaime Vera represents with an exclusively theoretical character the plainly Marxist side of our early socialism' (Marcos Sanz Agüero, 'Jaime Vera y el primer socialismo español' in *Boletín Informativo de Ciencia Política* 8 (1971), p. 115). The best discussion of the *Informe* is by Tomás Jiménez Araya, 'Introducción', in which he shows how Vera paraphrased, and in places simply copied, various passages from Marx and other authors with little attention to overall coherence or consistency.

28 For a comprehensive, though in places careless, survey of the translations of Marxist works into Spanish, see Pedro Ribas, *La introducción del marxismo en España* (Madrid, 1981).

29 See Guereña, 'Contribución'; Manuel Pérez Ledesma, prologue to Pablo Iglesias, *Escritos* (Madrid, 2 vols., 1975), vol. i, pp. 59–63.

30 George Lichteim, *Marxism in Modern France* (Columbia, 1966), p. 19. See also Luis Arranz, 'El guesdismo de Pablo Iglesias en los informes a la Comisión de Reformas Sociales' in *Estudios de Historia Social* 8–9 (January–June 1979); Lamo de Espinosa, *Filosofía y política en Julián Besteiro* (Madrid, 1973), pp. 182ff; Tony Judt, *Marxism and the French Left* (Oxford, 1986), pp. 24–114 *passim*.

31 Carlos Forcadell, in *Parlamentarismo y bolchevización* (Barcelona, 1978), p. 37, makes the important point that *all* European ideological currents which reached Spain were mediated by French influences.

32 There is an extensive literature on Iglesias. See the special issue of *Anthropos*, 45–7 (1985) for a bibliographical guide as well as further contributions. The description of Iglesias as a lay saint was coined by José Ortega y Gasset in the newspaper *El Liberal* following his election to the Cortes in 1910. See María Teresa Martínez de Sas, *El socialismo y la España oficial. Pablo Iglesias, diputado a Cortes* (Madrid, 1975), p. 127.

33 Joaquín Maurín, *Los hombres de la Dictadura* (Barcelona, 1977, but written in 1930), pp. 179, 180, 181. This view of Iglesias echoed that of Oscar Pérez Solís, a founder member of the Communist Party (who would ultimately end up fighting for Franco in the Civil War), who accused Iglesias of being responsible for the PSOE degenerating into a *caciquismo* dominated by certain leaders. See

Memorias de mi amigo Oscar Perea (no date, but 1929?), p. 228. Perezagua was a local leader of the PSOE in Vizcaya in the Basque Country, and a militant in the UGT, who was to become, along with Maurín, one of the harshest critics of *pablismo* and a supporter of the Third International.

34 Juan Andrade, *La burocracia reformista en el movimiento obrero* (Madrid, 1935); Morato, *Partido Socialista*, pp. 219–26; Juan José Morato, *Pablo Iglesias Posse – educador de muchedumbres* (Barcelona, 1977; first published 1931).

35 Carr, *Spain*, p. 532.

36 See Rafael Pérez de la Dehesa, *Política y sociedad en el primer Unamuno* (Barcelona, 2nd edn, 1973); C. Blanco Aguinaga, 'El socialismo de Unamuno, 1894–1897' in *Revista de Occidente* 41 (1966), and 'De nuevo: el socialismo de Unamuno (1894–1897)' in *Cuadernos de la Cátedra Miguel de Unamuno* 18 (1968); Elías Díaz, *Revisión de Unamuno. Análisis crítico de su pensamiento político* (Madrid, 1968); Miguel de Unamuno, *Escritos socialistas: artículos inéditos sobre el socialismo, 1894–1922* (Madrid, 1976); Dolores Gómez Molleda, *Unamuno socialista* (Madrid, 1978). See also, Perry Anderson, *Considerations on Western Marxism* (London, 1976), p. 28 n.4: 'The Spanish case, however, remains an important historical enigma. Why did Spain never produce a Labriola or a Gramsci...? Here it may merely be noted that...strikingly, while Croce was studying and advertising the work of Marx in Italy during the 1890s the nearest analogous intellectual in Spain, Unamuno, was likewise converted to Marxism. Unamuno indeed, unlike Croce, actively participated in the organisation of the Spanish Socialist Party in 1894–7. Yet whereas Croce's engagement with historical materialism was to have profound consequences for the development of Marxism in Italy, Unamuno's left no traces in Spain... Unamuno was a far lesser thinker. More generally, his limitations were symptomatic of the much wider absence in Spain of any major tradition of systematic philosophical thought – something that Spanish culture, for all the virtuosity of its literature, painting or music, had lacked from the Renaissance to the Enlightenment. It was perhaps the absence of this catalyst which prevented the emergence of any Marxist work of note in the Spanish labour movement of the twentieth century.'

37 Cited in S. Fernández Larraín (ed.), *Cartas inéditas de Miguel de Unamuno* (Madrid, 1972), p. 207. The reference to evolutionism reflects the influence of Darwin. For an interesting discussion of the influence of both Darwinism and positivism on Spanish Socialism, see the useful though flawed *Marxismo y positivismo en el socialismo español* by Eusebio Fernández (Madrid, 1981), especially pp. 149–82.

38 See Carlos Marx and Federico Engels, *Escritos sobre españa* (Barcelona, 1978); Juan José Carreras Ares, 'Los escritos de Marx sobre España' in Gil Novales (ed.), *La revolución burguesa en España* (Madrid, 1985), pp. 33–44.

39 Ironically, García Quejido was himself in part responsible for the lack of attention he has received from historians of the PSOE, for until the start of the twentieth century he helped to maintain the 'cult of *pablismo*' which led to the overshadowing of all other figures in the early Spanish Socialist movement. See Pérez Ledesma, *Pensamiento*, p. 10 n.1.

40 *El Socialista*, no. 1, 12 March 1886; see also Forcadell, *Parlamentarismo*, p. 38.

41 *El Socialista*, no. 5, 16 April 1886.
42 See Santiago Castillo, 'De "El Socialista" a "El Capital" ' in *Negaciones* 5 (1978), pp. 42ff.
43 See Manual Pérez Ledesma, 'La Unión General de Trabajadores: socialismo y reformismo' in *Estudios de Historia Social* 8–9 (1979), pp. 217–26; Manuel Pérez Ledesma, 'Partido y sindicato: unas relaciones no siempre fáciles' in Santos Juliá (ed.), *El socialismo en España* (Madrid, 1986), pp. 213–29.
44 Juan Pablo Fusi, 'El movimiento socialista en España (1879–1939)' in *Actualidad Económica* 845 (25 May 1974), p. 63. The UGT did not officially admit any formal link to the PSOE until 1918; see Heywood, 'Labour movement. . .'.
45 See Forcadell, *Parlamentarismo*, pp. 44–8. The only person to confront the problem was Andreu Nin, whose articles on the national question can be consulted in *Els moviments d'emancipació nacional* (Barcelona, 1935). On the dominance of Madrid-based orientations, particularly in the UGT, see Santos Juliá, 'Largo Caballero y la lucha de tendencias en el socialismo español (1923–1936)' in *'Annali' della Fondazione Giangiacomo Feltrinelli* (1983–1984), pp. 861–2.
46 This compares with the 1,427,000 votes received by the German socialists in 1899. On the PSOE's performance in the various elections, see Miguel Martínez Cuadrado, *Elecciones y partidos políticos de España (1868–1931)* (2 vols., Madrid, 1969), vol. 2, pp. 521–612 *passim*, but especially pp. 537–8, 544–6, 556–7, 565–7, 578–9, 585–6, 596–8, 604–6.
47 C.A.M. Hennessy, *Modern Spain* (London, 1965), p. 12.
48 'Regenerationism' was widely advocated in early twentieth-century Spain. Associated principally with Joaquín Costa, its central tenet was to introduce sweeping political reforms from above in order to 'cleanse' the existing political system of the corruption associated with the *turno pacífico*. For a more detailed discussion, see chapter 4 below. On Antonio Maura, see Maximiano García Venero, *Antonio Maura* (Madrid, 1953); Ricardo de la Cierva, *La derecha sin remedio (1801–1987)* (Barcelona, 1987), pp. 133–70. On Socialist anti-colonialism, see Bernabé López García, *El socialismo español y el anticolonialismo* (Madrid, 1976), pp. 7–26.
49 James Joll, *The Second International 1889–1914* (London, 1974), pp. 1–2; see also Gómez Llorente, *Aproximación*, pp. 186–221.
50 See Pérez Ledesma, *Pensamiento, passim*.
51 Morato, 'Las subsistencias en Madrid', *La Nueva Era*, 1901, pp. 433–8; 'Por distintos caminos', *La Nueva Era*, 1902, pp. 5–8.
52 Antonio García Quejido, 'La ley de los salarios, ¿está bien formulada?', in *La Nueva Era*, 1901, pp. 229–32, 269–72, 293–7, 325–9, 389–93.
53 Vicente Barrio, '¿Quiénes son los revolucionarios?', *La Nueva Era*, 1902, p. 94; see also, Manuel Vigil, 'Hay que ser lógicos y justos', *La Nueva Era*, 1902, pp. 174–6.
54 Letter from García Quejido to Unamuno, 16 September 1901, printed in Dolores Gómez Molleda, *El socialismo español y los intelectuales*, (Salamanca, 1981), p. 399.
55 See Juan Pablo Fusi, *Política obrera en el País Vasco (1880–1923)*, (Madrid, 1975), pp. 248–9.

56 See Tomás Meabe, *Fábulas del errabundo* (introduction and notes by V.M. Arbeloa and M. de Santiago; Bilbao, 1975).

57 Fusi, 'Movimiento socialista', p. 65; on the alliance, see Manuel Suárez Cortina, *El reformismo en España* (Madrid, 1986), pp. 22–58; Antonio Robles Egea, 'Formación de la Conjunción republicano-socialista de 1909' in *Revista de Estudios Políticos*, **29** (1982), pp. 145–61.

58 See Carr, *Spain*, pp. 477–89; Rama, *Crisis española*, pp. 46, 51; Carolyn P. Boyd, *Praetorian Politics in Liberal Spain* (Chapel Hill, 1979), pp. 3–25; Suárez Cortina, *Reformismo*, pp. 1–21.

59 On Socialism in Catalonia, see Xavier Cuadrat, *Socialismo y anarquismo en Cataluña (1899–1911). Los orígenes de la CNT* (Madrid, 1976).

60 For descriptive details, see Joan Connelly Ullman, *La Semana Trágica* (Barcelona, 1968); an alternative and more wide-ranging, interpretative account can be found in Joaquín Romero Maura, *'La Rosa de Fuego'. El obrerismo barcelonés de 1899 a 1909* (Barcelona, 1974), pp. 509–42; see also, Cuadrat, *Socialismo y anarquismo*, pp. 317–403.

61 See Antonio Elorza, 'Los esquemas socialistas en Pablo Iglesias' in *Sistema* 11 (1975), p. 64.

62 Pablo Iglesias, 'La situación política en España (conferencia)' in *El Socialista*, 19 November 1909; see also, Pablo Iglesias, *Escritos* (Madrid, 1975), vol. 2, pp. 231–9. It should be mentioned that the Conjunction suited the interests of the various Republican parties since it served to unite their increasingly divided forces. At the start of 1910, Unión Republicana was little more than a loose amalgam of progressivists, federalists, possibilists, centralists, governmentalists, and radicals. See Suárez Cortina, *Reformismo*, pp. 22ff, 40.

63 See Fusi, 'Movimiento socialista', p. 66.

64 On the extent of Church influence in Spain, see Frances Lannon, *Privilege, Persecution and Prophecy. The Catholic Church in Spain 1875–1975* (Oxford, 1987), pp. 119–97.

65 Gerald Brenan, *The Spanish Labyrinth*, pp. 188ff. See also, E.J. Hobsbawm, *Primitive Rebels* (Manchester, 1971), pp. 74–92.

66 For a brief, but very suggestive, article on this, see Santos Juliá, 'Raíces religiosas y prácticas sindicales' in *Revista de Occidente* **23** (April 1983), pp. 61–75.

67 Quoted in Alfonso Carlos Saiz Valdivielso, *Indalecio Prieto. Crónica de un corazón* (Barcelona, 1984), p. 177.

68 *Diario de sesiones de las Cortes Constituyentes de la República española* (25 vols.), p. 1527.

69 Juliá, 'Raíces religiosas', p. 63.

70 Juan López-Morillas, *The Krausist Movement and Ideological Change in Spain 1854–1874* (Cambridge, 1981), pp. 11–12.

71 See Gillian Rose, *Hegel contra Sociology* (London, 1981), introduction; Teresa Rodríguez de Lecea, 'El Krausismo español como filosofía práctica' in *Sistema*, **49** (1982), pp. 121ff.

72 I am indebted to Mary Vincent for information on Spanish Catholicism.

73 López-Morillas, *Krausist Movement*, p. 9.

74 Lannon, *Privilege, Persecution and Prophecy*, p. 39.

75 See Rodríguez de Lecea, 'Krausismo español', p. 122; Elías Díaz, *La filosofía*

social del Krausismo español (Valencia, 2nd edn, 1983), p. 46. See also, Fredrick B. Pike, 'Making the hispanic world safe from democracy: Spanish liberals and hispanismo', *The Review of Politics*, **33** (1971), pp. 307–22; Juan José Gil Cremades, *Krausistas y liberales* (Madrid, 1975).

76 See López-Morillas, *Krausist Movement*, pp. 65ff.

77 See Elías Díaz, 'De algunas personales relaciones entre PSOE y la Institución Libre de Enseñanza' in Fundación Pablo Iglesias, *Homenaje a Pablo Iglesias* (Madrid, 1979), pp. 55–64. Amongst the major figures who came through the ILE were Leopoldo Alas ('Clarín'), Antonio Machado, Federico García Lorca, Luis Buñuel, Salvador Dalí, and Salvador de Madariaga. See Pedro Cuesta Escudero, 'Ideario pedagógico' and Manuel Tuñón de Lara, 'Reflexiones sobre un proyecto cultural' in *Cuadernos de Pedagogía (Revista mensual de educación)* **22** (October 1976), pp. 4–15; Elías Díaz, 'La Institución Libre de Enseñanza y el Partido Socialista Obrero Español', in Díaz, *Socialismo*, pp. 7–40; Rodolfo Llopis, 'Francisco Giner de los Ríos y la reforma del hombre' in *Cuadernos del Congreso por la libertad de la Cultura*, **16** (January–February 1956), pp. 60–7; Vicente Cacho Viu, *La Institución Libre de Enseñanza* (Madrid, 1962), especially pp. 419–40, 465–99; José Castillejo, *Guerra de ideas en España* (Madrid, 1976; first published in English, 1937), pp. 79–100.

78 See Enrique Moral Sandoval, 'Pablo Iglesias: una aproximación crítica' in *Anthropos*, **45–7** (1985), p. 61; see also, Manuel Pérez Ledesma, '¿Pablo Iglesias, santo?', *Anthropos*, **45–7**, pp. 171–6. On the influence of Catholic terminology on the Spanish Socialists, see Forcadell, *Parlamentarismo*, p. 39. See also, C. de los Andes, 'Catolicismo y socialismo' in *Anales de la Real Academia de Ciencias Morales y Políticas*, **53** (1976).

79 For details, see Forcadell, *Parlamentarismo*, pp. 27–30.

80 On Besteiro, see Lamo de Espinosa, *Filosofía y política*, especially pp. 15ff. for the influence of the ILE and German philosophy.

81 Gómez Molleda, *Socialismo español*, p. 78.

82 See J.J. Castillo, introduction to Vera, *Ciencia*; Tuñón de Lara, 'Sobre la historia', p. 29.

83 Lichteim, *Marxism*, p. 20; see articles by Vera, Besteiro and Araquistáin in the special edition to mark the first anniversary of the death of Jaurès of *Acción Socialista*, Año II, no. 72 (1915).

84 Lichteim, *Marxism*, p. 31.

85 Tuñón de Lara, 'Sobre la historia', p. 31.

86 For further details of the 10th Congress, see chapter 2 below.

87 Forcadell, *Parlamentarismo*, p. 89.

88 See David Kirby, *War, Peace and Revolution. International Socialism at the Crossroads, 1914–1918* (London, 1986), p. 3.

89 On the 1910 elections, see Martínez Cuadrado, *Elecciones y partidos*, II, pp. 755–72.

2 Reform, revolution and the roots of rupture: the PSOE, 1914–19

1 See Manuel Suárez Cortina, *El reformismo en España* (Madrid, 1986), pp. 144–6. Suárez mentions the frustration of British correspondents, who

found that the local population was more interested in bullfights and fiestas than in propaganda in favour of the Allies. Leon Trotsky, who was arrested in Spain following his expulsion from France in 1916, complained that in Cádiz the local paper, *El Diario de Cádiz*, 'carried no information about the war, just as if it did not exist'. See Leon Trotsky, *My Life. An Attempt at an Autobiography* (Harmondsworth, 1975), p. 276.

2 On the economic impact of the war, see J.L. García Delgado and S. Roldán, *La formación de la sociedad capitalista en España (1914–1920)* (2 vols., Madrid, 1973); Josep Fontana and Jordi Nadal, 'Spain 1914–1970' in Carlo M. Cipolla (ed.), *The Fontana Economic History of Europe. Contemporary Economies 2* (Glasgow, 1973), pp. 460–73; Joseph Harrison, 'The failure of economic reconstitution in Spain, 1916–1923' in *European Studies Review*, 13 (1983), pp. 63–88.

3 See Joseph Harrison, *An Economic History of Modern Spain* (Manchester, 1978), pp. 89–104; Joseph Harrison, *The Spanish Economy in the Twentieth Century* (London, 1985), pp. 15–53; Juan Pablo Fusi, *Política obrera en el País Vasco 1880–1923* (Madrid, 1975), pp. 364ff.

4 J. Vicens Vives *et al.*, *Historia de España y América* (5 vols., Barcelona, 1972, 2nd edn), vol. 5, p. 249.

5 Edward Malefakis, *Reforma agraria y revolución campesina en la España del siglo XX* (Barcelona, 1982), p. 176; Xavier Paniagua and José A. Piqueras, *Trabajadores sin revolución. La clase obrera valenciana 1868–1936* (Valencia, 1986), pp. 127–31.

6 On Alba's relationship with Costa, see Andrés Saborit, *Joaquín Costa y el socialismo* (Madrid, 1970), p. 29; on the tax proposals, see Harrison, 'Failure of economic reconstitution', pp. 76ff.

7 On Cambó and the Assembly Movement, see below.

8 Instituto de Reformas Sociales (IRS), *Encarecimiento de la vida durante la guerra* (Madrid, 1919), *passim*; Fontana and Nadal, 'Spain', p. 466.

9 Martin Clark, *Modern Italy, 1871–1982* (London, 1984), p. 183.

10 Edward Mortimer, *The Rise of the French Communist Party 1920–1947* (London, 1984), p. 30; Helga Grebing, *History of the German Labour Movement* (Leamington Spa, 1985), pp. 92–7; Dick Geary, *European Labour Protest 1848–1939* (London, 1981), pp. 134–78; David Kirby, *War, Peace and Revolution. International Socialism at the Crossroads, 1914–1918* (London, 1986); Douglas J. Newton, *British Labour, European Socialism and the Struggle for Peace 1889–1914* (Oxford, 1985), pp. 307–38; George Haupt, *Socialism and the Great War: The Collapse of the Second International* (Oxford, 1972), pp. 183–249; James Joll, *The Second International 1889–1914* (London, 2nd edn, 1974), pp. 161–205.

11 Juan Antonio Lacomba Avellán, *La crisis española de 1917* (Madrid, 1970), pp. 57–8; Suárez Cortina, *Reformismo*, p. 145.

12 'Modos de ser neutral', *El Socialista*, 12 September 1914; see Carlos Forcadell, *Parlamentarismo y bolchevización. El movimiento obrero español 1914–1918* (Barcelona, 1978), pp. 89–91, 112; for the speech by Iglesias on 5 November, see Antonio Padilla Bolívar, *Pablo Iglesias y el parlamentarismo restauracionista* (Barcelona, 1976), pp. 246–7.

13 Gerald H. Meaker, *The Revolutionary Left in Spain 1914–1923* (Stanford, 1974), pp. 56–7. Torralba Beci would later be a founding member of the Communist PCOE in April 1921; see below, chapter 3.

14 Antonio Fabra Ribas, *El socialismo y el conflicto europeo* (Valencia, no date, but 1915?); see also, Forcadell, *Parlamentarismo*, p. 92; Meaker, *Revolutionary Left*, p. 110.

15 José Verdes Montenegro, the radical Marxist, is not to be confused with his contemporary Dr José Verdes Montenegro, whose political sympathies leaned to the Anarchists. For clarification, see Eusebio Fernández, *Marxismo y positivismo en el socialismo español* (Madrid, 1981), pp. 214ff.

16 See Fusi, *Política obrera*, pp. 350ff.

17 Meaker, *Revolutionary Left*, p. 356.

18 On Besteiro, see the outstanding study by Emilio Lamo de Espinosa, *Filosofía y política en Julián Besteiro* (Madrid, 1973); see also, José Antonio Balbontín, *La España de mi experiencia* (Mexico City, 1952), p. 138, where he states, 'Besteiro was one of the most peace-loving men I have known in my life. . . In a better run country, Besteiro would have been a great professor of metaphysics; in Spain he had to occupy himself with politics, like everybody else. . . He became a Marxist. . .but he never intended to make a violent revolution. He hated violence instinctively.'

19 Juan José Morato, *El Partido Socialista Obrero* (Madrid, 1976; first published, 1918), p. 207; Forcadell, *Parlamentarismo*, pp. 120, 121.

20 Fernández, *Marxismo*, pp. 124ff.

21 Both quotations from *El Socialista*, 31 October 1915.

22 The reports by Vigil and Verdes Montenegro in Forcadell, *Parlamentarismo*, Appendix III, pp. 345–8.

23 Letter from Araquistáin to Miguel de Unamuno, 30 July 1912, printed in Dolores Gómez Molleda, *El socialismo español y los intelectuales* (Salamanca, 1981), pp. 470–1.

24 See below, chapter 6; on Araquistáin during the 10th Congress, see Marta Bizcarrondo, *Araquistáin y la crisis socialista en la II República. Leviatán, 1934–1936* (Madrid, 1975), pp. 26ff.

25 Juan Losada, *Ideario político de Pablo Iglesias* (Barcelona, 1976), pp. 191–204.

26 Paloma Biglino, *El socialismo español y la cuestión agraria* (Madrid, 1986), pp. 139–48.

27 Neil Harding, *Lenin's Political Thought* (2 vols., London, 1977, 1981), vol. 2, pp. 18–19.

28 Luis Gómez Llorente, *Aproximación a la historia del socialismo español (hasta 1921)* (Madrid, 1976), p. 186.

29 Harding, *Lenin's Political Thought*, p. 16.

30 García Cortés published an article in *República Social* (Valencia), 28 January 1911, entitled 'Nuestro republicanismo', in which he stated, 'We socialists are republicans. . . In spite of our differences – which are large – Socialist republicans and bourgeois republicans can march together towards the conquest of the ideals we hold in common. Under certain circumstances, the union of socialists with bourgeois republican parties and even with monarchists who are sincere democrats. . .is something which becomes necessary

when liberty is at stake.' Reproduced in Paniagua and Piqueras, *Trabajadores sin revolución*, pp. 97–8.

31 Antonio González Quintana and Aurelio Martín Najera, *Apuntes para la historia de las Juventudes Socialistas de España* (Madrid, 1983), p. 28. Meabe, founder of the FJSE, died on the eve of the Congress.

32 IRS, *Huelgas y 'lock-out' en los diversos países* (Madrid, 1923), p. 40; García Delgado and Roldán, *Sociedad capitalista*, vol. 1, pp. 248–9.

33 Vicens Vives *et al.*, *Historia de España*, vol. 5, p. 359; Raymond Carr, *Spain 1808–1975* (Oxford, 2nd edn, 1982), pp. 413ff.

34 Morato, *Partido Socialista*, p. 119.

35 Ignacio Barrón, Santiago Castillo, Carlos Forcadell and Luis G. Germán, *Historia del socialismo en Aragón. PSOE–UGT 1879–1936* (Zaragoza, 1979), p. 14; Jesús M. Eguiguren, *El PSOE en el País Vasco (1886–1936)* (San Sebastián, 1984), p. 42.

36 Fusi, *Política obrera*, p. 368.

37 Adrian Shubert, *Hacia la revolución. Orígenes sociales del movimiento obrero en Asturias, 1860–1934* (Barcelona, 1984), pp. 142ff.

38 Xavier Cuadrat, *Socialismo y anarquismo en Cataluña. Los orígenes de la CNT* (Madrid, 1976), pp. 441–92; Forcadell, *Parlamentarismo*, pp. 209ff.

39 On the repression of Anarchism, see José Peirats, *Los anarquistas en la crisis política española* (Barcelona, 1976), pp. 16–17.

40 *Tierra y libertad*, 14 April 1915, quoted in Forcadell, *Parlamentarismo*, p. 220.

41 Angel Pestaña, 'La crisis sindicalista en España' in *Leviatán* 1 (May 1934).

42 Cuadrat, *Socialismo y anarquismo*, p. 496.

43 Colin Winston, *Workers and the Right in Spain, 1900–1936* (Princeton, 1985), especially pp. 216ff.

44 The only two journals set up in Barcelona, *La Guerra Social* (1900) and *La Internacional* (1908), under Fabra Ribas, both folded quickly. For a list of PSOE journals in print in 1918, see Morato, *Partido Socialista*, p. 218.

45 Amaro del Rosal, *Historia de la UGT de España 1901–1939* (2 vols., Barcelona, 1977), vol. 1, pp. 129–30, 128. Francisco Largo Caballero, *Mis recuerdos. Cartas a un amigo* (Mexico City, 1976; first published in 1954), p. 47, incorrectly states that the Congress was held in July. It should be said that Largo wrote his memoirs while both very ill and a prisoner in the Nazi concentration camp of Orianenburg.

46 Largo Caballero, *Mis recuerdos*, p. 47, says that it was agreed that should the government fail to respond to UGT demands, then the union would 'organise and carry out a revolutionary general strike'. In fact, the resolution was far vaguer than this. Carr, *Spain*, p. 502, accepts Largo's version as the basis for his account.

47 Contra Carr, *Spain*, p. 502, where he states 'the UGT threatened a general strike for higher wages, which, if ineffective, would be followed by a revolutionary strike. This new tone made a *rapprochement* with the Anarchists possible... More surprising was the alliance (June 1917) of Socialist and Reformist Republicans to impose, by a revolutionary strike if necessary, a ministry under Melquíades Alvarez.'

48 On Seguí, see Manuel Cruells, *Salvador Seguí, el Noi del sucre* (Barcelona, 1974); Meaker, *Revolutionary Left*, pp. 161ff.

49 Largo Caballero, *Mis recuerdos*, pp. 47–59.

50 See Carolyn Boyd, *Praetorian Politics in Liberal Spain* (Chapel Hill, 1979), pp. 44ff.

51 Largo Caballero, *Mis recuerdos*, p. 48; Meaker, *Revolutionary Left*, p. 42.

52 In English, the Juntas Militares de Defensa have been well covered by Boyd, *Praetorian Politics* and by Stanley Payne, *Politics and the Military in Modern Spain* (Stanford, 1967). The most comprehensive study is now Carlos Seco Serrano, *Militarismo y civilismo en la España contemporánea* (Madrid, 1984), see especially pp. 255–76. See also J.M. Capo, *Las Juntas Militares de Defensa* (Havana, 1923), which includes 'documents' by Benito Márquez, the leader of the Juntas.

53 Lacomba, *Crisis española*, p. 108.

54 Boyd, *Praetorian Politics*, p. 49.

55 The most accessible detailed account of the Assembly Movement is in Lacomba, *Crisis española*, pp. 165–212; see also, Jesús Pabón, *Cambó* (3 vols., Barcelona, 1952), vol. 1, pp. 497–582.

56 Joan B. Culla i Clarà, *El republicanisme Lerrouxista a Catalunya (1901–1923)* (Barcelona, 1986), pp. 310–30; Suárez Cortina, *Reformismo*, pp. 132–87.

57 Suárez Cortina, *ibid.*, pp. 40ff, 171–87.

58 See Lamo de Espinosa, *Besteiro*, p. 35.

59 *El Socialista*, 6 March 1917. Meaker, *Revolutionary Left*, p. 49, confuses this 5 March meeting with the 27 March meeting at which the joint UGT–CNT manifesto was published.

60 Del Rosal, *UGT*, pp. 143–6. Robert W. Kern, *Red Years/Black Years. A Political History of Spanish Anarchism 1911–1937* (Philadelphia, 1978), p. 28, confuses the issuing of the manifesto on 27 March with what he appears to believe was an actual strike, supposedly 'caused in good part by the electrifying news of the Russian revolution'.

61 The other signatories in Del Rosal, *UGT*, p. 146.

62 'Juicios socialistas sobre la revolución rusa', *El Socialista*, 12 April 1917.

63 Luis Araquistáin, 'La revolución rusa: pan, guerra, libertad' in *España*, 22 March 1917.

64 Dolores Ibárruri, *They Shall Not Pass* (London, 1966), p. 64.

65 Del Rosal, *UGT*, p. 147.

66 For details, see Boyd, *Praetorian Politics*, pp. 58–68.

67 See, for example, 'Declaraciones de Pablo Iglesias', *El Socialista*, 28 April 1917.

68 For details, see Lacomba, *Crisis española*, pp. 64ff; Suárez Cortina, *Reformismo*, pp. 178–9 n.95.

69 *El Socialista*, 24 May 1917 – emphasis added.

70 Besteiro's declarations to the Cortes, in Fermín Solana (ed.), *Historia parlamentaria del socialismo: Julián Besteiro* (2 vols., Madrid, 1975), vol. 1 (Política y Legislaturas de la Monarquía (1918–1923)), p. 70.

71 For details, see Suárez Cortina, *Reformismo*, pp. 171ff.

72 *El Socialista*, 24 and 26 May 1917; Forcadell, *Parlamentarismo*, pp. 203–5.

73 For details, see Lacomba, *Crisis española*, p. 225.

74 On Maura, see Carr, *Spain*, pp. 481–6, 501–8; Javier Tusell and Juan Avilés, *La derecha española contemporánea. Sus orígenes: el maurismo* (Madrid, 1986), pp. 103–30.

75 For details, see Lacomba, *Crisis española*, pp. 176–87; Pabón, *Cambó*, pp. 540ff.; Capo, *Juntas Militares*, pp. 6off.

76 Boyd, *Praetorian Politics*, p. 73. The Juntas actually wanted Maura to head a 'regenerationist' government in place of Dato.

77 Largo Caballero, *Mis recuerdos*, pp. 50–1. This seems rather unlikely; there is no reason to suppose that workers awaiting instructions from their UGT representative should pay attention to the Republican deputy Domingo.

78 On the provocation thesis, see Andrés Saborit, *La huelga de agosto de 1917* (Mexico City, 1967), p. 12; Besteiro in Solana (ed.), *Historia parlamentaria*, p. 80; Boyd, *Praetorian Politics*, p. 320.

79 Largo Caballero, *Mis recuerdos*, pp. 52–4.

80 Boyd, *Praetorian Politics*, p. 80.

81 Salvador de Madariaga, *Spain* (London, 1942), p. 237.

82 For further attacks on the PSOE by Madariaga, see below, chapter 5.

83 *El Liberal*, 10 August 1917; Boyd, *Praetorian Politics*, p. 83; Lacomba, *Crisis española*, p. 238.

84 Besteiro, in Solana (ed.), *Historia parlamentaria*, p. 80; Largo Caballero, *Mis recuerdos*, p. 51.

85 Details in Saborit, *Huelga de agosto*, p. 65.

86 Gómez Llorente, *Aproximación*, pp. 257–340, goes to great lengths to argue that the strike gave evidence of the PSOE's revolutionary nature: 'That the PSOE had parliamentary representation since 1910 does not mean, in truth, that it would await the transformation of society via Parliament' (pp. 221–2). Gómez, a radical PSOE militant in the latter years of the Franco regime, was presumably weighting his account as part of his struggle for control within the party with Felipe González and Alfonso Guerra. His account is quoted approvingly (and wrongly referenced) by Padilla Bolívar, *Pablo Iglesias*, pp. 252–3.

87 Besteiro, in Solana (ed.), *Historia parlamentaria*, p. 81 – emphasis added.

88 The manifesto can be consulted in Lamo de Espinosa, *Besteiro*, pp. 36–7.

89 Besteiro, 'Cosas Veredes', *El Socialista*, 10 August 1917. 'Cosas veredes' is old Spanish, part of a verse which starts 'Cosas veredes que farán fablar las piedras. . .', presumably 'True things which will make the stones speak. . .' The article, which refers approvingly to David Lloyd-George, can be consulted in Julián Besteiro, *Obras completas* (3 vols., Madrid, 1983), vol. 1, pp. 403–5. Eduardo Comín Colomer, *Historia del Partido Comunista de España* (3 vols., Madrid, 1965–7), vol. 1, p. 12, insists that the article was written by Torralba Beci, but produces no evidence to support the claim.

90 Largo Caballero, *Mis recuerdos*, pp. 52–3.

91 Miguel de Unamuno, 'En Salamanca: notas de un testigo' in *España*, 25 October 1917.

92 Fusi, *Política obrera*, pp. 369–77.

93 Boyd, *Praetorian Politics*, pp. 84–5.

94 On the strike in Asturias, see Shubert, *Hacia la revolución*, p. 150; see also two

letters by Manuel Llaneza in *El Minero de la Hulla* (August 1917 and September 1917); David Ruiz, *El movimiento obrero en Asturias* (Oviedo, 1968), pp. 152-8; Enrique Moradiellos, *El Sindicato de los Obreros Mineros de Asturias 1910-1930* (Oviedo, 1986), pp. 56-61.

95 Lamo de Espinosa, *Besteiro*, p. 42.

96 Boyd, *Praetorian Politics*, pp. 85-93; Capo, *Juntas Militares*.

97 'Sería bien triste...', *El Socialista*, 10 November 1917. Juan José Morato, *Pablo Iglesias Posse – educador de muchedumbres* (Barcelona, 1977; first published 1931), p. 180, surprisingly states 'In this period [1918] the triumph of the social revolution in Russia was like a ray of joy, an event which Iglesias saw with jubilation.' Comín Colomer, *Historia del PCE*, vol. 1, pp. 42-3, quotes this and other passages from Morato's hagiographic biography to support his own virulent anti-Socialism.

98 'La revolución rusa. Los límites de una radicalización', *El Socialista*, 28 March 1918.

99 Eduardo Torralba Beci, 'De la convulsión rusa' in *España*, 15 November 1917. The journal *España* was in fact financed by the Allies, which may help to explain its stance. See Enrique Montero, 'Luis Araquistáin y la propaganda aliada durante la Primera Guerra Mundial' in *Estudios de Historia Social*, 24-5 (1983).

100 Forcadell, *Parlamentarismo*, pp. 379-81.

101 The first issue of *Nuestra Palabra*, 6 August 1918, carried an article to mark the fourth anniversary of the death of Jean Jaurès, hardly a revolutionary figure. The journal was usually moderate in tone, in spite of its support for the Bolshevik revolution.

102 The most spectacular of these concerned Oscar Pérez Solís, who went from moderate to extreme leftist, only to end up fighting for Franco in the Civil War and being awarded a medal for his efforts. For his early career, see his autobiography, *Memorias de mi amigo Oscar Perea* (Madrid, no date, but 1929?); see also Meaker, *Revolutionary Left*, pp. 349-54. Torralba Beci also shifted from a position in the centre of the party to one on the far left.

103 See Forcadell, *Parlamentarismo*, p. 256.

104 Lamo de Espinosa, *Besteiro*, pp. 45-7.

105 For details of the debates and the programme, see issues of *El Socialista* between 24 November and 4 December, 1918; on the agrarian issue in particular, see Biglino, *Socialismo y cuestión agraria*, pp. 152-77.

3 Socialist schism and the development of organised Communism, 1919-23

1 On the impact in Europe of both the Bolshevik Revolution and the Versailles Treaty, see Arno J. Mayer, *Political Origins of the New Diplomacy 1917-1918* (New Haven, 1959); Arno J. Mayer, *Politics and Diplomacy of Peacemaking: Containment and Counter-Revolution at Versailles 1918-1919* (London, 1967); Gerhard Schulz, *Revolutions and Peace Treaties 1917-1920* (London, 1967). On the impact of the former on European politics, see Norman Stone, *Europe Transformed 1878-1919* (London, 1983), pp. 366-88. There is a massive literature on Bolshevism and the European workers' movement; see,

for example, Albert S. Lindemann, *The 'Red Years': European Socialism versus Bolshevism 1919–1921* (Berkeley, 1974); Neil McInnes, 'The Labour Movement, Socialists, Communists, Trade Unions' in Arnold J. Toynbee (ed.), *The Impact of the Russian Revolution 1917–67* (Oxford, 1967). For a most succinct and intelligent synthesis, see Dick Geary, *European Labour Protest 1848–1939* (London, 1984), pp. 134–78. On the influence of the Bolshevik Revolution on the Spartakist League, see Ben Fowkes, *Communism in Germany under the Weimar Republic* (London, 1984), pp. 8–23. On Gramsci and the Bolshevik Revolution, see Martin Clark, *Antonio Gramsci and the Revolution that Failed* (New Haven, 1977), pp. 51–2.

2 The classic study of labour unrest in Andalusia during the *trienio bolchevique* is Juan Díaz del Moral, *Historia de las agitaciones campesinas andaluzas* (Madrid, 1979; first published in 1928); an abridged version of the same has been published as *Las agitaciones campesinas del período bolchevista (1918–1920)* (Granada, 1985). See also, Jacques Maurice, 'A propósito del trienio bolchevique' in José Luis García Delgado (ed.), *La crisis de la Restauración. España entre la primera guerra mundial y la II República* (Madrid, 1986), pp. 337–47.

3 Between 1917 and 1923, there were three general elections and fifteen changes of government. For a list of heads of government, see Carolyn Boyd, *Praetorian Politics in Liberal Spain* (Chapel Hill, 1979), Appendix A, pp. 283–4.

4 Dato was assassinated on 8 March 1921; Seguí on 10 March 1923; Soldevila Romero on 4 June 1923. See respectively, Jesús Pabón, *Cambó* (3 vols., Barcelona, 1952), vol. 2, p. 212; Manuel Cruells, *Salvador Seguí, el Noi del sucre* (Barcelona, 1974), pp. 161–8, 191–4; Robert W. Kern, *Red Years/Black Years. A Political History of Spanish Anarchism 1911–1937* (Philadelphia, 1978), p. 60.

5 Raymond Carr, *Modern Spain 1875–1980* (Oxford, 1980), p. 88. On the economic impact of the end of the war, see Joseph Harrison, *An Economic History of Modern Spain* (Manchester, 1978), pp. 90ff.; Josep Fontana and Jordi Nadal, 'Spain, 1914–1970' in Carlo M. Cipolla (ed.), *The Fontana Economic History of Europe* (6 vols., London, 1976), 6(2), pp. 460–73.

6 The similarities should obviously not be overdrawn, and were consistently played down by Spanish Socialist leaders. However, Salvador de Madariaga, the moderate liberal who would later accuse the PSOE of responsibility for the outbreak of the Civil War, had published 'Spain and Russia: a parallel' in *New Europe*, 30 August 1917, pp. 198–204, in which he stated: 'The events of last week in Spain may be summed up in one sentence: If Spain had been a belligerent, there would be to-day in Madrid a Provisional Government with a Spanish Kerenski at its head.'

7 On the strike at La Canadiense, see Antonio Bar, *La CNT en los años rojos: Del sindicalismo revolucionario al anarcosindicalismo, 1910–1926* (Madrid, 1981), pp. 479–89; Manuel Buenacasa, *El movimiento obrero español, 1886–1926* (Barcelona, 1977; first published, 1928), pp. 53ff.; Instituto de Reformas Sociales, *Estadística de las huelgas. Memoria de 1919 y resumen estadístico comparativo del quinquenio 1915–1919* (Madrid, 1922), pp. 37–59 *passim*.

Joaquín Maurín, *Los hombres de la Dictadura* (Barcelona, 1977; first published, 1930), pp. 162–3, saw the CNT's action as a major error which saved the Socialist movement from extinction by creating splits within the Anarchist movement which in turn prevented the CNT from pressing home its advantage over the PSOE–UGT.

8 Albert Balcells, *El sindicalismo en Barcelona, 1916–1923* (Barcelona, 1965), pp. 15, 52.

9 The German SPD at this time had 1,180,208 members; see Helga Grebing, *History of the German Labour Movement. A Survey* (Abridged version, Leamington Spa, 1985), p. 115. It is not clear from Grebing's figures whether these figures for the SPD include the USPD and the Spartakists as well.

10 Figures in Amaro del Rosal, *Historia de la UGT de España, 1901–1939* (2 vols., Barcelona, 1977), vol. 2, p. 925, where a comparison is drawn with France (1,500,000 members of Socialist Federations affiliated to the Amsterdam International) and Britain (6,505,482).

11 It should be said that interpretation of membership figures is made more difficult by such unquantifiable factors as the extent to which non-payment of dues was a result of economic hardship. Thus, it could be the case that membership of the UGT went up in times of relative economic prosperity and down in periods of hardship. Lack of evidence makes it impossible to arrive at a definite judgement.

12 E.H. Carr, *The Bolshevik Revolution, 1917–1923* (3 vols., London, 1950), vol. 3; Franz Borkenau, *World Communism. A History of the Communist International* (Ann Arbor, 1962), pp. 182–207; Geary, *Labour Protest*, pp. 134–78.

13 Edward Mortimer, *The Rise of the French Communist Party 1920–1947* (London, 1984), pp. 54–69.

14 Alastair Davidson, *The Theory and Practice of Italian Communism* (London, 1982), pp. 75–101; Martin Clark, *Antonio Gramsci*, pp. 197–209.

15 David W. Morgan, *The Socialist Left and the German Revolution: A History of the German Independent Social Democratic Party, 1917–1922* (Ithaca, 1975); Grebing, *German Labour Movement*, pp. 87–110; Geary, *Labour Protest*, p. 141.

16 Helen Graham and Paul Preston, 'The Popular Front and the struggle against Fascism' in Helen Graham and Paul Preston (eds.), *The Popular Front in Europe* (London, 1987), pp. 1–2.

17 Manuel Suárez Cortina, 'La división del republicanismo histórico y la quiebra de la Conjunción republicano-socialista' in Santos Juliá (ed.), *El socialismo en España* (Madrid, 1986), pp. 141–60.

18 *El Socialista*, 25 January 1919.

19 On Branting, see James Joll, *The Second International 1889–1914* (London, 2nd edn, 1974), p. 198; on Besteiro at Berne, see Emilio Lamo de Espinosa, *Filosofía y política en Julián Besteiro* (Madrid, 1973), p. 48.

20 Julián Besteiro, 'Bolchevismo' in *El Socialista*, 1 May 1919; 'Mi crítico empieza a razonar', *Democracia*, 6 July 1935.

21 From a speech in the Cortes, quoted in *El Socialista*, 1 November 1918.

22 See Lamo de Espinosa, *Besteiro*, p. 209.

23 Pedro Ribas, *La introducción del marxismo en España, 1869–1939* (Madrid,

1981), p. 81. Ribas, pp. 49–50, mentions a letter from Pablo Iglesias to Bernstein in 1912, indicating 'cordial relations', but does not give any further details. Besteiro was dismissive of the Escuela Nueva, set up by Núñez de Arenas in 1911, on the grounds that it was 'revisionist'; see Lamo de Espinosa, *Besteiro*, p. 191. On Delorme, see Dolores Gómez Molleda, *El socialismo español y los intelectuales* (Salamanca, 1981), pp. 25, 65. Delorme left the PSOE to join the Republican group associated with Joaquín Dicenta's progressive journal, *Germinal*, where the revisionist ideas of Bernstein found their most receptive audience. On *Germinal*, see Donald L. Shaw, *The Generation of 1898 in Spain* (London, 1975), pp. 75–6.

24 On the work of the Institute in this period, see Juan Ignacio Palacio, 'Crisis política y crisis institucional: la experiencia del Instituto de Reformas Sociales en el período 1914–1924' in García Delgado (ed.), *Crisis de la Restauración*, pp. 271–89.

25 Luis Araquistáin recalled in 1953: 'I found myself one afternoon in the chamber of our Republican Cortes, stuck in my seat, waiting for the umpteenth speaker to finish in order to vote on something or other. To combat the tedium that was emanating from that perorator, whose name I neither can nor wish to remember, I was reading a German pamphlet in which there was a medical history of Karl Marx. Prieto was sitting next to me, seemingly asleep, but in reality listening very closely with his razor-sharp hearing, in order to interject some of his fearsome interruptions should the speaker slip into any of his own no less fearsome blunders. "Listen to what I've come across in this pamphlet," I said to him. "Just like you, Karl Marx also suffered from chronic piles." To which he replied immediately, impassive, virtually without opening his eyes, "I had to be Marxist in some respect." ' See Araquistáin, 'Prieto y el Marxismo', in *El Socialista* (Toulouse), 30 April 1953.

26 José Prat, 'Acción y pasión de Indalecio Prieto', Santos Juliá, 'Un líder político entre dirigentes sindicales', and Paul Preston, 'Demócrata por encima de todo: Indalecio Prieto y la creación del Frente Popular', all in *Revista MOPU*, no. 305 (Madrid, December 1983), pp. 26–41.

27 *El Sitio* (Bilbao), 22 March 1921.

28 The best study of the thought of De los Ríos is Virgilio Zapatero, *Fernando de los Ríos: Los problemas del socialismo democrático* (Madrid, 1974), esp. pp. 157–226. Elías Díaz, 'Fernando de los Ríos: socialismo humanista y socialismo marxista' in *Sistema* 10 (July 1975), pp. 115–26, points out that it would have been difficult for De los Ríos to gain access to the works of Lukács; there is no record of any translation into Spanish of the Hungarian Marxist's major work prior to the Civil War.

29 Fernando de los Ríos, *El sentido humanista del socialismo* (Introduction and notes by Elías Díaz, Madrid, 1976).

30 Anguiano, as one of the four members of the Socialist strike committee of August 1917 sentenced to life imprisonment the following month, was elected to the Cortes in 1918 as part of a campaign to ensure their release.

31 Leon Trotsky, *My Life: An Attempt at an Autobiography* (Harmondsworth, 1975), pp. 269, 271, 274.

32 This had been made clear with the journal, *Nuestra Palabra*, set up by Mariano

García Cortés and Ramón Lamoneda in August 1918. Its theoretical content was of a low level, instead, the journal simply supported the Bolsheviks, but on the basis of very limited information. See chapter 2, above. It is indicative of the ideological confusion that reigned within the Socialist movement that several figures who joined the Communist breakaway factions, for instance Lamoneda himself and Francisco García Lavid, soon returned to the Socialist fold. García Lavid would be involved in the tragic events of the November 1922 UGT Congress, in which a member of the FJSE was shot dead – see below.

33 Figures given in Luis Arranz Notario, 'La ruptura del PSOE en la crisis de la Restauración: debate ideológico y político' in Juliá (ed.), *Socialismo en España*, p. 175.

34 See Díaz del Moral, *Agitaciones campesinas*; Antonio M. Calero, *Movimientos sociales en Andalucía, 1820–1936* (Madrid, 1979), pp. 25–79.

35 Arranz, 'Ruptura del PSOE', pp. 175–6; on membership in the Basque Country, see Jesús M. Eguiguren, *El PSOE en el País Vasco, 1886–1936* (San Sebastián, 1984), p. 44; for Asturias, see Enrique Moradiellos, *El Sindicato de los Obreros Mineros de Asturias 1910–1930* (Oviedo, 1986), pp. 42ff.; Adrian Shubert, *Hacia la revolución. Orígenes sociales del movimiento obrero en Asturias, 1860–1934* (Barcelona, 1984), pp. 154ff.

36 The PSOE vote fell from 109,973 in 1918 to 106,774 in 1919. See Miguel Martínez Cuadrado, *Elecciones y partidos políticos 1868–1931* (2 vols., Madrid, 1969), vol. 2, pp. 801–15. The deputies were Iglesias, Besteiro, Largo Caballero, De los Ríos, Prieto and Anguiano.

37 Joseph Harrison, *The Spanish Economy in the Twentieth Century* (London, 1985), pp. 47–8; Moradiellos, *Obreros Mineros*, pp. 61–78.

38 On conditions in Andalusia, see articles by Pascual Carrión in *El Sol*, 27 April, 11 May, 1, 15 June, 6 July, 10, 24 August, 14 September and 12 October 1919, reprinted in Pascual Carrión, *Estudios sobre la agricultura española* (Madrid, 1974), pp. 107–53.

39 *El Socialista*, 1 July 1919.

40 Ovejero and Araquistáin would later reject the Comintern after the announcement of the 21 Conditions of membership. The latter was notably inconstant in his political affiliations, moving from moderate Socialism prior to 1919, to support for the Comintern, then abandonment of the PSOE altogether during the Dictatorship of Primo de Rivera, before returning and becoming one of the most notorious of the 'radicalisers' during the Second Republic. After the Civil War he reverted to a position of moderate Socialism. On his early career, see Marta Bizcarrondo, *Araquistáin y la crisis socialista en la II República. Leviatán (1934–1936)* (Madrid, 1975), pp. 13–72.

41 See Gerald Meaker, *The Revolutionary Left in Spain 1914–1923* (Stanford, 1974), p. 207.

42 Luis Portela, 'El nacimiento y los primeros pasos del movimiento comunista en España' in *Estudios de Historia Social*, 14 (1980); Antonio González Quintana and Aurelio Martín Najera, *Apuntes para la historia de las Juventudes Socialistas de España* (Madrid, 1983), pp. 33–7.

43 Juan Andrade, *Apuntes para la historia del PCE* (Barcelona, 1979), p. 22.

44 For details of the December Extraordinary Congress, see *El Socialista*, 12, 13, 14, 15 December 1919; Meaker, *Revolutionary Left*, pp. 225–33.

45 *El Socialista*, 13 December 1919; the comments were repeated in an article in *Democracia*, 27 September 1936.

46 *El Socialista*, 13, 14 December 1919; see also, Lamo de Espinosa, *Besteiro*, p. 50.

47 *El Socialista*, 15 December 1919. It is noteworthy that Prieto used a religious metaphor: 'Yo comulgo con todo el credo revolucionario ruso' (I share (literally, 'I take communion with') the entire Russian revolutionary creed). See above, chapter 1, for Catholic influences on Spanish Socialism, and the views of Prieto.

48 *El Socialista*, 15 December 1919.

49 The vote was 14,010 to 12,497; figures in *El Socialista*, 15 December 1919.

50 González Quintana and Martín Najera, *Juventudes Socialistas*, pp. 34–5.

51 Largo Caballero's letter quoted in Luis Gómez Llorente, *Aproximación a la historia del socialismo español (hasta 1921)* (Madrid, 2nd edn, 1976), pp. 463–4. See also Diego Abad de Santillán (pseudonym of Sinesio García Fernández), *Contribución a la historia del movimiento obrero español* (3 vols., Mexico, 1971), vol. 2, pp. 267–83.

52 On the CNT Congress, see Bar, *Años rojos*, pp. 479–555; Buenacasa, *Movimiento obrero*, pp. 59–72. Meaker, *Revolutionary Left*, p. 246, suggests that the PSOE decision not to join the Comintern may have influenced the CNT.

53 Buenacasa, *Movimiento obrero*, pp. 63–4.

54 On Ramírez, see Joaquín Maurín, *Revolución y contrarrevolución en España* (Paris, 1966; first published as *Hacia la segunda revolución*, 1935), p. 270.

55 On the foundation of the Communist Party, see Andrade, *Historia del PCE*, pp. 24ff.; Portela, 'El nacimiento'; Pelai Pagès, *Historia del Partido Comunista de España* (Barcelona, 1978), p. 21; Víctor Alba, *El Partido Comunista en España* (Barcelona, 1979), pp. 28–33; Eduardo Comín Colomer, *Historia del Partido Comunista de España* (3 vols., Madrid, 1965–7), vol. 1, p. 48; Joan Estruch Tobella, *Historia del PCE (1), 1920–1939* (Barcelona, 1978), pp. 19–23; Meaker, *Revolutionary Left*, pp. 253–64. A most extraordinary account can be found in Arthur Landis, *Spain! The Unfinished Revolution* (New York, 1975), pp. 27–9, where he states 'Little has been written of the Communist Party of Spain. . . Of that which has been written, the greater part is utter nonsense.' Landis then provides a virtuoso display of inaccuracy, stating that there were two PSOE Congresses in 1919 (there was only one), and confusing the 1921 Congress with that of 1920, leading him to overlook the fact that there were two separate Communist Parties, the first formed in April 1920 by the FJSE, and the second in April 1921 by *tercerista* opponents of *pablismo*. Instead, Landis conflates the two, and then incorrectly states that Nin and Maurín joined the 'new party', before concluding that a main reason for the slow growth of Communism was 'the simple fact that the Spanish Socialist Party, though reformist in nature, was still far more militant than its European counterparts, and had not, therefore, lost control of its worker adherents. . .'. As will be shown, this is genuine nonsense.

56 The new Executive Committee in Andrade, *Historia del PCE*, p. 26.
57 For details of this incident, Comín Colomer, *Historia del PCE*, vol. 1, pp. 51–2.
58 *El Socialista*, 24 June 1920; for details of the Congress, see issues of the party newspaper between 23 and 26 June 1920.
59 *El Socialista*, 24 June 1920.
60 *El Socialista*, 25 June 1920.
61 The vote was 8,296 in favour versus 5,016 against, with 1,615 abstentions; *El Socialista*, 26 June 1920. For details of the rumpus, see Meaker, *Revolutionary Left*, p. 272.
62 The new Executive Committee was comprised of Iglesias, García Quejido, Daniel Anguiano, C. Rodríguez González, Antonio López Baeza, Manuel Núñez de Arenas, Antonio Fabra Ribas, Andrés Ovejero, Luis Araquistáin and Fernando de los Ríos; *El Socialista*, 28 June 1920.
63 PSOE, *Congreso Extraordinario del PSOE 1921: Nacimiento del Partido Comunista Español* (Madrid, 1974), p. 94. See José Moll Marqués, 'Criterios para la unidad del socialismo español' in *Sistema*, **19** (July 1977), p. 72.
64 The vote was 110,902 to 17,919; see Del Rosal, *Historia de la UGT*, vol. 1, pp. 196–202. Antoni Jutglar, 'Pablo Iglesias, los diversos socialismos en España, y la visión de discrepantes en el seno del movimiento obrero' in *Anthropos*, **45–7** (1985), p. 185, sees this vote as surprising, saying that the 'moderate counter-offensive' was unexpected.
65 It was comprised of Iglesias, Besteiro, Largo Caballero, Saborit, Barrio, Trifón Gómez, Luis Fernández, Manuel Cordero, Juan de los Toyos, Francisco Núñez Tomás and Lucio Martínez; *El Socialista*, 2 July 1920.
66 Largo Caballero declaration to *El Liberal*, 8 July 1920.
67 'La CNT y la UGT firman un pacto de alianza', *El Socialista*, 4 September 1920; see also Buenacasa, *Movimiento obrero*, pp. 74–5.
68 Both Arranz, 'Ruptura del PSOE', p. 180 and Raymond Carr, *Spain, 1808–1975* (Oxford, 2nd edn, 1982), p. 514, state that the CNT–UGT pact was in response to the appointment of General Severiano Martínez Anido as Civil Governor of Barcelona, although this did not take place until November.
69 On the Sindicatos Libres, see Colin M. Winston, *Workers and the Right in Spain, 1900–1936* (Princeton, 1985), esp. pp. 108–70; Juan José Castillo, *El sindicalismo amarillo en España* (Madrid, 1977). On *pistolerismo*, Francisco Bastos Ansart, *Pistolerismo (historia trágica)* (Madrid, 1935), a fictionalised account; Pere Foix, *Los archivos del terrorismo blanco: el fichero Lasarte 1910–1930* (Madrid, 1931); Manuel Casal Gómez, *El origen y la actuación de los pistoleros en Barcelona (1918–1921)* (Madrid, n.d., but 1924?); Angel Pestaña, *Terrorismo en Barcelona* (Barcelona, 1979); León-Ignacio, *Los años del pistolerismo* (Barcelona, 1981); Murray Bookchin, *The Spanish Anarchists. The Heroic Years 1868–1936* (New York, 1978), pp. 186–202.
70 Winston, *Workers and the Right*, p. 139. Despite this comment, on the same page of what is rather an uneven study, Winston defends Martínez Anido in a bizarre manner: 'This image of a sadistic brute was certainly overdrawn... Martínez Anido's methods were extreme and flouted all normal standards of police and judicial procedure, but there is no evidence that he enjoyed his

repression or took pleasure in making it more bloody and horrific than he felt was required.'

71 Again, Winston makes a strange remark (p. 129) that the attempts by Amado and Bas to negotiate demonstrated that they 'sympathised with the CNT moderates led by Seguí', which seems unlikely given that they were appointees of a Conservative government. Instead, it is probable that they were attempting a pragmatic tactic of negotiation in the realisation that repression would produce a backlash and reduce the influence within the CNT of more moderate leaders.

72 On this period, see Carr, *Spain*, pp. 509–23; Shlomo Ben-Ami, *Fascism from Above. The Dictatorship of Primo de Rivera in Spain 1923–1930* (Oxford, 1983), pp. 1–52.

73 *El Socialista*, 18 December 1920; 'Partido Socialista Obrero. A los trabajadores españoles', *El Socialista*, 28 December 1920.

74 Francisco Largo Caballero, 'La lucha electoral en Madrid', *El Socialista*, 15 December 1920; 'Candidatos del gorro frigio', *El Socialista*, 18 December 1920; 'Del mitin del sábado. El discurso de Julián Besteiro', *El Socialista*, 14 December 1920.

75 Figures in Arranz, 'Ruptura del PSOE', p. 181. See also, Martínez Cuadrado, *Elecciones y partidos*, vol. 2, pp. 829–35.

76 Figures in Lamo de Espinosa, *Besteiro*, p. 53.

77 De los Ríos wrote a book on his experiences in Russia, *Mi viaje a la Rusia sovietista* (Madrid, 1970; first published, 1921).

78 'Comunicación del Presidium de la III Internacional dirigida al PSOE', *El Socialista*, 17 January 1921.

79 De los Ríos, *Mi viaje*, p. 102; see Zapatero, *De los Ríos*, pp. 68–9.

80 Meaker, *Revolutionary Left*, p. 302, reports how Zinoviev, president of the Comintern, was amazed at the honesty and frankness with which De los Ríos expressed his views. The demagogic Zinoviev recalled him thus: 'I can still remember a Spanish professor, de los Ríos, who came to Moscow as a representative of the Spanish party... Now this professor said with almost touching naivety: "You know, comrades, I personally am a reformist, but the Spanish workers are urging that they be admitted to the Communist International, and they have sent me here in order to get them admitted"... This professor was almost a saint; he used to tell everything with complete frankness.'

81 Full details of the meeting in PSOE, *Congreso Extraordinario*, pp. 5–57; see also, Zapatero, *De los Ríos*, p. 69.

82 See Winston, *Workers and the Right*, pp. 140–1; Prieto's attack in the Cortes on the *ley de fugas* was so harsh that Martínez Anido actually challenged the Socialist leader to a duel, which was forbidden by the Minister of War, Viscount de Eza. See Indalecio Prieto, *De mi vida* (Mexico, 1968), p. 309.

83 Pablo Iglesias, 'No nos dividamos'; 'Sobre la condición décima'; 'Sobre las condiciones tercera y cuarta'; 'El fin de las 21 condiciones' in *El Socialista*, 28 March, 4, 6, 9 April 1921.

84 Letter from Pablo Iglesias to Enrique de Francisco, 31 March 1921, reprinted

in Julián Zugazagoitia, *Pablo Iglesias: una vida heroica* (Madrid, 1976; first published, 1925), p. 156; see also the Appendix in *Cien cartas inéditas de Pablo Iglesias a Isidoro Acevedo* (Madrid, 1976), pp. 111–13.

85 On the selection of Basque delegates, see Juan Pablo Fusi, *Política obrera en el País Vasco 1880–1923* (Madrid, 1975), pp. 434–5.

86 For proceedings of the Congress, PSOE, *Congreso Extraordinario*, pp. 61–117. The Congress has been described in great detail, but only in terms of the debates rather than the composition of delegates, on which see below. See Meaker, *Revolutionary Left*, pp. 359–67; Miguel Peydro Caro, *Las escisiones del PSOE* (Barcelona, 1980), pp. 9–36; Gómez Llorente, *Aproximación*, pp. 520–58; Comín Colomer, *Historia del PCE*, vol. 1, pp. 60–70.

87 PSOE, *Congreso Extraordinario*, p. 85.

88 PSOE, *Congreso Extraordinario*, pp. 93–5.

89 PSOE, *Congreso Extraordinario*, pp. 97–8. Largo Caballero and Besteiro, it should be remembered, had resigned from the Executive Committee at the previous Congress. Normally, Executive members had unrestricted speaking rights, which in this case would have given the *terceristas* a notable advantage since they dominated the Executive Committee.

90 Meaker, *Revolutionary Left*, p. 366, wrongly states that Lamoneda's speech was followed directly by the vote.

91 PSOE, *Congreso Extraordinario*, pp. 99–102.

92 Those who left were Oscar Pérez Solís, Facundo Perezagua, Isidoro Acevedo, Lázaro García, Virginia González, Pedro García, Mariano García Cortés, Eduardo Torralba Beci, Evaristo Salmerón, José Luis Darriba, José Martínez Ponte, Luis Mancevo, Lorenzo Luzuruga, José López y López, Gonzalo Pedroso, Antonio Fernández de Velasco, Carlos Carbonell, Marcelino Pascua, Manuel Martín, Evaristo Gil, Feliciso López, Luis Hernández, Eduardo Vicente, Francisco Villar, Angel Bartol, Vicente Cases and José Rojas. See PSOE, *Congreso Extraordinario*, pp. 117–18. José Andrés-Gallego, *El socialismo durante la Dictadura 1923–1930* (Madrid, 1977), p. 37, gives different figures to the normally quoted 8,808 in favour versus 6,025 against. Using figures from PSOE, *Convocatoria y orden del día para el XII Congreso ordinario del PSOE* (Madrid, 1927), pp. 190ff., Andrés-Gallego gives figures of 8,812 in favour versus 2,311 against, with 192 abstentions. This seems unlikely, given a letter written by Pablo Iglesias to Enrique de Francisco on 15 April 1921, about which see below.

93 PSOE, *Congreso Extraordinario*, pp. 105–6, 115.

94 Letter from Pablo Iglesias to Enrique de Francisco, 15 April 1921, reprinted in Zugazagoitia, *Iglesias*, pp. 156–8. The claim about Alcira is quite extraordinary, and raises questions as to the whole structure of the PSOE and the manner in which the credentials of delegates were validated. The letter also clearly demonstrates Iglesias' bitterness towards his former close friend Acevedo: his crime was above all one of betrayal, for he was far from the most ardent of the supporters of the Comintern. See the outline by Isidro R. Mendieta, in *Cien cartas*, pp. 14–19.

95 For a more detailed breakdown of the figures, see Enrique Moral Sandoval, 'El

socialismo y la Dictadura de Primo de Rivera', in Santos Juliá (ed.), *El socialismo en España*, pp. 194–6. Paul Preston, *The Coming of the Spanish Civil War* (London, 1978; henceforth *CSCW*), p. 4, suggests that the schism was numerically not important; such a claim can be sustained only with regard to the UGT, which lost few members as a result of the schism.

96 This is the interpretation of Juan Pablo Fusi, 'El movimiento socialista en España 1879–1939' in *Actualidad Económica*, **845** (25 May 1974), p. 63, where he questions whether the UGT before 1931 was entirely a Socialist union.

97 On this interpretation with regard to Barcelona, see chapter 2, above.

98 Díaz del Moral, *Agitaciones campesinas*; Antonio Calero, *Movimientos sociales en Andalucía 1820–1936* (Madrid, 1976), p. 78.

99 On the foundation of the FNTT, see Preston, *CSCW*, p. 19; Paloma Biglino, *El socialismo español y la cuestión agraria 1890–1936* (Madrid, 1986), pp. 300–7; on how agrarian issues continued to be underplayed, despite the FNTT, see chapter 5, below.

100 Arranz, 'Ruptura del PSOE', p. 175.

101 On the peculiar circumstances in Oviedo, see Moradiellos, *Obreros Mineros*, pp. 64–78; Shubert, *Hacia la revolución*, pp. 161ff.; on the Basque Country, see Eguiguren, *PSOE en el País Vasco*, p. 50. There is a third, rather more mundane, reason for the lack of a fall in UGT membership, which is that the figures cannot be considered to be entirely reliable. Moreover, it is possible that in Asturias unemployment in the coalfields would have led to a lack of cash with which to pay membership dues.

102 Besteiro's reply to Domingo in *El Socialista*, 27 June 1921; see also Fermín Solana (ed.), *Historia Parlamentaria del Socialismo: Julián Besteiro* (2 vols., Madrid, 1975), vol. 2, pp. 876–80.

103 On the impact of Anual, see Boyd, *Praetorian Politics*, pp. 160–208; Carlos Seco Serrano, *Militarismo y civilismo en la España contemporánea* (Madrid, 1984), pp. 292–300.

104 See Andrade, *Historia del PCE*, pp. 29ff.; José Bullejos, *La Comintern en España* (Mexico, 1972), pp. 9–53; Víctor Alba, *Partido Comunista*, pp. 60–71; Estruch Tobella, *Historia del PCE*, pp. 14–37; Comín Colomer, *Historia del PCE*, vol. 1, pp. 101–58; Pagès, *Historia del PCE*, pp. 39–52; Meaker, *Revolutionary Left*, pp. 404–27; Rafael Cruz, 'La organización del PCE 1920–1934' in *Estudios de Historia Social*, **31** (1984), pp. 223ff.

105 Víctor Alba, *El marxismo en España (1919–1939)* (2 vols., Mexico, 1973), vol. 1, pp. 9–64.

106 On the Graziadei mission, see Meaker, *Revolutionary Left*, pp. 409–16.

107 Andrade, *Historia del PCE*, pp. 31–2; Pagès, *Historia del PCE*, pp. 38–40.

108 On the UGT Congress, see Del Rosal, *Historia de la UGT*, vol. 1, pp. 249–52.

109 Details in Meaker, *Revolutionary Left*, pp. 453–5. Pagès, *Historia del PCE*, p. 46, mentions that Juan Andrade effectively accused Bullejos of being responsible in a letter of 29 July 1965 to Luis Portela. Pagès himself suggests that responsibility probably lay with members of the Agrupación Comunista de Bilbao, of which Bullejos was leader, and observes that Bullejos makes no mention of the incident in *La Comintern*.

110 On the CSR, see Pagès, *Historia del PCE*, pp. 73–8.

111 On the 1923 elections, see Martínez Cuadrado, *Elecciones y partidos*, vol. 2, pp. 839–47. The number of PSOE deputies rose to seven – five in Madrid, one in Oviedo, and one in Vizcaya.

4 Dealing with a Dictator: organised Socialism, 1923–31

1 The Dictatorship of Primo de Rivera remains one of the least-studied periods of twentieth-century Spanish history. However, two outstanding monographs by Shlomo Ben-Ami have helped rectify the situation, and must be considered indispensable sources: *The Origins of the Second Republic in Spain* (Oxford, 1978), and *Fascism from Above. The Dictatorship of Primo de Rivera in Spain 1923–1930* (Oxford, 1983). Primo assumed power in order to prevent the publication of a report by a Cortes committee investigating 'responsibilities' for the military disaster at Anual in Morocco in 1921. The report was expected to be highly critical of the role of the King. It remains a matter of controversy how far Alfonso XIII was involved in events. Ben-Ami, *Fascism*, pp. 26, 61–5, argues that his role was 'decisive'. A recent study by Javier Tusell, *Radiografía de un golpe de estado* (Madrid, 1987), disputes this view and argues that the King was in no way involved. See in particular pp. 266–70, where Tusell summarises his disagreement with most prevailing interpretations of the Primo coup. Another recent study is James H. Rial, *Revolution from Above. The Primo de Rivera Dictatorship in Spain 1923–1930* (Cranbury, New Jersey, 1986), an analysis of Primo's reform programme which, remarkably, contains a mere two pages on labour legislation.

2 In broad terms, Primo's regime has usually been seen as *sui generis*, a failed effort at reform by an idiosyncratic but essentially well-meaning, though naive, general. Thus, Hampden Jackson, *The Post-War World. A Short Political History 1918–1934* (London, 1934), p. 99: 'Primo de Rivera made a most excellent Dictator. He was a big, bluff Andalusian, a talker and a worker and a leader, generous and shrewd and ignorant – the sort of personality most likely to appeal to an illiterate, hero-worshipping people sick of lobbying politicians and spineless government.' More persuasive analyses, laying stress on socio-political and socio-economic aspects of the Dictatorship, have been provided by Shlomo Ben-Ami in the works cited in note 1 above, as well as in the articles, 'The forerunners of Spanish fascism: Unión Patriótica and Unión Monárquica', recently republished in Martin Blinkhorn (ed.), *Spain in Conflict 1931–1939*, pp. 103–32, and 'The Dictatorship of Primo de Rivera: a political reassessment', in *Journal of Contemporary History*, 12 (1977), pp. 65–84. An approach which situates the Dictatorship in a more structural model of the development of Spanish capitalism is Paul Preston, 'Spain' in Stuart Woolf (ed.), *Fascism in Europe* (London, 1981), pp. 329–51.

3 'Nota de la Comisión Ejecutiva del PSOE', *El Socialista*, 22 September 1923. For 'official' perspectives on Primo's labour policy, see the works by his Labour Minister, Eduardo Aunós: *La reforma corporativa del Estado* (Madrid, 1935) and *La política social de la Dictadura* (Madrid, 1944). Also important for the viewpoint of a protagonist is José Calvo Sotelo, *Mis servicios al Estado. Seis años de gestión* (Madrid, 1930). Another valuable contemporary

204 Notes to pages 85–86

account is Gabriel Maura Gamazo, *Bosquejo histórico de la Dictadura* (Madrid, 1930).

4 See, for instance, Ricardo de la Cierva, *Historia del socialismo en España 1879–1983* (Barcelona, 1983), pp. 92–103; Manuel Cantarero del Castillo, *Tragedia del socialismo español* (Barcelona, 1971), pp. 103–6; Stanley Payne, *The Spanish Revolution* (London, 1970), pp. 77–80.

5 This was particularly irksome in regard to Francisco Largo Caballero – for many the *bête noire* of Socialism during the Republic – who was the most fervent defender of collaboration with Primo. See, for a recent example of anti-Largo literature which underplays his role during the Dictatorship, Julio Merino, *Los socialistas rompen las urnas. 1933* (Barcelona, 1986), esp. pp. 59–67. It should be added, of course, that the most virulent attacks on Largo's 'revolutionism' during the Second Republic derived from fellow Socialists and sympathisers of the Republic, such as Gabriel Mario del Coca and, later, Salvador de Madariaga. See chapters 5 and 6, below.

6 For apologetic literature by such Socialists as Antonio Ramos Oliveira, Manuel Cordero and Enrique de Santiago in the first years of the Republic, see chapter 5, below. See, as a representative example of the issue receiving scant attention from Socialist sympathisers, Manuel Tuñón de Lara, *El movimiento obrero en la historia de España* (Madrid, 1972), in which Socialist collaboration with the Dictatorship merits eleven pages (pp. 774–85) out of a total of 267 pages on the period 1920–36; Amaro del Rosal, *Historia de la UGT de España 1901–1939* (2 vols., Barcelona, 1977), in which just 33 pages out of 916 (vol. 1, pp. 260–93) are devoted to the issue. Some important exceptions to this rule are Santos Juliá, 'Largo Caballero y la lucha de tendencias en el socialismo español 1923–1936' in *'Annali' della Fondazione Giangiacomo Feltrinelli* (1983–4), pp. 857–85; Paul Preston, 'Los orígenes del cisma socialista: 1917–1931' in *Cuadernos de Ruedo Ibérico*, **49–50** (1976), pp. 11–40; Manuel Contreras, 'Líderes socialistas de la Dictadura a la República' in *Sistema*, **26** (September 1978), pp. 59–72; Enrique Moral Sandoval, 'El socialismo y la Dictadura de Primo de Rivera' in Santos Juliá (ed.), *El socialismo en España* (Madrid, 1986), pp. 191–211.

7 Joaquín Maurín, *Los hombres de la Dictadura* (Madrid, 1930); Juan Andrade, *La burocracia reformista en el movimiento obrero* (Madrid, 1935); Shlomo Ben-Ami, *Origins*, esp. chapter 3, 'A decisive reinforcement: reformist Socialism', pp. 104–53; José Andrés-Gallego, *El socialismo durante la Dictadura 1923–1930* (Madrid, 1977). Despite the greater sophistication of Preston's and Juliá's approaches, they basically share the interpretation of the Socialists', or at least Largo Caballero's, action as opportunistic.

8 Manuel Suárez Cortina, *El reformismo en España* (Madrid, 1986), pp. 282ff.

9 On the Republicans during the Dictatorship, see above all Ben-Ami, *Origins*, *passim*, and Juan Avilés Farré, *La izquierda burguesa en la II República* (Madrid, 1985), pp. 35–61; also, Stephen G.H. Roberts, 'Unamuno contra Primo de Rivera: 10 artículos de 1923–24' in *Sistema*, **75** (November 1986), pp. 83–112. Two important contemporary studies are Vicente Marco Miranda, *Las conspiraciones contra la Dictadura 1923–1930* (Madrid, 1930) and Ramiro Gómez Fernández, *La Dictadura me honró encarcelándome* (Madrid, 1930).

10 Manuel Azaña, *Obras completas* (4 vols., Mexico, 1966–8), I, p. 549.
11 *El Socialista*, 14, 18 September, 4 October 1923. Moral Sandoval, 'Socialismo', p. 196, says that the CNT strike call received little support even in those areas of greatest Anarchist influence. However, Carlos Llorens Castillo, *Historia del Partido Comunista de España* (Valencia, 1982), pp. 59–60, argues that the PCE played a much more important role in opposing the Primo coup than has generally been acknowledged.
12 Suárez Cortina, *Reformismo*, p. 281.
13 See articles by Ortega y Gasset in *El Sol* between September and November 1923; Ben-Ami, *Fascism*, pp. 72–8 *passim*, 93; Antonio Elorza, *La razón y la sombra. Una lectura política de Ortega y Gasset* (Barcelona, 1984), pp. 137–71 *passim*; Raymond Carr, *Spain 1808–1975* (Oxford, 2nd edn, 1982), pp. 574–81.
14 Carr, *Spain*, p. 473.
15 On the ILE, see chapter 1, above. For Costa and 'regenerationism', see Andrés Saborit, *Joaquín Costa y el socialismo* (Madrid, 1970), esp. pp. 47ff; Luis Araquistáin, *El pensamiento español contemporáneo* (Buenos Aires, 2nd edn, 1968), pp. 60ff.; Donald L. Shaw, *The Generation of 1898 in Spain* (London, 1975), *passim*; Carr, *Spain*, pp. 525–8.
16 The idea of Spain as a problem had been a fundamental concern of Spanish philosophers/men of letters since the latter part of the nineteenth century. The self-contemplative obsession with Spain and *Hispanidad*, or 'Spanishness', was a central feature of national philosophical concerns. Amongst the more important and influential works in this genre are Lucás Mallada, *Los males de la patria* (Madrid, 1890); Miguel de Unamuno, *En turno al casticismo* (Madrid, 1895); Angel Ganivet, *Idearium español* (Madrid, 1897); R. Picavea Macias, *El problema nacional* (Madrid, 1899); Rafael Altamira, *Psicología del pueblo español* (Madrid, 1902); José Ortega y Gasset, *España invertebrada* (Madrid, 1921). See Américo Castro, *The Spaniards. An Introduction to Their History* (Berkeley, 1971; first published as *The Structure of Spanish History* (Princeton, 1954)), pp. 324–79, together with Claudio Sánchez Albornoz, *España, un enigma histórico* (Madrid, 1956). See also, Ramón Menéndez Pidal, *The Spaniards in their History* (London, 1950); Pedro Laín Entralgo, *La generación del noventa y ocho* (Madrid, 1947), esp. ch. 6: 'La generación del 98 ante el problema de la Historia'; Richard Herr, *An Historical Essay on Modern Spain* (Berkeley, 1971), ch. 2: 'Historical explanations of contemporary Spain', pp. 28–34; Elorza, *La razón y la sombra*, esp. pp. 21–70.
17 On Azaña and Krausism, see the introduction by Juan Marichal to Azaña, *Obras*, II, pp. xxxiii–1; Manuel Azaña, *El problema nacional* (Alcalá de Henares, 1911; reproduced in facsimile in Vicente-Alberto Serrano and José-María San Luciano (eds.), *Azaña* (Madrid, 1980), pp. 21–580). On the influence of Krausism on Besteiro and De los Ríos, see respectively Emilio Lamo de Espinosa, *Filosofía y política en Julián Besteiro* (Madrid, 1973), pp. 135–53, and Virgilio Zapatero, *Fernando de los Ríos: Los problemas del socialismo democrático* (Madrid, 1974), pp. 129–39.
18 See Carolyn Boyd, *Praetorian Politics in Liberal Spain* (Chapel Hill, 1979), p. 70.

19 The references are to the poem *Autumn journal* by Louis MacNeice, written between August 1938 and January 1939, shortly before the end of the Spanish Civil War. See Louis MacNeice, *Collected Poems* (London, 1979), pp. 101–53.

20 *El Socialista*, 18 September 1923.

21 The original comment in *El Sol*, 27 September 1923; the reply in *El Socialista*, 28 September 1923. Part of the reply was cut out by the censors – hence the gap in the quote.

22 The decision was announced in *El Socialista*, 22 September 1923; see also, Andrés-Gallego, *Socialismo*, p. 74.

23 On similarities between the thought of Besteiro and Kautsky, see Lamo, *Besteiro*, pp. 197–211. On teleological determinism in Kautsky, see Massimo Salvadori, *Karl Kautsky and the Socialist Revolution 1880–1938* (London, 1976), pp. 20ff.

24 It should be said that the PCI had reacted in a similar manner to Mussolini's seizure of power, although the situation in Italy was somewhat different in that the Italian Left was already on the defensive by the time of the March on Rome; see Alistair Davidson, *The Theory and Practice of Italian Communism* (London, 1982), pp. 129ff.

25 Antonio Gramsci, *Selections from the Prison Notebooks* (London, 1971), p. 219.

26 Gramsci, *ibid.*, pp. 219ff.; Gramsci specifically mentioned Primo as an historical example, p. 217.

27 Lamo, *Besteiro*, pp. 57ff.

28 On his stay in England, which lasted from 24 February until 30 September, see Julián Besteiro, *Obras completas* (3 vols., Madrid, 1983), II, pp. 17–20.

29 The articles have been reprinted in Besteiro, *Obras*, II, pp. 23–140.

30 *El Socialista*, 1 May 1924. Besteiro meant by 'English revolution' the electoral success of the Labour Party and its participation in power.

31 *El Socialista*, 1 May 1924.

32 *El Socialista*, 26 January 1924.

33 Antonio Fabra Ribas, 'La misión del Labour Party', *El Socialista*, 12 February 1924.

34 *El Socialista*, 8 January 1924.

35 *El Socialista*, 26 March 1924.

36 Gabriel Alomar Villalonga, 'El Socialismo español en su prueba histórica', *El Socialista*, 8 April 1924.

37 See Jonathon Rée, *Proletarian Philosophers* (Oxford, 1984), pp. 46ff.

38 *El Sol*, 30 March 1924; similar themes were expressed in the 1 April issue.

39 See Santos Juliá, introduction to Francisco Largo Caballero, *Escritos de la República* (Madrid, 1985), p. x.

40 The approach was made via General Bermúdez de Castro, under-secretary at the War Ministry in the new regime. On the meeting itself, see Partido Socialista Obrero Español, *XII Congreso del PSOE, del 28 de junio al 4 de julio de 1928* (Madrid, 1929), pp. 74ff.; Ben-Ami, *Origins*, p. 107; Andrés-Gallego, *Socialismo*, pp. 78–87; Enrique Moradiellos, *El Sindicato de los Obreros Mineros de Asturias 1910–1930* (Oviedo, 1986), pp. 85–98.

41 For a concise outline of the evolution of Primo's regime from an intended

temporary Military Directory to a more ambitious attempt at permanency through a Civilian Directory, see Ben-Ami, *Origins*, pp. 10–25.

42 'Nota de la Comisión Ejecutiva del PSOE', *El Socialista*, 22 September 1923.

43 Andrés-Gallego, *Socialismo*, p. 87; Ben-Ami, *Origins*, p. 107.

44 *El Socialista*, 4, 5 October 1923.

45 Aunós, *Reforma corporativa, passim*. Aunós had studied the ideas of fascist corporatist legislation of the Catholic social thinker, La Tour du Pin, and based his scheme on these and on the *comités paritarios* created in Barcelona in 1919. See Pierre Malerbe, 'La Dictadura' in Manuel Tuñón de Lara (ed.), *Historia de España* (10 vols., Barcelona, 1981), vol. IX (*La crisis del estado: Dictadura, República, Guerra*), pp. 63–4; Ben-Ami, *Fascism*, pp. 290–1.

46 Ben-Ami, *Origins*, p. 107; Andrés-Gallego, *Socialismo*, p. 115; Juan Ignacio Palacio, 'Crisis política y crisis institucional: la experiencia del Instituto de Reformas Sociales en el período 1914–1924' in José Luis García Delgado (ed.), *La crisis de la Restauración en España* (Madrid, 1986), pp. 271–90.

47 Ben-Ami, *Origins*, p. 10: 'Once in power Primo kept insisting, as if his was a Roman dictatorship, that he would soon "return the country to normality".' What that normality might involve was never elaborated, but Primo's hatred of politicians and political parties would presumably have compromised a return to full parliamentary democracy.

48 Andrés-Gallego, *Socialismo*, p. 118.

49 Pablo Iglesias, 'Abstencionismo político. ¿Aprenderán los trabajadores equivocados?', *El Socialista*, 14 July 1925; see also Pablo Iglesias, *Escritos 2* (Madrid, 1975), pp. 411ff.

50. *El Socialista*, 13 September 1923; see also Moral Sandoval, 'Socialismo', pp. 195–8.

51 See Moral Sandoval, 'Socialismo', p. 204.

52 Francisco Largo Caballero, 'El control sindical y su finalidad', *El Socialista*, 27 September, 1923.

53 '¿Qué es la lucha parlamentaria revolucionaria?', *El Socialista*, 25 May 1921; '¿Qué es la colaboración de clases?', *El Socialista*, 25 October 1920; '¿Qué es la lucha de clases?', *El Socialista*, 22 October 1920.

54 *El Socialista*, 10 February 1925; see also, Lamo, *Besteiro*, pp. 60ff.

55 For a detailed discussion of the 'worker corporativism' definition, associated with Santos Juliá, see below, chapter 6. On accidentalism, see Frances Lannon, 'The Church's crusade against the Republic' in Paul Preston (ed.), *Revolution and War in Spain 1931–1939* (London, 1984), pp. 38–40, 55 n.5.

56 Ben-Ami, *Origins*, p. 107.

57 Letter from Prieto to the PSOE National Committee, 4 October 1924, printed in Andrés-Gallego, *Socialismo*, pp. 119–20.

58 See Zapatero, *De los Ríos*, p. 74.

59 Francisco Largo Caballero, *Mis recuerdos* (Madrid, 1976; originally published Mexico, 1954), p. 85.

60 Details in Andrés-Gallego, *Socialismo*, pp. 122–5; Ben-Ami, *Origins*, p. 108, makes a rare factual mistake over the date of Prieto's resignation, placing it in December, when it was discussed at a PSOE National Committee meeting, although it had been presented on the day Largo took up his post, 25 October.

61 It is, nonetheless, noteworthy that major divisions within the Socialist leadership were often ostensibly concerned with constitutional details.

62 Ben-Ami, *Origins*, p. 108.

63 Details in Aunós, *Política social*, pp. 33–83.

64 *El Socialista*, 1 March 1924.

65 *El Socialista*, 30 April 1924. Santos Juliá states in the introduction to Largo Caballero, *Escritos*, p. xxxviii, that Largo aimed to create a new organisation, half-syndical, half-political. I have found nothing in Largo's writings that gives explicit evidence of such an intention.

66 An argument along these lines was made by Luis Araquistáin in his article, 'El complejo sindicalista. ¿Por qué se producen tantas huelgas?', *El Sol*, 21 July 1931: 'advantage was taken of the legislation so that Socialist leaders could go around the country apparently to explain the advantages of the *comités paritarios* to the working class, but in reality to organise them and excite their revolutionary spirit'.

67 Francisco Largo Caballero, *Presente y futuro de la UGT de España* (Madrid, 1925).

68 Largo Caballero, *ibid.*, pp. 41–51.

69 Largo Caballero, *ibid.*, p. 237.

70 The decision had been taken in March 1924, and there had been a meeting in November of that year; see Andrés-Gallego, *Socialismo*, pp. 129, 133.

71 Largo Caballero, *Presente y futuro*, pp. 237–49.

72 Largo does not refer in any of his memoirs to the publication of *Presente y futuro*. This is presumably because of his desire to present himself as a consistently radical workers' leader – see note 39, above.

73 On the OCN, see Aunós, *Reforma corporativa*, pp. 122–39; Malerbe, 'La Dictadura', pp. 63–4; Ben-Ami, *Fascism*, pp. 290–6; Andrés-Gallego, *Socialismo*, pp. 205–16.

74 This point is made by Juliá in 'Largo Caballero y la lucha', p. 862; see also Manuel Pérez Ledesma, 'La primera etapa de la Unión General de Trabajadores 1888–1917. Planteamiento sindical y formas de organización' in Albert Balcells (ed.), *Teoría y práctica del movimiento obrero en España* (Valencia, 1977), pp. 113–71; Manuel Pérez Ledesma, 'Partido y sindicato: unas relaciones no siempre fáciles' in Santos Juliá (ed.), *El socialismo en España*, pp. 213–29. Colin M. Winston, *Workers and the Right in Spain, 1900–1936* (Princeton, 1985), pp. 260–1, refers to recent debates between Howard J. Wiarda, Philippe Schmitter and Frederick B. Pike on whether corporatism can be seen as a typical form of Ibero-Hispanic social organisation.

75 Winston, *Workers*, p. 265; Albert Thomas, it should be said, was considered to be very much on the right of the Socialist spectrum. See Edward Mortimer, *The Rise of the French Communist Party 1920–1947* (London, 1984), pp. 29, 42, 68.

76 The Asociación de Estudios Sociales y Económicos was not formally an employers' organisation, although it acted like one; see Ben-Ami, *Origins*, p. 109.

77 Speech by Largo Caballero at the PSOE 12th Congress, in PSOE, *XII Congreso*, pp. 94–106.

78 Winston, *Workers*, pp. 216ff.
79 Moradiellos, *Sindicato*, p. 110.
80 Luis G. Germán, 'La Dictadura y el socialismo en Aragón 1923–1929' in Ignacio Barrón *et al.*, *Historia del socialismo en Aragón* (Zaragoza, 1979), pp. 81–2.
81 Ben-Ami, *Origins*, p. 116; Lannon, *Privilege, Persecution, and Prophecy. The Catholic Church in Spain 1875–1975* (Oxford, 1987), pp. 173–4.
82 Figures in Andrés-Gallego, *Socialismo*, pp. 151–3. In 1922, Asturias and Vizcaya were the third-ranking areas behind Madrid in UGT affiliation, with 18,147 and 17,575 members respectively. By 1928, membership in Asturias had fallen to 12,808 and in Vizcaya to 9,938, putting the two regions behind Valencia and Castellón in the rankings.
83 Figures in Del Rosal, *Historia de la UGT*, vol. 2, p. 919. Caution should be exercised in judging these figures, since their reliability cannot be guaranteed. In any case, they give no indication of what the rank-and-file membership actually felt.
84 Paul Preston, *The Coming of the Spanish Civil War* (London, 1978; henceforth, *CSCW*) gives the following figures for growth in the UGT after the establishment of the landworkers' federation, the Federación Nacional de Trabajadores de la Tierra (FNTT) in April 1930:- 1929: 1,511 sections, 228,507 members; 1930: 1,734 sections, 277,011 members. Most of the growth derived from the influx of members to the FNTT.
85 On the solving of the Moroccan problem, see Carlos Seco Serrano, *Militarismo y civilismo en la España contemporánea* (Madrid, 1984), pp. 326–9; Shannon E. Fleming and Ann K. Fleming, 'Primo de Rivera and Spain's Moroccan Problem, 1923–27' in *Journal of Contemporary History*, 12 (1977), pp. 85–99; David S. Woolman, *Rebels in the Rif: Abd el Krim and the Rif Rebellion* (Stanford, 1969), pp. 161–24; Ben-Ami, *Origins*, pp. 2–3.
86 The others were Manuel Núñez Tomás, Lucio Martínez Gil, Santiago Pérez Ynfante, as well as Dolores Cebrián, wife of Julián Besteiro.
87 *El Socialista*, 11, 23 September 1927; Largo Caballero, *Mis recuerdos*, pp. 90–1.
88 Andrés-Gallego, *Socialismo*, pp. 156ff.
89 Aunós, *Política social*, p. 66.
90 Andrés-Gallego, *Socialismo*, pp. 158–62.
91 The entire proceedings of the Congress are included as an appendix in Andrés-Gallego, *Socialismo*, pp. 362–578.
92 Gabriel Morón, *El Partido Socialista ante la realidad política de España* (Madrid, 1929). Menéndez was Llaneza's greatest rival in Asturias.
93 This was one of several trips by De los Ríos to the United States and Latin America, funded by the Institución Libre de Enseñanza. In December 1926, De los Ríos had attended an International Philosophy Congress at Harvard, where he gave a paper on 'Religion and the Spanish State in the Sixteenth Century'; see Zapatero, *De los Ríos*, pp. 77–8.
94 *El Socialista*, 1 July 1928.
95 Aunós, *Política social*, p. 55.
96 *El Socialista*, 1 July 1928.
97 Andrés-Gallego, *Socialismo*, pp. 168–9.

98 PSOE, *XII Congreso*, pp. 15–18, 220–40; see also Preston, *CSCW*, p. 11.
99 Andrés-Gallego, *Socialismo*, p. 169; Rosal, *UGT*, pp. 288–94; Contreras, 'Líderes socialistas', pp. 62–3.
100 Ben-Ami, *Origins*, pp. 125–6.
101 *El Socialista*, 14, 17 August 1929; Morón, *Realidad política*; Andrés-Gallego, *Socialismo*, p. 170; Ben-Ami, *Origins*, p. 126; Contreras, 'Líderes socialistas', p. 64.
102 *El Socialista*, 14 August 1929.
103 This is essentially the view of both Ben-Ami and Andrés-Gallego.
104 In late 1926, Primo had suspended the entire artillery officer corps; see Ben-Ami, *Fascism*, pp. 356–64; Seco Serrano, *Militarismo y civilismo*, pp. 329–43.
105 Sánchez Guerra was the successor in the Conservative Party to Prime Minister Eduardo Dato, assassinated in 1923. See Rafael Sánchez Guerra, *El movimiento revolucionario en Valencia: relato de un procesado* (Madrid, 1930).
106 Frances Lannon, *Privilege*, pp. 175–6; Ben-Ami, *Fascism*, pp. 350–4. On the importance of educational issues to the Institucionistas, see the special issue of *Cuadernos de Pedagogía*, 22 (October 1976); Francisco Laporta, 'Fundamentos de la pedagogía institucionista', in *Historia 16* (1976), pp. 77–84.
107 Joseph Harrison, *An Economic History of Modern Spain* (Manchester, 1978), p. 103; Juan Hernández Andreu, *Depresión económica en España, 1925–1934* (Madrid, 1980), *passim*, and *España y la crisis de 1929* (Madrid, 1986), *passim*; Francesc Cambó, *La valoración de la peseta* (Madrid, n.d., but 1929?); Alejandro López López, *El boicot de la derecha a las reformas de la Segunda República* (Madrid, 1984), pp. 67–87.
108 Ben-Ami, *Fascism*, p. 372, calls this a 'jump on the opposition's bandwagon'. Saborit stated 'our vote was based on the examination of the political circumstances. Really it was a case of rectifying a correct policy out of pure opportunism', quoted in Preston, *CSCW*, p. 12.
109 Preston, *CSCW*, pp. 12–13. Ben-Ami, *Fascism*, pp. 375–6, rejects this view.
110 Details in Moradiellos, *Sindicato*, pp. 102–9; Adrian Shubert, *Hacia la revolución* (Barcelona, 1984), p. 167.
111 On the view that Largo was primarily concerned to defend the interests of the UGT and retain the support of its members, see Preston, *CSCW*, p. 11; Juliá, introduction to Largo Caballero, *Escritos*, p. xiii; Andy Durgan, 'The rise and fall of Largo Caballero' in *International Socialism*, 18 (Winter 1983), p. 88.
112 Ben-Ami, *Fascism*, p. 377.
113 Besteiro, 'La lucha de clases como hecho social y como teoría', lecture delivered on 16 May 1929 at the Madrid Casa del Pueblo, reprinted in *Obras*, II, pp. 495–512.
114 'Dictablanda' is a play on words, where the last four letters of 'dictadura' (dictatorship), which on their own form the word for 'hard', have been replaced by 'blanda' meaning 'soft'. On Berenguer see Miguel Maura, *Así cayó Alfonso XIII...* (Barcelona, 1962), pp. 37–128, *passim*; Dámaso Berenguer, *De la Dictadura a la República* (Madrid, 1946).
115 *El Socialista*, 8, 14 March 1930.
116 *El Socialista*, 28 June 1930, quoted in Ben-Ami, *Origins*, p. 131. The CNT was

being pushed in an ever more radical direction by the Federación Anarquista Ibérica (FAI), established in 1927 to reassert Anarchist 'purity' within the movement. I am grateful to Stuart Christie for providing me with a copy of his unpublished manuscript, 'We, the Anarchists... A study of the Iberian Anarchist Federation (FAI), 1927–1937' (London, 1985).

117 *El Socialista*, 4, 9, 22 February, 26 March 1930. The comments on personalism are ironic in the light of the highly personalistic rivalries which would dog the Socialist Party throughout the Republic.

118 On criticisms of Prieto, see Ben-Ami, *Origins*, pp. 140–1; Alfonso Carlos Saiz Valdivielso, *Indalecio Prieto. Crónica de un corazón* (Barcelona, 1984), p. 97.

119 On the Republicans, see Ben-Ami, *Origins*, pp. 154–205; Avilés Farré, *Izquierda burguesa*, pp. 47–61; Suárez Cortina, *Reformismo*, pp. 287ff.

120 The events from this point to the declaration of the Second Republic have been well covered in Preston, *CSCW*, pp. 14–25; Ben-Ami, *Origins*, pp. 206ff.

121 Preston, *CSCW*, p. 20.

122 Llaneza was to die on 24 January 1931. His long illness had left the SOMA increasingly under the influence of Ramón González Peña, a supporter of Prieto. See David Ruíz González, *El movimiento obrero en Asturias* (Oviedo, 1968), pp. 211–15, where 1931 is misprinted as 1930; Ramiro Suárez Iglesias, *Vida, obras y recuerdos de Manuel Llaneza* (Oviedo, 1933; reprinted 1979).

123 He was supported only by Saborit, Lucio Martínez Gil, Trifón Gómez, Anastasio de Gracia and Anibal Sánchez.

124 Details in Largo Caballero, *Mis recuerdos*, pp. 111–13; Cordero, *Socialistas*, pp. 80–7; Maura, *Así cayó*, p. 70; Ben-Ami, *Origins*, pp. 95–9, 148–51; Preston, *CSCW*, p. 20.

125 On the debates within the Socialist movement over the December 1930 strike, see chapter 5, below.

126 On the controversial issue of Besteiro's responsibility for the failure of the December rising, see Lamo de Espinosa, *Besteiro*, p. 75; Preston, *CSCW*, pp. 22–3.

127 On the growth in PSOE membership following the fall of Primo, see Jesús M. Eguiguren, *El PSOE en el País Vasco 1886–1936* (San Sebastián, 1984), pp. 53 and 62, where the following breakdown is given:

Region	Groups		Membership		
	1928	1932	1928	1932	
Andalucía	45	305	1,193	23,138	+1,100%
Aragón	3	29	177	1,471	+ 730%
Baleares	3	16	78	980	+1,156%
Canarias	1	28	67	1,927	+2,776%
Cataluña		20		1,196	
Castilla la Nueva	28	114	1,198	12,275	+ 539%
Castilla la Vieja	25	93	719	5,528	+ 669%
Extremadura	14	108	350	8,116	+2,219%
León	6	46	117	1,783	+1,424%
Fed. Asturiana	15	33	418	869	+ 108%

Region	Groups		Membership		
	1928	1932	1928	1932	
Fed. Gallega	9	78	499	3,500	+ 601%
Fed. Levantina	37	85	1,542	3,990	+ 158%
Fed. Vasco-Navarra	17	39	640	1,002	+ 57%
Totals	203	994	7,718	65,775	+ 752%

Eguiguren gives no figures for the years between 1928 and 1932. However, Marta Bizcarrondo, *Araquistáin y la crisis socialista en la II República. Leviatán 1934–1936* (Madrid, 1975), p. 156, gives the following figures for PSOE membership (without mentioning her source):

1928 (first half)	8,251
1928 (second half)	8,917
1929 (first half)	10,222
1929 (second half)	13,181
1930 (first half)	16,878
1930 (second half)	23,009
1931 (first half)	25,000
1931 (second half)	66,506
1932 (first half)	75,133
1932 (second half)	81,777 (= 891% rise between 1928 and 1932)

While it clearly emerges that the major take-off in growth occurred after the establishment of the Second Republic, there had still been a very large rise – over a 1,000% in some areas – in PSOE membership between 1928 and the declaration of the Republic.

5 Marxist mistakes: misinterpreting the Second Republic, 1931–4

1 The posts were held by Largo Caballero, Prieto and De los Ríos respectively. On the composition of the Provisional Government, see Joaquín Arrarás, *Historia de la Segunda República Española* (4 vols., Madrid, 1956–68), vol. 1 (4th edn, 1969), esp. pp. 39–58. See also, for a description of the party system in the new Republic, Manuel Ramírez, 'El sistema de partidos al instaurarse la República' in José Luis García Delgado (ed.), *La Segunda República española. El primer bienio* (Madrid, 1987), pp. 5–23.

2 See Santos Juliá, 'República, revolución y luchas internas' in Santos Juliá (ed.), *El socialismo en España* (Anales de Historia vol. 1) (Madrid, 1986), p. 234. On 16 December 1931, Prieto was moved from Economy to become Minister of Public Works, while De los Ríos went from Justice to head the Ministry of Education. Only Largo remained in his original post, which he held until September 1933.

3 *El Socialista*, 26 April 1931: 'It is a fatal law of the development of the political economy. The bourgeois Left and Right, once the Republic is consolidated, will unite to defend capitalist interests and we will be left isolated, on the Left, as the only revolutionary organisation.' A year later, in an editorial entitled 'La

colaboración socialista en gobiernos burgueses', the PSOE newspaper repeated this view; see *El Socialista*, 6 April 1932.

4 It is not the purpose of this chapter to give a minutely detailed account of the Socialist movement between the establishment of the Second Republic and the October rising. There already exists a considerable literature on this period, which will be referred to throughout the chapter. The aim here is to analyse the theoretical confusions within the Socialist movement and assess their effects.

5 For details, see above, chapter 4. See also Alfonso Carlos Saiz Valdivielso, *Indalecio Prieto. Crónica de un corazón* (Barcelona, 1984), pp. 82–104; Santos Juliá, 'Un líder político entre dirigentes sindicales', Paul Preston, 'Demócrata por encima de todo: Indalecio Prieto y la creación del Frente Popular', and José Prat, 'Acción y pasión de Indalecio Prieto' in *MOPU* (Revista del Ministerio de Obras Públicas y Urbanismo), **305** (December 1983), pp. 26–41.

6 Indalecio Prieto, *Discursos fundamentales* (selected with a prologue by E. Malefakis, Madrid, 1975), p. 45. See also, Valdivielso, *Prieto*, pp. 42, 63–82.

7 Juliá, 'República', p. 234. This chapter devotes slightly less attention to Prieto than to other leaders of the PSOE and UGT precisely because of his lack of interest in theoretical issues.

8 This is one of the main themes of Fernando de los Ríos, *El sentido humanista del socialismo* (Madrid, 1976; first published in 1926), see esp. pp. 220ff.; see also, Virgilio Zapatero, *Fernando de los Ríos: Los problemas del socialismo democrático* (Madrid, 1974). Elías Díaz, 'Fernando de los Ríos: socialismo humanista y socialismo marxista' in *Sistema*, 10 (July 1975), pp. 115ff., argues that the thought of De los Ríos was not so distant from that of Marx, detecting similarities between *El Sentido humanista* and 'The Paris manuscripts'. However, since the 'Paris manuscripts' must have been unknown to the Granada Socialist leader, he was unaware of such similarities.

9 See 'Por la libertad y la democracia' and 'Reflexiones sobre una posible reforma constitucional' in Fernando de los Ríos, *Escritos sobre democracia y socialismo* (Madrid, 1974), pp. 355ff.

10 Manuel Contreras, *El PSOE en la II República. Organización e ideología* (Madrid, 1981), p. 212.

11 *El Socialista*, 26 June 1931.

12 Luis Araquistáin, '¿Por qué hay tantas huelgas?' in *El Sol*, 21 July 1931. See Javier Tusell, prologue to Luis Araquistáin, *Sobre la guerra civil y en la emigración* (Madrid, 1983), p. 17; on Araquistáin more generally, see Marta Bizcarrondo, *Araquistáin y la crisis socialista de la Segunda República: Leviatán, 1934–1936* (Madrid, 1975; henceforth *ACSR*).

13 *Crisol*, 28 April 1931; quoted in Marta Bizcarrondo, 'En torno a un viejo tema: "reforma" y "revolución" en el socialismo español de la Segunda República' in García Delgado (ed.), *La Segunda República*, pp. 53–4.

14 For a revealing comment on the views of De los Ríos once disillusion with the Republic had set in, see Manuel Azaña, *Obras completas* (4 vols., Mexico, 1966–8), vol. IV, pp. 649–50: 'Fernando de los Ríos in a speech in Granada said that they renounced the Republic. That was the tone of the rest of them. The Republic was a swindle, just as bad as the monarchy, and they could expect nothing from it; the Republicans, bourgeois to the end, had deceived them.'

On the composition of the Republican forces, see Juan Avilés Farré, *La izquierda burguesa en la Segunda República* (Madrid, 1985), pp. 63–86; Manuel Suárez Cortina, *El reformismo en España* (Madrid, 1986), pp. 293–316; Manuel Tuñón de Lara, *Tres claves de la Segunda República* (Madrid, 1985), II: 'Poder político y aparatos de estado, 1931–1936', pp. 219–60.

15 See Arrarás, *República española*, vol. I, pp. 39–54; Avilés Farré, *Izquierda burguesa*, pp. 115–38; Alejandro Lerroux, *La pequeña historia de España 1930–1936* (Barcelona, 1985; first published, 1945), pp. 94ff.

16 This analysis draws heavily on Barrington Moore, *The Social Origins of Dictatorship and Democracy* (Harmondsworth, 1969), especially the section on 'Revolutions from above and fascism', pp. 433–52. See also Paul Preston, 'Spain', in S.J. Woolf (ed.), *Fascism in Europe* (London, 1981), pp. 329–51; Alberto Gil Novales, 'Las contradicciones de la revolución burguesa española' in Alberto Gil Novales (ed.), *La revolución burguesa en España* (Madrid, 1985), pp. 47–58. For a more detailed account of the development of capitalism in Spain, see above, chapter 1; see also, Paul Heywood, 'The development of marxist theory in Spain and the Frente Popular' in Martin S. Alexander and Helen Graham (eds.), *The French and Spanish Popular Fronts* (Cambridge, 1989), pp. 118–19.

17 See Juan Sisinio Pérez Garzón, 'La revolución burguesa en España: los inicios de un debate científico 1966–1939' in Manuel Tuñón de Lara (ed.), *Historiografía española contemporánea* (Madrid, 1980), pp. 91–138; see also Manfred Kossok, 'El ciclo de las revoluciones españolas en el siglo XIX. Problemas de investigación e interpretación a la luz del método comparativo' in Albert Gil Novales (ed.), *La revolución burguesa*, pp. 11–32.

18 See Tuñón de Lara, *Tres claves*, pp. 245ff.

19 This is highlighted in Paul Preston, 'The agrarian war in the south' in Paul Preston (ed.), *Revolution and War in Spain, 1931–1939* (London, 1984), pp. 159–81.

20 Manuel Cordero, *Los socialistas y la revolución* (Madrid, 1932); Antonio Ramos Oliveira, *Nosotros los marxistas. Lenin contra Marx* (Madrid, 1979; first published 1932); Enrique de Santiago, *La UGT ante la revolución* (Madrid, 1932). It is impossible to tell what impact any of these books may have had on rank-and-file Socialist militants; however, they do serve as an indication of important trends of thought within the leadership.

21 Cordero, *Los socialistas*, p. 25; on Cordero's reputation, see Paul Preston, *The Coming of the Spanish Civil War* (London, 1978, henceforth *CSCW*), pp. 18, 208 n.77; Valdivielso, *Prieto*, p. 98, where he mentions criticism of Cordero for dining with Severiano Martínez Anido, the hated former Civil Governor of Barcelona; Juan Andrade, *La burocracia reformista en el movimiento obrero* (Madrid, 1935), pp. 242, 245. A contrasting, and far more positive, view can be found in Julio Alvarez del Vayo, *Freedom's Battle* (London, 1940), p. 69.

22 De Santiago, *La UGT*, pp. 8–9; see also Bizcarrondo, *ACSR*, p. 152.

23 Joaquín Maurín, *Los hombres de la Dictadura* (Barcelona, 1977; first published 1930), esp. pp. 159–200; see also, Andrade, *Burocracia*.

24 Ramos Oliveira, *Nosotros los marxistas*, pp. 214–20.

25 Bizcarrondo, *ACSR*, p. 153, sees Ramos Oliveira's position as mixing elements of Trotskyism and Krausism; see also Marta Bizcarrondo, 'La Segunda República: ideologías socialistas' in Santos Juliá (ed.), *Socialismo*, pp. 259–60.

26 Gabriel Morón, *El Partido Socialista ante la realidad política española* (Madrid, 1929).

27 Gabriel Morón, *La ruta del socialismo en España: ensayo de crítica y táctica revolucionaria* (Madrid, 1932), see esp. pp. 24–35.

28 See Adrian Shubert, *Hacia la revolución. Orígenes sociales del movimiento obrero en Asturias, 1860–1934* (Barcelona, 1984), p. 196.

29 Javier Bueno, *El estado socialista: nueva interpretación del comunismo* (Madrid, 1931), pp. 9–13.

30 For details on these debates, see Juan-Simeón Vidarte, *Las Cortes Constituyentes de 1931–1933* (Barcelona, 1976), pp. 59ff.; Contreras, *El PSOE*, pp. 218–30; Preston, *CSCW*, pp. 60–1.

31 *El Sol*, (Madrid, 15 March 1930; on *pablismo*, see earlier chapters; also, Paul Heywood, 'De las dificultades para ser marxista: el PSOE, 1879–1921' in *Sistema*, **74** (1986), pp. 17–49.

32 *El Socialista*, 5 June 1932.

33 On the influence of Krausism and the ILE on Spanish Socialism, see chapters 1 and 4, above; also Elías Díaz, 'De algunas personales relaciones entre PSOE y la Institución Libre de Enseñanza' in Fundación Pablo Iglesias, *Homenaje a Pablo Iglesias* (Madrid, 1979), pp. 55–63; on Besteiro and the ILE, see Emilio Lamo de Espinosa, *Filosofía y política en Julián Besteiro* (Madrid, 1973), pp. 78, 204ff.

34 Julián Besteiro, 'Por qué he llegado a ser socialista', in Besteiro, *Obras Completas* (3 vols., Madrid, 1983), vol. II, pp. 565–74. On Besteiro's Marxism, see Lamo de Espinosa, *Filosofía y política*, pp. 213–74. An extraordinary work on Besteiro is Carlos Díaz, *Besteiro: el socialismo en libertad* (Madrid, 1976), which sees him as manifesting a strong anarchist current in his thought, but also as being influenced by the Socialist thought of Oswald Mosle [*sic*] – in 1933. See pp. 62ff., 81. Elsewhere, Díaz provides a virtuoso quasi-intellectual, though quite impenetrable, 'exegesis' of Besteiro's Marxist philosophy, based on the assertion that criticisms of Besteiro's Marxism demonstrate 'crass historicism'. Díaz claims to avoid this trap by talking rather gnostically of two Spains: constructive–dogmatic and iconoclastic. See pp. 93ff.

35 See Lamo, *Filosofía y política*, p. 209; chapter 4, above. In 1934, Besteiro wrote the prologue to Sir Stafford Cripps, *Problemas del socialismo* (Madrid, 1934), a collection of essays by British Socialists. The prologue can be found in Besteiro, *Obras completas*, vol. III, pp. 119–25.

36 See Helga Grebing, *History of the German Labour Movement* (revised edn, Leamington Spa, 1985), pp. 76ff.; Massimo Salvadori, *Karl Kautsky and the Socialist Revolution 1880–1938* (London, 1979), pp. 20ff.

37 Cited in Enrique López Sevilla (ed.), *El PSOE en las Cortes Constituyentes de la Segunda República* (Mexico, 1969), pp. 295–300.

38 On Spanish Socialists and the dictatorship of the proletariat, see above, chapter 3.

39 On the influence of Kautsky on Besteiro, see Lamo, *Filosofía y política*, pp. 154–212.
40 For a clear exposition of Marx's views, see Hal Draper, *Karl Marx's Theory of Revolution. Vol. 3: The Dictatorship of the Proletariat* (New York, 1986), p. 330.
41 Besteiro spent some months in England in 1924, studying the Workers' Educational Association. See chapter 4, above; also, Lamo, *Filosofía y política*, pp. 57–8.
42 On the 1931 Extraordinary Congress, see PSOE, *El Partido Socialista ante las Constituyentes: recopilación de los discursos pronunciados en el Congreso Extraordinario celebrado en el Cinema Europa de Madrid, los días 10, 11 y 12 de julio de 1931, con asistencia de los delegados provinciales* (Madrid, n.d., but 1931?); Contreras, *El PSOE*, pp. 225–30; Vidarte, *Cortes Constituyentes*, pp. 59ff.; Marta Bizcarrondo, 'Democracia y revolución en la estrategia socialista de la Segunda República' in *Estudios de Historia Social*, **16–17** (January–June 1981), p. 249.
43 Bizcarrondo, 'Democracia', p. 249.
44 PSOE, *Actas de las sesiones celebradas por el XIII Congreso ordinario del Partido Socialista Obrero Español, del 6 al 13 de octubre de 1932* (Madrid, 1932); Vidarte, *Cortes Constituyentes*, pp. 484ff.; Preston, *CSCW*, p. 77; Bizcarrondo, 'Democracia', p. 351; Contreras, *El PSOE*, pp. 232–45.
45 José Manuel Macarro Vera, 'Causas de la radicalización socialista en la Segunda República' in *Revista de Historia Contemporánea* (Seville), 1 (December 1982), p. 194.
46 Contrast the views of Stanley Payne, *The Spanish Revolution* (London, 1970), p. 93, and Richard A.H. Robinson, *The Origins of Franco's Spain: The Right, the Republic and Revolution, 1931–36* (Newton Abbot, 1970), p. 83.
47 PSOE, *XIII Congreso*, pp. 386–98.
48 Largo Caballero quoted a letter written to him by Isa Brante, in which it was stated that Kautsky was in favour of the PSOE remaining in government. See PSOE, *XIII Congreso*, p. 445; Macarro Vera, 'Causas de la radicalización', p. 204.
49 Quoted in Preston, *CSCW*, p. 77.
50 See Alejandro López López, *El boicot de la derecha a las reformas de la Segunda República* (Madrid, 1984); Mercedes Cabrera, *La patronal ante la Segunda República* (Madrid, 1983), pp. 12–79; Preston, *CSCW*, pp. 26–50; José R. Montero, *La CEDA. El catolicismo social y político en la Segunda República* (2 vols., Madrid, 1977), vol. 1, pp. 179ff.; Frances Lannon, 'The Church's crusade against the Republic' in Paul Preston (ed.), *Revolution and War*, pp. 35–58; Frances Lannon, *Privilege, Persecution, and Prophecy. The Catholic Church in Spain 1875–1975* (Oxford, 1987), pp. 179–97.
51 See Montero, *CEDA*; Preston, *CSCW*; Paul Preston, 'Alfonsist monarchism and the coming of the Spanish Civil War', and Martin Blinkhorn, 'Carlism and the Spanish crisis of the 1930s', in *Journal of Contemporary History*, VII, 3–4 (1972), both reprinted in Martin Blinkhorn (ed.), *Spain in Conflict 1931–1939. Democracy and its Enemies* (London, 1986), pp. 160–82, 183–205; Paul

Preston 'El "accidentalismo" de la CEDA: ¿Aceptación o sabotaje de la República?' in Paul Preston, *Las derechas españolas en el siglo XX: autoritarismo, fascismo y golpismo* (Madrid, 1986), pp. 111–26; Martin Blinkhorn, *Carlism and Crisis in Spain 1931–1939* (Cambridge, 1975); Sheelagh Ellwood, *Prietas las filas. Historia de Falange Española, 1933–1983* (Barcelona, 1984), pp. 21–71.

52 See Mercedes Cabrera, 'Las organizaciones patronales ante la conflictividad social y los Jurados Mixtos' in Josep Fontana *et al.*, *La Segunda República. Una esperanza frustrada* (Valencia, 1987), pp. 65–82.

53 See Juan Muñoz, 'La reforma bancaria de Indalecio Prieto' in García Delgado (ed.), *La Segunda República*, pp. 153–66; see also Bizcarrondo, 'Democracia', p. 263.

54 José María Serrano Sanz, 'La política comercial ante la crisis del veintinueve: el primer bienio republicano', in García Delgado (ed.), *II República*, pp. 135–51.

55 Figures given in Bizcarrondo, *ACSR*, pp. 156–7.

56 Paloma Biglino, *El socialismo español y la cuestión agraria 1890–1936* (Madrid, 1986), pp. 300ff.

57 See Amaro del Rosal, *Historia de la UGT de España 1901–1939* (2 vols., Barcelona, 1977), vol. I, pp. 347–53; Preston, *CSCW*, p. 78; Vidarte, *Cortes Constituyentes*, pp. 495–500.

58 There has been much written on the PSOE and the agrarian question. Among the most important works are Edward E. Malefakis, *Agrarian Reform and Peasant Revolution in Spain* (New Haven, 1970); Paul Preston, *CSCW, passim*; Paul Preston, 'Agrarian war' in Preston (ed.), *Revolution and War*; Eduardo Sevilla-Guzmán, *La evolución del campesinado en España* (Barcelona, 1979). See also, Biglino, *Socialismo y cuestión agraria*; Tuñón de Lara, *Tres claves* (1: La cuestión agraria), pp. 21–215.

59 See Santos Juliá, 'Objetivos políticos de la legislación laboral' and Julio Aróstegui, 'Largo Caballero, ministro de Trabajo' in García Delgado (ed.), *La Segunda República*, pp. 27–47, 59–74.

60 See Heywood, 'De las dificultades'; also chapter 1, above.

61 The lack of differentiation between agrarian and industrial measures emerged as a point of discussion at an International Conference on the Popular Front in France and Spain, held at the University of Southampton in April 1986. The proceedings of the conference, edited by the organisers Martin Alexander and Helen Graham, have been published by Cambridge University Press: see note 16, above.

62 See Preston, 'Agrarian war' in Preston (ed.), *Revolution and War*, p. 168.

63 On the Austro-Marxists, see Tom Bottomore and Patrick Goode (eds.), *Austro-Marxism* (Oxford, 1978); Leszek Kolakowski, *Main Currents of Marxism* (3 vols., Oxford, 1978), vol. II, pp. 240–304.

64 See Bottomore and Goode, *Austro-Marxism*, pp. 25–7; Bizcarrondo, 'Democracia', p. 256.

65 See Bottomore and Goode, *Austro-Marxism*, p. 28.

66 Rudolf Hilferding, *Nuevas tácticas para el nuevo capitalismo* (Madrid, 1928). A translation of *Der Weg zum Socialismus*, with a prologue by A. Revesz, was

published as *El camino hacia el socialismo* (Madrid, 1930); Antonio Ramos Oliveira translated *Kapitalismus und Sozialismus nach dem Weltkreig* as *Capitalismo y socialismo en la posguerra* (Madrid, 1932); see Pedro Ribas, *La introducción del marxismo en España 1869–1939* (Madrid, 1981), pp. 78, 107.

67 The 'radicalisation' of the PSOE has become the source of a prolonged historiographical debate. The idea that this radicalisation was in large measure responsible for the collapse of the Second Republic and the outbreak of the Civil War in 1936 first found 'objective' expression in Salvador de Madariaga, *Spain* (London, 1942), p. 348: 'What made the Spanish Civil War inevitable was the Civil War within the Socialist Party. This is no exaggeration.' It was given greater academic respectability by the publication of three books in 1970: Edward E. Malefakis, *Agrarian Reform and Peasant Revolution in Spain*, with a concluding chapter attacking Socialist irresponsibility, which arguably goes against the evidence provided by the author in the rest of the book; Richard A.H. Robinson, *The Origins of Franco's Spain* (Newton Abbot, 1970), an attempt to establish the democratic credentials of Gil Robles and the CEDA as opposed to the revolutionary stance of the PSOE; Stanley Payne, *The Spanish Revolution*, an often inaccurate account of the PSOE during the Second Republic and the Civil War. All three authors were contributors to Raymond Carr (ed.), *The Republic and the Civil War in Spain* (London, 1971). These books provided major support for another contributor to the Carr volume, Ricardo de la Cierva, the prolific Spanish historian charged with leading Francoist historiography away from the more extremist pronouncements of the post-war years. The reply to what for a time became the prevailing orthodoxy on Socialist 'irresponsibility' came principally in Paul Preston, *The Coming of the Spanish Civil War* (London, 1978), an effective rejoinder to Robinson's work; also in an extensive series of articles and books by Marta Bizcarrondo and Santos Juliá. For a comprehensive list, see Rafael Casado González and Matilde Vázquez Cea, 'Fuentes impresos para la historia del socialismo en España' in Santos Juliá (ed.), *El socialismo en España* (Madrid, 1986), pp. 453–5. On the debate in general, see Paul Preston, 'War of words: the Spanish Civil War and the historians' in Preston (ed.), *Revolution and War*, pp. 1–13. For a wider ranging historiographical debate on the collapse of the Second Republic, see the review article by Joaquín Romero Maura, 'El debate historiográfico acerca de la segunda República' in *Revista Internacional de Sociología* (Madrid, 2nd series, 3–4, July–December 1972); Santos Juliá, 'Segunda República: por otro objeto de investigación', in Tuñón de Lara (ed.), *Historiografía española*, pp. 295–314; Shlomo Ben-Ami, 'The Republican "take-over": prelude to inevitable catastrophe?' in Preston (ed.), *Revolution and War*, pp. 14–34.

68 On Casas Viejas, see Jerome R. Mintz, *The Anarchists of Casas Viejas* (Chicago, 1982), esp. pp. 178ff. on Anarchist strike calls.

69 Quoted in Mintz, *ibid.*, p. 180.

70 See Preston, *CSCW*, pp. 51–92, *passim*; Biglino, *Socialismo y cuestión agraria*, pp. 374–82; Edward Malefakis, *Reforma agraria y revolución campesina en la España del siglo XX* (Barcelona, 2nd edn, 1982), pp. 329–65.

71 On the CEDA, see Montero, *La CEDA*; Javier Tusell, *Historia de la*

democracia cristiana en España 1. Los antecedentes. La CEDA y la II República (Madrid, 1974); Preston, *CSCW*, pp. 92–130.

72 Quoted in Preston, *The Spanish Civil War* (London, 1986), p. 31.

73 'El camino de la democracia burguesa', *El Socialista*, 22 March 1933.

74 Juan-Simeón Vidarte, *El bienio negro y la insurrección de Asturias* (Barcelona, 1978), p. 39. Macarro Vera also argues that fascism was not seen as that important by the Spanish Socialists, referring to the article written by Luis Araquistáin, 'The struggle in Spain', *Foreign Affairs*, 12(3) (April 1934), pp. 458–71. In the article, Araquistáin wrote: 'In Spain there can be no fascism of the Italian or German type. There are no demobilized men, as there were in Italy; there are no hundreds of thousands of young university men with no future, nor millions of unemployed, as in Germany. There is no Mussolini, nor even a Hitler; there are no imperialist ambitions nor sentiments of revenge, no problems of expansion, nor even a bad Jewish problem. Out of what could Spanish fascism be concocted? I cannot imagine the recipe' (p. 470). The article was unrepresentative of PSOE opinion, nor, indeed, did it square with Araquistáin's own views expressed elsewhere – for instance, his October 1933 lecture, 'El derrumbamiento del socialismo alemán' (on which, see below), as well as a further article, 'The October Revolution in Spain', again published in *Foreign Affairs*, 13(2) (January 1935), pp. 247–61.

75 *El Socialista*, 1 May and 31 October, 1933.

76 Araquistáin expressed his faith in Marxism in a letter sent to Angel Ossorio, editor of *El Sol*, on 3 January 1935. See preliminary study by Javier Tusell to Araquistáin, *Sobre la guerra civil*, p. 19, and the prologue, also by Tusell, to Archivo Histórico Nacional, *Papeles de Don Luis Araquistáin Quevedo* (Madrid, 1983), p. xiii. In 1920, in the first edition of *España en el crisol*, Araquistáin had said that Spain's ills were not economic, but moral. Bizcarrondo detects the influence of José Ortega y Gasset and Max Adler: see 'Democracia', p. 264. See also Santos Juliá, *La izquierda del PSOE 1935–1936* (Madrid, 1977), p. 266.

77 See Antonio González Quintana and Aurelio Martín Najera, *Apuntes para la historia de las Juventudes Socialistas de España* (Madrid, 1983), pp. 45ff.

78 *Renovación*, 18 March 1933; see also Bizcarrondo, 'Democracia', p. 250.

79 *El Obrero* (El Ferrol), 30 September 1933.

80 *Renovación*, 16 September 1933.

81 See Bizcarrondo, 'Democracia', p. 279.

82 The speech can be found in Francisco Largo Caballero, *Discursos a los trabajadores* (Barcelona, 1979; first published 1934), pp. 33–51. However, caution should be exercised, since the various speeches which were included in the book were revised and merged; for details of the changes, see Bizcarrondo, *ACSR*, pp. 138–9. Macarro, 'Radicalización', p. 205 n.63, disagrees with Preston over the start of Largo Caballero's radicalisation – see Preston, *CSCW*, p. 78. Santos Juliá dates it from September 1933 in his introduction to Francisco Largo Caballero, *Escritos de la República* (Madrid, 1985), p. 1, but from 1934 in *Izquierda del PSOE*.

83 On the Erfurt Programme, see Salvadori, *Kautsky*, pp. 26–41; Grebing, *German Workers*, pp. 74–7; Draper, *Dictatorship of the Proletariat*, pp. 317–

23. The very first sentence of the programme stressed the 'natural necessity' of the economic development of bourgeois society leading to the socialisation of the means of production.

84 *El programa de Erfurt* (Madrid, 1933). The introduction has been reprinted in Besteiro, *Obras completas*, vol. III, pp. 45–8.

85 Largo Caballero, *Discursos a los trabajadores*, p. 74.

86 Besteiro's speech in *Obras completas*, vol. III, pp. 17–42.

87 Besteiro's speech at Torrelodones in *Obras completas*, vol. III, pp. 75–98; see Lamo, *Filosofía y política*, p. 90.

88 Besteiro, 'Los caminos', *passim*; see also Macarro Vera, 'Radicalización', p. 209.

89 Details of the speech in Gabriel Mario de Coca, *Anti-Caballero. Una crítica marxista de la bolchevización del partido socialista obrero español* (Madrid, 1975, with introduction and notes by Marta Bizcarrondo; originally published, 1936), pp. 78–80, 173–6; see also Preston, *CSCW*, pp. 86–7.

90 Mario de Coca, *Anti-Caballero*, pp. 174, 175.

91 For details, see Vidarte, *Cortes Constituyentes*, pp. 631ff.; Preston, *CSCW*, pp. 88–9.

92 Macarro Vera, 'Radicalización', p. 218; Juliá, 'República, revolución', pp. 238–9, reports a suggestion by Azaña that the Socialists were not expelled, but left the government of their own volition.

93 Macarro Vera, 'Radicalización', p. 221–2.

94 See Juliá, introduction to Largo Caballero, *República*, pp. li–lii.

95 Mario de Coca, *Anti-Caballero*; Engels' *Herrn Eugen Dührings Umwälzung der Wissenschaft* was originally translated by José Verdes Montenegro as *Anti-Dühring o la revolución de la ciencia* (Madrid, 1913). Two further translations were published in 1932, and a fourth in 1935.

96 Reported in *El Socialista*, 30 October 1933; see also Bizcarrondo, 'Democracia', p. 269.

97 Indalecio Prieto, *Del momento: posiciones socialistas* (Madrid, n.d. but 1935?), p. 35 (this was a collection of speeches and articles made during the Republic); see also Bizcarrondo, 'Democracia', p. 276.

98 On the election results and their immediate aftermath, see Juan-Simeón Vidarte, *El bienio negro*, pp. 30–69; Manuel Tuñón de Lara, *La España del siglo XX* (Paris, 1966), pp. 286–91.

99 Largo Caballero, *Discursos a los trabajadores*, p. 16.

100 Fernando Claudín, 'Spain – the untimely revolution', in *New Left Review*, **74** (July–August 1972), p. 11.

101 The letter is reprinted in Eduardo Comín Colomer, *Historia del Partido Comunista de España* (3 vols., Madrid, 1965–7), vol. I, pp. 287–301.

102 Open letter from ECCI to PCE, in Comín Colomer, *Historia del PCE*, vol. I, pp. 295, 296; see also, Claudín, 'Untimely revolution', p. 2; José Bullejos, *España en la segunda República* (Madrid, 1979), pp. 41–2.

103 On the Sanjurjo coup, see Mariano Aguilar Olivencia, *El ejército español durante la segunda república* (Madrid, 1986), pp. 306–26; Arrarás, *Segunda República*, vol. I, pp. 505–39. There is a large literature on the dramatic shifts in

Comintern policy; see, for example, E.H. Carr, *The Twilight of the Comintern 1930–1935* (London, 1982), pp. 3–155; Fernando Claudín, *The Communist Movement. From Comintern to Cominform* (2 vols., New York, 1975), vol. I, *passim.*

104 On these expulsions, see Enrique Matorras, *El comunismo en España* (Madrid, 1935), pp. 121–44; Andrade, *Apuntes*, pp. 45–55; Joan Estruch Tobella, *Historia del PCE (1920–1939)* (Barcelona, 1978), pp. 72–4; and the virulently anti-Communist Alba, *El Partido Comunista en España* (Barcelona, 1979), pp. 130–33. For events in Seville, see José Manuel Macarro Vera, *La utopía revolucionaria: Sevilla en la Segunda República* (Seville, 1985), pp. 253–66.

105 Díaz's loyalty to the Communist cause is reflected in the volume of his speeches, *Tres años de lucha* (3 vols., Barcelona, 1978; first published, Toulouse, 1947). Hernández, on the other hand, left a highly bitter account of his experiences in *Yo fui un ministro de Stalin* (Madrid, 1974) and *En el país de la gran mentira* (Madrid, 1974) – both published originally as one volume (Mexico, 1953). Perhaps ironically, Díaz 'fell' to his death in Tiflis, Soviet Union, in 1942, while Hernández escaped to live out his life in Mexico, where he died in 1971.

106 Ricardo de la Cierva, *Historia del socialismo en España 1879–1983* (Barcelona, 1983), p. 137, incorrectly asserts under the heading 'The truth about the alianzas obreras' that they were set up by the PSOE in February 1934 on the initiative of Francisco Largo Caballero.

107 Maurín was a former schoolteacher whose early political inclinations had been Anarchist, but whose later commitment to Marxism–Leninism led him to abandon the CNT and join the Federación Comunista Catalano-Balear (FCCB), the Catalan section of the PCE, in 1924. The FCCB soon fell into dispute with the PCE over what Maurín saw as the latter's blind obedience to Moscow, whose intransigently sectarian line, he argued, would prove costly in Spain. As a result, in 1928 the FCCB was expelled from the PCE, taking with it nearly half that party's membership. In March 1931 the FCCB merged with the diminutive Partit Comunista Català (PCC), a dissident Marxist party headed by Jordi Arquer, to form the BOC. On Maurín, who remains something of a mysterious figure, see the highly hagiographic studies by Víctor Alba, *Dos revolucionarios: Andreu Nin/Joaquín Maurín* (Madrid, 1975) and Manuel Sánchez, *Maurín, gran enigma de guerra y otros recuerdos* (Madrid, 1976). A recent study of his political thought is Antoni Monreal, *El pensamiento político de Joaquín Maurín* (Barcelona, 1984). Also of importance is Andrew Durgan, 'Dissident Communism in Catalonia, 1930–1936' (Unpublished PhD thesis, Queen Mary College, University of London, 1989).

108 Nin, from Vendrell in Tarragona, was also a former schoolteacher. Originally a Republican sympathiser, Nin first joined the PSOE in 1911, becoming secretary of the FJSE soon afterwards. By 1919, he had become disillusioned with the PSOE's 'sickening reformism', and joined the CNT in Barcelona as a member of the Liberal Professions Union, which he had helped to set up. Thereafter, in the summer of 1921, he went to Moscow to attend the founding Congress of the Red International of Labour Unions, or Profintern, of which

he became a delegated member, based in Berlin. His ever closer collaboration with Trotsky, whom he had met in Moscow, led to Nin being expelled from the Profintern, of which he had become secretary, in 1928. He remained in the Soviet Union a further two years before returning to Spain, where he set up in Barcelona the Oposición Comunista de Izquierda, later to become the ICE. See Francesc Bonamusa, *Andreu Nin y el movimiento comunista en España (1930–1937)* (Barcelona, 1977), pp. 11–21. See also the anthology of the ICE's short-lived theoretical journal, *Comunismo*, published by Editorial Fontamara, *Revista Comunismo (1931–1934)* (Barcelona, 1978), with a brief, but useful, introduction by Jesús Pérez.

109 This is the central theme of Joaquín Maurín, *La revolución española* (Barcelona, 1977; first published, 1932); see esp. pp. 170–88.

110 *La Batalla*, 18 May 1933; Joaquín Maurín, 'La Alianza Obrera. Orígenes, características y porvenir' in *La Nueva Era*, 1(1), January 1936.

111 See Preston, *CSCW*, pp. 196–7. See also, Víctor Alba, *La Alianza Obrera. Historia y análisis de una táctica de unidad en España* (Madrid, 1977), pp. 13–185; Víctor Alba, *El marxismo en España (1931–1939)* (2 vols., Mexico, 1973), vol. I, pp. 135–79.

112 Vidarte, *Cortes Constituyentes*, pp. 66off.

113 The programme in full can be consulted in Partido Comunista de España, *Guerra y revolución en España 1936–39* (4 vols., Moscow, 1966–77), vol. I, pp. 52–4. Preston, *CSCW*, p. 105, in a surprising judgement calls Prieto's proposals 'relatively mild'.

114 Besteiro's proposals in Besteiro, *Obras*, III, pp. 607–9.

115 Saborit, Gómez, Muiño, Cernadas and Muñoz Giraldos also resigned in solidarity with Besteiro; see Besteiro, *Obras*, III, p. 609; Preston, *CSCW*, pp. 105–6; Bizcarrondo, 'Democracia', pp. 286ff.

116 The five points can be consulted in Besteiro, *Obras*, III, p. 606.

117 Vidarte, *Bienio negro*, pp. 185ff.

118 Alba, *Alianza Obrera*, pp. 112–13; Alba, *Marxismo en España*, vol. I, pp. 135–79.

119 *Adelante*, 13 February 1934.

120 See L. Fersen (pseudonym of Luis Fernández Sendón), 'La actitud del Partido Socialista y la situación política', *Comunismo*, 32 (February 1934).

121 *El Socialista*, 21 April 1934.

122 See Ricard Viñas, *La formación de las Juventudes Socialistas Unificadas (1934–1936)* (Madrid, 1978), pp. 11–15. Viñas mentions Jesús Hernández instead of Carlos Hernández, presumably an inadvertent confusion with the Communist leader.

123 See Bizcarrondo, 'Democracia', p. 304.

124 Margarita Nelken, 'Reformismo o marxismo', *Espartaco*, 3 (September 1934).

125 Claudín was replaced at the second meeting by Agustín Zapirain; see Fernando Claudín, *Santiago Carrillo. Crónica de un secretario general* (Barcelona, 1983), pp. 20–7.

126 See Antonio M. Calero, *Movimientos sociales en Andalucía 1820–1936* (Madrid, 1979), pp. 86–91; José Manuel Macarro Vera, *La utopía revolucionaria*; Luis Garrido González, 'Colectividades socialistas en la provincia de

Jaén 1933–1939' in *Actas I Congreso de Historia de Andalucía* (2 vols., Córdoba, 1979), vol. II; Luis Garrido González, *Colectividades agrarias en Andalucía: Jaén 1931–1939* (Madrid, 1979); Biglino, *Socialismo y cuestión agraria*, pp. 406–41.

127 See Preston, *CSCW*, pp. 112ff.

128 For details, see Biglino, *Socialismo y cuestión agraria*, pp. 442–67; Tuñón de Lara, *Tres claves*, pp. 130–53; Malefakis, *Reforma agraria*, pp. 386–92.

129 On the strikers' demands, see Preston, *CSCW*, pp. 114–5.

130 Tuñón de Lara, *Tres claves*, pp. 143–8, 163–5; Biglino, *Socialismo y cuestión agraria*, pp. 465–7.

131 The Madrid Alianza was founded in May 1934. See Pelai Pagès, *El movimiento trotskista en España 1930–1935* (Barcelona, 1977), p. 177.

132 José Luis Arenillas, 'La crisis del Partido Socialista Español' in *Comunismo*, 37 (August 1934).

133 This point is forcefully argued in Preston, *CSCW*, p. 118.

134 See Bizcarrondo, 'Democracia', pp. 298ff.

135 Consistent with the lack of attention devoted to agrarian issues was a tendency, evident in the writings and speeches of *all* the Spanish Marxists, to speak of 'peasants' and 'the peasantry' as homogeneous, self-explanatory entities. This probably reflected a belief that Marx and Engels themselves held such a view, as evidenced by such famous remarks as: 'A smallholding, a peasant and his family; alongside them another smallholding, another peasant and another family... In this way, the great mass of the French nation is formed by simple addition of homologous magnitudes, much as potatoes in a sack form a sack of potatoes.' (*The Eighteenth Brumaire of Louis Bonaparte*, in Karl Marx, *Surveys From Exile* (Harmondsworth, 1973), p. 239). Such interpretations have been lambasted by Hal Draper, *Karl Marx's Theory of Revolution. Vol. 2: The Politics of Social Classes* (New York, 1978), p. 317: 'One of the hoariest of the myths of marxology is the belief that Marx and Engels simply dismissed the peasantry as rural troglodytes without interest – the "Marx against the peasants" legend.' See in particular, chs. 12–14.

136 See preface to Ed. Fontamara, *Comunismo*, p. 18; on the political trajectory of García Palacios, see *ibid.*, p. 574.

137 Leon Trotsky, *The Revolution in Spain* (Communist League of America, 1931), reprinted in Leon Trotsky, *The Spanish Revolution (1931–1939)* (New York, 1973), pp. 67–88.

138 Leon Trotsky, 'The Spanish Revolution and the dangers threatening it', *The Spanish Revolution in Danger*, 28 May 1931, in Trotsky, *Spanish Revolution*, pp. 111–34. On Trotsky's view of the role of the peasantry within his theory of permanent revolution, see Baruch Knei-Paz, *The Social and Political Thought of Leon Trotsky* (Oxford, 1978), pp. 129–40.

139 Maurín, *Revolución española*, pp. 130–49; the quote is on p. 149. Maurín's description of Castile as being marked by monoculture was not strictly accurate, although cereal production certainly dominated.

140 See Leszek Kolakowski, *Main Currents of Marxism*, vol. II, pp. 405–12; Neil Harding, *Lenin's Political Thought* (2 vols. bound as one, London, 1983), 'Vol. I', pp. 216–18.

141 See Víctor Alba, *La Nueva Era* (Madrid, 1977), pp. 345–52.
142 Montero, *CEDA*, vol. ii, pp. 225–40; Arrarás, *Segunda República*, vol. ii, pp.
     461–82; Vidarte, *Bienio negro*, pp. 163–84; Preston, *CSCW*, pp. 120–1; Albert
     Balcells, *Cataluña contemporánea II (1900–1939)* (Madrid, 1981), pp. 33–4,
     127–33.
143 For details of the October insurrection, see below, chapter 6.

6 Marxism marginalised: the PSOE and the creation of the Popular Front, 1934–6

1 There is a massive literature on the Asturian rising of October 1934. Amongst
   recent works, the best introduction and overview is Germán Ojeda (ed.),
   Octubre 1934. Cincuenta años para la reflexión (Madrid, 1984), a collection of
   articles from a conference held in Oviedo under the auspices of the Fundación
   José Barreiro in 1984. The book also contains a useful bibliography. Also
   important is the monographic edition of *Estudios de Historia Social*, 31 (1984),
   dedicated to the October rising. For a recent view from the Right, see Enrique
   Barco Teruel, *El 'golpe' socialista* (Madrid, 1984). A contrasting approach, on
   the long-term social origins of the rising, is developed by Adrian Shubert,
   Hacia la revolución (Barcelona, 1984), the English version of which has been
   published as *The Road to Revolution in Spain* (Chicago, 1987).
2 On the formation of the *Alianza obrera*, see chapter 5, above. See also Víctor
   Alba, *La Alianza Obrera. Historia y análisis de una táctica de unidad en
   España* (Barcelona, 1977), esp. pp. 138ff.
3 See José María Gil Robles, *Discursos parlamentarios* (Madrid, 1971), pp.
   439ff.; José R. Montero, *La CEDA* (Madrid, 1977), vol. ii, pp. 410–11; Javier
   Tusell, *Historia de la democracia cristiana en España* (Madrid, 1974), vol. i, pp.
   244–52.
4 See the PCE's official history of the Civil War, *Guerra y revolución en España*
   (4 vols., Moscow, 1966–77), vol. i, pp. 66–78; Joaquín Arrarás, *Historia de la
   Segunda República española* (4 vols., Madrid, 1956–68), vol. iv, 2 – 'El Frente
   Popular hechura de la Internacional comunista' ('The Popular Front, creature
   of the Communist International'), pp. 17–28. The view has gained acceptance
   amongst a number of historians, such as Gabriel Jackson, *The Spanish
   Republic and the Civil War, 1931–1939* (Princeton, 1967), pp. 185–6; Stanley
   Payne, *The Spanish Revolution* (New York, 1970), p. 167. It should be
   acknowledged that the PCE was helped in its assumption of a greater political
   role by Largo Caballero's denial at his trial of any participation in the October
   rising – see below.
5 This view had been effectively argued by Santos Juliá and Paul Preston. See
   Juliá, *Orígenes del Frente Popular en España (1934–1936)* (Madrid, 1979), esp.
   pp. 27–41, 134–49; Juliá, 'Sobre la formación del Frente Popular en España',
   Sistema, 73 (July 1986), pp. 67–81; Preston, 'Manuel Azaña y la creación del
   Frente Popular (1933–1936)' in Vicente Alberto Serrano and José María San
   Luciano (eds.), *Azaña* (Madrid, 1980), pp. 269–85; Preston, 'The Creation of
   the Popular Front in Spain' in Helen Graham and Paul Preston (eds.), *The
   Popular Front in Europe* (London, 1987), pp. 84–105.

6 Of course the ultimate irony is that General Franco rose precisely against the 'red threat' represented by the PSOE as supposed Marxist lackeys of the so-called international Communist conspiracy. Thus, there was no distinction drawn between the various component parts of the Popular Front, which was seen as the harbinger of 'cruel, inhuman, barbarous, anti-Spanish, anti-Christian' Communist revolution. For a florid description of the full scale of alleged Communist horrors, see Jesús Iribarren (ed.), *Documentos colectivos del Episcopado español, 1870–1974* (Madrid, 1974), pp. 228–35.

7 Given Prieto's rather enormous girth, this feat of athleticism is worthy of admiration. For further details, see Alfonso Carlos Saiz Valdivielso, *Indalecio Prieto. Crónica de un corazón* (Barcelona, 1984), p. 175. Ignacio Hidalgo was the husband of the remarkable Constancia de la Mora, grand-daughter of Antonio Maura and Spanish aristocrat turned Communist, whose experiences during the Civil War were published in her autobiography, *In Place of Splendour* (New York, 1939).

8 See, for example, Richard A.H. Robinson, *The Origins of Franco's Spain* (Newton Abbot, 1970), p. 261; Paul Preston, *The Coming of the Spanish Civil War* (London, 1978; henceforth *CSCW*), p. 134 mentions Caballero's 'acute personal resentment of Prieto' as one of several reasons for the former's 'radicalisation'; Santos Juliá, 'Corporativistas obreros y reformadores políti-cos: crisis y escisión del PSOE en la II República', *Studia Histórica*, 1(4) (1983), p. 50, states that while 'it would be ridiculous to reduce the confron-tation to merely a personal question', the personal incompatibility between the two leaders had a 'decisive effect' on the form in which the schism occurred.

9 Santos Juliá, *ibid.*; Juliá, 'Los socialistas en la crisis de los años treinta', *Zona Abierta*, 27 (1983), pp. 63–77; Juliá, 'Continuidad y ruptura en el socialismo español del siglo xx', *Leviatán*, 17 (1984), pp. 121–30; Juliá, 'Largo Caballero y la lucha de tendencias en el socialismo español', *'Annali' della Fondazione Giangiacomo Feltrinelli 1983–1984* (Milan, 1985), pp. 857–85; Juliá, 'República, revolución y luchas internas' in Santos Juliá (ed.), *El Socialismo en España* (Madrid, 1986), pp. 231–54. Although the terminology employed is different, Juliá's description of the differing concerns of 'worker corporativ-ists' and 'political reformists' in places closely parallels the analysis of Paul Preston in *CSCW*, chapters 1, 3 and 4.

10 Juliá, 'República, revolución', p. 234; See Manuel Azaña, *Obras completas* (4 vols., Mexico, 1966–8), vol. ii, pp. 631–43.

11 Juliá, 'Corporativistas obreras', pp. 50–1.

12 Juliá, *ibid.*, p. 47.

13 Juliá does not confront the question directly. Marta Bizcarrondo, who has also written extensively on the PSOE during the Second Republic, sees Prieto's position in these terms: see, for example, Bizcarrondo, 'Democracia y revolu-ción en la estrategia socialista de la II República', *Estudios de Historia Social*, 16–17 (January–June 1981), pp. 277–8. In similar vein, Preston, *CSCW*, p. 132.

14 Years later, Prieto stated at the Círculo Pablo Iglesias in Mexico City: 'I am free of blame for the genesis of that movement, but I must take full responsi-bility for its preparation and development. . .I accepted tasks from which others fled because there hung over them the risk not only of losing their

liberty but the more painful shadow of losing their honour. Nevertheless, I undertook those tasks. I collaborated in that movement heart and soul. . .'. Quoted in Preston, 'Creation of the Popular Front', p. 94.

15 See Helen Graham, 'The Spanish Popular Front and the Civil War' in Graham and Preston (eds.), *The Popular Front in Europe*, p. 107: 'In reality, the dispute had much less to do with differences of political doctrine or tactics than it did with organisational rivalries in the socialist movement.' See also Santos Juliá, *La izquierda del PSOE 1935–1936, passim*, but esp. ch. 6, pp. 287–304, and the review of Juliá's book by Andrés de Blas Guerrero in *Sistema*, 23 (March 1978).

16 On both the poverty and the subtleties of Marxist analyses of fascism, see the excellent introduction to David Beetham, *Marxists in Face of Fascism* (Manchester, 1983), pp. 1–62. On Thalheimer, see Martin Kitchen, *Fascism* (London, 1976), chapter 7; on Trotsky, Robert Wistrich, 'Leon Trotsky's Theory of Fascism', *Journal of Contemporary History*, 11(4) (1976); on Gramsci, *Selections from the Prison Notebooks* (London, 1971), *passim*, and introduction by Quintin Hoare and Geoffrey Nowell-Smith.

17 See Beetham, *Marxists in Face of Fascism*, pp. 40–50; also Leszek Kolakowski, *Main Currents of Marxism* (3 vols., Oxford, 1981), vol. 3, chapter 3: 'Marxism as the ideology of the Soviet state', esp. pp. 105–16. Largo's position might be seen as in some ways analogous to that of Hilferding when he drew up the so-called Prague Manifesto in January 1934 against the legalist line of Kautsky.

18 Víctor Alba, *El marxismo en España 1919–1939* (2 vols., Mexico, 1973), pp. 135–79, *passim*.

19 Xavier Paniagua and José A. Piqueras, *Trabajadores sin revolución* (Valencia, 1986), p. 273; Bizcarrondo, 'Democracia', p. 326.

20 Luis G. Germán, 'El Socialismo en Aragón' in Ignacio Barrón *et al.*, *Historia del socialismo en Aragón* (Zaragoza, 1979), pp. 115–16; Salvador Forner Muñoz, *Industrialización y movimiento obrero. Alicante 1923–1936* (Valencia, 1982), pp. 363ff.

21 *La Batalla*, 20 September 1935.

22 *Los combates de octubre*, Resolución del Buro Político del Partido Comunista de España (n.p., n.d., but Madrid, 1934). See Marta Bizcarrondo (ed.), *Octubre del 34: Reflexiones sobre una revolución* (Madrid, 1977), introduction, pp. 68–70.

23 On the distinction between the singular (Maurín) and plural (PCE) designation of the *Alianza(s)*, see Marta Bizcarrondo, *Araquistáin y la crisis socialista en la II República. Leviatán (1934–1936)* (Madrid, 1975; henceforth *ACSR*), p. 193.

24 PCE, *Guerra y revolución*, vol. I, p. 62.

25 For the French Communists, see Jacques Danos and Marcel Gibelin, *June '36. Class Struggle and the Popular Front in France* (London, 1986; translated from 1972 edition by Peter Fysh and Christine Bourry), pp. 35ff.

26 See Juliá, 'Sobre la formación', pp. 70–3; E.H. Carr, *The Twilight of the Comintern, 1930–1935* (London, 1982), pp. 310ff.; Eduardo Comín Colomer, *Historia del Partido Comunista de España* (3 vols., Madrid, 1965–67), vol. II, pp. 389–418.

27 On Codovilla, see Sheldon B. Liss, *Marxist Thought in Latin America* (California, 1984), pp. 56–9.

28 The quote from Blum in Beetham, *Marxists in Face of Fascism*, p. 20.

29 See *ibid*. p. 22; E.H. Carr, *Twilight*, pp. 123ff.

30. *Ibid.*, p. 198.

31 Juliá, 'Sobre la formación', p. 71, quotes PCE leader José Díaz: 'after strenuous efforts we managed to set up the *comité de enlace* with them. We were not deceiving ourselves. We knew that they had agreed under duress and that they would not hold to the agreements, and also that it would be very difficult to get them to accept anything practical. . . In the Socialist Party we have not done anything much at the top level – the Executive Commission has sabotaged all our efforts.'

32 Juliá, 'Sobre la formación', p. 72. Juan-Simeón Vidarte makes no reference to his role in his memoirs, while Amaro del Rosal, vice-secretary of the UGT, mentions in his *Historia de la UGT en España 1901–1939* (2 vols., Barcelona, 1977), p. 423, that Largo Caballero was all in favour of formal unity, but was afraid of losing '*control*' of the movement.

33 Juliá, 'Sobre la formación', p. 72.

34 *Ibid.*

35 See Juan Avilés Farré, *La izquierda burguesa en la Segunda República* (Madrid, 1985), p. 251; Cipriano de Rivas Cherif, *Retrato de un desconocido* (2nd edn, Barcelona, 1981), pp. 293–302.

36 Azaña, *Obras*, vol. III, pp. 587–604.

37 See Preston, 'Creation of the Popular Front', pp. 84–105.

38 Letter in Indalecio Prieto *et al.*, *Documentos socialistas* (Madrid, 1935), pp. 19–26; Juan-Simeón Vidarte, *El bienio negro y la insurrección de Asturias* (Barcelona, 1978), pp. 389–93.

39 The circular in Vidarte, *Bienio negro*, pp. 396–8; the claim is on pp. 393–4, and repeated in Juan-Simeón Vidarte, *Todos fuimos culpables* (2 vols., Barcelona, 1978), vol. I, p. 25.

40 On De los Ríos' brief re-entry to political life, see Virgilio Zapatero, *Fernando de los Ríos: Los problemas del socialismo democrático* (Madrid, 1974), pp. 108ff. Santos Juliá, 'República, revolución', p. 248, sees the letter as the real start of the 'Caballerista' faction. The other signatories were Tomás, Pretel, Díaz Alor and Del Rosal.

41 For details, see Robinson, *Origins of Franco's Spain*, pp. 196ff.; Preston, *CSCW*, pp. 156–7.

42 See Juliá, *Izquierda del PSOE*, p. 316.

43 Ramón Lamoneda remains a rather mysterious figure; there is a surprising dearth of information on him, given his senior role in the PSOE and his importance during the Civil War. Stanley Payne, *Spanish Revolution*, p. 167, has both his name and ideological beliefs wrong: 'The wave of Bolshevisation-. . .accelerated Communist penetration of the Spanish Socialist party. . . Carlos Lamoneda, who had been a member of the Communist party from 1921 to 1933, served as secretary for the group of Socialist deputies that remained in the Cortes. He and another leading crypto-Communist, Alvarez del Vayo, dominated relations between the parliamentary representation and the party at

large.' Payne's description is riddled with inaccuracies – Ramón Lamoneda, born in Begíjar (Jaén), rejoined the PSOE in the early years of the Primo de Rivera Dictatorship after a brief flirtation with the nascent PCE in the early 1920s. Far from being a crypto-Communist, Lamoneda was a supporter of Prieto against Caballero. Moreover, the so-called 'Communist penetration of the Socialist party' failed to take place, as admitted even by the PCE – see note 31, above. Ricardo de la Cierva, *Historia del socialismo en España. 1879–1983* (Barcelona, 1983), p. 174, also incorrectly refers to Lamoneda 'moving over secretly to "bolshevism"'. For a brief summary of Lamoneda's political career, see *Historia 16, La Guerra Civil* (24 vols., 1986–7), vol. 15, 'Las Dos Zonas (December 1937)', p. 94.

44 A long article by Enrique de Francisco, attacking Prieto's record, was turned down by the editor in July 1935. It was subsequently published in the Caballerista journal, *Claridad*. See Bizcarrondo, 'Democracia', p. 358.

45 Bizcarrondo, 'Democracia', p. 350, states that the articles were published in response to the increased circulation of a journal called *Octubre*. I have been unable to find any reference to this journal in the Fundación Pablo Iglesias, the Hemeroteca Nacional or the Biblioteca Nacional (Madrid). Nor have I found a reference to it in any other secondary work on the period.

46 Prieto, *Posiciones socialistas*; see also, Bizcarrondo, 'Democracia', pp. 348–50.

47 The speech can be found in Julián Besteiro, *Obras completas* (3 vols., Madrid, 1983), vol. III, pp. 229–334. See also Emilio Lamo de Espinosa, *Filosofía y política en Julián Besteiro* (Madrid, 1973), p. 99, where he refers to Besteiro's misfortune in being elected to replace Gabino Bugallal y Arango, former president of the Conservative Party during a period in which Besteiro had twice been arrested and vilified under that party's rule (1917 and 1920). Protocol demanded that Besteiro offer a eulogy of his predecessor, the source of easy debating points for the left opposition within the PSOE.

48 Besteiro, *Obras*, III, p. 245.

49 Besteiro, *Obras*, III, pp. 229–334 *passim*; see Bizcarrondo, 'Democracia', pp. 16–17, 243ff.

50 Elorza was later shot by the Francoists. See Bizcarrondo, 'Democracia', p. 347.

51 It is virtually impossible to establish the precise date of publication of the pamphlet. Few works refer to the date at all, while – surprisingly – Ricard Viñas, *La formación de las Juventudes Socialistas Unificadas (1934–1936)*, p. 157, gives October 1934 as the date, which is clearly wrong.

52 Juventudes Socialistas de España, *Octubre: segunda etapa* (Madrid, n.d., but 1935). The demands can also be consulted in Bizcarrondo (ed.), *Octubre*, p. 154; see also, Comín Colomer, *Partido Comunista*, vol. II, pp. 459–484.

53 Letter from FJSE (Oviedo) to the Comisión Ejecutiva of the FJSE in Madrid, 5 March 1935, reproduced in Antonio González Quintana and Aurelio Martín Najera, *Apuntes para la historia de las Juventudes Socialistas de España* (Madrid, 1983), p. 55.

54 Carlos de Baraibar, *Las falsas 'posiciones socialistas' de Indalecio Prieto* (Madrid, 1935).

55 On Baraibar, see Bizcarrondo, *ACSR*, p. 237.

56 Prieto *et al.*, *Documentos socialistas*.

57 On 31 March, Ramón González Peña sent a letter of support to Prieto; for details, see Preston, *CSCW*, p. 136.

58 Luis Araquistáin, 'El profesor Besteiro o el marxismo en la Academia', *Leviatán*, 13 (May 1935). A reprint of the article can be found in Araquistáin, *Marxismo y socialismo en España* (Barcelona, 1980), pp. 26–7, a collection of all the articles Araquistáin wrote in *Leviatán*. The other articles in the series against Besteiro were 'Un marxismo contra Marx' and 'La esencia del marxismo' in *Leviatán*, nos. 14 and 15 (June, July 1935). Besteiro's reply came in the shape of two articles, 'Leviatán, el socialismo mitológico' and 'Mi crítico empieza a razonar' in *Democracia* (15 June, 6 July 1935), and the publication of his inaugural lecture at the Academy, *Marxismo y antimarxismo* (Madrid, n.d., but 1935).

59 This accusation was taken up by Payne, *Spanish Revolution*, pp. 136–7, and La Cierva, *Historia del socialismo*, p. 136. For a rather dismissive view of Araquistáin's capabilities, see Juliá, *Izquierda del PSOE*, pp. 265ff.

60 See, for example, Paul Preston (ed.), *Leviatán (antología)* (Madrid, 1976); Marta Bizcarrondo, *ACSR*; Marta Bizcarrondo, *Leviatán y el socialismo de Luis Araquistáin* (Glashütten im Taunus, 1974); Araquistáin, *Marxismo y socialismo*.

61 Unfortunately, in light of the lack of reliable data, it is impossible to assess how widely read was *Leviatán* and what was the nature of its impact – if any – on ordinary PSOE militants.

62 *Democracia*, 1 (15 June 1935).

63 See Bizcarrondo, 'Democracia', p. 354.

64 Saborit, 'Nada más y nada menos que socialista', *Democracia*, 8 (3 August 1935).

65 '¿Dónde están las tendencias ideológicas?', *Democracia*, 7 (27 July 1935).

66 Again, the lack of circulation figures makes it difficult to assess the impact of *Democracia* on party militants.

67 On Gabriel Mario de Coca, see above, chapter 5.

68 *Claridad*, 1, 4 (July, August 1935); see Bizcarrondo, 'Democracia', p. 359.

69 *Claridad*, 2 (20 July 1935).

70 Carlos de Baraibar, 'El estado a la luz del marxismo', *Claridad*, 6 (17 August 1935).

71 See *Claridad*, 22 (7 October 1935), 23 (14 October 1935).

72 The speeches, which were held in Mestalla (Valencia), Lasesarre (Baracaldo, nr. Bilbao) and Comillas, can be consulted in Azaña, *Obras*, III, pp. 229–93. They attracted combined audiences of nearly 700,000 people. See Avilés Farré, *Izquierda burguesa*, p. 270.

73 The success of Azaña's 'discursos' raises a very important point which, although it lies beyond the scope of this work, is in need of detailed investigation. One of the least studied aspects of the Socialist movement during the Second Republic is the question of grass-roots militant activism: what did PSOE members actually think; how were they affected by the divisions within the leadership of the party; what were local-level relations between Socialists and Anarchists, etc. The answers to these questions can come only through a series of detailed local studies, a number of which have

started to appear in Spain. Unfortunately, many of these (for example, Ignacio Barrón *et al.*, *Historia del socialismo en Aragón* (Zaragoza, 1979), Jesús M. Eguiguren, *El PSOE en el País Vasco (1886–1936)* (San Sebastián, 1984), Xavier Paniagua and José A. Piqueras, *Trabajadores sin revolución. La clase obrera valenciana 1868–1936* (Valencia, 1986)) remain very abstract and generalised, covering the Republic in sketchy detail and still at the level of leadership discussions and clashes. There are exceptions, such as Salvador Forner Muñoz, *Industrialización y movimiento obrero. Alicante 1923–1936* (Valencia, 1982), and, above all, Santos Juliá, *Madrid, 1931–1934. De la fiesta popular a la lucha de clases* (Madrid, 1984), but in general the picture remains patchy for most of Spain. However, it is generally asserted that the *bienio negro* saw the development of increased militancy amongst the working class and peasantry, and that the pressure this brought about was a major inducement to the radicalisation of the PSOE, and in particular its participation in the October 1934 uprising. Nonetheless, there is less agreement as to what pressure was most significant. Two leading analysts of the Left during the Republic, Paul Preston and Santos Juliá, reach differing conclusions. While Preston lays stress on the pressure brought to bear on the PSOE leadership by the radical stances of the southern peasantry and of FNTT members in particular, Juliá sees the greater influence coming from displaced urban workers in a period of social and industrial upheaval. (For brief outlines of these positions, see Juliá, 'Economic crisis, social conflict and the Popular Front: Madrid 1931–6' and Preston, 'The agrarian war in the south' in Paul Preston (ed.), *Revolution and War in Spain, 1931–1939* (London, 1984).) Both arguments are persuasive, but contain problems. If the rural radicalisation thesis is correct, this fails to explain why the PSOE failed to support the peasant strike of 1934, nor the mechanisms for transmitting pressure to the Caballeristas *after* October 1934 while the radical leaders of the party were in jail in Madrid. The dislocated urban workers thesis faces the same problem of explaining mechanisms of transmission, but also fails to account for the very evident support accorded Azaña and Prieto in predominantly industrial areas. Moreover, if the working class in Spain was so radical as to act as a pressure on the PSOE to adopt maximalist positions, this raises questions as to why it failed in general to support the October 1934 rising and why it offered support in such large numbers to a Popular Front coalition which was markedly moderate. Neither Preston nor Juliá lays sufficient stress on the ideological constrictions of Marxism during the 1930s and the impact that these had upon the PSOE leadership.

74 Arrarás, *Segunda República*, vol. III, p. 219, mentions *David* Strauss and Perlo; José María Gil Robles, *No fue posible la paz* (Barcelona, 1968), p. 299 has Perl; Eduardo Comín Colomer, *Historia secreta de la segunda República* (Barcelona, 1959), p. 396, mentions 'the jews Strauss and Perlowitz'; Alejandro Lerroux, *La pequeña historia de España 1930–1936* (Barcelona, 1985; first published, 1945), pp. 243–4, 260–2, mentions only Strauss. Even an article by José Miguel Fernández Urbina, 'Straperlo y Taya' in *Historia 16, La Guerra Civil* (24 vols., Madrid, 1986–7), vol. II, simply has 'Perlo', mentioned once, with no further explanation. This is all the more remarkable given that the

word *estraperlo* has passed into the Spanish language to mean 'black market'. The Vox Diccionario General Ilustrado de la Lengua Española (Barcelona, 1973), states that the word derives from *Strauss, Pérez* and *López*.

75 See Avilés Farré, *Izquierda burguesa*, pp. 269–70.

76 See, for example, Víctor Alba, 'Marxism' in James W. Cortada (ed.), *Historical Dictionary of the Spanish Civil War, 1936–39* (Connecticut, 1982), p. 323.

77 On the unification process in general, see Ricard Viñas, *Formación de las Juventudes Socialistas.*

78 See E.H. Carr, *Twilight*, p. 317; Preston, *CSCW*, pp. 142–3.

79 Azaña, *Obras*, vol. III, p. 602.

80 This goes against most prevailing interpretations. See, for example, Preston, *CSCW*, p. 144; Preston, 'Formation of the Popular Front' in Graham and Preston (eds.), *Popular Front*, p. 102: 'The adherence of Largo Caballero would not have been possible without the efforts of the communists... Accordingly, they worked hard to get him to drop his opposition, even sending Jacques Duclos to try to persuade him.' Jacques Duclos himself gives this version in his memoirs, quoted in E.H. Carr, *The Comintern and the Spanish Civil War* (London, 1984), pp. 2–3. Against these views, see Juliá, 'Sobre la formación', pp. 76–7; Manuel Tuñón de Lara, 'La España del Frente Popular', *Historia 16, La Guerra Civil* (24 vols., Madrid, 1986–87), vol. II, pp. 39–40.

81 Bizcarrondo, 'Democracia', pp. 338ff.; Del Rosal, *UGT*, pp. 437–8.

82 Bizcarrondo, 'Democracia', pp. 342–4.

83 The proposals were published in *La Libertad*, 13 April 1935, by Izquierda Republicana, Unión Republicana, and the Partido Nacional Republicano.

84 Fernando Claudín, 'Spain – the untimely revolution' in *New Left Review*, 74 (July–August 1972), p. 11.

85 See letter from Trotsky to the International Secretariat, 1 November 1934, in Leon Trotsky, *The Spanish Revolution (1931–1939)* (New York, 1973), p. 202. The depth of Trotsky's disillusionment with Nin over his refusal to comply with his wishes can be gauged from a letter by Trotsky to Victor Serge, 3 June 1936, in which he stated 'You can easily imagine how happy I was when Nin came abroad. Over various years I have maintained regular correspondence with him... I think that my letters to Nin over two or three years would constitute a volume several hundred pages long: that suffices to demonstrate the importance I attached to Nin and my friendship with him... Of course, no one is obliged to be a revolutionary. But Nin was leader of the Bolshevik–Leninist organisation in Spain, and for that reason alone had taken on serious responsibilities from which he slipped away in practice, while throwing sand in my eyes through his letters.' Quoted in Leon Trotsky, *La Revolución Española 1930–1940. León Trotsky* (2 vols., Barcelona, 1977; introduction and prologue by Pierre Broué), vol. I, p. 346.

86 Leon Trotsky, 'The Revolution in Spain', 24 January 1931 and 'The character of the Revolution', 18 June 1931, both reproduced in Trotsky, *Spanish Revolution*. Trotsky's view of developments in Spain was informed by his theory of 'permanent revolution', which rejected the stagist conception of the Comintern and of the Socialists.

87 On the details of the creation of the JSU, see Ricard Viñas, *La formación de las Juventudes Socialistas Unificadas (1934–1936)*, pp. 1–68; on its significance, Helen Graham, 'The Socialist Youth in the JSU: the experience of organizational unity, 1936–8', in Martin Blinkhorn (ed.), *Spain in Conflict, 1931–1939. Democracy and its Enemies* (London, 1986), pp. 83–102.

88 For references to the POUM as Trotskyist, see Gabriel Jackson, *The Spanish Republic and the Civil War, 1931–1939* (Princeton, 1967), p. 285; Edward Malefakis, 'The Parties of the Left and the Second Republic' in Raymond Carr (ed.), *The Republic and the Civil War in Spain* (London, 1971), p. 38; Rhea Marsh Smith, *Spain. A Modern History* (Michigan, 1965), p. 450. Even more inaccurate is the suggestion in Juan-Simeón Vidarte, *Las Cortes Constituyentes de 1931–1933* (Barcelona, 1976), pp. 734–5, that the POUM was created in 1930, at Trotsky's suggestion, and led by Nin.

89 Bonamusa, *Andreu Nin*, p. 259; see also, Andrew Durgan, 'Dissident Communism in Catalonia, 1930–1936' (Unpublished PhD thesis, Queen Mary College, University of London, 1989). In fact, prior to the Civil War, the POUM remained a relatively unimportant group. According to Payne, *The Spanish Revolution* (London, 1970), p. 170, it had around 7,000 members at the end of 1935. Nonetheless, it has received widespread, though superficial, attention in the literature on the Spanish Republic and Civil War. This attention derives almost entirely from the POUM's role in the 'May Events' of 1937 in Barcelona, when it became embroiled in a wider struggle between the Stalinist PCE and the revolutionary Anarcho-syndicalists of the CNT. The brutal assassination of Andreu Nin by the NKVD, the subsequent liquidation of the POUM, and – it must be acknowledged – the continued popularity of George Orwell's *Homage to Catalonia*, have contributed to the construction of something of a myth around both Nin and the POUM.

90 Santiago Carrillo in *La Batalla*, 2 August 1935; see Trotsky, *Revolución española*, vol. 1, p. 326.

91 Luis Araquistáin, 'Paralelo histórico entre la revolución rusa y la española', *Leviatán*, 22 (1 March 1936).

92 Juliá, *Izquierda del PSOE*, pp. 211ff.

93 See Colin Mercer, 'Revolutions, reforms or reformulations? Marxist discourse on democracy' in Alan Hunt (ed.), *Marxism and Democracy* (London, 1980), pp. 101–37.

94 For details, see Preston, *CSCW*, pp. 144–5; Prieto had by this stage returned secretly to Spain.

95 Pascual Tomás also resigned; see Juliá, introduction to Francisco Largo Caballero, *Escritos de la República* (Madrid, 1985), p. lvii.

96 Juliá, 'Sobre la formación', p. 78.

97 *El Socialista*, 16 January 1936. The Manifesto of the Popular Front can be consulted in Vidarte, *Bienio negro*, pp. 507–14.

98 Javier Tusell, 'The Popular Front Elections in Spain, 1936' in Stanley G. Payne (ed.), *Politics and Society in Twentieth-Century Spain* (New York, 1976), pp. 110–1. For a more detailed consideration, see Tusell, *Las elecciones del Frente Popular en España* (2 vols., Madrid, 1971). See also Manuel Tuñón de Lara, *La España del siglo XX* (Paris, 1966), pp. 383–93. The results were as follows:

Popular Front 257 deputies (85 PSOE, 76 Izquierda Republicana, 34 Unión Republicana, 20 Esquerra Republicana, 15 PCE, 5 Unió Socialista de Catalunya, 5 Acció Catalana, 3 Galician independents, 1 Partit Catalá Proletari, 1 POUM and 1 Left independent); Right 139 (94 CEDA, 12 Monarchists, 11 Traditionalists, 2 Catholic independents, 1 Nationalist, 7 Independent Rightists); Centre 57 (26 Centrists (Portela Valladares), 11 Lliga Regionalista, 8 Radicals, 6 Progressivists, 2 Basque Nationalists, 1 Democratic Liberal, 1 Conservative Republican, 2 Independents). On post-electoral disputes over the results, see Preston, *CSCW*, pp. 182–4.

99 See Paloma Biglino, *El socialismo español y la cuestión agraria 1890–1936* (Madrid, 1986), pp. 488–92; Edward Malefakis, *Reforma agraria y revolución campesina en la España del siglo XX* (Barcelona, 1982), pp. 418–41; Preston, *CSCW*, pp. 177–201.

100 On the events at Yeste and unrest in Badajoz, see Preston, *CSCW*, p. 190; Malefakis, *Reforma agraria*, pp. 425, 435.

101 On Calvo Sotelo, see Paul Preston, 'Alfonsist monarchism and the coming of the Spanish Civil War', *Journal of Contemporary History*, 7(3–4), 1972, reprinted in Blinkhorn (ed.), *Spain in Conflict*, pp. 160–82; Richard A.H. Robinson, 'Calvo Sotelo's *Bloque Nacional* and its manifesto', *The University of Birmingham Historical Journal*, x(2), 1966.

102 See Preston, *CSCW*, *passim*, but esp. p. 178. See also, Montero, *CEDA*, *passim*.

103 On the reaction of landowners and employers, see Alejandro López López, *El boicot de la derecha a las reformas de la Segunda República* (Madrid, 1984), pp. 338–57; Mercedes Cabrera, *La patronal ante la Segunda República* (Madrid, 1983), pp. 287–306; on the Church, see Frances Lannon, *Privilege, Persecution, and Prophecy. The Catholic Church in Spain 1875–1975* (Oxford, 1987), chapters 7 and 8 *passim*; on the army, see Mariano Aguilar Olivencia, *El ejército español durante la segunda república* (Madrid, 1986), pp. 469–57.

104 On the Falange, see Sheelagh Ellwood, *Prietas las filas. Historia de Falange Española, 1933–1983* (Barcelona, 1984), pp. 72ff.; Sheelagh Ellwood, 'Falange Española, 1933–9: from fascism to Francoism' in Blinkhorn (ed.), *Spain in Conflict*, pp. 206–23; Stanley G. Payne, *Falange. A History of Spanish Fascism* (Stanford, 1967), pp. 89–100. On the other main group of extremists on the Right, the Carlists, see Martin Blinkhorn, *Carlism and Crisis in Spain 1931–1939* (Cambridge, 1975), pp. 228–50.

105 This had been a condition imposed by Largo Caballero for acceptance of PSOE participation in the Popular Front; see, 'Puntos de vista para una coalición electoral', *Claridad*, 2 November 1935. See also Andrés de Blas Guerrero, *El socialismo radical en la II República* (Madrid, 1978), pp. 153–74.

106 The precise details of the deposition of Alcalá-Zamora remain unclear. In broad terms, there are two views: on the one hand it has been seen as a manoeuvre by leftist elements in the PSOE seeking to remove the last guarantee of moderation and also to seek revenge for the President's acceptance of CEDA ministers in October 1934. This view is based on a conversation between Luis Araquistáin and Juan Marichal, reported in the latter's introduction to Manuel Azaña, *Obras*, III, pp. xxxii; see also, Azaña, *Obras*, IV, p. 719.

It is used as the basis for Hugh Thomas' account in *The Spanish Civil War* (London, 3rd edn, 1977), pp. 171–2. On the other hand, more recent research suggests that in fact Prieto was one of the main movers behind the removal of Alcalá-Zamora, in the hope that he would be able to succeed Azaña as Prime Minister when the latter became President. See Preston, *CSCW*, pp. 184–5; Saiz Valdivielso, *Prieto*, p. 190; Juliá, *Izquierda del PSOE*, p. 108.

107 See Preston, *CSCW*, p. 191; Graham, 'Spanish Popular Front' in Graham and Preston (eds.), *Popular Front in Europe*, pp. 109–11.

108 Vidarte, *Todos fuimos culpables*, I, pp. 119–22; Saiz Valdivielso, *Prieto*, pp. 192–3.

109 Vidarte, *Todos fuimos culpables*, I, p. 122.

110 See Santos Juliá, introduction to Largo, *Escritos de la República*, pp. lxi–lxii.

111 Saiz Valdivielso, *Prieto*, pp. 190ff.; see also articles by Preston, Juliá and José Prat in *MOPU* (Revista del Ministerio de Obras Públicas y Urbanismo), 305 (December 1983), pp. 26–41.

112 See Vidarte, *Todos fuimos culpables*, I, pp. 67–70; Preston, *CSCW*, p. 191; Juliá, introduction to Largo Caballero, *Escritos de la República*, pp. lviii–lx.

113 See Viñas, *Formación de Juventudes Socialistas Unificadas*; Graham, 'Socialist Youth' in Blinkhorn (ed.), *Spain in Conflict*, pp. 83–102; Fernando Claudín, *Santiago Carrillo. Crónica de un secretario general* (Barcelona, 1983), pp. 20–7; Vidarte, *Todos fuimos culpables*, I, pp. 71–2.

114 Graham, 'Socialist Youth' in Blinkhorn (ed.), *Spain in Conflict*, pp. 89–91.

115 Alba, *Marxismo en España*, I, pp. 276–7; Preston, *CSCW*, p. 197; Durgan, 'Dissident Communism'.

116 Juliá, introduction to Largo, *Escritos de la República*, p. lxii.

Bibliography

I PRIMARY SOURCES

(i) Newspapers, periodicals, theoretical journals

(a) PSOE

El Socialista (Madrid, 1886–1934; 1936)
La Nueva Era (Madrid, 1901–2)
Acción Socialista (Madrid, 1914–15)
Nuestra Palabra (Madrid, 1918–19)
Renovación (Madrid, 1932–6)
Espartaco (Madrid, 1933)
Leviatán (Madrid, 1934–6)
Claridad (Madrid, 1935–6)
Tiempos Nuevos (Madrid, 1934–6)
Democracia (Madrid, 1935)
Los Marxistas (Madrid, 1935)

(b) Dissident Communist

Comunismo (Madrid, 1931–4)
La Nueva Era (Barcelona, 1931–2/1935–6)
La Batalla (Barcelona, 1933–6)

(c) PCE

Mundo Obrero (Madrid, 1931–6)

(d) Others (occasional numbers consulted)

La Federación (Barcelona)
La Emancipación (Madrid)
La Lucha de Clases (Bilbao)
Justicia Social (Reus)
El Liberal (Bilbao)
El Sitio (Bilbao)
El Sol (Madrid)

(ii) Documents

(a) Official government, party and trade union publications

Alba, Víctor (ed.), *La Nueva Era. Antología de una revista revolucionaria. 1930–36* (Madrid, 1977)

———*La revolución en la práctica. Documentos del POUM* (Madrid, 1977)

Instituto de Reformas Sociales (IRS), *Encarecimiento de la vida durante la guerra* (Madrid, 1919)

———*Estadística de las huelgas. Memoria de 1919 y resumen estadístico comparativo del quinquenio 1915–1919* (Madrid, 1922)

———*Huelgas y 'lock-out' en los diversos países* (Madrid, 1923)

Juventudes Socialistas de España, *Octubre: segunda etapa* (Madrid, n.d., but 1935)

Partido Comunista de España (PCE), *Los combates de octubre*, Resolución del Buro Político del Partido Comunista de España (n.p., n.d., but Madrid, 1934)

Partido Socialista Obrero Español (PSOE), *Programa del Partido Socialista Obrero, Congreso de 23–25 de agosto de 1888* (Barcelona, n.d.)

———*Congreso Extraordinario del PSOE 1921: Nacimiento del Partido Comunista Español* (Madrid, 1974)

———*Convocatoria y orden del día para el XII Congreso ordinario del PSOE* (Madrid, 1927)

———*XII Congreso del PSOE, del 28 de junio al 4 de julio de 1928* (Madrid, 1929)

———*El Partido Socialista ante las Constituyentes: recopilación de los discursos pronunciados en el Congreso Extraordinario celebrado en el Cinema Europa de Madrid, los días 10, 11 y 12 de julio de 1931, con asistencia de los delegados provinciales* (Madrid, n.d., but 1931?)

———*Convocatoria y orden del día para el XIII Congreso del PSOE* (Madrid, 1932)

———*Actas de las sesiones celebradas por el XIII Congreso ordinario del Partido Socialista Obrero Español, del 6 al 13 de octubre de 1932* (Madrid, 1932)

Preston, Paul (ed.), *Leviatán (antología)* (Madrid, 1976)

Unión General de Trabajadores (UGT), *Actas. Vol. I: 1888–1892* (Barcelona, 1977)

———*Actas. Vol. II: 1899–1904* (Madrid, 1985)

———*Actas. Vol. III: 1905–1909* (Madrid, 1982)

———*Actas. Vol. IV: 1910–1913* (Madrid, 1985)

———*Memoria y orden del día del XIV Congreso ordinario* (Madrid, 1920)

———*Memoria y orden del día del XV Congreso ordinario* (Madrid, 1922)

———*XVI Congreso de la UGT. Sesiones de 10 al 15 de septiembre de 1928* (Madrid, 1929)

———*Actas de las sesiones celebradas por el XVII Congreso Ordinario, verificado en el teatro Fuencarral de Madrid en el mes de octubre de 1932* (Madrid, 1932)

(b) Diaries, letters, speeches

Acevedo, Isidoro. *Cien cartas inéditas de Pablo Iglesias a Isidoro Acevedo* (Madrid, 1976; prologue by Isidro R. Mendieta; first published 1929)

Archivo Histórico Nacional. *Papeles de Don Luis Araquistáin Quevedo* (Madrid, 1983; prologue by Javier Tusell)

Azaña, Manuel. *Obras completas* (4 vols., Mexico, 1966–8)

Besteiro, Julián. *Obras completas* (3 vols., Madrid, 1983)
Díaz, José. *Tres años de lucha* (3 vols., Barcelona, 1978; first published Toulouse, 1947)
Fernández Larraín, S. (ed.). *Cartas inéditas de Miguel de Unamuno* (Madrid, 1972)
Iglesias, Pablo. *Escritos y discursos. Antología crítica* (Madrid, 1984; selection and introduction by Enrique Moral Sandoval)
Largo Caballero, Francisco. *Discursos a los trabajadores* (Barcelona, 1979; first published 1934)
López Sevilla, Enrique (ed.). *El PSOE en las Cortes Constituyentes de la Segunda República* (Mexico, 1969)
Prieto, Indalecio. *Con el Rey o contra el Rey* (Mexico, 1972)
——*Dentro y fuera del gobierno* (Mexico, 1975)
——*Discursos fundamentales* (Madrid, 1975; selected with a prologue by E. Malefakis)
Prieto, Indalecio *et al. Documentos socialistas* (Madrid, 1935)
Solana, Fermín (ed.). *Historia parlamentaria del socialismo: Julián Besteiro* (2 vols., Madrid, 1975)

(iii) Memoirs and theoretical works by protagonists

Alvarez del Vayo, Julio. *Freedom's Battle* (London, 1940)
Andrade, Juan. *La burocracia reformista en el movimiento obrero* (Madrid, 1935)
Araquistáin, Luis. 'The struggle in Spain', *Foreign Affairs*, **12(3)** (April 1934)
——'The October Revolution in Spain', *Foreign Affairs*, **13(2)** (January 1935)
——*Marxismo y socialismo en España* (Barcelona, 1980)
——*Sobre la guerra civil y en la emigración* (Madrid, 1983; prologue by Javier Tusell)
Azaña, Manuel. *El problema nacional* (Alcalá de Henares, 1911)
Balbontín, José Antonio. *La España de mi experiencia* (Mexico City, 1952)
Baraibar, Carlos de. *Las falsas 'posiciones socialistas' de Indalecio Prieto* (Madrid, 1935)
Besteiro, Julián. Introduction to *El programa de Erfurt* (Madrid, 1933)
——*Marxismo y antimarxismo* (Madrid, n.d., but 1935)
Bueno, Javier. *El estado socialista: nueva interpretación del comunismo* (Madrid, 1931)
Bullejos, José. *La Comintern en España* (Mexico, 1972)
——*España en la segunda República* (Madrid, 1979)
Cordero, Manuel. *Los socialistas y la revolución* (Madrid, 1932)
Fabra Ribas, Antonio. *El socialismo y el conflicto europeo* (Valencia, n.d., but 1915?)
Gascón, Antonio and Priego, Victoria. *Por hoy y por mañana: leves comentarios a un libro firmado por Carlos de Baraibar* (Madrid, 1935)
Hernández, Jesús. *Yo fui un ministro de Stalin* (Madrid, 1974; first published Mexico, 1953)
——*En el país de la gran mentira* (Madrid, 1974; first published Mexico, 1953)
Ibárruri, Dolores. *They Shall Not Pass* (London, 1966)
Iglesias, Pablo. *Escritos* (2 vols., Madrid, 1975; introduction by Manuel Pérez Ledesma)

Largo Caballero, Francisco. *Presente y futuro de la UGT de España* (Madrid, 1925)
——*Mis recuerdos. Cartas a un amigo* (Madrid, 1976; first published Mexico, 1954)
——*Correspondencia secreta* (Madrid, 1961; annotated version of *Mis recuerdos* with prologue and notes by Mauricio Carlavilla)
——*Escritos de la República* (Madrid, 1985; prologue by Santos Juliá)
Lorenzo, Anselmo. *El proletariado militante* (Madrid, 1974; first published in 2 vols., 1901, 1923)
Mario de Coca, Gabriel. *Anti-Caballero. Una crítica marxista de la bolchevización del partido socialista obrero español* (Madrid, 1975; introduction and notes by Marta Bizcarrondo; first published 1936)
Marvaud, Angel. *La cuestión social en España* (Madrid, 1975; first published 1910)
Marx, Carlos and Engels, Federico. *Escritos sobre España* (Barcelona, 1978)
Matorras, Enrique. *El comunismo en España* (Madrid, 1935)
Maurín, Joaquín. *Los hombres de la Dictadura* (Barcelona, 1977; first published 1930)
——*La revolución española* (Barcelona, 1977; first published Madrid, 1932)
——*Revolución y contrarrevolución en España* (Paris, 1966; first published 1935 as *Hacia la segunda revolución*)
Meabe, Tomás. *Fábulas del errabundo* (Bilbao, 1975; introduction and notes by V.M. Arbeloa and M. de Santiago)
Molina, Ramón (ed.). *Polémica Maurín–Carrillo* (Barcelona, 1978; first published 1937)
Mora, Constancia de la. *In Place of Splendour* (New York, 1939)
Morato, Juan José. *El Partido Socialista Obrero* (Madrid, 1976; first published 1918)
——*La cuna de un gigante* (Madrid, 1984; first published 1925)
——*Pablo Iglesias Posse – educador de muchedumbres* (Barcelona, 1977; first published 1931)
Morón, Gabriel. *El Partido Socialista ante la realidad política de España* (Madrid, 1929)
——*La ruta del socialismo en España: ensayo de crítica y táctica revolucionaria* (Madrid, 1932)
Nin, Andreu. *Els moviments d'emancipació nacional* (Barcelona, 1935)
——*Los problemas de la revolución española* (Paris, 1971; edited with an introduction by Juan Andrade)
——*La revolución española* (Barcelona, 1978; edited with an introduction by Pelai Pagès)
Pérez Solís, Oscar. *Memorias de mi amigo Oscar Perea* (Madrid, n.d., but 1929?)
Prieto, Indalecio. *Del momento: posiciones socialistas* (Madrid, n.d., but 1935?)
——*Convulsiones de España* (3 vols., Mexico, 1967–9)
——*De mi vida* (Mexico, 1968)
Ramos Oliveira, Antonio. *Nosotros los marxistas. Lenin contra Marx* (Madrid, 1979; first published 1932)
Ríos, Fernando de los. *Mi viaje a la Rusia sovietista* (Madrid, 1970; first published 1921)

——*El sentido humanista del socialismo* (Madrid, 1976; introduction and notes by Elías Díaz; first published 1926)

——*Escritos sobre democracia y socialismo* (Madrid, 1974)

Santiago, Enrique de. *La UGT ante la revolución* (Madrid, 1932)

Serrano Poncela, Segundo. *El partido socialista y la conquista del poder* (Barcelona, 1935)

Trotsky, Leon. *The Spanish Revolution (1931–1939)* (New York, 1973)

——*La Revolución Española 1930–1940. León Trotsky* (2 vols., Barcelona, 1977; introduction and prologue by Pierre Broué)

——*La revolución española* (Madrid, 1977)

Unamuno, Miguel de. *Escritos socialistas: artículos inéditos sobre el socialismo 1894–1922* (Madrid, 1976)

Vera, Jaime. *Ciencia y proletariado. Escritos escogidos de Jaime Vera* (Madrid, 1973; introduction by Juan José Castillo)

Vidarte, Juan-Simeón. *Las Cortes Constituyentes de 1931–1933* (Barcelona, 1976)

——*No queríamos al rey* (Barcelona, 1977)

——*El bienio negro y la insurrección de Asturias* (Barcelona, 1978)

——*Todos fuimos culpables* (2 vols., Barcelona, 1978; first published 1973)

2 SECONDARY SOURCES

Abad de Santillán, Diego (Sinesio García Fernández). *Contribución a la historia del movimiento obrero español* (3 vols., Mexico, 1971)

Aguilar Olivencia, Mariano. *El ejército español durante la segunda república* (Madrid, 1986)

Alba, Víctor. *El marxismo en España (1919–1939)* (2 vols., Mexico, 1973)

——*Dos revolucionarios: Andreu Nin/Joaquín Maurín* (Madrid, 1975)

——*La Alianza Obrera. Historia y análisis de una táctica de unidad en España* (Madrid, 1977)

——*El Partido Comunista en España* (Barcelona, 1979)

Altamira, Rafael. *Psicología del pueblo español* (Madrid, 1902)

Anderson, Perry. *Considerations on Western Marxism* (London, 1976)

Andes, C. de los. 'Catolicismo y socialismo', *Anales de la Real Academia de Ciencias Morales y Políticas*, **53** (1976)

Andrade, Juan. *Apuntes para la historia del PCE* (Barcelona, 1979)

Andrés-Gallego, José. *El socialismo durante la Dictadura 1923–1930* (Madrid, 1977)

Anthropos, **45–7** (Barcelona, 1985; special issue on Pablo Iglesias)

Araquistáin, Luis. *El pensamiento español contemporáneo* (Buenos Aires, 1962)

Aróstegui, Julio. 'Largo Caballero, ministro de Trabajo' in José Luis García Delgado (ed.), *La Segunda República. El primer bienio* (Madrid, 1987)

Arranz Notario, Luis. 'El guesdismo de Pablo Iglesias en los informes a la Comisión de Reformas Sociales', *Estudios de Historia Social*, **8–9** (January–June 1979)

——'La ruptura del PSOE en la crisis de la Restauración: debate ideológico y político' in Santos Juliá (ed.), *El socialismo en España*, Anales de Historia, vol. 1 (Madrid, 1986)

Arrarás, Joaquín. *Historia de la Segunda República española* (4 vols., Madrid, 1956–68)

Artola, Miguel. 'El sistema político de la Restauración' in José Luis García Delgado (ed.), *La España de la Restauración* (1986)

Aunós, Eduardo. *La reforma corporativa del Estado* (Madrid, 1935)
——*La política social de la Dictadura* (Madrid, 1944)

Avilés Farré, Juan. *La izquierda burguesa en la Segunda República* (Madrid, 1985)

Aviv, Aviva and Isaac. 'Ideology and political patronage: workers and working-class movements in Republican Madrid, 1931–34', *European Studies Review*, 11(4) (1981)
——'The Madrid working class, the Spanish Socialist Party and the collapse of the Second Republic (1934–1936)', *Journal of Contemporary History*, 16(2) (1981)

Balcells, Albert. *El sindicalismo en Barcelona, 1916–1923* (Barcelona, 1965)
——*Cataluña contemporánea* (2 vols., Madrid, 1981)

Balcells, Albert (ed.) *Teoría y práctica del movimiento obrero en España* (Valencia, 1977)

Bar, Antonio. *La CNT en los años rojos: Del sindicalismo revolucionario al anarcosindicalismo, 1910–1926* (Madrid, 1981)

Barco Teruel, Enrique. *El 'golpe' socialista* (Madrid, 1984)

Barrio, Angeles. 'La CNT de Asturias, León y Palencia y la Alianza Obrera de 1934', *Estudios de Historia Social*, 31 (1984)

Barrón, Ignacio, Castillo, Santiago, Forcadell, Carlos and Germán, Luis G. *Historia del socialismo en Aragón. PSOE–UGT 1879–1936* (Zaragoza, 1979)

Bastos Ansart, Francisco. *Pistolerismo (historia trágica)* (Madrid, 1935)

Beetham, David. *Marxists in Face of Fascism* (Manchester, 1983)

Ben-Ami, Shlomo. 'The Dictatorship of Primo de Rivera: a political reassessment', *Journal of Contemporary History*, 12 (1977)
——*The Origins of the Second Republic in Spain* (Oxford, 1978)
——*Fascism From Above. The Dictatorship of Primo de Rivera in Spain 1923–1930* (Oxford, 1983)
——'The Republican "take-over": prelude to inevitable catastrophe?' in Paul Preston (ed.), *Revolution and War in Spain 1931–1939* (London, 1984)
——'The forerunners of Spanish fascism: Unión Patriótica and Unión Monárquica', reprinted in Martin Blinkhorn (ed.), *Spain in Conflict 1931–1939. Democracy and its Enemies* (London, 1987)

Berenguer, Dámaso. *De la Dictadura a la República* (Madrid, 1946)

Biglino, Paloma. *El socialismo español y la cuestión agraria 1890–1936* (Madrid, 1986)

Bizcarrondo, Marta. 'Julián Besteiro, socialismo y democracia', *Revista de Occidente*, 94 (1971)
——'La crisis socialista en la II República', *Revista del Instituto de Ciencias Sociales*, 21 (1973)
——*Leviatán y el socialismo de Luis Araquistáin* (Glashütten im Taunus, 1974)
——*Araquistáin y la crisis socialista de la Segunda República. Leviatán, 1934–1936* (Madrid, 1975)

———'Democracia y revolución en la estrategia socialista de la Segunda República', *Estudios de Historia Social*, 16–17 (January–June 1981)

———'La Segunda República: ideologías socialistas' in Santos Juliá (ed.), *El socialismo en España* (Anales de Historia, vol. 1) (Madrid, 1986)

———'En torno a un viejo tema: "reforma" y "revolución" en el socialismo español de la Segunda República' in José Luis García Delgado (ed.), *La Segunda República. El primer bienio* (Madrid, 1987)

———*Octubre del 34: Reflexiones sobre una revolución* (Madrid, 1977)

Blanco Aguinaga, C. 'El socialismo de Unamuno, 1894–1897', *Revista de Occidente*, 41 (1966)

———'De nuevo: el socialismo de Unamuno 1894–1897', *Cuadernos de la Cátedra Miguel de Unamuno*, 18 (1968)

Blas Guerrero, Andrés de. *El socialismo radical en la II República* (Madrid, 1978)

Blinkhorn, Martin. 'Carlism and the Spanish crisis of the 1930s' in *Journal of Contemporary History*, 7 (1972)

———*Carlism and Crisis in Spain 1931–1939* (Cambridge, 1975)

Blinkhorn, Martin (ed.). *Spain in Conflict 1931–1939. Democracy and its Enemies* (London, 1986)

Bonamusa, Francesc. *Andreu Nin y el movimiento comunista en España (1930–1937)* (Barcelona, 1977)

Bookchin, Murray. *The Spanish Anarchists. The Heroic Years 1868–1936* (New York, 1978)

Borkenau, Franz. *World Communism. A History of the Communist International* (Ann Arbor, 1962)

Bottomore, Tom and Goode, Patrick (eds.). *Austro-Marxism* (Oxford, 1978)

Bottomore, Tom et al. *A Dictionary of Marxist Thought* (Oxford, 1983)

Boyd, Carolyn P. *Praetorian Politics in Liberal Spain* (Chapel Hill, 1979)

———' "Responsibilities" and the Second Spanish Republic', *European History Quarterly*, 14 (1984)

Braunthal, Julius. *History of the International* (London, 1967)

Brenan, Gerald. *The Spanish Labyrinth* (Cambridge, 2nd edn, 1950)

Buenacasa, Manuel. *El movimiento obrero español 1886–1926* (Barcelona, 1977; first published 1928)

Cabrera, Mercedes. *La patronal ante la Segunda República* (Madrid, 1983)

———'Las organizaciones patronales ante la conflictividad social y los Jurados Mixtos' in Josep Fontana et al., *La Segunda República. Una experiencia frustrada* (Valencia, 1987)

Cacho Viu, Vicente. *La Institución Libre de Enseñanza* (Madrid, 1962)

Calero, Antonio M. *Movimientos sociales en Andalucía 1820–1936* (Madrid, 1976)

Calvo Sotelo, José. *Mis servicios al Estado. Seis años de gestión* (Madrid, 1930)

Cambó, Francesc. *La valoración de la peseta* (Madrid, n.d., but 1929?)

Cantarero del Castillo. M. *Tragedia del socialismo español* (Barcelona, 1971)

Capo, J.M. *Las Juntas Militares de Defensa* (Havana, 1923)

Carr E.H. *The Bolshevik Revolution, 1917–1923* (3 vols., London, 1950)

———*The Twilight of the Comintern, 1930–1935* (London, 1982)

———*The Comintern and the Spanish Civil War* (London, 1984)

Carr, Raymond. *The Spanish Tragedy* (London, 1977)
——*Modern Spain 1875–1980* (Oxford, 1980)
——*Spain 1808–1975* (Oxford, 2nd edn, 1982)
Carr, Raymond (ed.). *The Republic and the Civil War in Spain* (London, 1971)
Carreras Ares, Juan José. 'Los escritos de Marx sobre España' in Alberto Gil
    Novales (ed.), *La revolución burguesa en España* (Madrid, 1985)
Carrión, Pascual. *Estudios sobre la agricultura española* (Madrid, 1974)
Casado González, Rafael and Vázquez Cea, Matilde. 'Fuentes impresos para la
    historia del socialismo en España' in Santos Juliá (ed.), *El socialismo en España*
    (Anales de Historia, vol. 1) (Madrid, 1986)
Casal Gómez, Manuel. *El orígen y la actuación de los pistoleros en Barcelona 1918–
    1921* (Madrid, n.d., 1924?)
Castillejo, José. *Guerra de ideas en España* (Madrid, 1976; first published in
    English 1937)
Castillo, Juan José. *El sindicalismo amarillo en España* (Madrid, 1977)
Castillo, Santiago. 'De "El Socialista" a "El Capital" ', *Negaciones*, 5 (1978)
Castro, Américo. *The Spaniards. An Introduction to Their History* (Berkeley,
    1971; first published as *The Structure of Spanish History*, Princeton, 1954)
Cerdá, M., García Bonafé, M. and Piqueras, J.A. *Historia fotográfica del socialismo
    español* (Valencia, 1984)
Christie, Stuart. 'We, The Anarchists. . . A study of the Iberian Anarchist Feder-
    ation (FAI) 1927–1937' (Unpublished manuscript, 1985)
Cierva, Ricardo de la. *Historia del socialismo en España 1879–1983* (Barcelona,
    1983)
——*La derecha sin remedio (1801–1987)* (Barcelona, 1987)
Cierva, Ricardo de la *et al. Bibliografía sobre la Guerra de España y sus antecedentes*
    (Barcelona, 1968)
Cipolla, Carlo M. *The Fontana Economic History of Europe* (6 vols.; Glasgow,
    1973)
Clark, Martin. *Antonio Gramsci and the Revolution that Failed* (New Haven,
    1977)
——*Modern Italy, 1871–1982* (London, 1984)
Claudín, Fernando. 'Spain – the untimely revolution', *New Left Review*, 74 (July–
    August, 1972)
——*The Communist Movement. From Comintern to Cominform* (2 vols.; New
    York, 1975)
——*Santiago Carrillo. Crónica de un secretario general* (Barcelona, 1983)
Cohen, G.A. *Karl Marx's Theory of History. A Defence* (Oxford, 1978)
Comín Colomer, Eduardo. *Historia secreta de la segunda República* (Barcelona,
    1959)
——*Historia del Partido Comunista de España* (3 vols.; Madrid, 1965–1967)
Connelly Ullman, Joan. *La Semana Trágica* (Barcelona, 1968)
Contreras, Manuel. 'Líderes socialistas de la Dictadura a la República', *Sistema*, 26
    (September 1978)
——*El PSOE en la II República. Organización e ideología* (Madrid, 1981)
Cortada, James W. (ed.). *Historical Dictionary of the Spanish Civil War, 1936–39*
    (Connecticut, 1982)

Costa, Joaquín. *Oligarquía y caciquismo* (2 vols.; Madrid, 1975)

Cruells, Manuel. *Salvador Seguí, el Noi del sucre* (Barcelona, 1974)

Cruz, Rafael. 'La organización del PCE 1920–1934', *Estudios de Historia Social*, 31 (1984)

Cuadernos de Pedagogía, 22 (October 1976; special issue on the Institución Libre de Enseñanza)

Cuadrat, Xavier. *Socialismo y anarquismo en Cataluña. Los orígenes de la CNT* (Madrid, 1976)

Cuesta Escudero, Pedro. 'Ideario pedagógico', *Cuadernos de Pedagogía (Revista mensual de educación)*, 22 (October 1976)

Culla i Clarà, Joan B. *El republicanisme Lerrouxista a Catalanya (1901–1923)* (Barcelona, 1986)

Danos, Jacques and Gibelin, Marcel. *June '36. Class Struggle and the Popular Front in France* (London, 1986)

Davidson, Alastair. *The Theory and Practice of Italian Communism* (London, 1982)

Degras, Jane (ed.). *The Communist International (1919–1943)* (London, 1956–65)

Deutscher, Isaac. *The Prophet Outcast. Trotsky: 1929–1940* (Oxford, 1963)

Díaz, Carlos. *Besteiro: el socialismo en libertad* (Madrid, 1976)

Díaz, Elías. *Revisión de Unamuno. Análisis crítico de su pensamiento político* (Madrid, 1968)

——'Fernando de los Ríos: socialismo humanista y socialismo marxista', *Sistema*, 10 (July 1975)

——'De algunas personales relaciones entre PSOE y la Institución Libre de Enseñanza' in Fundación Pablo Iglesias, *Homenaje a Pablo Iglesias* (Madrid, 1979)

——*Socialismo en España: el Partido y el Estado* (Madrid, 1982)

——*La filosofía social del Krausismo español* (Valencia, 2nd edn, 1983)

Díaz del Moral, Juan. *Historia de las agitaciones campesinas andaluzas* (Madrid, 1976; first published 1928)

Draper, Hal. *Karl Marx's Theory of Revolution. Vol. I: State and Bureaucracy* (New York, 1977)

——*Karl Marx's Theory of Revolution. Vol. II: The Politics of Social Classes* (New York, 1978)

——*Karl Marx's Theory of Revolution. Vol. III: The Dictatorship of the Proletariat* (New York, 1986)

Droz, Jacques (ed.). *Historia General del Socialismo* (5 vols.; Barcelona, 1979)

Durgan, Andrew. 'The rise and fall of Largo Caballero', *International Socialism*, 18 (Winter 1983)

——'Dissident Communism in Catalonia, 1930–1936' (Unpublished PhD thesis, Queen Mary College, University of London, 1989)

Eguiguren, Jesús M. *El PSOE en el País Vasco 1886–1936* (San Sebastián, 1984)

Ellwood, Sheelagh. *Prietas las filas, Historia de Falange Española, 1933–1983* (Barcelona, 1984)

——'Falange Española, 1933–9: from fascism to Francoism' in Martin Blinkhorn (ed.), *Spain in Conflict 1931–1936. Democracy and its Enemies* (London, 1986)

Elorza, Antonio. 'Los esquemas socialistas en Pablo Iglesias', *Sistema*, 11 (1975)

——'Los primeros programas del PSOE, 1879–1888', *Estudios de Historia Social*, 8–9 (January–June 1979)

——*La razón y la sombra. Una lectura política de Ortega y Gasset* (Barcelona, 1984)

Elorza, Antonio, Ralle, Michel and Serrano, Carlos (eds.). 'Mouvements ouvriers espagnols et questions nationals, 1868–1936' – special issue of *Le Mouvement Social*, 128 (1984)

Elster, Jon. *Making Sense of Marx* (Cambridge, 1985)

Esenwein, George. 'Anarchist ideology and the Spanish working-class movement (1880–1900): with special reference to the ideas of Ricardo Mella' (Unpublished PhD thesis, London School of Economics, University of London, 1986)

Estruch Tobella, Joan. *Historia del Partido Comunista de España, 1920–1939* (Barcelona, 1978)

Fatherree, Ben H. 'Trotskyism in Spain, 1931–1937' (Unpublished PhD thesis, Mississippi State University, 1978)

Fernández, Eusebio. *Marxismo y positivismo en el socialismo español* (Madrid, 1981)

Fleming, Shannon E. and Fleming, Ann K. 'Primo de Rivera and Spain's Moroccan problem, 1923–1927', *Journal of Contemporary History*, 12 (1977)

Foix, Pere. *Los archivos del terrorismo blanco: el fichero Lasarte 1910–1930* (Madrid, 1931)

Fontana, Josep and Nadal, Jordi. 'Spain 1914–1970' in Carlo M. Cipolla (ed.), *The Fontana Economic History of Europe. Contemporary Economies 2* (1973)

Fontana, Josep *et al. La Segunda República. Una experiencia frustrada* (Valencia, 1987)

Forcadell, Carlos. *Parlamentarismo y bolchevización* (Barcelona, 1978)

Forner Muñoz, Salvador. *Industrialización y movimiento obrero. Alicante 1923–1936* (Valencia, 1982)

Fowkes, Ben. *Communism in Germany under the Weimar Republic* (London, 1984)

Fundación Pablo Iglesias. *Cien años de socialismo en España. (Bibliografía)* (Madrid, 1979)

Fusi, Juan Pablo. 'El movimiento socialista en España 1879–1939', *Actualidad Económica*, 845 (25 May 1974)

——*Política obrera en el País Vasco 1880–1923* (Madrid, 1975)

Ganivet, Angel. *Idearium español* (Madrid, 1897)

García Delgado, José Luis (ed.). *La España de la Restauración* (Madrid, 1985)

——*La crisis de la restauración. España entre la primera guerra mundial y la Segunda República* (Madrid, 1986)

——*La Segunda República española. El primer bienio* (Madrid, 1987)

García Delgado, José Luis and Roldán, S. *La formación de la sociedad capitalista en España (1914–1920)* (2 vols.; Madrid, 1973)

García Durán, Juan. *La guerra civil española: Fuentes* (new edn, Barcelona, 1985)

García Venero, Maximiano. *Antonio Maura* (Madrid, 1953)

Garrido González, Luis. *Colectividades agrarias en Andalucía: Jaén 1931–1939* (Madrid, 1979)
——'Colectividades socialistas en la provincia de Jaén 1933–1939' in *Actas del Primer Congreso de Historia de Andalucía* (2 vols.; Córdoba, 1979)
Geary, Dick. *European Labour Protest 1848–1939* (London, 1984)
Germán, Luis G. 'La Dictadura y el socialismo en Aragón 1923–1929' in I. Barrón *et al. Historia del socialismo en Aragón PSOE–UGT 1879–1936* (Zaragoza, 1979)
Gil Cremades, Juan José. *Krausistas y liberales* (Madrid, 1975)
Gil Novales, Alberto. 'Las contradicciones de la revolución burguesa española' in Alberto Gil Novales (ed.), *La revolución burguesa en España* (Madrid, 1985)
Gil Robles, José María. *No fue posible la paz* (Barcelona, 1968)
——*Discursos parlamentarios* (Madrid, 1971)
Gómez Casas, Juan. *La Primera Internacional en España* (Madrid, 1974)
Gómez Fernández Ramiro. *La Dictadura me honró encarcelándome* (Madrid, 1930)
Gómez Llorente, Luis. *Aproximación a la historia del socialismo español (hasta 1921)* (Madrid, 1976)
Gómez Molleda, Dolores. *Unamuno socialista* (Madrid, 1978)
——*El socialismo español y los intelectuales* (Salamanca, 1981)
González Quintana, Antonio and Martín Najera, Aurelio. *Apuntes para la historia de las Juventudes Socialistas de España* (Madrid, 1983)
Graham, Helen. 'The Socialist Youth in the JSU: the experience of organizational unity, 1936–8', in Martin Blinkhorn (ed.), *Spain in Conflict 1931–1939. Democracy and its Enemies* (London, 1986)
——'The Spanish Popular Front and the Civil War' in Helen Graham and Paul Preston (eds.), *The Popular Front in Europe* (London, 1987)
Graham, Helen and Preston, Paul. 'The Popular Front and the struggle against Fascism' in Helen Graham and Paul Preston (eds.), *The Popular Front in Europe* (London, 1987)
Gramsci, Antonio. *Selections from the Prison Notebooks* (London, 1971)
Grebing, Helga. *History of the German Labour Movement* (Leamington Spa, 1985)
Guereña, Jean-Louis. 'Contribución a la biografía de José Mesa: De "La Emancipación" a "L'Egalité" 1873–1877', *Estudios de Historia Social*, **8–9** (January–June 1979)
Harding, Neil. *Lenin's Political Thought* (2 vols.; London, 1977, 1981)
Harrison, Joseph. *An Economic History of Modern Spain* (Manchester, 1978)
——'The failure of economic reconstitution in Spain, 1916–1923', *European Studies Review*, **13** (1983)
——*The Spanish Economy in the Twentieth Century* (London, 1985)
Haupt, Georges. *Socialism and the Great War: The Collapse of the Second International* (Oxford, 1972)
Hennessy, C.A.M. *Modern Spain* (London, 1965)
Hernández Andreu, Juan. *Depresión económica en España, 1925–1934* (Madrid, 1980)

——*España y la crisis de 1929* (Madrid, 1986)

Herr, Richard. *An Historical Essay on Modern Spain* (Berkeley, 1971)

Heywood, Paul. 'De las dificultades para ser marxista: el PSOE, 1879–1921', *Sistema*, 74 (1986)

——'The development of marxist theory in Spain and the Frente Popular' in Martin S. Alexander and Helen Graham (eds.), *The French and Spanish Popular Fronts* (Cambridge, 1989)

——'The labour movement in Spain before 1914' in Dick Geary (ed.), *Labour and Socialist Movements in Europe before 1914* (London, 1989)

Hilferding, Rudolf. *Nuevas tácticas para el nuevo capitalismo* (Madrid, 1928)

Hills, George. *Spain* (London, 1970)

Hindess, Barry. *Parliamentary Democracy and Socialist Politics* (London, 1983)

Historia 16. La Guerra Civil (24 vols.; 1986–7)

Hobsbawm, Eric. *Primitive Rebels* (Manchester, 1971)

Hunt, Alan (ed.). *Marxism and Democracy* (London, 1980)

Hunt, Richard N. *The Political Ideas of Marx & Engels. I: Marxism and Totalitarian Democracy 1818–1850* (London, 1975)

——*The Political Ideas of Marx & Engels. II: Classical Marxism, 1850–1895* (London, 1984)

Jiménez Araya, Tomás. 'La introducción del marxismo en España: el Informe a la Comisión de Reformas Sociales de Jaime Vera', *Anales de Economía*, 15 (July–September 1972)

Jackson, Gabriel. *The Spanish Republic and the Civil War, 1931–1939* (Princeton, 1967)

Jackson, Hampden. *The Post-War World. A Short Political History 1918–1934* (London, 1934)

Joll, James. *The Second International 1889–1914* (London, 2nd edn, 1974)

Judt, Tony. *Marxism and the French Left* (Oxford, 1986)

Juliá, Santos. *La izquierda del PSOE 1935–1936* (Madrid, 1977)

——*Orígenes del Frente Popular en España (1934–1936)* (Madrid, 1979)

——'Segunda República: por otro objeto de investigación' in Manuel Tuñón de Lara *et al. Historiografía española contemporánea* (Madrid, 1980)

——'Corporativistas obreros y reformadores políticos: crisis y escisión del PSOE en la II República', *Studia Histórica*, 1 (1983)

——'Largo Caballero y la lucha de tendencias en el socialismo español 1923–1936', *'Annali' della Fondazione Giangiacomo Feltrinelli (1983–1984)* (Milan, 1985)

——'Un líder político entre dirigentes sindicales' in *MOPU* (Revista del Ministerio de Obras Públicas y Urbanismo), 305 (Madrid, December 1983)

——'Raíces religiosas y prácticas sindicales', *Revista de Occidente*, 23 (April 1983)

——'Los socialistas en la crisis de los años treinta', *Zona Abierta*, 27 (1983)

——'Continuidad y ruptura en el socialismo español del siglo xx', *Leviatán*, 17 (1984)

——'Economic crisis, social conflict and the Popular Front: Madrid 1931–6' in Paul Preston (ed.), *Revolution and War in Spain, 1931–1939* (London, 1984)

——*Madrid, 1931–1934. De la fiesta popular a la lucha de clases* (Madrid, 1984)

——'Sobre la formación del Frente Popular en España', *Sistema*, **73** (July 1986)
——'República, revolución y luchas internas' in Santos Juliá (ed.), *El socialismo en España* (Madrid, 1986)
——'Objetivos políticos de la legislación laboral' in José Luis García Delgado (ed.), *La Segunda República española. El primer bienio* (Madrid, 1987)
Juliá, Santos (ed.) *El socialismo en España* (Anales de Historia, vol. 1) (Madrid, 1986)
Jutglar, Antoni. *Ideologías y clases en la España contemporánea 1874–1931* (2 vols.; Madrid, 1969)
——'Pablo Iglesias, los diversos socialismos en España, y la visión de discrepantes en el seno del movimiento obrero', *Anthropos*, **45–7** (1985)
Kelly, Michael. *Modern French Marxism* (Oxford, 1982)
Kern, Robert W. *Liberals, Reformers and Caciques in Restoration Spain, 1875–1909* (Albuquerque, 1974)
——*Red Years/Black Years. A Political History of Spanish Anarchism 1911–1937* (Philadelphia, 1978)
Kirby, David. *War, Peace and Revolution. International Socialism at the Crossroads, 1914–1918* (London, 1986)
Kitchen, Martin. *Fascism* (London, 1976)
Knei-Paz, Baruch. *The Social and Political Thought of Leon Trotsky* (Oxford, 1978)
Kolakowski, Leszek. *Main Currents of Marxism* (3 vols.; Oxford, 1978)
Kossok, Manfred. 'El ciclo de las revoluciones españolas en el siglo XIX. Problemas de investigación e interpretación a la luz del método comparativo' in Alberto Gil Novales (ed.), *La revolución burguesa en España* (Madrid, 1985)
Lacomba Avellán, Juan Antonio. *La crisis española de 1917* (Madrid, 1970)
Laín Entralgo, Pedro. *La generación del noventa y ocho* (Madrid, 1947)
Lamberet, Renée. *Mouvements ouvriers et socialistes (Chronologie et bibliographie) L'Espagne (1750–1936)* (Paris, 1953)
Lamo de Espinosa, Emilio. *Filosofía y política en Julián Besteiro* (Madrid, 1973)
Landis, Arthur. *Spain! The Unfinished Revolution* (New York, 1975)
Lannon, Frances. 'The Church's crusade against the Republic' in Paul Preston (ed.), *Revolution and War in Spain 1931–1939* (London, 1984)
——*Privilege, Persecution, and Prophecy. The Catholic Church in Spain 1875–1975* (Oxford, 1987)
Laporta, Francisco. 'Fundamentos de la pedagogía institucionalista', *Historia 16* (1976)
Lenin, V.I. *Selected Works I* (Moscow, 1963)
León-Ignacio. *Los años del pistolerismo* (Barcelona, 1981)
Lerroux, Alejandro. *La pequeña historia de España 1930–1936* (Barcelona, 1985; first published 1945)
Lichteim, George. *Marxism in Modern France* (Columbia, 1966)
Lindemann, Albert S. *The 'Red Years': European Socialism versus Bolshevism 1919–1921* (Berkeley CA, 1974)
Liss, Sheldon B. *Marxist Thought in Latin America* (California, 1984)
Llopis, Rodolfo. 'Francisco Giner de los Ríos y la reforma del hombre', *Cuadernos del Congreso por la libertad de la cultura*, **16** (January–February 1956)

Llorens Castillo, Carlos. *Historia del Partido Comunista de España* (Valencia, 1982)

López García, Bernabé. *El socialismo español y el anticolonialismo* (Madrid, 1976)

López López, Alejandro. *El boicot de la derecha a las reformas de la Segunda República* (Madrid, 1984)

López-Morillas, Juan. *The Krausist Movement and Ideological Change in Spain 1854–1874* (Cambridge, 1981)

Losada, Juan. *Ideario político de Pablo Iglesias* (Barcelona, 1976)

Löwy, Michael. *The Politics of Combined and Uneven Development* (London, 1981)

Macarro Vera, José Manuel. 'Causas de la radicalización socialista en la Segunda República', *Revista de Historia Contemporánea* (Seville), 1 (December 1982)

——*La utopía revolucionaria. Sevilla en la Segunda República* (Seville, 1985)

Madariaga, Salvador de. 'Spain and Russia: a parallel', *New Europe*, 30 August 1917

——*Spain* (London, 1942)

Malefakis, Edward. *Agrarian Reform and Peasant Revolution in Spain* (New Haven, 1970)

——'The Parties of the Left and the Second Republic' in Raymond Carr (ed.), *The Republic and the Civil War in Spain* (London, 1971)

——*Reforma agraria y revolución campesina en la España del siglo XX* (Barcelona, 1982)

Malerbe, Pierre. 'La Dictadura' in Manuel Tuñón de Lara (ed.), *Historia de España*, vol. IX, *La crisis del estado: Dictadura, República, Guerra* (Barcelona, 1981)

Mallada, Lucás. *Los males de la Patria* (Madrid, 1890)

Marco Miranda, Vicente. *Las conspiraciones contra la Dictadura 1923–1930* (Madrid, 1930)

Martínez Cuadrado, Miguel. *Elecciones y partidos políticos 1868–1931* (2 vols.; Madrid, 1969)

Martínez de Sas, María Teresa. *El socialismo y la España oficial. Pablo Iglesias, diputado a Cortes* (Madrid, 1975)

Martínez Val, José María. *Españoles ante el comunismo* (Barcelona, 1976)

Marx, Karl. *The Revolutions of 1848* (Harmondsworth, 1973)

——*Surveys from Exile* (Harmondsworth, 1973)

——*The First International and After* (Harmondsworth, 1974)

——*Early Writings* (Harmondsworth, 1975)

——*Capital: Volume I* (Harmondsworth, 1976)

Marx, Karl and Engels, Friedrich. *Selected Works* (Moscow, 1962)

Maura, Miguel. *Así cayó Alfonso XIII...* (Barcelona, 1962)

Maura Gamazo, Gabriel. *Bosquejo histórico de la Dictadura* (Madrid, 1930)

Maurice, Jacques. 'Sobre la penetración del marxismo en España', *Estudios de Historia Social*, 8–9 (January–June 1979)

——'A propósito del trienio bolchevique' in José Luis García Delgado (ed.), *La crisis de la Restauración. España entre la primera guerra mundial y la II República* (Madrid, 1986)

Meaker, Gerald H. *The Revolutionary Left in Spain 1914–1923* (Stanford, 1974)

Menéndez Pidal, Ramón. *The Spaniards in their History* (London, 1950)

Mercer, Colin. 'Revolutions, reforms or reformulations? Marxist discourse on democracy' in Alan Hunt (ed.), *Marxism and Democracy* (London, 1980)

Merino, Julio. *Los socialistas rompen las urnas. 1933* (Barcelona, 1986)

Mintz, Jerome. *The Anarchists of Casas Viejas* (Chicago, 1982)

Moll Marqués, José. 'Criterios para la unidad del socialismo español', *Sistema*, 19 (July 1977)

Monreal, Antoni. *El pensamiento político de Joaquín Maurín* (Barcelona, 1984)

Montero, Enrique. 'Luis Araquistáin y la propaganda aliada durante la Primera Guerra Mundial' in *Estudios de Historia Social*, 24–5 (1983)

Montero, José Ramón. *La CEDA. El catolicismo social y político en la Segunda República* (2 vols.; Madrid, 1977)

Moore, Barrington, Jr. *The Social Origins of Dictatorship and Democracy* London, 1967)

Moore, Stanley. *Three Tactics* (New York, 1963)

Moradiellos, Enrique. *El Sindicato de los Obreros Mineros de Asturias 1910–1930* (Oviedo, 1986)

Moral Sandoval, Enrique. 'Pablo Iglesias: una aproximación crítica', *Anthropos*, 45–7 (1985)

——'El socialismo y la Dictadura de Primo de Rivera' in Santos Juliá (ed.), *El socialismo en España* (Anales de Historia vol. 1) (Madrid, 1986)

Morgan, David W. *The Socialist Left and the German Revolution: A History of the German Independent Social Democratic Party, 1917–1922* (Ithaca, 1975)

Morodo, Raúl. 'Introducción al pensamiento político de Araquistáin', *Boletín Informativo de Ciencias Políticas*, 7 (1971)

Mortimer, Edward. *The Rise of the French Communist Party 1920–1947* (London, 1984)

Munis, Grandizo. *Jalones de Derrota, Promesa de Victoria* (Madrid, 1977; first published 1948)

Muñoz, Juan. 'La reforma bancaria de Indalecio Prieto' in José Luis García Delgado (ed.), *La Segunda República española. El primer bienio* (Madrid, 1987)

Nadal, Jordi. 'The failure of the Industrial Revolution in Spain 1830–1914' in Carlo M. Cipolla (ed.), *The Fontana Economic History of Europe*, vol. IV (Glasgow, 1973)

Newton, Douglas J. *British Labour, European Socialism and the Struggle for Peace 1889–1914* (Oxford, 1985)

Ojeda, Germán. *Asturias en la industrialización española, 1833–1907* (Madrid, 1985)

Ojeda, Germán (ed.). *Octubre 1934. Cincuenta años para la reflexión* (Madrid, 1984)

Ortega y Gasset, José. *España invertebrada* (Madrid, 1921)

Pabón, Jesús. *Cambó* (3 vols., Barcelona, 1952)

Padilla Bolívar, Antonio. *Pablo Iglesias y el parlamentarismo restauracionista* (Barcelona, 1976)

——*El movimiento socialista español* (Barcelona, 1977)

——*El movimiento comunista español* (Barcelona, 1979)

Pagès, Pelai. *El movimiento trotskista en España 1930–1935* (Barcelona, 1977)
——*Historia del Partido Comunista de España* (Barcelona, 1978)
Palacio, Juan Ignacio. 'Crisis política y crisis institucional: la experiencia del
    Instituto de Reformas Sociales en el periodo 1914–1924' in José Luis García
    Delgado (ed.), *La crisis de la Restauración en España* (1986)
Paniagua, Xavier and Piqueras, Jose A. *Trabajadores sin revolución. La clase obrera
    valenciana 1868–1936* (Valencia, 1986)
Partido Comunista de España. *Guerra y revolución en España 1936–1939* (4 vols.,
    Moscow, 1966–1977)
Payne, Stanley. *Falange. A History of Spanish Fascism* (Stanford, 1967)
——*Politics and the Military in Modern Spain* (Stanford, 1967)
——*The Spanish Revolution* (London, 1970)
Peirats, José. *Los anarquistas en la crisis política española* (Barcelona, 1976)
Pérez de la Dehesa, Rafael. *Política y sociedad en el primer Unamuno* (Barcelona,
    2nd edn, 1973)
Pérez Garzón, Juan Sisinio. 'La revolución burguesa en España: los inicios de un
    debate científico' in Manuel Tuñón de Lara (ed.), *Historiografía española
    contemporánea* (Madrid, 1980)
Pérez Ledesma, Manuel. *Pensamiento socialista español a comienzos de siglo*
    (Madrid, 1974)
——'La primera etapa de la Unión General de Trabajadores 1888–1917. Plan-
    teamiento sindical y formas de organización' in Albert Balcells (ed.), *Teoría y
    práctica del movimiento obrero en España* (Valencia, 1977)
——'La Unión General de Trabajadores: socialismo y reformismo', *Estudios de
    Historia Social*, 8–9 (1979)
——'¿Pablo Iglesias, santo?', *Anthropos*, 45–7 (1985)
——'Partido y sindicato: unas relaciones no siempre fáciles' in Santos Juliá (ed.),
    El socialismo en España (Anales de Historia, vol. 1) (Madrid, 1986)
——*El obrero consciente. Dirigentes, partidos y sindicatos en la II Internacional*
    (Madrid, 1987)
Pestaña, Angel. *Terrorismo en Barcelona* (Barcelona, 1979)
Peydro Caro, Miguel. *Las escisiones del PSOE* (Barcelona, 1980)
Picavea Macias, R. *El problema nacional* (Madrid, 1899)
Piccone, Paul. *Italian Marxism* (London, 1983)
Pike, Fredrick B. 'Making the hispanic world safe from democracy: Spanish liberals
    and hispanismo', *The Review of Politics*, 33 (1971)
Portela, Luis. 'El nacimiento y los primeros pasos del movimiento comunista en
    España', *Estudios de Historia Social*, 14 (1980)
Prat, José. 'Acción y pasión de Indalecio Prieto' in *MOPU* (Revista del Ministerio
    de Obras Públicas y Urbanismo), 305 (Madrid, December 1983)
Preston, Paul. 'Alfonsist monarchism and the coming of the Spanish Civil War',
    Journal of Contemporary History, 7 (1972)
——'Los orígenes del cisma socialista: 1917–1931', *Cuadernos de Ruedo Ibérico*,
    49–50 (1976)
——*The Coming of the Spanish Civil War* (London, 1978)
——'The struggle against Fascism in Spain: *Leviatán* and the contradictions of

the Spanish Left, 1934–1936', *European Studies Review*, **9**(1) (1979)

——'Manuel Azaña y la creación del Frente Popular (1933–1936)' in Vicente-Alberto Serrano and José María San Luciano (eds.), *Azaña* (Madrid, 1980)

——'Spain' in S.J. Woolf (ed.), *Fascism in Europe* (London, 1981)

——'Demócrata por encima de todo: Indalecio Prieto y la creación del Frente Popular' in *MOPU* (Revista del Ministerio de Obras Públicas y Urbanismo), **305** (Madrid, December 1983)

——*The Spanish Civil War* (London, 1986)

——*Las derechas españolas en el siglo XX: autoritarismo, fascismo y golpismo* (Madrid, 1986)

——'The Creation of the Popular Front in Spain' in Helen Graham and Paul Preston (eds.), *The Popular Front in Europe* (London, 1987)

Preston, Paul (ed.). *Revolution and War in Spain, 1931–1939* (London, 1984)

Rama, Carlos M. *La crisis española del siglo XX* (Mexico, 2nd edn, 1962)

Ramírez, Manuel. *Las reformas de la IIa República* (Madrid, 1977)

Ramírez, Manuel (ed.). *Estudios sobre la II República española* (Madrid, 1975)

Rée, Jonathon. *Proletarian Philosophers* (Oxford, 1984)

Rial, James H. *Revolution From Above. The Primo de Rivera Dictatorship in Spain 1923–1930* (Cranbury, New Jersey, 1986)

Ribas, Pedro. 'Sobre la introducción del marxismo en España', *Estudios de Historia Social*, **5–6** (1978)

——*La introducción del marxismo en España 1869–1939* (Madrid, 1981)

Rivas de Cherif, Cipriano de. *Retrato de un desconocido* (Barcelona, 2nd edn, 1981)

Roberts, Stephen G.H. 'Unamuno contra Primo de Rivera: 10 artículos de 1923–24' in *Sistema*, **75** (November 1986)

Robinson, Richard A.H. 'Calvo Sotelo's *Bloque Nacional* and its manifesto', *The University of Birmingham Historical Journal*, **10**(2) (1966)

——*The Origins of Franco's Spain: The Right, the Republic and Revolution, 1931–36* (Newton Abbot, 1970)

Robles Egea, Antonio. 'Formación de la Conjunción republicano-socialista de 1909', *Revista de Estudios Políticos*, **29** (1982)

Rodriguez de Lecea, Teresa. 'El Krausismo español como filosofía práctica' in *Sistema*, **49** (1982)

Romero Maura, Joaquín. *'La Rosa de Fuego'. El obrerismo barcelonés de 1899 a 1909* (Barcelona, 1974)

——'*Caciquismo* as a political system' in Ernest Gellner and John Waterbury (eds.), *Patrons and Clients* (London, 1977)

Rosal, Amaro del. *Historia de la UGT de España 1901–1939* (2 vols.; Barcelona, 1977)

Rose, Gillian. *Hegel contra Sociology* (London, 1981)

Rubio Cabeza, Manuel. *Diccionario de la Guerra Civil Española* (2 vols.; Barcelona, 1987)

Ruiz González, David. *El movimiento obrero en Asturias* (Oviedo, 1968)

——'Clase, sindicatos y partidos en Asturias (1931–1934)', *Estudios de Historia Social*, **31** (1984)

Saborit, Andrés. *La huelga de agosto de 1917* (Mexico City, 1967)

——Joaquín Costa y el socialismo (Madrid, 1970)

Saiz Valdivielso, Alfonso Carlos. Indalecio Prieto. Crónica de un corazón (Barcelona, 1984)

Salvadori, Massimo. Karl Kautsky and the Socialist Revolution 1880–1938 (London, 1979)

Sánchez, Manuel. Maurín, gran enigma de guerra y otros recuerdos (Madrid, 1976)

Sánchez Albornoz, Claudio. España, un enigma histórico (Madrid, 1956)

Sánchez Guerra, Rafael. El movimiento revolucionario en Valencia: relato de un procesado (Madrid, 1930)

Sanz Agüero, Marcos. 'Jaime Vera y el primer socialismo español', Boletín Informativo de Ciencia Política, 8 (1971)

Seco Serrano, Carlos. Militarismo y civilismo en la España contemporánea (Madrid, 1984)

Serrano, Vicente-Alberto and San Luciano, José María (eds.). Azaña (Madrid, 1980)

Serrano Sanz, José María. 'La política comercial ante la crisis del veintinueve: el primer bienio republicano' in José Luis García Delgado (ed.), La Segunda República española. El primer bienio (Madrid, 1987)

Sevilla-Guzmán, Eduardo. La evolución del campesinado en España (Barcelona, 1979)

Shaw, Donald L. The Generation of 1898 in Spain (London, 1975)

Shubert, Adrian. Hacia la revolución. Orígenes sociales del movimiento obrero en Asturias, 1860–1934 (Barcelona, 1984)

——The Road to Revolution in Spain (Chicago, 1987)

Smith, Rhea Marsh. Spain. A Modern History (Michigan, 1965)

Spriano, Paolo. Stalin and the European Communists (London, 1985)

Stone, Norman. Europe Transformed 1878–1919 (London, 1983)

Suárez Cortina, Manuel. 'La división del republicanismo histórico y la quiebra de la Conjunción republicano–socialista' in Santos Juliá (ed.), El socialismo en España (Anales de Historia, vol. 1) (Madrid, 1986)

——El reformismo en España (Madrid, 1986)

Suárez Iglesias, Ramiro. Vida, obras y recuerdos de Manuel Llaneza (Oviedo, 1933; reprinted 1979)

Thomas, Hugh. The Spanish Civil War (London, 3rd edn, 1977)

Tortella, Gabriel. 'La economía española a finales del siglo xix y principios del siglo xx' in José Luis García Delgado (ed.), La España de la Restauración (1986)

Trotsky, Leon. My Life: An Attempt at an Autobiography (Harmondsworth, 1975)

Tuñón de Lara, Manuel. La España del siglo XX (Paris, 1966)

——El movimiento obrero en la historia de España (Madrid, 1972)

——'Reflexiones sobre un proyecto cultural', Cuadernos de Pedagogía (Revista mensual de educación), 22 (1976)

——'Sobre la historia del pensamiento socialista entre 1900 y 1931' in Albert Balcells (ed.), Teoría y práctica del movimiento obrero en España 1900–1936 (Valencia, 1977)

——Tres claves de la Segunda República (Madrid, 1985)

Tuñón de Lara, Manuel et al. Historiografía española contemporánea (Madrid, 1980)

Tuñón de Lara, Manuel (ed.). *Historia de España* (10 vols.; Barcelona, 1981)
Tusell, Javier. *Las elecciones del Frente Popular en España* (2 vols.; Madrid, 1971)
——*Historia de la democracia cristiana en España* (2 vols.; Madrid, 1974)
——'The Popular Front Elections in Spain, 1936' in Stanley Payne (ed.), *Politics and Society in Twentieth-Century Spain* (New York, 1976)
——*Radiografía de un golpe de estado* (Madrid, 1987)
Tusell, Javier and Avilés, Juan. *La derecha española contemporánea. Sus orígenes: el maurismo* (Madrid, 1986)
Unamuno, Miguel de. *En turno al casticismo* (Madrid, 1895)
Varela Ortega, José. 'Los amigos políticos: funcionamiento del sistema caciquista', *Revista de Occidente*, **127** (October 1973)
——*Los amigos políticos* (Madrid, 1977)
Vicens Vives, Jaime *et al. Historia de España y América* (5 vols.; Barcelona, 1972, 2nd edn)
Vilar, Pierre. *Spain. A Brief History* (Exeter, 1977)
——'El socialismo en España (1917–1945)' in Jacques Droz (ed.), *Historia General del Socialismo* (5 vols.; Barcelona, 1979)
——'El socialismo española de sus orígenes a 1917' in Jacques Droz (ed.), *Historia General del Socialismo* (5 vols.; Barcelona, 1979)
Viñas, Ricard. *La formación de las Juventudes Socialistas Unificadas (1934–1936)* (Madrid, 1978)
Winston, Colin. *Workers and the Right in Spain, 1900–1936* (Princeton, 1985)
Wistrich, Robert. 'Leon Trotsky's Theory of Fascism', *Journal of Contemporary History*, **11** (1976)
Woolman, David S. *Rebels in the Rif: Abd el Krim and the Rif Rebellion* (Stanford, 1969)
Zapatero, Virgilio. *Fernando de los Ríos: Los problemas del socialismo democrático* (Madrid, 1974)
Zugazagoitia, Julián. *Pablo Iglesias: una vida heroica* (Madrid, 1976; first published 1925)

Index